Studies in Islamic History

No. 1

MOSLEM SCHISMS AND SECTS
PART TWO

MOSLEM SCHISMS AND SECTS

(Al-Fark Bain al-Firak)

Being the

HISTORY OF THE VARIOUS PHILOSOPHIC SYSTEMS DEVELOPED IN ISLAM

BY

Abu-Manṣūr ʻAbd-al-Ḳāhir ibn Ṭāhir al-Baghdādi (d. 1037)

PART II

Translated from the Arabic with introduction and notes by
ABRAHAM S. HALKIN

PORCUPINE PRESS
Philadelphia

First edition 1935
(Tel Aviv: Palestine Publishing Co., Ltd., 1935)

Reprinted 1978 by
PORCUPINE PRESS, INC.
Philadelphia, Pennsylvania 19107

Library of Congress Cataloging in Publication Data

Ibn Tāhir al-Baghdādī, 'Abd al-Qâhir, d. 1037.
Moslem schisms and sects = al-Farq bain al-Firak.

(Studies in Islamic history ; no. 1).
Reprint of pt. 2, 1935 ed. published in Tel-Aviv, Israel.
Originally presented as the translator's thesis, Columbia, 1935.
Bibliography: p.
Includes index.
1. Islamic sects. I. Title. II. Series: Studies in Islamic history (Philadelphia) ; no. 1.
BP191.I2213 1977 297.8 78-3673
ISBN 0-87991-450-5

Manufactured in the United States of America

To the Memory
of My Father.

PREFACE.

The abrupt opening of the translation with Chapter Four of Section Three is due entirely to the fact that up to this point the present work was translated by Kate Chambers Seelye, New York, 1919. The selection of that particular point as a proper conclusion was probably influenced by the consideration that it completed the study of the outright Mu'tazilite groups, whereas the remaining chapters of this section deal with groups which, while betraying points of contact with the "mother-sect", nevertheless display quite independent characteristics. Unfortunately, the book in its present form is still incomplete. The unique MS. which underlies the edition lacks two chapters at the end, as can be gathered from a perusal of the contents in Section Five on page 158.

To offset the very serious shortcomings of the Printed Edition, — a fault which everyone who has referred to the book recognizes readily, — the translator has utilized the following supplementary material: a photostatic copy of the MS. which was of inestimable value in establishing the correct text; the epitome, again incomplete, of the present work of our author, edited by Philipp K. Hitti; the recently published edition of our author's lengthy study of orthodox theology, his *Usul al-Din*; and finally, the Berlin and Paris MSS. of Isfaraini's study of heresiography which exploited our present work very generously. In addition, use was made, wherever possible or wherever they seemed plausible, of the emendations suggested by Goldziher and Brockelmann in the *Zeitschrift der deutschen morgenländischen Gesellschaft,* LXV (1911) and in *Le monde oriental,* XIX (1925), respectively, as well as of those by Casanova made in a private communication to Prof. Richard Gottheil.

In preparing the notes for the text, the translator strove in so far as possible to verify all statements, whether historic or otherwise, by checking a large variety of source material; to clarify all obscure or vague remarks; to illuminate more definitely persons, places and events to whom reference was made; and, in general, to make the contents of the work meaningful for the reader who is less than a specialist in the field. Altogether a serious effort was made to employ a maximum of supplementary reference material. The Introduction, on the other hand, is not the product of meticulous research, but rather in the nature of a personal judgment based on a comparatively long period of study of Ash'arite theology.

The method of transcription employed is the now generally prevalent one, found, e. g., in the Encyclopedia of Islam, with the exception of the *j* in place of the usual *dj* and *dh* in place of the *d* with a line under it. The reader will doubtless note that, owing to technical difficulties, all exact transcription had to be dispensed with in the Table of Contents, the Introduction, the Bibliography and the Index. It is sincerely hoped that this regrettable procedure will not prove a serious drawback.

It is a pleasure to conclude these prefatory remarks with an expression of gratitude and thanks to Prof. Gottheil who gave me of his time and advice, to Professor Gray of Columbia University and Professor Hitti of Princeton University who made valuable suggestions in the course of their reading of the work, and, finally, to my wife who was a source of encouragement while the work was in progress and participated actively and eagerly in the reading of the proofs and in the preparation of the Index. They are all entitled to a share in whatever merit the work may possess, without any responsibility for its defects and faults.

TABLE OF CONTENTS.

INTRODUCTION.

Abd-al-Kahir al-Baghdadi is an adherent of the Ash'arite school of theology, the orthodox party of his day. There were indeed the Hanbalites, under whatever name they appeared, who were even more orthodox than the Ash'arites, and minced no words in accusing the latter of heresy in matters of religion. But they constituted a minor group, of the sort which in all generations regards as its sacred duty the vociferous protest against the least semblance of compromise. It boasted several capable exponents of its position even in the days of Baghdadi, but altogether it was treated with disdain as a group of ignorant corporealists who arrogantly claimed to be the cultural heirs of the pious Ahmad b. Hanbal.

Without question the Ash'arites were champions of Orthodoxy, "adherents of the straight religion and the straight path". More than that, they were practically the dominant group in Islam. The day of the Mu'tazila was over. After they had enjoyed a brilliant career of some two centuries their star set, and subsequent defenders were only faint shimmerings of a more glorious past. With the passing of time the extent of Ash'arite indebtedness to Mu'tazilism became more obscured and its protagonists were discussed and regarded as a practically extinct party of wanderers from that truth which in the eyes of the victors preceded the errors of the Mu'tazila as it did every other interpretation of Islam. There were also the philosophers who were beginning to see through the inadequacies of both the physies and the metaphysics of the Ash'arites although at the time of our author they had not yet enounced the metamorphosed Aristotelian doctrine. But they were not at the time of Baghdadi, nor were they ever destined to be, serious rivals of Ash'arism. Even though they challenged it, exposed its errors and discussed its deficiencies, they did not care to undermine its position. On the contrary, they preferred (for very telling reasons) to leave those who were not endowed with higher understanding entertain the untenable dogmas to which they clung, while they and the few elect would aspire to the truth.

The Sufis formed a substantial body within Islam in the days of our author. But they did not actively or officially oppose themselves as rivals of Ash'arite Islam. And while their starting point as well as their doctrines were far removed from strait-laced orthodoxy, it was as if a secret understanding existed between the two groups not to be publicly hostile to each other. Further, Sufi was a blanket term. By definition it could not really become a fixed creed, and as a result of that it included under its embracing title innumerable shades of opinion, some of which, it must be added, were extremely unorthodox. However, these latter outraged not only Ash'arites but even Sufis of authority. With the exception of these the others were accepted, some with greater readiness than others. Altogether the Sufis were regarded in a spirit of tolerance if not actually with an inner respect and reverence.

By the age of Baghdadi Ash'arism had become a fixed creed. The age of speculation was over. The formulators of the doctrine in all its aspects were deceased, and both physics and metaphysics, politics and ethics, eschatology and immortality were specific and exact concepts. It was still to be blessed with Ghazali, who was to leave his indelible impress on its theology, but that contribution partook of the intangible, it belonged to the realm of the heart. It did not alter the theology, it regenerated it, – temporarily, – with the dew of Sufiism. And unfortunately the work of a Ghazali must by its very nature remain the gain of a few blessed souls striving for a more intimate communion. As for the mass of worshippers, the mystic strain of Ghazali could accomplish as little as the intellectual principles of dogma in deepening and revitalizing their religious experiences. The philosophic method at first employed by Ghazali in his exposition of theology did not alter essentially, or even appreciably, the component parts of the creed, while his later reversal which amounted to a stern rebuke of rationalized religion passed unheeded by a people who were much more cognizant of the results of the rational process, in themselves very close to the faith of the fathers, than of the process itself, or its justification. Even the Mu'tazilite influences discernible in Fakhr al-Din al-Razi's approach to some of the problems of Ash'arite theology, such as the Word of God and the immunity of prophets from sin, did not inaugurate a new orientation in Kalam. The work of its early thinkers established the principles of Ash'arite physics, metaphysics and ethics, and the system appeared finished to its adherents.

Baghdadi is decidedly an epigon. Ash'arism is no longer speculation, it is creed. Like Shafi'ism in Fikh, it is the straight road in Kalam followed by Muhammad and all good people since his time. Extremely orthodox in the practices of Islam, our author maintains the same unswerving position on the theoretical side. It has become with him an 'Akida, differing from the earlier ones only in that it includes even the corollaries of the main principles, thus becoming longer and more detailed. The creed is laid down in imperative fashion : whoever disagrees is either an outright heretic, a sinner of one shade or another, or one steeped in error. Kalam had so caught up with Fikh as to be able to reclaim its ancient name of Fikh al-Akbar, major Fikh. Like the legal Fikh it could be formulated and made binding just as the various books of ritual law were designed, deliberately or unwittingly, to conclude the developmental period and to establish authoritative codes.

Baghdadi lacks originality or depth even as an epitomist. He discovers no new principles, reveals no new ramfications from the cardinal principles, but seems altogether contented with the conclusions reached by those of his predecessors who became authorities in the Ash'arite school. Not that his exposition of Orthodox Islam either in this book or in the much larger *Usul al-Din* is devoid of argumentation. On the contrary, the bulk of the latter is mainly the result of a recital and a refutation of antagonistic views. But the calibre of the discussion is exactly what dampens the eagerness of the interested reader. It is mediocre in the extreme. Where an idea appears it is generally traceable to another source. Baghdadi does not hesitate to utilize the works of others, even as medieval writers generally had different standards by which to gauge an author's property. We meet with little philosophy in his presentation, which consists of a statement of the Orthodox position, a list of divergent views and a retort to the heterodox, on the whole annoyingly superficial. The result of comparing his work with those of some of his contemporaries is truly distressing. Over against the keen analysis and ardent refutation of Ibn Hazm, the lucid presentation of Shahrastani and the profound treatment of Al-Iji, Baghdadi's handling of his subject appears ineffectual.

If in the face of all this Baghdadi's work enjoyed such popularity that it was in turn abridged and recast, edited and translated, it is due in part to these very shortcomings. It is comparatively brief so that with easy effort a reader may obtain a conspectus of the vast field of Muslim heterodoxy and orthodoxy ; it is elementary and superficial, challenging the reader's intellectual capacity to no great extent ; it is factual rather than speculative and affords the reader a "catalogue raisonné" of all the disputed points ; it is popularly written and only rarely falls into a cumbersome manner of expression. Perhaps in the same shortcomings we can also find certain advantages for the modern reader, since he too is eager to know the bare facts in addition to the philosophic background.

It is now generally accepted that in a sense the term Ash'arites for the Mutakallims of Islam is a misnomer. Ash'ari himself, a former disciple of Mu'tazilism who reverted to Orthodoxy, occupies a position which may only indirectly entitle him to the fatherhood of Orthodox Kalam. In his *Ibana,* a polemical confession of faith, he stands squarely in the territory of Ahmad Ibn Hanbal and makes an explicit avowal to that effect. The first temptation to treat that avowal as a means of escaping the charge of innovation, as we often find among earlier and later medieval thinkers, is hardly justified by a reading of the *Ibana.* It is composed in its entirety in a tone of unswerving Hanbalism, a restatement of the conservative Orthodoxy. And while in his large work on heresiography and on the orthodox physics and theology he does not display the ardor for polemics of the *Ibana,* we seek in vain for points of contact between Ash'ari and the school subsequently bearing his name. Perhaps Ash'ari's contribution to Kalam and his right to be called its father rest in the main on his method and not on his conclusions. Unlike the "salaf", the ancients, or his revered master Ahmad b. Hanbal, Ash'ari shows a readiness to argue and does not merely withdraw behind a blind adherence to text and tradition which allow of no argumentation. But the type of argument employed by him is not characterized by a philosophic, speculative approach. It is textual, deriving its decisiveness from the Holy Book or from tradition. Moreover, in adducing such textual proof Ash'ari insists on the plain meaning of the words. The Kur'an was revealed in Arabic for the benefit of Arabs, and the sole arbiter of the intent of any word or phrase is the interpretation common among Arabs. *Ta'wil,* or allegorization, is thus ruled out as uncompromisingly as by the Hanbalites. A statement in the Kur'an is adequate rebuttal, in Ash'ari's estimate, of a philosophic argument produced by the Mu'tazilites, a comparison of two verses apparently contradicting each other is a powerful enough challenge to a Mu'tazilite reconciliation of the verses. In truth, except for his willingness to argue, even when the array of arguments is lamentably circumscribed, one finds little ground for honoring Ash'ari with the parentage of Ash'arite theology.

In its conclusions and even in its method his school obviously abandons his position. While he, a renegade Mu'tazilite, was able to embrace the doctrine of orthodoxy with the extremism and zeal of a neophyte, his so-called disciples could not close their eyes to the trenchant criticism of the rationally minded Mu'tazilites, nor could they disregard the dictates of reason as fanatically as their master. Rationalism had at least established the right of human reason to be consulted in the formulation of theologic doctrine. If the group that regarded itself as intermediate between narrow-minded conservatism and devastating rationalism was to pretend that it could maintain its title, it had to placate reason, it had to perform just what the theory of compromise entitled one to expect: that it would prove the orthodoxy of old tenable even from a rational standpoint. As a starting-point, therefore, they found it necessary to establish the right of reason to participate in the discussion, to lay down the conciliatory principle that intellect was not *ab initio* hostile to tradition; that, on the contrary, as a creation of God it could be utilized in behalf of God and His revelation. If, nevertheless, there was much in the Asharite theology which later philosophers regarded as puerile and senseless it was due not to this premise but to the very idea of compromise; a situation, may it be remarked, which was destined to repeat itself when the later philosophic position was submitted to the dissecting scalpel, and in other cases as well, wherever compromise was the working hypothesis. But of this later.

The movement of Kalam, both in the hands of Ash'ari and in the hands of his successors was perhaps primarily a reaction against Mu'tazilism, but one which conceded the very important premise that a theory could not be expected to thrive merely on an obscurantist attitude of defying experience and intellectual activity. Kalam therefore found it necessary to go over the same ground as the Mu'tazilites, to examine the physical world, to investigate the ethical bases of society, to inquire into the person of God and His revelation to man. However, the Ash'arites assumed the role of apologists for the faith, defenders of Orthodox Islam. This latter point is what became so decisive in their theologic speculation. They were out not to discover truth, but to establish it; not to investigate the compatibility of reason and faith but to erect their philosophy upon a presumed compatibility. And while in these efforts, in a large way, there is nothing particularly unique, since they are ever so common, one cannot fail to discover in the specific character of the Kalamistic approach an aspect which does render it unique, at least among Islamic movements. So far as was humanly possible and in so far as their knowledge qualified them, the Mu'tazilites gave unchecked freedom to their speculation. The philosophers of a later day, particularly Averroes, philosophised primarily, and sought to force theology into a philosophic mould. No one can deny that in the process of conciliation as effected by Averroes or by Maimonides the theology of the ancients was treated more violently than their philosophy. But quite the contrary is to be found in Ash'arite Kalam. As apologists for Islam they strove most zealously to retain all accretions to the faith of the fathers, and it is difficult to avoid the conclusion that they manipulated the facts to suit the theory and juggled words to escape the necessity of formulating definite concepts or the discomfort of mutually contradictory premises.

In proof of the first charge their theory of knowledge and their theory of the physical universe may be briefly surveyed. Leaving aside the various classifications of knowledge, its division into divine and human, the subdivision of the latter into natural, or axiomatic, and acquired, the further subdivision of the latter into intuitive and sensual, we may dwell specifically on his analysis of acquired knowledge, for it is there that Baghdadi exhibits his tendency to suit his theory to his theology. Acquired or mental knowledge is of four types: 1) Deductive knowledge, i. .e., the purely mental process whereby logic and its ancillary arts guide one to the affirmation of such truths as the creàtion of the universe, the nature of the Maker, the admissibility of prophecy, etc., 2) Empirical knowledge, and deductive knowledge based on experience; 3) Revelation, which, our author explains, belongs to mental knowledge since prophecy on which the validity of revelation rests is intellectually demonstrable; 4) Intuitive knowledge with which some are inexplicably gifted as an uneducated person's appreciation of the technique of poetry.

Still another source of knowledge is the reports of others. The Kalamists list three classes of reports. The first comprises those handed down successively through the ages by credible reporters. The conditions required for qualifying a report in this first group (*Tawatur*) are that the veracity of the transmitters down the ages remain beyond suspicion and challenge, and that the first one to have told it has either seen it or heard it himself or that he has had positive knowledge of it. With these two requirements filled, a report of that kind is so certain a fact that our author does not hesitate to call it "necessary" because "doubt regarding it is as little justified as regarding knowledge derived intuitively or through the senses." Such knowledge obligates one not only to act in accordance with it if it is prescriptive, but to accept it as a fact. Examples of this type of knowledge are our information about lands which we have not visited or times which antedate us. The second type consists of reports (*Ahad*) whose transmitters are credible and whose contents are not contrary to reason, but lack an uninterrupted chain of transmitters through the ages. Such require action but not belief. We may cite as an example most of the derivative laws resting on reports of individuals. The third type (*Mustafid*) includes those which have had wide circulation, although they are not supported by an uninterrupted chain of authorities. If such a report is plausibe, it obligates both action and belief, but it is acquired and not necessary knowledge. In this category will be included the reports of those whose miracles testify to their veracity such as prophets, or reports of those to whose veracity a prophet bears testimony, or reports told at first by trustworthy people and later circulated by many, so that they assume the characteristics of *Tawatur*. As examples of the last we may adduce the stories about God's visibility, or the intercession of the Prophet on the Day of Judgment, or the Pool and the Balance, or certain principles of Fikh.

With this scheme of knowledge Baghdadi succeeds in saving as gospel truth every shred of tradition and every bit of jurisprudence, every story of saint, every legend of the past incorporated in the lore of Islam and every miracle of the Prophet or prophets which imaginative minds throughout the ages have invented. In this alone we seem to feel the artificial nature of his philosophic set-up, the conscious effort to evolve a philosophy which will confirm faith. This feeling is strengthened by the additional fences which Baghdadi constructs; by the numerous conditions he sets up to make sure that none of the beliefs current among other nations, which Islam has for one reason or another denied, will lay claim to being true since it fulfills the conditions set up by our author; by the arbitrary rejection of opposing arguments. A few illustrations will make this clearer. A *Tawatur* report as we have seen, is one resting on authorities whom it is simply absurd to suspect of agreeing on a lie. Hence, Baghdadi continues to argue, the story of Jesus' crucifixion is false. The reasoning in establishing this is highly enlightening. Although the story about Jesus' crucifixion has assumed the proportions of *Tawatur* it goes back in the final analysis to four people who were allegedly witnesses of the event. But if there were four people present the Jews would no doubt have abstained from the act. It is told that thirty Jews were present at the crucifixion. Now deliberate agreement on this number is very possible and deliberate agreement on the weakness of the four against the thirty is certainly possible. Indeed, that there was someone crucified is true, but the question is whether it was Jesus. This whole involved argument is explicable on only one ground: that the Kur'an denies that Jesus was crucified but adheres to the teachings of the Docetics that some one else was crucified in his place. His virgin birth, his immortality – attested by the same book which bears witness to his crucifixion – are not questioned because the Kur'an and Muhammadan tradition have accepted them. Or consider the case of the traditionist Abu Huraira, one of the most fertile minds and most generous contributors to the *Hadith*. Abu Huraira's veracity was contested in the generations immediately following his. That his traditions are accepted as the most practical expedient it is still within our power to understand. But when Abu Huraira, in company with all the Companions of the Prophet, is declared to be honest beyond the shadow of a doubt, while he who still challenges his authority is declared a heretic, we are working with principles of knowledge which fall far short not only of our theory of philosophic principles, but even of those which the medieval period evolved. Another illustration : Baghdadi establishes another strange law of knowledge : when a *Tawatur* supports a story which is likewise intellectually demonstrable it no longer possesses the force of compelling knowledge and of making it axiomatic. This is the way Baghdadi explains why the *Tawatur* reports about Islam have failed to convince all the non-Muslims. (This is also a splendid illustration of Baghdadi's naive conviction that he was operating with universals and of the genuineness of his orthodoxy.) Finally Baghdadi has laid down the thesis that *Ahad* reports are valid enough to compel action but not belief. Yet he immediately hastens to inform us that in matters of Fikh no attention is to be paid to the criticism or the divergence of the Dissidents. Why ? Because such attention is to be paid in questions of Kalam but not of Fikh !

The philosophy of revelation may conveniently lead us into a discussion of his theory of the physical world. The Mu'tazilites developed a philosophy in which revelation became a necessary part of the order of the universe over which a just God interested in man's welfare holds sway. It fits in with the logic of their premises, regardless of whether or not the premises themselves conform to our conceptions. Moreover, they made an honest attempt to explain revelation, as indeed, miracles in general, without rudely disturbing the order of the universe. The ultra-Orthodox consistently denied any order in this world other than the ever active will of God, and for them it was not necessary to seek any other explanation for revelation than that God willed it and performed it. But the Ash'arites found themselves indisposed to join their forces either with the one party or the other. They did seek an orderly universe, they admitted the existence of one, and withal they strove to maintain their belief in the power of God to disturb the order and to interfere with its working, all on the basis of a rationally understood hypothesis. Hence they developed a view of the physical universe which strangely laid as its foundation the atomic conception of the ancients. Truly a wonder that the theory which served Epicurus and Lucretius adequately enough in their denial of God and the affirmation of chance was utilized by Ash'arite Muslims centuries later as the best vehicle for interpreting their orthodoxy philosophically. They achieved it by admitting on the one hand the fortuitous nature of the physical components of the universe, but by recognizing, on the other hand, the order which reigns in the universe. The result was a providential God such as Tradition had taught them to conceive. It was all done thoroughly on the basis of certain principles which Maimonides summed up succintly. Briefly their conception of the physical world is as follows :

The universe, which is a term for everything other than God, is composed of substances and accidents, or properties, the substance being the essential part of every object, and the property the additional element. Substances are divisible compounds and the lowest irreducible substance is the atom, although it is disputed whether the atom possesses dimensions or whether it is necessary to combine two or more atoms in order that they become dimensional. Although the accidents are properties added to the substance, the separate existence of the latter is entirely abstract. Actually no body can be devoid of properties, especially of the categories of motion or rest, composition and color. Moreover, the apparent diversity of substance is due entirely to the properties. Stripped of those, there would be homogeneity of matter and even the four basic elements of earth, water, air and fire are further reducible as can be shown through the transmutation of one to the other.

The novel concept of Ash'arite physics is its view that properties possess only momentary existence. From instant to instant, – and, it may be remarked in passing, it regarded time in the same way as matter, namely, as reducible to an indivisible "atom", the instant, – the properties attendant on the substance perish and new ones are created. What brought the Ash'arite school to this conclusion philosophically may be read in Baghdadi. But probably, as Maimonides has pointed out, a deeper cause underlay their premise: the denial of causality. For, since there is no natural law which necessitates the existence of a property for as long as the object exists there is no other way of explaining why accidents should endure longer than an instant, – especially in view of the fact that some properties endure only an instant, – except by declaring that God creates a property of non-existence in the atom which makes it perish. But this possibility leads to an absurdity since it involves for at least a fraction of a second the simultaneous co-existence of the given property as well as its non-existence. According to Ash'arite theology it is not the substances which lead to the existence of properties but vice versa. Objects cannot exist without properties and the perishing of an object is due entirely to the cessation of creation of the attendant accidents. Now, having established the incontrovertible linking of properties and substances, and having, moreover, proved that properties are, and were, created in time, they demonstrate, to their own satisfaction, that the substances too are created. Since the entire universe consists only of those two categories it is proved that the entire universe has been created in time. One is duly impressed with their argument against the upholders of the hylic hypothesis which predicates the existence of matter devoid of, and prior to, properties. "Tell us," Baghdadi says to them, was the hylic substance originally one or more ? If the answer is one, we can object: How did the one become many through the creation of properties ? Properties change the quality, but do not change the quantity ! If, on the contrary, the answer is more than one, then the objection is that substance cannot be devoid of agreement and differentiation both of which are properties." With that accomplished it becomes relatively simple, and convincing, that for a created universe a Creator is required, and thus the existence of God is established.

To return to the problem of cause and effect. The Ash'arites denied any relation between any two apparently interlinked incidents. The fact that two incidents always follow each other in time does not necessitate the conclusion that the second is the generated effect of the first. Pain follows a blow; falling follows a hurled stone; wetness follows the pouring of water. But in all these cases it is the customary rather than the necessary that we observe. In reality there is no inevitable relation between the three first actions and the three second actions, respectively. It is in these cases, and in each case, the result of an act of God, and it is admissible that at any time, if God should choose to disturb His imposed order, a blow will not be followed by pain. The principle of admissibility is another of the important instruments in the Ash'arite creed. Any thing which is rationally (although the philosophers have very loudly called it to the attention of the Kalamists that they mean imaginatively) admissible is a reality. Revelation now becomes exceedingly simple to prove. God disturbed His own universe. But with what violent treatment of nature and experience!

We have also accused the Ash'arites of playing with words and substituting them in place of a comprehensible concept, and it devolves upon us to substantiate this accusation. It is true that in a general way words had a more real quality in Medieval days. They were realities, and as such, an expression carried a real weight as something existent either in the physical world or in the mind. One may cite in illustration some of the arguments offered against dissenters. In answer to the sceptics who deny reality, the following "formidable" argument is raised: Is the denial of reality a reality? If they say, yes, they have admitted one reality, and if they say, no, the retort is: Since your denial has no reality, it is not true, and its converse – the recognition of reality – is true. Or, take the gibe at a representative of a group which maintained that every one who disagreed with it was a liar: Am I right when I assert that you are an honorable man born of wedlock? – No, you are lying. You are right. – But nevertheless a distinction ought to be made between sophistry and absurdity. And it must be admitted that in at least two doctrines – although more can be listed – they maintain an attitude which, to all intents and purposes, is absurd.

One is the problem of God's attributes. Whether out of poetic imagination or ignorance of logic, Muhammad did not hesitate to employ epithets and descriptive adjectives in qualifying God. They did not disturb either his conception of God's unity with which he was no doubt intoxicated, or his peace of mind because of the contradictions which later minds, sharpened by contact with Christian theology and Greek philosophy, found to be "inherent" in such an attitude unless somehow explained. Even the first generations after Muhammad did not appear to be upset by it. To the numerous anthropomorphic expressions with which the Kur'an teems they liberally contributed their share of charming legends and other "traditions". But when people began to think they were compelled to define their terms more plainly. And when that tendency grew active it became evident that to apply rationalism to the problem of God's anthropomorphism and His attributes, and to carry through a consistent and honest analysis would involve a step tantamount to a break with the simple and direct language of the Apostle and the Ancients. Consequently the development of rationalism generated an articulate counter-movement sponsored by those who were the defenders and spokesmen of the early conception.

This was in broad lines the array of forces prior to the rise of Ash'ari. The traditionists refused to discuss. They paid their respects to reason with the admission that there was no comparison between anything applied to God and anything applied to man but they insisted very emphatically that all the anthropomorphic expressions, the epithets, the descriptive adjectives and the legendary material were really and literally true. They did not know how and they could not explain it; so they decided that they would not explain but would faithfully adhere to, and repeat, whatever was found in the Book and in Tradition regarding God and His attributes without explanation and without qualification, but always with the understanding that they were not implying any parallel and comparison with any human attribute or action. In consonance with their opinion these people frowned on translations of such terms into foreign languages.

At the other end we meet the Mu'tazilites. As rationalists they could not afford to seek shelter in an attitude expressible in "It is true, but I cannot explain". A stand of this kind, while perhaps reasonable, is not rational. Yet reason dictates that God be conceived of as absolutely free of any quality or qualification. For a quality, being something which describes, is added to the substance, and addition to the Person of God, Who is indivisible unity, is absurd unless we care to sink into the errors of polytheism. Moreover, description is delimitation and that again is equivalent to tampering with the infinite power of God. In view of all this, it was clear to the Mu'tazilites that there could be no talk of attributes as realities, much less of sensations and of physical acts or physical traits. If in the face of this presumption, a long series of verses appeared in the Kur'an which pointed to the contrary, confirmed and even augmented by statements and traditions of later generations, there were only two ways out: allegorization, where the authenticity of the statement could not be called into question, and denial where the uncomfortable statement might be said to be spurious. Some of the extreme traditions which were examples of crass anthropomorphism unless rendered harmless by being characterized as poetry – a process not very popular in those days – were simply discredited. In this act the Mu'tazilites were not really disreputable heretics since the struggle around the establishment of the canon of tradition is a historically established fact rendered even better known through modern investigation. Where denial was out of consideration there was the gentler treatment of "explaining away". Physical properties were spiritualized, antropomorphic allusions were interpreted, and God's unity and incorporeality were maintained ardently and thoroughly. Some things, of course, are true of God. He is living, He possesses power, He possesses will. But what this means is either – as some Mu'tazilites believed – that this is the way God's Person appears to human understanding, or – as others believed – that whatever can be predicated of God is not in any way distinct from Himself, indeed is Himself. They were often violent with regard to the verses of the Kur'an but they defended themselves on the ground that since Islam was so monotheistic, there could be no thought of lending any other meaning to the plainly anthropomorphic words and phrases.

In this problem the Ash'arites attempt to play the role of conciliators, with greater respect for the requirements of tradition than for the dictates of reason. True, it must be remarked that in this issue, more than in any other, the Ash'arites renounced the teachings of their patron. His passionate arguments in support of the face and hands of Allah proved as unconvincing to them as to the Mu'tazilites. They, too, now took it for granted that even "bila kaifa" tactics could not rid the physical attributes of God of their unsavoriness to the intelligent person. They therefore followed the Mu'tazilites and explained those things allegorically. Furthermore, while they did not utilize the critical apparatus of the Mu'tazila and were consequently confronted with a greater number of traditions and statements, they applied the method of interpretation to these as well.

There remained, however, seven attributes in which they could not follow the Mu'tazila but chose to adhere to the view enounced by Al-Ash'ari himself. The seven attributes of God are : Power, Knowledge, Will, Life, Seeing, Hearing, Speech. Al-Ash'ari was rather consistent. These attributes, like the physical attributes, are realities. But a difficulty was encountered here which had not been present hitherto. What exactly were they ? Were they separate entities distinguishable from one another, or merely different faces of the same coin? That al-Ash'ari preferred the first answer is a matter of course. And his so-called followers could not, if they were to remain faithful to their ideal, but defend the view of their predecessors. And herein lay their failure. Predicating the existence of attributes which were separate entities, while at the same time they insisted on God's Unity and freedom from composition and incorporeality, they were compelled to evolve the formula that "His attributes are neither He nor not He". What that formula means not even they could tell. It was an escape through words, which added little credit to them.

Finally there was the problem of human free will. Is man a free agent or are his hands tied and his acts only metaphorically performed by him ? Both the implications and complications of the problem are not difficult to see. On the one hand the entire doctrine of reward and punishment ought to hinge on the solution of the problem ; only a free agent can be held responsible for his acts and given his retribution. On the other hand, the assumption of free will in man creates the difficulty of defining the respective domains of power of man and of God and the further complication of the apparent exclusion of divine foreknowledge. The Kur'an, too, proves to be of little aid in unraveling the knot. It supports both views, and one cannot readily decide whither Muhammad tended, unless one grants here also, as has been suggested elsewhere, that it is historically wrong to seek exact definitions in the Kur'an. There can be little doubt that Muhammad was literally overwhelmed by the omnipotence of God and His participation in, let alone His awareness of, every human act. Yet Muhammad was not hindered from preaching the doctrine of human responsibility and of retribution.

This stand of the Prophet guided the Orthodox. They too believed and were not baffled by the contradiction. Both theses are true. Even the will to do good or evil is implanted by God in man, not as a general capacity for desiring the one or the other, but as a specific preference inspired by God now for a good act and now for an evil one. But just as God's power is a fact, so man's reward and punishment are a fact. This is the doctrine preached by Muhammad and this is the doctrine sponsored by his faithful followers. The Kur'an and tradition are the sole arbiters, just as they are the source in general for decisions of what constitutes good and evil. Only that is good which God approves of, and evil is what God abhors. To look for logic in the several component parts of this briefly sketched doctrine would be futile. Yet one cannot fail to be impressed with the compelling force of a kind of primitive logic underlying the entire structure: the inescapable necessity of bowing before the supreme power of an omnipotent and omniscient Creator. One can discover no other way than to accept what He offers, to believe what He tells us, and to conduct ourselves as He guides us by standards set up by Him and according to directions which He has revealed to us.

The solution of the intricate thesis along logical lines was attempted by two parties, each upholding the premise with which it was more profoundly impressed. The Kadarites, later developed into Mu'tazila, were the champions of free-will. On their banner was inscribed the motto: God's Unity and Justice, and in both cases comprehensible to mankind. We have already noted how thoroughly the concept of Unity forced them to deal with attributes. Similarly their concept of justice inspired them with courage and determination to premise certain axiomatic truths. God is just, and being just He cannot deprive man of his freedom and then hold him responsible for his acts. He can not, in justice, make man the powerless play-ball of a predetermined fate. Yes, God is the creator of the entire Universe, but He has willingly placed in the hands of man that domain of activity which consists in his deciding for himself what he chooses to do at one time and what at another. God knows beforehand all that will happen but He has willingly consented to limit His knowledge in the case of human acts. Justice requires that man retain the right to exercise free will and it is in his capacity of being a free agent that he can be held accountable for morality and ethical living.

Over against them we find the Jabarites, a comparatively small group impressed above all with the omnipotence of Allah and the parallel impotence of man. Only metaphorically may man be spoken of as the agent of any of the acts he performs, for in fact he is only the helpless instrument through whom God does what He chooses.

When Ash'arite Kalam took the field, it subscribed fully to the doctrine of the ancients. But unlike the ancients, it was urged to explain, to create a rational background for its stand. So the Ash'arites assume the reality of *aksab*, of acquired acts, presumably performed by the one consequently held accountable for them. However, in order to avoid the uncomfortable position of granting to man the right to perform acts, they categorically deny that man is the creator and performer. Quite on the contrary it is God who really performs the human act. The full weight of this contention becomes even more compelling when it is remembered that the Mutakallims also deny cause and effect, or generated effects. It therefore means that from the time the intention to do is created by God in man's mind up to the moment when the final results of the action become apparent through the act there are numerous single acts all of which are not only inspired but actually executed by God. They are thus faced by the dilemma of how man can be said to be the performer. And once again they rely on words. While creating the act, God creates along with it the power in man to perform that act. But that power is simultaneous with the act, nor is the act traceable to that power created in man. God is the author of both. What, then, is man's share in the act? In an attempt to clarify the point an illustration is given of a very heavy boulder which one especially strong man is capable of carrying. Now, if this man is aided by a weak person, the result is that actually the strong man does all the work. Yet the weaker one feels that he too is cooperating. But in addition to the general lameness of the example there is the further consideration that the analogy is not consistent. In the illustration the strong man is not the bestower of the weaker man's strength, whereas God is the performer not only in His own capacity but also in the capacity of the individual of whose power He is the

Author. Essentially, therefore, the Kalamists are playing with words. Even if the explanation were restated to express the idea that it seems to man as if he were the actual doer and in that sense he is a free agent, it would be evident that we are deceiving ourselves with words, just as the ordinary man usually deceives himself. And the same dilemma is confronted in the discussion of good and evil or in dissussing guidance or sustenance or the other topics which fall under the general heading of God's justice.

The foregoing does not pretend to serve as an exposition of Ash'arite theology or even as a systematic critique. It is rather a summary of the impressions carried away by a student of their theology. It must, however, be stated quite definitely that to the mind of the writer the failure of the Kalamists is only a matter of degree as compared with the efforts of the other rationalizing schools. More than in the choice of a particular philosophy or process of reconciliation there lurks the initial question of whether a reconciliation of any kind may be looked to to harmonize two such divergent realms as reason and faith. That there is an almost natural yearning for that peace on the part of those who are torn between the two or are drawn to both is an almost established fact. But the wish does not always generate its fulfillment — certainly not in such form as will prove convincing even to an unbiased onlooker.

The doctrine of the Ash'arites has enjoyed a long life and a stable reputation in Islam. But it is clear that these are due mainly to the particular history of Ash'arite theology : to a gradual overshadowing of the philosophic veneer, a religious garb covering the philosophic tenets, and an ever growing identification of Ash'arism with the religion of the ancients. It was the religious conservatism of the doctrine which saved the day for it rather than its philosophic presentation. The turbulent minds of succeeding generations were compelled to go to other sources. Those who found rest in Ash'arism were in the main neither great thinkers nor very seeking spirits. They were cut out to follow the religion of their fathers and were at ease in the pursuit of it.

CHAPTER FOUR

THE SECTS OF THE MURJIYYA AND A DISCUSSION OF THEIR DOCTRINES

The Murjites are divided into three classes[1]. One professes postponement in respect of faith and accepts the view of the Mu'tazilite Ḳadarites on free will[2]. Its protagonists are Ghailān[3], Abu Shimr and Muḥammad ibn Shabīb of Baṣra. This class is included among those referred to in the tradition which has come down regarding the curse on the Ḳadarites and the Murjites[4]; it deserves the curse from both angles. Another class professes postponement in faith and determinism[5] in works, following the views of Jahm ibn Ṣafwān[6], and therefore belongs to the Jahmiyya. The third rejects both determinism and the Ḳadarite doctrine. The latter forms five sects in accordance with their divergences from one another: the Yūnusiyya, the Ghassāniyya, the Thaubāniyya, the Tūmāniyya, and the Marīsiyya[7].

---

[1] Shahr., I, 104, lists four classes, adding to those here a group from the Khawārij. The combination of Khārijism and Murjiism is odd and rests on a loose application of the term. The reference is probably to Shabīb b. Yezīd al-Shaibāni who withheld from pronouncing either Ṣālih or his opponents (two Khārijite groups; see Ash'ari, 120—3) right, and was therefore branded as a "Murjite Khāriji", ib., 123. Shahr. himself calls Ghailān a Khārijite, 106, and Maḳrīzi says that Thaubān was also one, and was called *Jāmi' al-Naḳā'iṣ* because of his simultaneous adherence to Mu'tazilism.

[2] Reading بالقدر with MS.; Ed. وما يقدر.

[3] On these Ḳadarites see below.

[4] This reading seems more correct than the one in *Mukhtaṣar*, 122, which punctuates between the two words قدرية and مرجئة, since the author is dealing here particularly with Ḳadarites who are also Murjites. Isf. A., 46 b, supports this reading.

[5] Reading وبالجبر with MS.; Ed. وبالخبر.

[6] On him and his adherents see below, 13—15.

[7] Together with the four Ḳadarite Murjites and Jahm b. Ṣafwān, our author enumerates ten groups. Ash'ari, who identifies Abu Shimr's views with those of the Yūnusiyya, counts twelve, including the Najjāriyya, the Karrāmiyya, and the Ḥanīfiyya (132—41). *Bad'wal-Ta'rīkh* names

They are called Murjites because they regard works of secondary importance to faith[1]. *Irjā'* (postponement) is employed in the same sense as *Ta'khīr* (delay). We say: I postponed it (*'arjaitu* or *'arja'tuhu*), that is, delayed it[2]. It is reported that the Prophet said: Cursed are the Murjites by the mouth of seventy prophets[3]. —Who are the Murjites, O Apostle? he was asked, and replied: Those who say[4] faith consists in a verbal confession, meaning those who maintain that faith is only

---

the Raḳashiyya (see Naubakhti, 9) the Ziyādiyya, the Karrāmiyya and the Mu'ādhiyya, V, 152—4. Maḳrizi, 350, names seven sects. In a brief treatise on the sects published by Dedering in *Le Monde Oriental* XXV (1931), 35—43, and written by one Al-Kirmānī, whom the editor believes to have lived before 525 A. H., we also find ten groups, but in place of the Jahmiyya he includes the Ḥanīfiyya. Iji, 359—61, counts a sect 'Ubaidiyya in place of the Marīsiyya and does not include the Jahmiyya.

[1] Although the Murjites are treated here and in other discussions as a dogmatic division in Islam, the view is generally accepted that its rise is to be sought in the political developments in early Islam when the undeserving 'Umayyads became the rulers. Refusing to condemn them outright, yet seeing the injustice of their usurpation, they chose to remain non-committal. See *Muh. St.*, II, 89—92; Macdonald, *Muslim Theology*, 122—7; *Vorlesungen*[2], 78 f. Van Vloten, however, while not denying the political factor, would trace its origin to the division between Arabs and Persians — the jealousy between them is well known. He also urges the recognition of a dogmatic standpoint even in its early stages. See his article on *Irjā'* in *ZDMG*, XLV (1891), 161—71. There is still an echo of the political basis of this group in Shahr.'s report that "it is said that *Irjā'* also signifies the ranking of 'Ali fourth instead of first and for this reason the Murjites and Shī'ites are opposed to each other", 104. Definite proof of their early political program is afforded by the recently published *Firaḳ al-Shī'a* of Naubakhti, 6, although he also adds the dogmatic factor.

[2] To this explanation Iji, Maḳrīzi and Shahr. add the element of hope also implicit in the verb. Maḳrīzi, 349 bottom, calls them "extremists in confirming promise and hope and in denying retribution" غلاة في اثبات الوعد والرجاء ونفي الوعيد. Shahr. places the Wa'īdiyya in contrast to them, 16. Cf. *Mukhtaṣar*, 123, note 1.

[3] This tradition — without an *Isnād*? — is recorded by Ibn Ḳuṭaiba in a fuller form: Two divisions among my people will not be benefited by my intercession. May they be cursed by the mouth of seventy Prophets: [they are] the Murjites and Ḳadarites *Mukhtalif al-Ḥadīth*, 97. In his article on Murjite and Anti-Murjite Traditions in *ZA*, XXVI (1911), 169—74, Kern does not cite any tradition similar to this one.

[4] Arab. زعموا, Goldziher remarks that this verb „ist, wie arabische Gelehrte sagen, ‚eine Kunya für den Begriff der Lüge'." *Muh. St.* II, 51.

a confession and nothing more. The five sects which we have listed accuse one
another of error and the other sects believe them all to be in error. We shall 191
now treat of them in detail, God willing.

The Yūnusiyya. — These are the followers of Yūnus ibn 'Awn[1] who maintained that faith pertains to the heart and mouth and consists of a knowledge of, love for, and humility to God in the heart, together with a confession by word of mouth that He is one and there is nothing like unto Him[2]. This is not dependent on evidence of prophets[3]. If, however, the evidence comes, then[4] the recognition of their veracity and the general knowledge of what came from them forms part of faith, but a detailed knowledge of what came from them does not constitute faith nor part of it. They hold that no single tenet among the tenets of faith can be called faith or part of it, but that all of them together constitute faith[5].

The Ghassāniyya. — They are the followers of Ghassān, the Murjite[6], who maintained that faith consists in a confession of, love for, and reverence towards God[7], and renunciation of pride before Him. He held that faith can be increased

---

[1] Sam'āni (603 b) calls him Al-Shamari and Ash'ari (133) calls him Al-Samari. There are several places mentioned in Yaḳūt, III, 132—3, by the name Samara, but none of them is cited by the author as the native city of Yūnus. Shahr., ib., gives him the *nisba* Numairi and so does Iji, ib., although he makes him his (or its) son. In Maḳrīzi, 350, he appears as Ibn 'Umar.

[2] Some of the other authorities such as Ash'ari, Shahr., and Sam'āni mention as a specific tenet of Yūnus the renunciation of pride, only implied by Baghdādi in his word humility. Iblīs, acc. to Yūnus, is guilty of non-belief only because of his insolence despite his confession in God.

[3] Adding عليه with *Mukhtasar* 123. Its conjecture that the second clause should read فان قامت عليه حجتهم now finds its confirmation in MS. and Ash'ari, 134.

[4] Reading فالتصديق with MS.; Ed. بالتصديق.

[5] Ash'ari, ib., ascribes this view to his disciples, denying that Yūnus himself held it.

[6] He was a Kūfite and his followers had their centre there, Sam'āni, 408 b. Maḳrīzi makes him a disciple of Muḥammad al-Shaibāni and also informs us that he denied the prophetic character of Jesus (ib.).

[7] The other authorities also add the doctrine that belief in the Apostle and his law is required. The statements cited Ash'ari, 138—9, Iji, 360, Sam'āni, ib., Shahr. 105, that a man is a believer if, for example, he recognizes that Muḥammad is a prophet, but does not know whether he was sent to the Ethiopians or the Arabs, serves as an illustration of their view.

but not decreased[1]. He differed with the Yūnusiyya in calling every tenet a part of faith. In his book Ghassān states that his view on this question[2] agrees with that of Abu Ḥanīfa[3]. But it is an error on his part[4], because Abu Ḥanīfa said: Verily, faith is knowledge and confession of God and of His Apostles and of what has come down from God and His Prophets generally, not specifically. It cannot be increased nor decreased, nor can people excel one another in it, whereas Ghas-
192 sān declared that it can be increased but not decreased.

The Tūmāniyya. — These are the followers of Abu Mu'ādh al-Tūmāni[5] who maintained that faith is what preserves one from non-belief, and it is a term applied to certain tenets. Anyone who neglects them in whole or in part becomes an infidel. All of them together constitute faith, but no single tenet can be called faith or part of it. He said: Any commandment, the transgression of which the community is not agreed in terming non-belief, is part of the canon-laws but is not faith. According to his claim, anyone transgressing a commandment which is

---

[1] So all authorities except Sam'āni who reads (ib.) "can be increased and decreased". Maḳrīzi's reading "can neither be increased nor decreased" is an obvious misprint since he places it in contrast to Abu Ḥanīfa's view, as our author does.

[2] Reading الباب with MS.; Ed. الكتاب.

[3] With MS. Ed. misreads his name as *Ḥanafiyya* both times.

[4] Our author, a thoroughgoing orthodox, is apparently eager to deny any similarity between the Ḥanīfite and Murjite systems. Although he limits it only to this point, his silence about a similarity between Abu Ḥanīfa and Ghassān is nevertheless significant. Shahrastāni, more philosophically-minded, makes an attempt to soften the full effect of branding the famous jurist a Murjite by modifying it to mean a Sunnite Murjite or by regarding it as a name which the Mu'tazila applied to him because of his views on Ḳadar. Iji, 360, goes still further and calls this claim of Ghassān libel, explaining it as a desire on his part to attach himself to a great man. Al-Ash'ari, however, a frank opponent of Abu Ḥanīfa, shows no hesitancy in discussing the two under the same heading (138—9), and similarly, Ibn Ḥazm, his direct opponent in Fiḳh, who does not hesitate to include Al-Ash'ari as well as Abu Ḥanīfa, *Shiites*, I, 29 and II, 8. Cf. *Ghunya*, 103. For his doctrines see Maṭurīdi, 9—10; Abu Ḥanīfa, 33—5, and commentaries; these fully justify the view that he is a Murjite. Evidence of the elasticity of the name Murjite is given by the fact that Naubakhti includes both Mālik ibn Anās and al Shāfi'i among the Murjites.

[5] Tūmān is a village in Egypt. Yaḳūt, I, 897, mentions it specifically as the birthplace of Abu Mu'ādh. Maḳrīzi names him a philosopher, ib.

not faith is said to have sinned but is not called an outright sinner, since he did not transgress it as one who disavows[1]. He also held that one who strikes a prophet or kills him becomes an infidel, not by reason of the striking or killing but because of the enmity and hatred of him and the disregard[2] for his truth.

The Thawbāniyya. — These are tho followers of Abu Thawbān, the Murjite[3], who held that faith is confession and knowledge of God and of His Apostles and of everything the doing of which is rationally obligatory. The knowledge of works, whose neglect is rationally admissible, does not form part of faith. They dissent from the Yūnusiyya and Ghassāniyya in making a thing rationally incumbent even before the revealed Law makes it binding.

The Marīsiyya. — They are the Murjites of Baghdād, adherents of Bishr al-Marīsi[4]. In jurisprudence he adopted the system of Abu Yūsuf al-Ḳāḍi[5]. But when he declared openly that the Ḳur'ān was created, Abu Yūsuf severed relations with him. The Ṣifātiyya also accused him of error for it. When he 193
agreed[6] with the Ṣifātiyya that God is the Author of the deeds of man and that the power to act is acquired simultaneously with the performance of the act, the

---

[1] That is, the sin is in the attitude he takes to the transgression and not in the actual act of commission. See Ash'ari, 140; Shahr., 107; Iji, 361. Ash'ari also reports of him that the Ḳur'ān, acc. to him, is an unoriginated and uncreated occurrence-in-time; the same is true of God's will and love, 300 and 583.

[2] Ed. واستحفاقه (a non-existent verb); MS. not clear. The reading chosen here is supported by Al-Ash'ari, 140: واستخفافه.

[3] Maḳrīzi, ib., names him successively Murjite, Khārijite and Mu'tazilite, adding that he was called a collector of faults and shunner of good qualities.

[4] Bishr b. Ghaiyāth b. Abu Karīma al-Marīsi (Yaḳūt, IV, 515, reads it Al-Marrīsi) is said to have been of Jewish parentage. Marrisa is a village in Egypt, Yakut, ib. Ikhall, I, 260, seems disinclined to accept this derivation since Marrisa acc. to him is inhabited by negroes. He cites a report that Bishr was the son of a Jewish goldsmith in Kūfa (*Mīzān*, I, 150, makes him a fuller and dyer). Bishr was a Ḥanīfite, nevertheless his views on the creation of the Ḳur'ān necessitated his concealment during the Khalīfate of Hārūn al-Rashīd and Al-Amīn for a period of some twenty years. Ibn Ḥazm regards him as closest to the orthodox of all the Mu'tazilites, *Shiites*, I, 29.

[5] He was Bishr's teacher and author of the famous *Kitab al-Kharaj*. His full name is Abu Yūsuf Ya'ḳūb b. Ibrahīm (Maḳrīzi, ib.; *Mukhtaṣar*, 12, 125, note 2). Cf. *Mīzān*, ib.

[6] Both Ed. and MS. read the verb in the plural.

Mu'tazila called him a heretic. He was thus an outcast from both the Ṣifātiyya and the Mu'tazila[1]. He used to say of faith that it is an avowal both within the heart and by word of mouth, just as Ibn Rawendi said that non-belief is disavowal and denial[2]. They both believed that kneeling before an idol is not abjuration but is merely evidence of it. These five sects make up the Murjites who reject both determinism[3] and free will.

The Ḳadarite Murjites, like Abu Shimr[4], Ibn Shabīb[5], Ghailān[6] and Ṣāliḥ Ḳubba[7] differ among themselves in regard to faith. Abu Shimr[8] says that faith is a knowledge and confession of God and of whatever has come down from Him upon which the community is agreed, such as prayer, the poor-rate, fasting, the pilgrimage, the prohibition against the flesh of carcasses and against blood, and the flesh of swine, incest, and so on; also, a confession of the justice of God,[9] His unity, and a denial of any resemblance between Him and any creature, — all of which is rationally known. By justice[10] he has reference to his views on free will, and by unity he means divesting God of His eternal attributes. All this, he said, is faith. Anyone doubting it is a heretic and anyone harassed by doubts

---

[1] Isf. 47a, relates that he used to discuss with Al-Shāfi'i, but when the latter learned that he was partly in agreement with the Sunnites and partly with the Ḳadarites he said to him: You are half a believer and half a heretic.

[2] Ash'ari, 141.

[3] Reading الجبر; Ed. and MS. الخبر.

[4] This is the pronunciation given by Sam'āni, 338a. Although he calls him a Ḳadarite, his views on faith are identical with those of the Yūnusiyya, with whom Ash'ari, 134, classes him in the discussion. Horten, *Systeme*, 304-5, places his death in 860 A.D.

[5] Muḥammad ibn Shabīb was a contemporary of Abu Shimr, Horten, *l.c.*, 308.

[6] Iji, 360, names him either Merwān or Abu Merwān ibn Ghailān, although several lines below he also accepts the possibility that his own name was Ghailān. He was one of the foremost theologians and reformers of his time and became a martyr for his doctrines. Horten, *l.c.*, 121-5. Naubakhti, 6, names his father Merwān.

[7] A disciple of Al-Naẓẓām. Cf. Horten, *l.c.*, 307.

[8] Ed. ابن مبشر; MS. not clear. The reading here is required by the context.

[9] Both Ed. and MS. read عدل الايمان. But, aside from the fact that the terms justice and unity are always applied to Allah, they make no sense with the MS. reading. Read عدل الله.

[10] Reading بالعدل instead of بالعقل contra Ed. and MS.

regarding the doubter is also a heretic[1] and so on forever. He held that this knowledge does not constitute faith save in conjunction with a verbal confession. Despite this innovation, Abu Shimr would not say of anyone sharing his views on free will who sinned that he is an outright sinner, but he would say that he is a sinner in this or that respect[2]. To the orthodox Muslims this group is the most
heretical among the Murjites since it combines both errors of free will and post- 194
ponement. The justice of God to which Abu Shimr refers is real polytheism because thereby he means to establish two great creators other than God. The divine unity to which he refers is a denial of attributes because he wishes thus to divest God of His knowledge, His power, His vision, and His other eternal attributes. What he says about his opponents, that they are heretics, and that he who doubts their heresy is a heretic himself, closely agrees with what the Sunnites say of him: that he himself is a heretic and that whoever doubts it is a heretic.

Ghailān, the Ḳadarite, combined free will and postponement[3] and believed that faith consists in the secondary knowledge of God, love of and humility before Him and a confession of belief in what the Apostle announced and in what has come down from God. The primary knowledge, he held, is innate and cannot be called faith[4]. In his History of Heretical Sects, Zurḳān[5] states that, according to Ghailān, faith is a confession by word of mouth but that knowledge of God is inherent and is an act of God; it cannot be called faith. Ghailān also held that faith can be neither increased nor decreased, nor can people excel one another in it.

Muḥammad Ibn Shabīb held that faith is a confession of God and a knowledge of His Apostles and of all that has been revealed by Him: prayer, the poor-rate, fasting and pilgrimage, which the Muslims have accepted, and everything else regarding which they do not differ[6]. Faith. he said, is compound

---

[1] Ash'ari, 152.

[2] Ash'ari, 134.

[3] In general he agreed with the doctrines of Abu Shimr, Ash'ari, 136.

[4] The first knowledge is that things are created and controlled, Ash'ari, ib.

[5] One of the disciples of al-Naẓẓām. He is said to have been very well-versed in Theology. Arnold, *al-Mu'tazila*, 35. Ritter in *Islam*, XVIII (1929). 38.

[6] With the exception of the greater stress laid by him on works, this creed is very much like that of Yūnus. Ash'ari, 137.

and people may excel one another in it[1]. A single tenet may be part of faith.
He who transgresses it is a heretic because he renouncas part of faith; one can
be a believer only[2] by adhering to all of it. Al-Ṣāliḥi held that faith is solely
195 knowledge of God and heresy only ignorance of Him. A statement to the effect
that God is one of three is not in itself heresy[3], although it will be made only
by a heretic. Whoever disavows the Apostle is not a believer, not because this
is absurd but because the Apostle said: He who does not believe in me is not
a believer in God[4]. He believed that prayer, the poor-rate, fasting and pilgrimage
are acts of obedience but do not constitute worship; there is no worship except
belief in Him, that is, knowledge of Him. Faith, according to him, is a unit,
which can be neither increased nor decreased. In the same way heresy is a unit.
These are the doctrines of the Murjites in matters of faith, and they are called so
because they make works secondary to faith.

---

[1] *Ib.*, 133.

[2] Reading إلا although both Ed. and MS. lack it.

[3] IH, II, 3, attributes this view to Jahm b. Ṣafwān, Al-Karrām and Al-Ash'ari. See Ash'ari, 132-3,

[4] The tradition is related by Aḥmad b. Ḥanbal, V, 382 top; Tayālisi, No. **242.**

CHAPTER FIVE

THE DOCTRINES OF THE NAJJĀRIYYA[1] SECTS

These are the followers of Al-Ḥusain ibn Muḥammad al-Najjār[2]. They agree with us in some fundamental dogmas and with the Ḳadarites in others. On certain principles they maintain a unique position. They are of one mind with us in their belief that God is the Creator of the acquired acts of man[3], and that the power to act is acquired simultaneously with the act[4]; nothing comes into existence unless God wills it. They also agree with us on the question of retribution and the admissibility of forgiveness to sinners and on most problems concerning what 196
it is proper and what it is wrong[5] for God to do.

They share the Ḳadarite views about divesting God of His knowledge, power, life, and His other eternal attributes; about considering visibility absurd[6] and about believing that the word of God is created. The Ḳadarites call them heretics be-

---

[1] They are called Ḥusainiyya by Ash'ari, 283,

[2] His full name is Ḥusain (Maḳrīzi, 350, IH, III, 2, *Ghunya*, 103: Ḥasan) b. Muḥammad b. 'Abdallāh al-Najjār Abu 'Abdallāh (Sam'āni also adds Al-Rāzi, probably a mistake for Al-Rayyi). He is said to have been a weaver or a maker of balances. He had frequent discussions with Al-Naẓẓām, whose disciple he was. In a serious discussion Al-Naẓẓām, angered by Al-Najjār's refusal to grant him a certain argument, kicked him and cursed anyone who would teach him anything. Al-Najjār left heated, caught cold and died. *Fihrist*, 179, and Maḳrīzi, 350; (the latter apparently from *Fihrist*).

[3] It is this question which the heated discussion developed.

[4] Ash'ari, 283.

[5] Reading والتجوير with MS.; Ed. والتحوير.

[6] Acc. to IH, III. 2, Al-Najjār taught that His visibility in the world to come was possible but that he was not convinced of it. Ash'ari, 283, and Shahr., 262, explain that he thought it possible only if God should transfer to the eye the characteristics of the heart, and then it could have a visible perception of Him.

cause of what they believe in common with us and we call them heretics by reason of their partial agreement with the Ḳadarites.

That which makes the Najjāriyya a distinct unit in religious matters is their opinion that faith consists of a knowledge of God and His prophets and those of His commandments upon which the Muslims are unanimously agreed, coupled with humility before Him, and a confession by word of mouth. He who shows ignorance of any of these truths after evidence in proof of them has reached him, or he who knows them yet does not confirm them, is guilty of Kufr (disbelief). They say: Every single article of faith is an act of obedience but is not faith; only all of them together compose faith. But a single article isolated from the rest is neither faith nor obedience. Faith can be increased but not decreased[1].

Al-Najjār held that the body is made up of an agglommeration of accidents, being those accidents from which a body cannot be disjoined[2]: color, taste, odor, and those other properties, or their opposites, of which a body cannot be divested. No property, or its opposite, of which a body may be devoid, such as knowledge or ignorance, and the like, can in any way be regarded as part of the body. He also maintained that the Word of God is an accident if recited, and a body if written[3]. If it were written in blood, this blood shaped into letters would become the Word of God, although it was not a word when it was only shed blood[4].

These are the fundamental principles of the Najjāriyya. Afterwards they split up into many sects because of the divergences among them as to the explanation[5]
197 of the creation of the Ḳur'ān and to the proper attitude to the doctrines of their opponents; and they declared one another heretical. The best known among them

---

[1] Ash'ari, 136., Isf. 47a omit the negative before ينقص, but it is probably the copyist's error.

[2] This view is very similar to Ḍirār's, see below 16, and *Usūl*, 47. The latter adds that acc. to Al-Najjār a thing may exist as a property in one state and as a substance in another (in this he was no doubt influenced by his teacher Al-Naẓẓām, see Horten, *ZDMG*, LXIII [1909], 780-1). Ḍirār's and Al-Najjār's views are expounded more fully, Ash'ari, 305-6. They are cautious enough to explain that this process of agglomeration is to be conceived of as occurring at the beginning of the production of the accidents and not since their existence.

[3] Ash'ari, 594 (ascribed to Ḍirār, as in the conception of bodies).

[4] Sam'āni, 554a, brands this theory as utter heresy since it implies that unclean substances like blood or wood can become the Word of God.

[5] Reading العبارة with MS. and Isf.; Ed. العبادة.

are the Burghūthiyya, the Za'farāniyya, and the Mustadrika, — a subdivision of the second.

The Burghūthiyya.—They are the followers of Muḥammad ibn 'Īsa, nicknamed Burghūth (flea)[1]. He adhered to most of Al-Najjār's doctrines but opposed him with regard to terming the acquirer an agent; he abstained from this, while Al-Najjār affirmed it without qualifications. He also assumed a contradictory position on generated effects, for he believed that they are God's acts by necessity in the sense that God formed the stone so that it must fly if it is hurled[2], or that He endowed animals with a nature which must suffer pain when hurt. Al-Najjār adopted our view on effects, maintaining that they are God's acts by choice, and not the result of a characteristic in the body, which is called the cause[3].

The Za'farāniyya. — They are the followers of Al-Za'farāni[4] who lived in Rai. He had a way of contradicting one of his statements by another. He would say that God's Word is not of His essence, and whatever is outside God's essence is created. Yet despite this he said: A dog is preferable to one who says God's Word is created[5]. Some historians relate that this Al-Za'farāni desired to be known everywhere. He therefore hired a man to go to Mecca at the time of the fairs to vilify and curse him so that his name would become familiar among pilgrims from distant lands[6]. The stupidity of his adherents in Rai is such that some of

---

[1] IH, III, 22, calls him *Al-Kātib*.

[2] Reading دفع with MS.; Ed. وقع.

[3] For the orthodox view on effects see Ed. 328 (below 194).

[4] Probably after a town Za'farāniyya (there are several by that name, Yāḳūt, II, s. v.) From an incident recounted in *Nujūm* (see below), he probably lived in the second half of the third century A. H., so that he was almost a contemporary of Al-Najjār. One is tempted to identify him with Al-Ḥasan b. Muḥammad (or Al-Faḍl. *Lisān al-Mīzān*, II, 244), a discredited Rāwi, who died about 260. But Sam'āni does not relate the sect to him (275 b). Perhaps our al-Za'farāni is to be identified with a man of similar name and similar views on the Ḳur'ān, mentioned by Goldziher, *ZDMG*, LXII (1908), 7. This identification supports the above dates.

[5] On this Isf. remarks: ومن كان كلامه على هذا النمط كان الكلام في عقله لا في دينه, 47 b. Shahr. by his ambiguous ولعلهم ارادوا بذلك الاختلاف (62), may perhaps mean that they sought to draw a distinction between God and the Ḳur'ān, without admitting its creation. Cf. *Systeme*, 148.

[6] This incident is related *Nujūm*, II, 226—7, and the one pronouncing the curse is given as Abu 'Abbās al-Sarrāj, a famous traditionist, who died 312 or 313 (Sam'āni, 295 a).

them refuse to eat raisins in deference to Al-Za'farāni; for they believe that he
198 relished them. "We shall not eat what he liked," they would say.

The Mustadrika. — They are a group of people among the Najjāriyya who believe that they have clarified what was obscure to their forerunners, in as much as the latter had abstained from asserting unhesitatingly that the Kur'ān is created. The Mustadrika maintain that it is created, but they have broken up into two divisions regarding this. One argues that the Prophet stated definitely that God's Word is created in so far as the arrangement of these letters goes, but he believed it, when saying this word, regarding his arrangement of its letters[2]. Whoever does not grant that the Prophet asserted as much is a heretic. The other division insists that the Prophet did not definitely state that God's Word is created in so far as the arrangement of letters goes, but that he was convinced of it and indicated it. Anyone believing that he actually said, in so many words, God's Word is created is a heretic.

There are some members of the Mustadrika in Rai who think that the views held by their antagonists are all false so that if one of them said of the sun that it is the sun, he would still be lying. 'Abd-al-Ķāhir relates: I once held a discussion with one of them in Rai and asked him: Tell me, what is your attitude to my statement that you are an intelligent person born of wedlock and not of fornication. Am I right? He said: You are lying. This answer of yours is correct, I told him. He kept silence in shame. Praised be Allah for **it.**

---

[2] This passage is altogether unclear. The Arabic text is a follows: زعمت ان النبي... قد قال ان كلام الله مخلوق على ترتيب هذه الحروف. ولكنه اعتقد ذلك بهذه اللفظة على ترتيبه حروفها. Apparently it means that the word of God as recited and read is created, but that there is an eternal Ķur'ān existing which God revealed to Muḥammad. Cf. Shahr. 62; Iji. 361; *Systeme* 148.

CHAPTER SIX

THE JAHMIYYA, THE BAKRIYYA AND THE DIRĀRIYYA AND AN EXPOSITION OF THEIR DOCTRINES

The Jahmiyya are followers of Jahm ibn Ṣafwān[1] who believed in the compulsory nature and inevitableness of our acts and denied altogether our power to act. He held that paradise and hell will come to an end and perish[2]. He also maintained that faith consists only of a knowledge of God, while non-belief is simply ignorance of Him[3]. He said: No act or deed belongs to anyone other than God. They are attributed to creatures only metaphorically[4]. We say, the sun went down and the mill turned, without implying that they are agents or that it lies in their power to do what they have been described as doing. He further maintained that God's knowledge is something come-into-existence[5]. He

[1] Jahm b. Ṣafwān Abu Miḥraz (acc. to Ṭab., II, 1924: Abu Muḥriz), Maula of the Banu Rāsib, and secretary to Al-Hārith b. Suraij (Wellhausen, *Arab Kingdom*, 464) during the latter's governorship in Khurāsān, was a native of Balkh, but first made his views public in Tirmidh and for this reason he is frequently called Al-Tirmidhi (he is also called Al-Samarkandi). See IH, III, 129; Sam'āni, 145 b; *Lisān al-Mīzān*, II, 142.

[2] Ash'ari, 289 and 148—9; *Bad'wal-Ta'rīkh*, V. 154—5 (Ar. 146); *Usūl*, 333; Iji, 362; Shahr., 61. His views on Paradise are refuted IH, IV, 84. See *Intisār*, 12.

[3] Ash'ari 132 and 279; Shahr., ib. As our author has pointed out (Ed., 190, above) his views on faith are those of a Murjite.

[4] Ash'ari. 279; *Bad'-wal-Ta'rīkh*, ib.; Shahr., 60—1; Isf. 49 a; Cf. IH, III, 23 top, and the refutation of the Jahmiyya on the remainder of the page and foll.

[5] The reason for his theory is this: If we assume, that He knows entities before they come into existence, we shall have to assume one of two things about His knowledge when the entity is created: Either a change takes place, becoming a knowledge of something present and not future, as before, or He remains ignorant of it now that it is actual. Since both are absurd, we must grant a created knowledge. But to avoid change this knowledge must be created not

refused to define God as a Something, or as the Living, the Knowing or the Willing. His explanation is: I shall not qualify Him by an attribute which may be generally applied to others, such as the existent or the living, knowing or williug, and others like them[1]. But he described Him as the Powerful One, the Bringer into Existence, the Agent, Creator, Giver of life or death, because these attributes are exclusively His. Like the Ḳadarites he contended that God's Word is created and he did not call God the Speaker of that word. We condemn him as a heretic for
200 all of his errors and the Ḳadariyya declare him a Kāfir for his assertion that God is the Creator of the acts of mankind. The several divisions of our community therefore coincide in charging him with unbelief. In addition to his blunders, which we have related, Jahm used to carry a weapon and make war on the ruler[2]. Together with Shuraiḥ[3] ibn al-Ḥārith he proceeded against Naṣr ibn Sayyār[4], but Salm ibn Aḥwaz al-Māzini[5] killed him towards the end of the epoch of the 'Umayyad dynasty. At present his followers are in Tirmidh[6]. In our time, Isma'īl ibn Ibrahīm ibn Kabūs al-Shīrāzi al-Daili went forth to preach to them the doctrine of our

---

in Him but in another subject. Shahr., 60; Cf. Iji, ib. and IH, II, 127—9; Shahr. and Ibn Rawendi see a similarity between this view and that of Hishām al-Ḥakam, and al Khayyāṭ grants it, but denies that Jahm was a Mu'tazilite--*Intiṣār*, 126.

[1] Ash'ari, 280; *Uṣūl*, Iji, *Bad'wal-Ta'rīkh*, Shahr. ib.; In *Ibāna*, 54—5, Al-Ash'ari charges that Jahm really meant to deny that God was knowing, living, etc., but that fear for his life compelled him to employ this explanation.

[2] This refers to his position in the service of al-Ḥārith, who rebelled against the 'Umayyads. Cf. Wellhausen, l. c. 464 ff.

[3] The name of this man is twisted. It should be Al-Ḥārith Ibn Suraij (Ed. and MS. Shuraiḥ) who was a rebel governor of Khurāsān since 115 (ib), and employed Jahm as his Kātib, ib. Wellhausen lays great stress on Ḥārith's Murjite theories.

[4] Reading Sayyār with MS.; Ed. يسار (Yassār). Naṣr b. Sayyār, a famous general, was sent to quell the rebellious Khurāsān and subdue Ḥārith. Having failed to bribe him recourse was had to war. Wellhausen, *l. c.* 474 ff, esp. 485—88. Naṣr was appointed governor of Khurāsān in 125.

[5] Ed. اجون; MS. اجوز; a brave soldier and faithful to the 'Umayyads. He lent his assistance to Naṣr, and in the battle between Al-Ḥārith and Naṣr, Salm took Jahm prisoner. His execution in 128 is told in Tab. II, 1924, *Lisān al-Mīzān*, II, 142. From it Salm's great hatred for Jahm is apparent, no doubt because of his rebelliousness.

[6] Ed. Nahawend; MS. gloss. بترمذ, This is supported by all authorities.

Sheikh Abu-l-Ḥasan al-Ash'ari, and a number of them have heeded his call and identified themselves with the orthodox. Praised be Allah for it.

The Bakriyya. — They are the followers of Bakr ibn Ukht 'Abd-al-Wāḥid ibn Ziyād[1]. He agrees with Al-Naẓẓām in his assertion that man is the spirit and not the body in which the spirit resides, but he agrees with us in rejecting the belief in generated effects and in making God the producer of pain when the blow falls. He thinks it possible for a blow to come with no consequent pain or cut, in conformity with our attitude. But he adhered to some unique errors for which the entire community declares him a heretic. Among them is his statement that God will be seen at the time of the Resurrection in a form which He will create, and that He will address His creatures in that form[2]. He also declared that deadly sins committed by Muslims[3] are acts of hypocrisy and that the sinner is a hypocrite[4] and a worshipper of the devil, even though he a be Sunnite. He maintained that, in addition to his being a hypocrite, the sinner is giving God the lie and disavowing Him, and for that reason will be eternally condemned to the lowest depths of hell. Nevertheless, he is a believing Muslim. Then he pursued this 201
heterodox innovation still further and said that the sins of 'Ali, Ṭalḥa and Al-Zubair were non-belief and polytheism but that they were forgiven[5] in accordance with the transmitted tradition that God looked down upon the warriors at Badr and said: "Do what you please, for I have forgiven you."[6] Another of his errors, and one in which he contradicts all rational beings, is his assertion that children in the cradle do not feel pain even if they are cut or burned[7]. He thought it possible that they experience pleasure while they are being hit or cut despite the apparent

---

[1] With *Mukhtaṣar*, 128; Ed, and MS, زيد, Acc. to Ed., 16, he was a contemporary of Wāṣil b. 'Aṭā'. Goldziher points out the interesting fact that the Bakriyya was a "one-man" sect. *ZDMG*, LXI (1907), 73.

[2] See *Intiṣār*, 144; Ash'ari, 287; Maḳrīzi, 349.

[3] Ar.; *Ahl al-Ḳibla*; it is a more general term than Ahl al-Sunna and may even include the Khawārij. Dozy, *Supplément*, s. v. *Ḳibla*.

[4] Ash'ari, 286; IH, III, 229.

[5] IH, IV, 45, mentions only Ṭalha and Zubair in this connection; but see Ash'ari, 287 and 457, and Naubakhti, 13.

[6] Aḥmad b. Ḥanbal, II, 295—6.

[7] Ash'ari, 286—7; Maḳrīzi, ib.

crying and screaming. Finally he erred in introducing into law a prohibition against eating garlic and onions[1] and he required an ablution after rumbling had been heard in the bowels[2]. There is no notice taken of it in Fiḳh by the orthodox, contrary to the people of fancy.

The Ḍirāriyya. — They are the followers of Ḍirār ibn 'Amr[3] who supported our stand that the acts of mankind are created by God and acquired by man and that the belief in generated effects is baseless. He agreed with the Mu'tazila that the power to act exists before the act. He even went further by maintaining that it persists before, during and after the act, and that it forms part of the one exerting it. He also followed Al-Najjār, since they both contend that the body is an agglomeration of accidents such as color, taste, odor and others of which a body cannot be devoid[4]. But he stood alone in a number of impious statements. He said, for example, that on the day of resurrection God will be seen with a sixth sense with which the faithful will behold God's essence[5]. He said: God's
202 essence is such as none other than He can know, but the faithful will see it with a sixth sense. In this he was followed by Ḥafḍ al-Fard[6]. He also denied the Ḳur'ānic readings of Ibn Mas'ūd and Ubai ibn Ka'b[7] and he argued that God did not reveal them and he accused these two Imāms from among the Companions of

---

[1] Ash'ari, ib., informs us that he forbade a person under such circumstances to approach a mosque. The law may be of Hindoo origin. CF. *Shiites*, II, 76.

[2] Ib.

[3] Like Bakr he was also a contemporary of the first Mu'tazilite.

[4] *Uṣul*, 47; for further details of Ḍirār's view see Ed. 196 (above 10).

[5] This view, for which all the Mutakallims condemn him, is quite acceptable to *IH* who, in stating that mankind will receive a special faculty in the world to come, adds; Some of those who profess this view call it the sixth sense, III, 2. See *Intiṣār*, 133—4.

[6] He is described in *Fihrist*, 180, as one of the staunchest Jabarites and similar in his views to Al Najjār. *Intiṣār*, ib., asserts definitely that he, as well as Ḍirār, was not a Mu'tazilite The two are generally mentioned together.

[7] The editors of the two, respectively, out of the four pre-'Uthmānic recensions of the Ḳur'ān. Ibn Mas'ūd's Ed. was adopted in Kūfa and Ubai's in Damascus. For their lives as well as for a detailed discussion of the nature of their work see Noeldeke-Schwally, *Geschichte des Qorans*, I? 27—12.

error in their recensions[1]. Another impiety was his suspicion of the common folk in the Muslim community, for he asserted: I do not know; perhaps the inner thoughts of the common people are nothing but polytheism and non-belief. He also declared that what we mean when we say that God is knowing or living is that He is not ignorant nor dead[2], and he drew similar parallels for all the other attributes of God, without establishing a meaning or deriving an advantage other than denial of the qualities by contradicting them.

---

[1] Shahr., 63.
[2] *Ib*

CHAPTER SEVEN

THE DOCTRINES AND CHARACTERISTICS OF THE KARRĀMIYYA

The Karrāmiyya in Khurāsān form three groups, the Ḥaḳāḳiyya, the Ṭarā'iḳiyya, and the Isḥāḳiyya, These three divisions do not regard one another as heretical although the other sects condemn them as Kāfirs. For this reason we have counted them as one sect. Its founder, known as Muḥammad ibn Karrām[1], was banished from Sijistān[2] to Gharjistān[3]. His followers in his time were the feeble-minded of Shūramain[4] and Afshīn, and they came with him[5] to Nīshāpūr
203 during the governorship of Muḥammad ibn Ṭāhir ibn 'Abdallah ibn Ṭāhir[6]. A part of the population in the rural districts of Nīshāpūr followed him in his innovations,

---

[1] He was born in Nīshāpūr where his father was a vintner (*Lisān al-Mīzān*, V, 354, challenges this explanation of his father's name, claiming that it was rejected by the Karrāmiyya themselves. See also Iji, 362). He grew up in Sijistān and went from there to Khurāsān. Then he stayed in Mecca for five years until he was finally imprisoned there by Ṭāhir b. 'Abdallah. After his release he went to Syria and from there to Nīshāpūr, but was again arrested, this time by Muḥammad Ibn 'Abdallah ibn Ṭāhir, and was detained in prison for some eight years. When he obtained his freedom he went to Jerusalem where he died in 255. He was a pious and ascetic individual. The Sunnites describe him as a person whose exterior is fine but whose interior is vile. Sam'āni, 476 b—77 a; *Lisān*, 353—5; IA, VII, 149; *Nujūm*, II, 24; Isf. 50 a.

[2] Ed. and MS. سغستان.

[3] The common name for Gharjushār, a district west of Herāt and south of Ghazna. Yaḳūt, III, 785; Muḳaddasi, 309.

[4] Or Suramain which, together with Afshīn, constitute the two important cities of Gharjushār. On the variants of the two names see Istakhri, 271 and notes; and Muḳaddasi, 309. See Yaḳūt, ib.

[5] Reading معه with Ms.; Ed. مع.

[6] He was appointed governor of Khurāsān by Musta'īn in 248, IA, VII, 77. It was he who imprisoned him, see first note.

and also a part of the weavers[1] and distressed ones[2] of the villages. The errors of his followers at the present day are so diverse that we cannot enumerate them by fours or sevens but we should have to go thousands beyond thousands. We shall only mention the well-known among them, and these we shall relate with disgust. Ibn Karrām urged his followers to ascribe corporeality to the Object of his Worship. He held that He is a body, possessing an end and limit below, where He comes in contact with His throne. This is similar to the doctrine of the Dualists, since their God, whom they call Light, is limited on the side which borders on darkness[3]; but is not limited in the five other directions. In one of his books Ibn Karrām has described[4] the Object of his Worship as a substance, just as the Christians believe that God is a substance. In this vein he wrote in the preface to his book, which is entitled *The Tortures in the Grave*, that God is a Unit of essence and a Unit of substance[5]. His adherents at the present time do not permit the general public to use the word 'substance' for God, fearing demoralization as a result of its publication. But the application of the term body to Him is more demoralizing than the use of the word 'substance'. Their refraining from calling Him substance, while asserting that He is a body, is like Shaiṭān al-Ṭāķ[6], the Rāfiḍite, refraining[7] from calling God a body while maintaining that He is of human form. No rule can be set as to the avoidance (of a term) when any one selected is bad.

---

[1] I. e. the ignorant. See *ZDMG*, LXV (1911), 360.

[2] Reading والزنهم with MS.; Ed. والدتهم. Goldziher *(ZDMG, ib.)*, reads واذلتهم.

[3] Reading الظلام with *Mukhtaṣar*, 132 and Isf. ib.; MS. and Ed. الكلام. This doctrine has been especially developed by the Manicheans, see Jackson, ***Researches in Manichaeaism***, 222—4.

[4] An exposition of his views nearly as full as our author's will be found in Shahr., 80—5. In addition to the similarity between the Karrāmiyya and Christians which our author indicates, Sam'āni compares them to the Jews, the Hishāmiyya und Jawāliķiyya (see next chapter) in their doctrine which ascribes a body to God, 477a.

[5] Reading الجوهر with MS. and Isf. 50b; Ed. الجواهر; Shahr., 80.

[6] His real name is Muḥammad ibn Nu'mān; IH, II, 112 calls him Ibn Ja'far, but see *Intiṣār*, 177, and *Shiites*, II, 29. Naubakhti counts him, among others, as a supporter of Mūsa al-Kāthim's claims to the Caliphate, 66.

[7] Ed. adds the word تسمية before Shaiṭān which is not in MS., and is probably due to dittography.

Ibn Karrām writes in his work that God touches His throne and that the throne is a place for Him. But his followers have substituted the word contiguity
204 (*Mulākāt*) tor the word touching (*Mumāssat*) and explained: The existence of a body between Him and the throne is true only if the throne declines[1] downward[2]. This is the significance of touching, the use of which they avoid. His followers differ regarding the meaning of Istiwā (firmness) which is used in His Word "the Merciful One sits firmly (Istawa) on His throne"[3]. Some of them are of the opinion

---

[1] Reading ينحط with MS. and *Uṣūl*, 77; Ed. يحيط.

[2] I. e., contiguity does not mean that there is another body between Him and the throne, unless the throne declines downward. *Uṣūl*, ib. On the distinction between touching and contiguity, Isf. *ib.*, remarks: "I wish I knew what is the difference between them".

[3] Sura 20, v. 5. This verse which Goldziher has characterizcd as "the subject of heated disputes in Muḥammadan schools" (*David Kaufmann Festschrift*, 87) serves as an outstanding example of the cleavage between the literalists and rationalists. (A good illustration of this is afforded by the fact that in demonstration of the truth of literalism the six Istiwā verses were posted on the mosque in Ḥamadān. — cited by Goldziher, *ZDMG*, LXII [1908], 8). The attitude of the Ḥanbalites and Mālikites is simple. Refusing to go the full length of the Karrāmiyya they adopted the classic remark of Mālik's (see Ibn Taimiyya, *Rasā'il* I, 432.): I know that God sits on His throne but I do not know how (later adopted as a technical term: *bila kaifa*). This was adopted as the official stand of the more orthodox groups, esp. the Ḥanbalites; see Ṣabūni in *Rasā'il Munīriyya* I, 110—112. It is voiced most clearly by Al-Ash'ari, *Ibāna*, 42—7. His adherents have more modified views on the subject. Baiḍāwi, for example, I, 327, vacillates between the two, explains "*istawa*" as "*istawla*" but adds at the same time that "men who hold views consider *Istiwā* as an attribute of God '*bila kaifa*' ". Our author Baghdādi is still more moderate. He translates "*Istawa 'ala 'Arshihi*" to mean that the rule was firmly in God's control, *Uṣūl*, 113. Ghazāli (*Greencia* 103—*4*) identifies '*arsh* with God's power. Even the Zahirite ibn Ḥazm forsakes his adherence to a literal interpretation and adopts the interpretation that God completed His creation with the throne (II, 125). This explanation is also suggested by Maṭurīdi, 17, though he himself prefers one similar to Ghazāli's (ib., 16). Abu Ḥanīfa also belives in the throne as interpreted by the previously cited theologians. Iskandari, 10—12. The Mu'tazila, of course, deny the Istiwā', explaining it to mean istawla, "made himself master" (Ash'ari, 157 and 211—12, *Uṣūl*, 112; IH, ii, 122, 123). The most plausible explanation is probably Goldziher's that it is borrowed from the Jewish idea that when the Sabbath came He rested and sat on his throne (עד שבא שבת ונתעלה וישב על כסא כבודו). It seems therefore that Ibn Ḥazm comes nearest to the original meaning. For a rejection of the several metaphoricat interpretations see Ibn Taimiyya, *l. c.*, II, 31 ff.

that the throne is a place for Him and that if He created many thrones alongside of the existing one and all corresponding with it, they would all become a place for Him, for He is greater than all of them. This view forces them to the conclusion that His throne at the present is equal to only part of His width. But there are others who say that He is no larger than His throne on the side where He touches it and no part of Him overhangs it; this requires that His measure be equal to the measure of the throne. There was one among the Karrâmiyya in Nīshāpūr known as Ibrahīm ibn Muhājir, who defended this opinion and took its side in discussions[1].

Ibn Karrâm and his adherents hold that the Object of their Worship is a subject in which created entities exist. They believe that His utterances, His will, His visual and auditory perceptions, His contiguity to the uppermost surface[2] of the Universe, are all accidents originated in Him and He is the place for these creations which originated in Him[3]. His command to anything, "Be", they term an act-of-creating that which has been created and of bringing-forth that which has been brought forth, and of causing-destruction[4] to that which has perished after existing. They refrain from describing the properties originating in Him as created or made or come-into-existence. They also hold that no body or accident is originated in this world without the arising of many accidents in the essence of their Worshipped One, such as the will to produce that existence, His saying 205
to it "Be" in the manner in which He knows it is to exist eventually[5]. The utterance itself consists of many letters, each one of which is a property originating in Him. There is also the vision with which He will see the produced object; if that vision were not created in Him, He could not see the object; also His hearing of what is created if it is audible. They likewise maintain that no accident perishes in this world without the occurrence of many accidents in

---

[1] The details of the discussion which took place in presence of Maḥmūd of Ghazna (who was their patron; cf. Macdonald, *Muslim Theology*. 170) between Ibn Muhājir and Abu Isḥāḳ Isfaraini are related, Isf. 50b—51a.

[2] Reading صفيحة with Isf.; Ed. and MS. صحيفة.

[3] See Shahr. 81 f.

[4] Reading واعداما with Goldziher; Ed. and MS. واعلاما.

[5] I. e., the words specifying what and how the substance is to be.

their Worshipped One. One is His will that it perish; another, His command to that whose extinction He desires "Become non-existent" or "Perish". This utterance also consists of many letters, every one of which is an accident originating in Him. The creations originating in God's essence are, from their standpoint, duplicates of the bodies and accidents in the Universe [1].

The Karrāmiyya differ regarding the possibility of the extinction of those existences which. in their opinion, originate in God's substance. Some of them regard their non-existence as possible, but most of them consider it absurd [2]. However, both groups agree that God's essence will not become devoid, in the future, of the creations inhering in Him, although It was devoid of them at the beginning of time. This is similar to the opinion of those who uphold the Hylic hypothesis, that primordial matter was eternally a substance devoid of properties until the accidents came to be in it; it shall henceforth not be devoid of them.

The Karrāmiyya differ regarding whether it is possible for the bodies in the Universe to perish, and most of them think it impossible, thus conforming to
206 those of the Dahriyya and the philosophers who believe that the heaven and the stars are a fifth element which is not subject to decay or destruction [3]. People are surprised at the assertion of the Mu'tazila of Baṣra that God can cause all bodies to perish all at once, but He cannot cause some to perish while others survive. But this surprise is naught in comparison with the view of the Karrāmiyya that He is incapable of causing a body to perish at all. Even more astonishing than all this is the fact that Ibn Karrām described his Worshipped One as possessing weight. He has written in the *Book of the Tortures in the Grave* as a comment on God's Word "when the heavens shall be cleft asunder" [4] that they are rent asunder by the weight of the Merciful One pressing upon them.

---

[1] Isf. accounts for this strange theory by linking it with the theory of the Magians that when Yazdān contemplated that a rival might come forth in the Universe, He took it to heart. As a result of it corruption was created in His essence and He made Satan from it., 51 b.

[2] Reading احال with Goldziher; Ed. and MS.; واجاز both phrases, see *Uṣūl*, 50 and the refutation of this view, 52; from Isf. ib. we can gather that in general they held it to be absurd: ke objects that that will make an object existent and non-existent at the same time. See Shahr. 82--3.

[3] The Orthodox doctrine is stated Ed. 319 and 338 (below 181 and 208).

[4] Sura 82, v. 1.

Ibn Karrām and the majority of his adherents believe that God has been eternally qualified by the names derived by philologists from His acts, despite the absurdity of the eternal existence of acts. He has been eternally a creator, sustainer and benefactor, even without the existence of acts of creation, sustenance and benefit. He has been eternally a creator because of a creative faculty (*Khāliḳiyya*) in Him, and sustainer, because of a sustaining faculty (*Rāziḳiyya*) in Him. They explain His creative faculty to mean His power to create and His sustaining faculty as the power to grant sustenance. This power is eternal, whereas the acts of creating and sustaining originate in Him in time through this power of His. They say: By the act-of-creation the created object in the Universe becomes created, and by the act-of-sustainiug the sustained one is sustained. Even more astonishing than this is their distinction between the Speaker (*Mutakallim*) and the Sayer (*Ḳā'il*) and, similarly, between the Word and the Utterance. For they say: Verily, God has ever been a Speaker and a Sayer, but they distinguish between the meaning of the two names. They teach that He has always been a Speaker because of a Word, which is His power-to-utter, and He has been eternally a Sayer 207
because of a faculty-to-utter (*Ḳā'iliyya*) and not because of the utterance[1]. His faculty to utter is His power-to-utter, but His utterance consists of letters originating in Him. The utterance of God, according to them, is therefore created in Him, but His Word is eternal[2].

'Abd al-Ḳāhir relates: I discussed this point with one of them and said to him: Since you are of the opinion that the Word is the power-to-utter, and the silent person in his state of silence is, according to you, capable of uttering, you are therefore forced to admit that the silent person is a speaker. He admitted it. Among the subtleties of the Karrāmiyya in this connection is their following argument: We admit, generally speaking, that God has been eternally a creator and a sustainer, but we do not admit that He has never ceased to create the created and sustain the sustained in a particular relation. We recognize this relation only from the time when the created objects or the sustained objects already existed. By analogy with this, they maintain that God never ceased to be worshipped but He has not been eternally worshipped by worshippers, becom-

[1] Reading بقول with MS.; Ed. يقول.

[2] Isf. 52 b.; See *EI*, II, 773.

ing so only when the worshippers and their worship came into existence. Ibn Karrām in his *Book of the Tortures in the Grave* prefixes a certain chapter with an astonishing title, calling it "A Chapter on the 'Qualitiness' (كيفوفية) of God". The intelligent person does not know what to wonder at, whether at his audacity in accepting without reserve the word *quality* as an attribute of God or at his vileness in expressing *quality* by *qualitiness*. He has a number of examples of this sort of usage, among which we find his statement in the section entitled Refutation of the Traditionists on Faith which reads as follows: "If their books (صحوفيتهم) should say, faith is word and deed, we shall say to them so and so". In the same way he has designated in one of his books the place of the Object
208 of his Worship by the term *ubiquitousness* (حيثوثية). These ugly expressions match his ugly doctrine[1].

He and his followers, in discussing the objects of God's power, maintain that His power extends only over those created objects which are brought forth in His essence, such as His will, His utterances. His perceptions, and His contiguity to that with which He comes in contact, But the created bodies and properties in the world are in no way the objects of God's power, nor does His power extend over them all despite their created state. For He created every being in the world with His utterance "Be" and not with His power. In this innovation they have no predecessors. True, people before them have differed regarding the powers of God. Thus the Orthodox say[2] that every created being is the object of God's power before it was brought forth, He being the originator with His power, of all originated entities[3]. Mu'ammar held that all bodies are the objects of God's power before He created them but that the accidents are neither created by Him nor objects of His power. Most of the Mu'tazila assert that bodies, colors, tastes, smells, and the other types of accidents are objects of God's power, but they withhold from describing Him as possessing power over the objects of power ascribed to beings other than He[4]. The Jahmiyya say: All things brought forth are the objects of God's power and there is no possessor

[1] Ib. 52a; Isf. adds a few more examples.

[2] Adding قفال after مذاهب with MS.; missing in Ed.

[3] Ed. 322-3 (below 185—6).

[4] Referring to the controversy over human acts *(aksāb)*; see Ed. 327-8

of power and no agent other than He[1]. But no one before the Karrāmiyya spoke about the limitation of God's power to created objects which originate in His essence, according to them. Far be God from their views.

In the field of God's justice and injustice[2] they have also proposed some astonishing theses. One of them is that the first entity which God created must have necessarily been a living body, endowed with reason[3]. They maintain that 209
if He had begun by creating inanimate objects He would not be wise. In this heresy they exceed the Ḳadariyya and their contention that there are certainly created beings for whom it is reasonable to assume understanding, but that the first creation need not necessarily have been a living being endowed with reason. With this heresy they have repudiated true tradition to the effect that the first things which He created were the Tablet and the Pen; then He made the Pen trace upon the Tablet all that will take place on the day of resurrection[4]. They maintain that if God had created mankind while knowing that not one of them would believe in Him, His creation would have been a sport. But it pleased Him to create all of them because He knew that some of them would believe in Him. The Orthodox retort that if He had created the unbelievers and not the believers, or if He had created the believers and not the infidels, it would still have been possible, and would not have impugned His justice[5]. The Karrāmiyya maintain that God's justice does not allow the deprivation of the lives of children about whom He knows that if He spared them to the time of their maturity they would be believers[6]. Nor is it right of Him to bring death upon an infidel who, if he had been spared for a period of time, would have become a believer unless an act of righteousness to someone else is involved in the premature death which he brings upon him[7]. By this doctrine they are compelled to admit

---

[1] Ed. 199 (above 13).

[2] Reading والتجوير with MS.; Ed. والتحوير.

[3] Iji, 362.

[4] This tradition which Goldziher, who discusses it in *ZA*, XXII (1908), 321, calls "ein sehr verbreitetes Ḥadīth" is recorded with various readings in Ṭab. I, 29—38.

[5] This is expounded more fully Ed. 331 (below 198—9).

[6] Ash'ari, 250.

[7] Ib. and 249—50.

that God must have caused the death of Ibrahīm, the son of the Prophet, before his maturity, because He knew that if He had spared him he would not have been a believer[1]. In this way they slander all children of prophets, who died prematurely.

Among their follies on the subject of prophecy and the apostolate is their belief that prophecy and apostleship are two attributes inherent in the prophet or
210 the apostle; they are not the revelation to him, nor his miracles nor his immunity from sin. They hold that everyone who is affected by this attribute must necessarily be sent by God[2]. They distinguish between the apostle and the sent one in that the apostle is he in whom that attribute inheres, and the sent one is he who is charged with carrying the apostleship into execution. They next occupy themselves with the problem of the prophets' immunity from sin. They teach that they are immune from every sin which disqualifies them from giving testimony or which renders punishment necessary, but they are not immune from lesser sins[3]. Some of them say that they cannot possibly sin while conveying the message, but others think it admissible. They believe that the Prophet was guilty of a lapse in delivering His Word: "And Manāt is the third, the last",[4] and in adding: "These are the exalted females whose intercession is to be sought after". The orthodox explain that this word was an interlocution by Satan who interpolated it between the parts of the Prophet's sermon. Our sheikh, Abu-l-Ḥasan al-Ash'ari, has asserted in one of his books that after the descent of prophecy upon them, prophets are immune from both deadly and minor sins.

The Karrāmiyya also believe that when a prophet's call is announced, it is incumbent upon everyone who hears it from him, or upon everyone whom a

---

[1] See *Muh. St.*, II, 105—6.

[2] Isf. 53 a contends that by this definition they deny to the Prophet the acquired acts on the merit of which he becomes worthy of prophecy and thus deny his reward. In Ibn Karrām's entire heretical conception of prophecy and apostleship Tor Andrae would recognize the θεῖος ἄνθρωπος of the Pneumatics. *Die Person Muhammeds*, 292—4.

[3] On the question of the prophets' immunity from sin see Ed. 333 (below 201—2).

[4] Sura 53, v. 20. The second half of the verse cited in the Text does not occur in the Ḳur'ān; but see Lane, s. v. غرنيق. An elucidating discussion of the entire problem in connection with this verse will now be found in Tor Andrae's recently published *Mohammed sein Leben und Glaube*, 14—19,

report of him reaches, to put his trust in him and to confess his belief in him without waiting for a recognition of his proof[1]. They stole this innovation from the Ibāḍiyya among the Khawārij who argue that the prophet's utterance about himself: "I am a prophet" is in itself[2] proof which requires no other sign[3]. The Karrāmiyya further hold that one whom the call of the prophet has not reached
is bound to believe the rational axioms and to believe that God sends messengers 211
to mankind[4]. Most of the Ḳadariyya have already anticipated them in the view regarding the necessity of believing in certain rational principles, but no one before them has declared that it is necessary to believe in the existence of prophets before reports of their existence have arrived. The Karrāmiyya also maintain that if God had confined the charge unto mankind to one messenger from the beginning of time to the Day of Judgment, and continued the law of the first messenger, He would not be just. The Sunnites reply that if God had done this it would be admissible just as the law of the Seal of the Prophets to His community until the Day of Judgment is admissible.

Ibn Karrām tackled next the question of the Imāmate. He allowed the incumbency of two Imāms at the same time despite the ensuing quarrels, the engagements in battle, and the divergences in law[5]. He uses as proof the fact that both 'Ali and Mu'āwiya were Imāms at the same time[6]. The adherents of each of the two were obliged to obey the other even though one of them was just and the other a usurper. His followers say that 'Ali was the Imām in conformity to the Sunna, while Mu'āwiya was an Imām in contradiction to the Sunna, yet it was the duty of the followers of each of them to obey the other. Is there anything more wonderful than the duty to obey something that contradicts the Sunna?

The Karrāmiyya also attacked the problem of faith. They hold that it

---

[1] For the relations between this view and a possible skepticism about prophetic miracles see Andrae, ***Person Muhammeds,*** 115—16.

[2] Reading بِنفسه with MS; Ed. لنفسه

[3] Ed. 86.

[4] Shahr., 84.

[5] Shahr., 85; Iji, 363; *Usūl,* 274.

[6] For the Orthodox attitude to this phenomenon see Ed. 342 (below 214).

consists only of a single confession made at the beginning of time. Its repetition is not regarded as an act of faith except from an apostate who confesses it after his apostasy[1]. They maintain that it is the confession which was made for the first time by the offspring from the loins[2] of the Prophet when they declared:
212 Certainly[3]. They believe that this declaration endures forever, becoming ineffective only in case of apostasy. They also believe that he who confesses in both parts of the Shahāda is a believer even if he is a convinced heretic with respect to the apostleship[4]. They also hold that the hypocrites, concerning whose disbelief God has revealed many verses in which He condemns them as infidels, are believers indeed and that their faith is as pure as that of the prophets and the angels[5]. Regarding the people of fancy who oppose their views as well as the views of the Sunnites they teach that their punishments in the world to come are not eternal. In truth, however, the people of fancy will witness the perpetual sufferings of the Karrāmiyya in hell.

Ibn Karrām further introduced stupidities without precedent in the Fiḳh. Among them is his statement that it is sufficient for the traveller[6] to say the *Allāh Akbar* twice without kneeling, bowing, standing, sitting or reciting the Shahāda or the Salutation[7]; also his declaration that it is proper to offer prayer in dirty clothes and on dirty ground and with a dirty body[8]. Yet he required ablutions for *Aḥdāth* and not for *Anjās*[9]. He also ruled that the washing of the dead and prayer after them are customs not ordained by law. What is obligatory

---

[1] Reading بعد ردته with MS.; Ed. بقدرته.

[2] Reading صلب with MS.; Ed. طلب.

[3] Referring to Sura 7, v. 171. See the traditions around this verse, Tirmidhī, II, 180—81. See Iji, ib; Isf. 53a-b; The Prophet is apparently Adam.

[4] Ash'ari, 141; Shahr. 84; Isf. 53a, Iji, ib; IH, II, 112.

[5] Same sources as above.

[6] Reading مسافر with Ed.; MS. مسايف.

[7] See Juynboll, 70, for the Shāfi'ite regulation for a traveller; for the various technical terms, ib. 75—80; See Muzāni (*Umm*, I, 121—30 margin).

[8] See Shāfi'ite requirements Juynboll, 71—2.

[9] *Aḥdāth* and *Anjās* are two types of impurity. The former includes semenal discharges, contact with a woman to whom one is not married, etc. The second is applied to contact with unclean objects. Juynboll, 72—4, esp. 72, note 2.

consists merely in shrouding and burying them[1]. He also recognized the validity of prayer, fasting, or the pilgrimage unaccompanied by concentration[2], maintaining that the devotion inherent in Islām since its beginning compensates for the devotion required with every commandment in Islām.

In our time a sheikh of the Karrāmiyya, Ibrahīm ibn Muhājir by name, has devised unprecedented errors. He believes that all of God's names are accidents in Him and, similarly, the name of anyone who is designated by it is an accident within the bearer. He holds that the name *Allāh* is an accident inhering in a primordial body, *Al-Raḥmān* (the Merciful One) a second accideut, *Al-Raḥīm* 213
(the Compassionate) a third, and Al-*Khāliḳ* (the Creator) a fourth. Thus every name of God is an accident distinct from the other. *Allāh,* in his view, is not *Al-Raḥmān,* and *Al-Raḥmān* is not *Al-Raḥīm,* and *Al-Khāliḳ* is not *Al-Rāziḳ* (the Sustainer). He holds further that "adulterer" is an accident in a body to which adultery is attributed and, similarly, "thief" is an accident in one against whom a charge of theft is made. But the body is neither adulterer nor thief. The flogged or amputated person, according to him, is not the adulterer nor the thief. He also holds that motion and the mover are two accidents in the body; in the same way blackness and the black are two accidents in the body, and so knowledge and the knower, power and the powerful, life and the living, are all accidents but not bodies. Knowledge, to his mind, does not reside in the knower but in him who is the place for the knower, and motion does not abide in the moving object but in that which is the place for the moving object.

'Abd-al-Ḳāhir relates: I held a disputation on this question with this Ibrahīm ibn Muhājir in the presence of Nāṣir al-Dawla, Abu-l-Ḥasan Muhammad ibn Ibrahīm ibn Sīmjūr, General of the Sāmānid army, in the year 370[3]. In it I

[1] Acc. to the Shāfi'ites all the four practices are required by law, ib., 170.

[2] Arab. *Niya* (very similar to Heb. *Kawwāna*) Acc. to Muḥammadan law, not only are an inner preparation and full-heartedness required with external practices but an actual declaration to the effect. See Hughes, *Dictionary of Islam*, 434.

[3] He had held the generalship for a long time (the first record of it in the year 354, IA, VII, 417; he had previously been chief of Khurāsān, was removed, but reinstated) until he was finally removed in 371. He is accused of having become too strong and independent. IA, IX, 7—8. He did not accept his removal and became a rebel until he was killed in 372. Ib., 17—20. See also 'Utbi, 95—119.

forced him to admit that the person flogged for adultery is not the adulterer and that the person whose hand is amputated for theft is not the thief. Then I forced him to admit that the Object of his Worship is an accident since, according to him, the Worshipped One is a name, and the names of God in his view are accidents inherent in a primordial body. He retorted: The Worshipped One is an accident in a primordial body but I worship the body and not the accident. But I answered him: In that case[1] you do not worship Allah, because Allah,
214 according to you, is an accident and you maintain that you worship the body and not the accident.

The ignominies of the Karrāmiyya are very numerous. But we have cited a sufficient number of them in this chapter, and Allah knows best.

---

[1] Reading إذاً with Ms; Ed. اذن.

CHAPTER EIGHT

THE DOCTRINES OF THE ANTHROPOMORPHISTS AMONG THE VARIOUS DIVISIONS

Know, may God make you prosper, that the *Mushabbiha* (anthropomorphists) fall under two categories, one of which likens the essence of the Creator to the essence of others, and another which draws a similarity between His attributes and the attributes of others. Each of these two is split up into many subdivisions. The Mushabbiha whose error consists in comparing His essence to that of others comprise a number of groups. The rise of the doctrine of anthropomorphism is linked with several groups among the *Ghulāt Rawāfiḍ*[1]. One of them is the Sabbābiyya who called 'Ali God and identified him with the essence of God. When he committed a number of them to the flames they declared: Now we know that you are God for none but God punishes with fire[2]. Another is the Bayāniyya, adherents of Bayān ibn Sam'ān who believed that his Worshipped One is a person of light[3] and possesses limbs which have a human form; He will perish completely save His face. Still another is the Mughīriyya, followers of Mughīra ibn Sa'īd al-'Ijli who believed that the Object of his Worship possesses limbs and that they are shaped like the letters of the alphabet. Then there are the Manṣūriyya, followers of Abu Manṣūr al-'Ijli, who likened himself to his Lord, believing that he was raised to heaven. He also thought that God patted him 215

---

[1] All the sects of the *Ghulāt Rawāfiḍ* are treated more fully in the next section and therefore no details will be given about them in this chapter.

[2] The tradition is related in Bukhāri, II, 352; the Prophet once sent a detachment with instructions that if they found certain men they were to burn them. As they were preparing to leave, he said to them: I told you to burn them, but only God punishes with fire; if you find them kill them. Cf. *Bad'wal-Tarīkh*, V, 131 (Arabic 125).

[3] Reading نور with MS.; Ed. ثور.

on his head with His hand and said: O my son, convey a message from Me. Among them are also the Khaṭṭābiyya who profess the divine character of the Imāms and of Abu-l-Khaṭṭāb al-Asadi, also those who profess the divinity of 'Abdallah ibn Mu'āwiya ibn 'Abdallah ibn Ja'far. They include the Ḥulūliyya who believe that God inheres in the person of the Imāms, and who, in consequence of it, worship the Imāms; the Hulūliyya who are called Ḥulmāniyya and are traced to Abu Ḥulmān[1] al-Dimishḳi, who maintained that God inheres in every beautiful form; he used to prostrate himself before every beautiful form. Among them are the Muḳanna'iyya Mubayyiḍa situated in Ma-warā-n-nahr, who assert that Al-Muḳanna' was a god and that he assumes a particular form in every age. There are also the 'Azāḳira[2] who believe in the divinity of Ibn Abu-l-'Azāḳir who was executed in Baghdād. All of these groups which we have mentioned in this chapter are excluded from Islam although they externally claim relationship with it. We shall specify in detail[3] the doctrines of each of these groups in the fourth section of this book when we get to it, God willing.

In addition, there are sects among the Mushabbiha whom the theologians have included among the sects of Islam because they affirm the obligatory character of the precepts in the Ḳur'ān, since they recognize the binding force of the fundamentals of the Law of Islam such as prayer, fasting and the pilgrimage, and because they confirm the prohibitive nature of the forbidden things. They regard them as Muslims despite the fact that they err and are heretics with respect to some of the intellective principles. This division includes the Hishāmiy-
216 ya[4], which traces its origin to Hishām ibn al-Ḥakam al-Rāfiḍi[5]. He compared his Worshipped One to a human being[6] and believed as a result that He

[1] With MS.; Ed. حكماية and حكمان.

[2] Ed. العذاقرة; MS. doubtful, but see below 84.

[3] Reading تفصيل with Ed.; MS. تفسير.

[4] Ed., 47—51 (Seelye, 67—70).

[5] Died c. 200 A. H. He lived in Kūfa and this fact is cited by Ibn Ḥazm several times to strengthen the validity of his testimony (e. g. *Shiites*, I, 63 and 72). For more biographical details see *Shiites* II, 65—6 and *Intiṣār*, 177—8. Acc to *Intiṣār*, 41, he was a friend of Abu Shākir al-Daiṣāni, the father or grandfather of the founder of the Ḳarmatian movement. See Ed., 266 (below 108).

[6] His antropomorphic views are treated in detail, Ash'ari 31—3; Maḳrīzi, 348 (He says that they are also called Ḥakamiyya).

measures seven spans by His own span and that He is a body having ends and limits. He is describable in terms of length, width and depth and is endowed with color, taste and odor. It has been reported in his name that the Object of his Worship is like an ingot[1] of silver or like a revolving pearl[2]. It has been reported of him that he pointed out Mount Abu Ḳubais as being larger than He[3]. It is also reported of him that he maintained that the rays emanating from his Worshipped One fall upon whatever He sees[4]. A detailed account of his anthropomorphic views has already been given by us in the special[5] study of the doctrines of the Imāmiyya.

It includes the Hishāmiyya who are associated with Hishām ibn Sālim al-Jawālīḳi[6]. He was of the opinion that the Object of his Worship is cast in the shape of a human and that His upper half is hollow and the lower solid[7]. He has black hair and a heart from which wisdom flows[8]. Another one of them is the Yūnusiyya which owes its existence to Yūnus ibn 'Abd al-Raḥmān al-Ḳummi[9]. He held that God is borne by those who bear His throne although He is heavier than they, just as the crane is supported by its two legs although it is heavier than they[10]. There are the Mushabbiha who are related to Daud

---

[1] Reading كسيكة with MS.; Ed. كسكية.

[2] Ash'ari, 33, calls attention to the fact that in one year he held five different doctrines on the nature of God. See *Shiites*, I, 53.

[3] Abu Ḳubais is the highest mountain near Mecca, Yaḳūt, I, 101f. See Ed. 48 and Ash'ari, ib.

[4] Ash'ari, 33, explains that this is how He knows what is under the earth and adds that if it were not for his idea of rays the doctrine would be orthodox.

[5] Ed. تفصيل; MS. تفاصيل.

[6] Or Juwālīḳi (*Shiites*, II, Index, s.v. *Hishām*; Strothmann reads: Juwailiḳi, *EI*, IV, 352b), Acc. to Ṭūsi, who cites a polemical work against him, written by Hishām b. al-Ḥakam (*Intiṣār*, 176), he lived in the second century. Naubakhti lists him, Hishām b. al-Ḥakam, 'Ubaid b. Zurāra [b. A'yun?] and others as supporters of Mūsa al-Ḳāṭhim's claims to the Imamate, 66.

[7] This view is ascribed by Ash'ari, 153 and Shahr., 97, to al-Jawāribi (see below). Maḳrīzi, ib., agrees with our author.

[8] Ash'ari reports that he also ascribed the five senses to God, and so also Maḳrīzi.

[9] Both *Fihrist*, 220 and Ash'ari, 35, name him Mawla of the family of Yaḳṭīn. On the family see *Fihrist*, 224.

[10] Ash'ari, ib.; Ed., 53 (*Seelye*, 72; both Ed. الكرسى and Seelye (the throne) miss the point in the comparison).

al-Jawāribi [1]. He described his Worshipped One as possessing all the human organs except the pudenda and the beard [2]. There are also the Ibrahīmiyya who trace their origin to Ibrahīm ibn Abu Yaḥya al-Aslami [3]. He belonged to a group of traditionists but he erred in anthropomorphism and was therefore branded as a liar in many of his traditions. Another one of them is the Ḥā'iṭiyya among the Ḳadariyya. They are linked with Aḥmad ibn Ḥā'iṭ who was one of the Mu'tazilites
217 who regarded themselves as disciples [4] ot Al-Naẓẓām. He likened 'Īsa ibn Maryam to his Lord, believing him to be the second God, and that it is he who will call mankind to account on the day of resurrection. Still another one is the Karrāmiyya and its declaration that God is a body possessing an end and limit, that He is the place for all created entities, and that He is contiguous to His throne. We have already given an adequately detailed account of their doctrines. All of these compare God's essence to that of His creatures.

As for the Mushabbiha who liken His attributes to the attributes of His created beings, they consist of a number of groups. One of them likens the Will of God to the will of His creatures. This is the doctrine of the Mu'tazila of Baṣra who hold that God wills the objects of His Will with a created will. They believe that His Will is of the same genus as ours. However, they contradict this assertion by saying that it is possible for God's Will to be created not-in-a-subject; the creation of our will is possible only in a subject. This therefore

---

[1] This name appears in a number of variants but Al-Ash'ari's reading adopted above is, no doubt, the correct one, as it is supported by Shahr., 143, *Mīzān*, I, 326; *Lisān al-Mīzān*, II, 427 and *Intiṣār*, 67. Isf. B. also reads Jawāribi but Isf. P, Ḥawāri. See *Shiites*, II, 67—8. —*Mīzān* and *Lisān al-Mīzān*, ib., relate that he is the chief of the antropomorphists and is condemned to hell. In a tradition he is classed with Bishr al-Marīsi.

[2] Sam'āni, s. v. Hishāmi; Shahr., 77.

[3] Ibrahīm ibn Muḥammad ibn Abu Yaḥya (died 184 A. H.) is a Rāwi who was suspected of Mu'tazilism, Jabarism, and Rāfiḍism. Most traditionists did not credit his transmissions. When Mālik was asked about the authenticity of his reports he answered that neither they are to be trusted nor his religious behavior. Others call him a liar outright. It is noteworthy however that Al-Shāfi'i, who knew of his Ḳadarite views, heard and studied his traditions and later utilized them although he mentions the Rāwi by his Kunya or merely by the name Ibrahīm. See *Mīzān* I, 77—9.

[4] Reading المنتسبة with Ed.; MS. المشابهة. On the Hā'iṭiyya see Ed., 260—1 (below 99-100).

contradicts their doctrine that His Will is of the same genus as our will, because when two things are alike and of one class, then that which is possible for either of them is admissible for both and what is impossible for either is impossible for both. The Karrāmiyya exceeded the Mu'tazila of Baṣra in comparing the Will of God to the will of His creatures, by believing that His will is of the same genus as ours and that it is created in Him just as our will is created in us. In consequence of this they maintain that God is the subject of all creation. Far be God from this.

Another group is represented by those who draw a resemblance between God's Word and the word of His creatures [1]. They hold that God's speech consists of sounds and letters belonging to the same species as the sounds and letters which are ascribed to mankind. They teach the creation of His Word, and 218
all of them, with the exception of Al-Jubbāi, declare the eternity of God's speech to be absurd. One of them, Al-Naẓẓām, said: There is nothing miraculous in the composition of God's Word just as there is nothing remarkable about the composition of the speech of mankind. The majority of the Mu'tazilites believe that the Ethiopians, Turks and Khazars [2] are capable of producing a Ḳur'ān similar to ours or even more rhetorical [3], only they lack the knowledge required for the compilation of such poetry. But this knowledge may well be within their power. The Karrāmiyya joined the Mu'tazila in affirming the creation of God's Word, but they distinguish between utterance and speech by declaring that the utterance of God, far be He from it, is of the same species as the sounds and letters produced by mankind, and that His speech is His capacity to originate the Word. They exceed the Mu'tazila in their doctrine about the originated character of God's utterance in His essence, proceeding on the basis of their fundamental principle that God may be conceived as the subject of all created entities.

Another group among them are the Zurāriyya, followers of Zurāra ibn A'yun al-Rāfiḍi [4]. They teach the creation of all of God's attributes and assert that they

---

[1] Ed., 325—6 (below 100—4); Shahr., 78—9.

[2] Ed. الخزر.

[3] *Intiṣār*, 79; the author denies this charge against the Mu'tazila.

[4] Acc. to *Fihrist*, 220, his real name is 'Abd Rabbihi and his father was a Greek (or Roman) slave. He is characterized as one of the outstanding Shī'ites in Fiḳh and Ḥadīth.

belong to the same genus as our attributes. They believe that God was not eternally living nor knowing nor powerful nor willing nor hearing nor seeing. He became entitled to these attributes only when He created for Himself life, power, knowledge, will, hearing and seeing, just as one of us becomes living, powerful, hearing, seeing and willing when life, power, will, knowledge, hearing and seeing are created in Him[8]. There is another group among the Rawāfiḍ which
219 teaches that God does not know a thing until it comes into existence. They therefore require that His knowledge be created just as it is necessary for the knowledge of any knower among us to be created. If we should prolong this chapter it will become elongated and the train of its garments will increase. We have already given a detailed exposition of the doctrines of the M'utazila and the Mushabbiha and of the other people of fancy in our book which is called Book of Religions and Dogmas. What we have related of these things in this chapter is adequate, and Allah knows best.

---

[8] Ash'ari, 36. He names his adherents التيمية. As Friedländer points out (*Shiites*, II, 66) Zurāra's view is adopted from Hishām b. al-Ḥakam. Cf. Ed. 49 (Seelye, 68).

SECTION FOUR

AN INQUIRY INTO THE FACTIONS WHICH CLAIM TO BELONG TO ISLAM BUT DO NOT[1]

The discussion in this section will center on the differences of opinion among theologians as to who is to be reckoned within the community and faith of Islam. We have already mentioned previously that some people think that membership within the community[2] of Islam is granted to everyone who confesses the prophecy of Muḥammad and that everything which was revealed through him is true, regardless of what his views besides that may be. This is the system[3] of Al-Kaʿbi in his treatise.[4] The Karrāmiyya think that membership in the community is extended to everyone who says: There is no God but Allah, Muḥammad is the Prophet of Allah, regardless of whether he is sincere in it or believes the contrary. These two groups are forced to include the ʿĪsawiyya[5] and the Shadhkāniyya[6]

---

[1] MS. adds هى before منها; omitted in Ed.

[2] Reading امة with MS. Ed. ملة.

[3] Reading with MS. اختيار; Ed. اختبار. For translation see Rāzi, 161.

[4] Ed., 8 (Seelye, 27); for his biography see Samʿāni, 485 a.

[5] Followers of ʿĪsa of Ispahān. For his system see Shahr., 168.

[6] Without entering into the history of the long discussion around the identity of this group and its relation to the Yudghāniyya (see e. g. *REJ*, XXIX [1894], 207, and LX [1910], 311), it will be best to quote Poznansky, probably the best authority on this subject; "Together with the Yudghāniyya, the Ḳaraite Japhet b. ʿAli (and similarly other Ḳaraites) include the Shadghāniyya. Acc. to Graetz they are the Mushkāniyya, but I prefer the view of Schreiner (*REJ*, XXIX, 207), that they are the Sharkāniyya or the Shadghāniyya, concerning whose founder the Arabic author ʿAbd-al-Ḳāhir al-Baghdādi relates that he maintained that God sent Muḥammad to the Arabs and the other nations, revealed the Ḳur'ān to him and enjoined the fundamentals of the Islamic Law on him. In that case it is possible that the Shadghāniya are part of the Mushkāniyya. Japhet further relates that they also taught (like the Yudghāniyya) that we are not required to

among the Jews within the community of Islam, because these affirm that there is no God but Allah and Muḥammad is the Apostle of Allah, believing however that Muḥammad was sent to the Arabs. They acknowledge that what he enjoined is true.

Others among the jurists teach that inclusion in the Community of Islam can be extended to whomever believes in the obligatory character of the five prayers directed toward the Kaʿba. But this is not true because most of the
221 apostates who apostasized by refusing to pay the poor-rate in accordance with the Covenant of the Companions, nevertheless recognized the necessity of offering prayer in the direction of the Kaʿba. They only reverted from the faith by their denial of the compulsory poor-rate. These are the apostates among the Banū Kinda and Tamīm.[1] The apostates mong the Banū Ḥanīfa and the Banū Asad have become heretics for two reasons. In the first place they rejected the compulsory poor-rate, and in the second, they acknowledged the prophetic character of Musailima and Ṭulaiḥa.[2] The Banū Ḥanīfa rejected in addition the compulsory morning and evening prayers and heaped heresy on heresy.[3]

The approved view, according to us, is that membership in the Community of Islam is extended to everyone who affirms the creation of the Universe[4], the unity and pre-existence of its Maker, and that He is just and wise, rejecting at the

---

observe the laws of purity and impurity in the Diaspora and that festivals are celebrated only for commemorative reasons. Another strange thing related of the Shadghāniyya is that in their view a sinner has to fast forty days because the meaning of 'he is to strike him forty' (Deut., XXV, v. 3) is fasting; .... the fast must be observed in the month of Shebat. — At any rate we may well consider the Yudghāniyya, the Mushkāniyya and the Shadghāniyya as one sect." *Reshumoth*, edited by Druaynov, I, 215.

[1] See Shahr. 13. On the matter of the *Ridda* see Caetani, *Annali dell'Islam*, vol. II (sub anno 11), § 83 ff.

[2] On these prophets see below (201). As Becker has pointed out their names were Maslama and Ṭalḥa, but were turned into diminutives as a mark of scorn. *Cambridge Mediaeval History*, II, 336.

[3] On those apostate sects see Müller I, 173—183; see also Ed., 333 and 335 (below 201 and 204).

[4] A much more extended treatment of the orthodox creed is afforded in Section V of this book. See also *Ibāna*, 7—13, and a translation from Al-Nasafi in MacDonald, *Muslim Theology*, 308—315.

same time both Tashbīh (anthropomorphism) and Ta'ṭīl (divesting of attributes). He must also acknowlege the prophecy of all His prophets and the veracity of the prophecy and apostolate of Muḥammad to all mankind, and the perpetuation[1] of his Law; that everything which was revealed to him is true and that the Ḳur'ān is the source of all the precepts of His Law. He must also recognize the duty of the five prayers in the direction of the Ka'ba, of the poor-rate, of the fast of Ramaḍan and of the pilgrimage to the House, which are required of the community as a whole. Whoever professes all this is included within the people of the community of Islam. After this he is to be observed; if he does not adulterate his faith with an abominable innovation which leads to heresy, then he is a Sunnite Unitarian. But if he joins to it some abominable innovation he is to be watched. If it is along the lines of the heterodoxy of the Bāṭiniyya,[2] the Bayāniyya, the Mughīriyya, the Manṣūriyya, the Janāḥiyya, the Sabbābiyya, or the Khaṭṭābiyya among the Rawāfiḍ; or if he follows the doctrine of the Ḥulūliyya or the doctrine of the believers
in metempsychosis or the rites of the Maimūniyya or the Yezīdiyya among the 222
Khawārij or the Ḥimāriyya among the Ḳadariyya; or if he is of those who forbid in their own name anything whose lawfulness the Ḳur'ān has indicated or of those who allow in their own name anything which the Kur'ān has forbidden, he is not regarded as one of the Community of Islam[3]. But if his heterodoxy is of the type of the Zaidiyya or Imāmiyya Rawāfiḍ or of the heterodoxies of most of the Khawārij or the Mu'tazila or of the Najjāriyya, the Jahmiyya, the Ḍirāriyya, or the Corporealists among the community, he is counted as one of the community of Islam with respect to certain laws; namely, he may be buried in the cemetery of the Muslims and he is to receive his share of the spoils if he makes a raid with Muslims. He is not prevented from entering the mosques of the Muslims or from praying in them. In other respects he is excluded from the Muslim community. Prayers on his behalf or in his memory are not lawful; his meats may not be

[1] Reading تأبيد with MS ; Ed. تأييد, and so throughout the book where the word تأييد appears in Ed. I cannot see the reason why Hitti prefers the reading of our Ed. to his MS, reading which conforms to that of our Ms. *Mukhtaṣar*, 140.

[2] All of the sects listed here are treated in the following chapters of this section.

[3] For the regulations governing the various sects of Islam see Ed., 348 ff. (below 218 ff).

eaten nor can any woman [following any of the above heresies] be married to a Sunnite nor may anyone of them marry a Sunnite woman.

The sects which pretend to belong to Islam externally, while in reality they are excluded from the community, are twenty in number. This is their list: Sabbābiyya, Bayāniyya, Ḥarbiyya, Mughīriyya, Manṣūriyya, Janāḥiyya, Khaṭṭābiyya, Ghurābiyya, Mufawwiḍa[1] [Dhammiyya[2] Shurai'iyya, Namīriyya], Ḥulūliyya, the believers in metempsychosis, Ḥā'iṭiyya, Ḥimāriyya[3], Muḳanna'iyya, Ruzāmiyya, Yezīdiyya,
223 Maimūniyya, Bāṭiniyya, the Ḥallājiyya, the Azāḳiriyya[4] and the Licentious. Generally, each of these sects has branched out into many sub-sects which we shall specify in detail in a separate[5] chapter, God willing.

---

[1] With MS.; Ed., Mufawwiḍiyya.

[2] The three sects in brackets do not appear in Ed.

[3] With MS.: Ed., Ḥimādiyya.

[4] With MS.; Ed., Adhāḳiriyya.

[5] Reading مهدة with MS.; Ed. مهدِة.

CHAPTER ONE

THE DOCTRINE OF THE SABBĀBIYYA[1] AND THEIR EXCLUSION FROM ISLAM[2]

The Sabbābiyya are followers of 'Abdallah ibn Sabā'[3] who exaggerated with respect to 'Ali, maintaining that he was a prophet. Then he exaggerated still further believing that he was a God[4]. He spread propaganda for this belief among the erring Kūfites. The story of this group was reported to 'Ali who ordered a number of them to be burnt in two pits[5], so that one of the poets sang concerning it:

May misfortunes hurl me wherever they will
So long as they hurl me not into the two pits.

However, 'Ali feared to burn the rest of them lest the people of Syria

---

[1] Generally and more correctly called Sabā'iyya after its founder. The spelling Sabābiyya or Sabbābiyya is explained in *Shiites* II, 41, as a derivative from سب meaning to accuse or denounce and applied to this sect because of its hostile attitude to the three Khalīfs who preceded 'Ali. Cf. also *l. c.*, appendix A., p. 142.

[2] For a critical study of ibn Sabā' as well as àn appraisal of the motives behind the various statements made by sect-historians see Friedländer's article in *ZA*, XXIII and XXIV, (1909—1910). In connection with it, Friedländer has translated most of this chapter XXIII, pp. 308—313 and ediited it completely, as well as Isf., XXIV, 38—43.

[3] His full biography is given *EI*, I, s. v.; also Friedländer, *ZA*, XXIV, 19 ff. He relates him to the Felashas of Abyssinia on the basis of his mother's name (Sawdā'-Black) and his teachings which are a mixture of Jewish and Christian views, 26 ff., esp. 27.

[4] He is reported to have said to 'Ali: انت انت (you are you), a manifestly Ṣufiistic utterance, Ash'ari, 15, and Shahr. I, 132 (Haarbrücker 200). According to *Bad'wal-Ta'rīkh*, V, 131 (Arabic 125) he expressed himself even more fully: You are thé God of the Universe, you are our Creator and Supporter, you grant us life and send death upon us. Friedländer, *ZA*, XXXIII, 319, rejects this as definitely unauthentic.

[5] Despite all the authorities who report this auto-da-fe, Friedländer doubts its historicity suspecting it to be an Imāmite invention (*ZA*, XXIII, 316 ff). Cf. this view as expounded by Massignon, *Passion d'al-Halladj*, I, 138 ff. and below, 83.

rejoice over his calamities[1] and, moreover, he dreaded the opposition of his adherents. So he banished ibn Sabā' to Sabbat-al-Madain.[2] When 'Ali was killed, ibn Sabā' held that the slain one was not 'Ali but a devil who appeared to the people
224 in the likeness of 'Ali[3]. 'Ali himself ascended to heaven just as 'Īsa ibn Mariam had ascended there. He said: Just as the Jews and Christians lie[4] in affirming the execution of 'Īsa, so the Nāṣibs[5] and Khawārij lie in alleging 'Ali's assassination. However, the Jews and Christians saw a crucified person whom they confused with 'Īsa. Similarly those who affirm the killing of 'Ali saw a slain person who resembled him, so that they were of the opinion it was 'Ali. But 'Ali, in truth, ascended to heaven, and he will surely come down to earth[6] and take revenge of his foes.

Some of the Sabbābiyya believe that 'Ali is in the clouds[7], that the thunder is his voice, and the lightning his whip[8]. Whenever anyone of them hears the sound of thunder he says: Peace be upon you, O Prince of the Faithful! It is told in the name of 'Āmir ibn Shurāḥīl[9] al-Sha'bi[10] that when Ibn Sabā' was told: Behold, 'Ali was killed, he replied: Even[11] if you bring us his brain in a bag we

---

[1] This refers to the civil wars in progress at the time between 'Ali and the 'Umayyads.

[2] Town in Persia about ten farasangs from Ushrūsāna, the birth-place of the famous general Al-Afshīn, and twenty farasangs from Samarḳand, Yakūt, III, s. v.

[3] This belief is probably traceable to the Manichees who held the same about Jesus, *Shiites*, II, 29—30 and *ZA*, XXIV (1910), 1—2, and to the Gnostic docetic doctrine.

[4] With Ed. كذبت; MS. ذهبت.

[5] People who make a tenet of the hatred for 'Ali, including the Khawārij generally and a number of Sunnites. They are the counterpart of the Rawāfiḍ who venerate 'Ali and disparage Abu Bekr, 'Omar and 'Uthmān. See Goldziher's excursus on them in *Literaturgeschichte*, 491—95; *Tāj-al-'Arūs*, I, part 4, 11; and *Shiites*, II, 159.

[6] See Friedländer's discussion of the Raj'a (return), *Shiites*, II, 23—28, esp. 25.

[7] Ib. 42—3.

[8] With MS. سوطه; Ed. صوته.

[9] Ed. شراجيل; MS. possibly correct.

[10] Resident of Kūfa, one of Muḥammad's most zealous adherents, a jurist and a poet. He is said to have transmitted traditions from 150 Companions of the Prophet. Born 20 or 31 A. H, died 103. His hostile attitude to the 'Umayyads is cited *Muh. St.*, II, 40. See also Wellhausen, *Oppositionsparteien*, 77.

[11] MS. لن, which Friedländer corrects to لئن; Ed. إن.

shall not admit the truth of his death,[1] for[2] he shall not die until he descends from heaven and rules over the entire world.[3] This group holds that the expected Mahdi is in truth 'Ali and no one else. Regarding this group Isḥāḳ ibn Suwaid al-'Adawi[4] recited his Ḳaṣīdah in which he declares himself free from the Khawārij and the Rawāfiḍ and the Ḳadariyya. The following verses are taken from it:

I declare myself free from the Khawārij; I am not one of them; —
From the Ghazzāl[5] among them and from ibn Bāb;[6]
And from the people who, when they mention 'Ali,
Send greetings to the clouds.
But I love with all my heart — for I know that that is the truth —
The Apostle of God and al-Ṣiddīḳ[7], a love
For which I expect in the future a goodly reward.

Al-Sha'bi tells that 'Abdallah ibn Sawdā'[8] supported the doctrine of the Sab- 225
bābiyya. Ibn Sawdā' was originally a Jew, a native of Herat[9] but he feigned

---

[1] *ZA*, XXIII, 321 ff. where this anecdote is discussed.

[2] With MS. لأنه; omitted in Ed.

[3] *ZA*, XXIII, 321 ff. The more usual phrase in general and in this connection is حتى يملأ الارض عدلا كما ملئت جورا (until he fills the world with justice as it is now filled with injustice). Naubakhti, 19, Shahr, 132; *Shiites*, I, 45. On Baghdādi's variant see ib. II, 30—31.

[4] Poet, member of the Ḳuraish (*Muruj*, II, 142—3, and *al-Tanbīh* (Ed. de Goeje) 109, in both of which a similar verse is quoted in which the genealogy of the Nizār tribe is traced to Isaac son of Abraham. Tab. II, 280 and 252 uses him as an authority for traditions related by Hubaira ibn Jubair so that al-'Adawi lived about 50 A. H.

[5] Alluding to Wāṣil ibn 'Aṭā, the first Mu'tazilite, who was named thus because he would follow the spinning women (غزالين) to recognize the chaste among them in order to give them alms. *Kamil* (Ed. Wright) 546.

[6] Wāṣil's pupil 'Amr ibn 'Ubaid ib. 546. On the relationship between the Khawārij and these two Mu'tazilites, see *ZA*, XXIII, 311. *Kamil* ib. explains that it is because they and the Khawārij alike were innovators (اهل البدع والاهواء).

[7] I. e. Abu Bekr, in contrast to the Rawāfiḍ who rank 'Ali above Abu Bekr.

[8] Friedländer points out that our author and his imitator Isf. are the only two authorities who count Ibn al-Sawdā' as an individual distinct from Ibn Sabā' while in reality it is merely another name for the latter, after his mother. *Shiites*, II, 18—19; *ZA*, XXIII, 21.

[9] Friedländer in *ZA*, XXIII, 23, records that Baghdādi is the only one to trace him to Herat. All other historians regard him as Yemenite and some, even more specifically, as hailing from Ṣan'a.

Islam, wishing to gain influence[1] and authority among the people of al-Kūfa. He related to them that he discovered in the Torah that every prophet is given an heir[2] and that ʿAli was the heir of Muḥammad and that he was the most perfect heir just as Muḥammad had been the most perfect prophet. When the ʿAlid party heard this from him they said to ʿAli: Verily he is an admirer of yours. ʿAli, therefore, raised his rank and seated him under the stairs of his Mimbar [in the Mosque[3]]. Then he was informed of Ibn Sawdā's extravagant attitude towards him and he planned to kill him, but Ibn ʿAbbās dissuaded him from doing it, saying to him: If you kill him, your supporters will part company with you, and since you are set on resuming war with the Syrians, you will have to honor your men. Since he feared the sedition which Ibn ʿAbbās foresaw as a result of his[4] and Ibn Sabā's execution he banished the two into al-Madain. After the assassination of ʿAli, the riff-raff were seduced by them[5]. Ibn Sawdā' said to them: By Allah, two springs will certainly gush for the benefit of ʿAli in the Mosque of al-Kūfa; one of them will pour forth honey and the other oil[6], and his party will scoop up from both.

The critical Sunnite scholars[7] say that Ibn Sawdā' felt deeply attached to the

---

[1] *Mukhtasar* makes a note to the effect that it indicates the Jewish influence on Muslim sectarianism, but it appears that he bases his conclusion on material which Friedländer repudiates. See above 41, n. 4.

[2] Other writers also inform us that as a Jew, Ibn Sabā' had believed Joshua to be Moses' heir and then, as a Muslim, held the same view regarding Muḥammad and ʿAli. On the parallel between Joshua and ʿAli see *ZA*, XXIII, 320, and Naubakhti, 20.

[3] This is a mark of honor. See Becker in *Orientalische Studien Theodor Noeldeke gewidmet*, I, 335.

[4] This establishes beyond doubt that Baghdādi thinks of two individuals. But it is clear that he misunderstood the source from which he drew, where the two names were probably employed interchangeably. Else the sudden appearance of Ibn Sabā' strikes us as unnatural. The argument against Ibn Sabā's execution is recorded also in Naubakhti, 19 See note 6 below

[5] Reading بهم. with Ed. and *Mukhtaṣar*, 143.; MS. به. which Friedländer, *ZA*, XXIII, (1909), 313 terms "recht holperig".

[6] On this belief in two fountains see *Shiites*, II, 38—39. Acc. to Naubakhti, *ib.*, the appeal was made on the ground of Ibn Sabā's devotion to ʿAli and his hatred of his opponents.

[7] Friedländer uses this statement as proof that the preceding material came from Shīʿite sources. This will strengthen the theory of Imāmite influence.

Jewish religion and he sought to corrupt the Muslims and their religious principles by fanciful interpretations concerning 'Ali and his children so that they might believe in him as the Christians believe in 'Īsā. He identified himself with the Sabbābiyya among the Rawāfiḍ when he found them most extravagant[1] in the heresy of the people of fancy, and he stealthily introduced his blunders by means of allegorization.

'Abd-al-Ḳāhir says: How can people who claim that 'Ali was a god or a 226
prophet belong to the Islamic sects? Indeed, if it is possible to include these in the category of the Islamic sects, then it should be equally possible to admit into the ranks of Islam those who proclaim the prophetic character of Musailima the Liar.

We say to the Sabbābiyya: If he who was killed by 'Abd-al-Raḥmān ibn Muljam[2] was a devil who appeared to the people in the likeness of 'Ali, why then do you curse Ibn Muljam? Ought you not much rather to praise him? For indeed, the killer of a devil ought to be praised for his deed, not censured for it. We say to them: How can your assertion that thunder is the voice of 'Ali and lightning his whip be true when the sound of thunder was heard and lightning perceived in the age of the Philosophers prior to the period of Islam? That is why they discuss thunder and lightning in their treatises and differ regarding their causes. It may be said to Ibn Sawdā': According to you and those Jews with whom you sympathize, 'Ali is not greater in rank than Mūsa and Hārūn and Yūsha' ibn Nūn, yet the death of those three is conceded and neither honey nor oil flows for their benefit in place of the sweet water which flowed from a hard rock for Mūsa and his people in the desert. What is it then that preserved 'Ali from death while his son al-Ḥusain and his supporters died of thirst[3] in Ḳarbelā[4] and no water flowed for them, let alone honey and oil?

---

[1] With Goldziher اغرق; MS. and Ed. اعرف which Friedländer follows.

[2] 'Abd-al-Raḥmān ibn Muljam al-Sarimi, a Khāriji, assassinator of 'Ali, *EI*, I, 282, s. v. 'Ali, and more fully Mueller, ***Islam***, I, 332—33.

[3] Although Ḥusain's death actually came when he was decapitated, his resistance was nevertheless broken by the lack of water, since Yezīd's forces made the Euphrates inaccessible to him (Lammens, ***Le Califat de Yezid Ier***, 153 and 162—170). This incident has been developed in the Shī'ite Passion Play into a major motif.

[4] A place on the border of the desert near Kūfa. Its etymology is not known. Yaḳūt, IV, 249.

227

CHAPTER TWO

THE BAYĀNIYYA AMONG THE GHULĀT [1] AND THEIR EXCLUSION FROM THE SECTS OF ISLAM

They are the followers of Bayān [2] ibn Sam'ān al-Tamīmi. It is they who believe that the Imāmate passed from Muḥammad ibn al-Ḥanafiyya to his son Abu Hāshim 'Abdallah ibn Muḥammad [3], then it passed from Abu Hāshim to Bayān ibn Sam'ān as his bequest to him. [4]. But they differed regarding the nature of their chief Bayān. Some of them think that he was a prophet and that he annulled a part of Muḥammad's Revealed Law. Others are of the opinion that he was a god. The latter relate that Bayān told them that the spirit of God transmigrated [5] through the prophets and the Imāms until it came to Abu Hāshim 'Abdallah ibn Muḥammad ibn al-Ḥanafiyya, then it was transferred from the latter

---

[1] Shahr. counts this sect among the moderate Shī'a, although a few lines below he adds that its founder was of the Ghulāt, 113—14. Ash'ari also lists them both among the Ghulāt and among the moderates, 5 and 23.

[2] Bayān (or Banān or Bunān. cf. *Shiites*, II, 88; but he is not right in his generalization as to the "consensus of opinion" about the reading بنان ; add to his references Bayān in Ash'ari, 5; Sam'āni, 98a; *Bad' wal-Ta'rikh*, V. 130 [Arabic]; IA, V, 154—5; *Usul*, 351; and Banān, *Ghunya*, 61) ibn Sam'ān al-Mahdi (Shahr. 113; *Mizān al-I'tidal*, I, 166; Iji, 344) of the Banu Tamīm appeared in Irāḳ after one hundred A. H. (*Mizān* ib.) Naubakhti, 25, tells of a certain Bayān who was a straw-gatherer, and was burned by Khālid al-Ḳasri. Ritter properly identifies him with Ibn Sam'ān, but it is somewhat surprising that he claimed the bequest from Muḥammad b. 'Ali b. Ḥusain, i. e., al-Bāḳir.

[3] Ed. 27—42, Seelye, 47—60; On Abu Hāshim compare *Shiites*, II, 89.

[4] Ash'ari adds وانه لم يكن له ان يوصي بها الى عقبه (he had no posterity to bequeath it to).

[5] On the relation between transmigration (Tanāsukh) and the Return (Raj'a) see *Shiites* II, 26—28 (Friedländer takes issue with Wellhausen [*Oppositionspartheien*, 93] who identifies the two).

to him, that is, himself. He thus claimed divinity for himself[1] after the manner of the Ḥulūliyya. He further believed that it is he who is referred to in the Ḳur'ān in His words: "This is a clear statement (Bayān) for man and a guidance and an admonition to those who guard against evil[2]". He asserted: I am the clear statement and I am the guidance and the admonition.

He maintained he knew [God's] Greatest Name[3] and that he could rout armies with it, and that he could invoke Venus with it and she would answer 228
him. He thought that the eternal God is a man of light[4], and that He will perish entirely save His face. In accordance with his view he interpreted His words: "Everything perishes but His face",[5] and His words: "Everyone on it must pass away and the face of your Lord will endure forever"[6]. The story of Bayān was brought to Khālid ibn 'Abdallah al-Ḳasri[7] while he was governor of 'Irāḳ. He employed cunning against Bayān until he seized and impaled him[8].

---

[1] *Mīzān*, ib. Shahr. 114, and Naubakhti, 30 relate that he wrote to Muḥammad al-Bāḳir asking him to become an adherent of his. Shahr. and Naubakhti add that al-Bāḳir made the messenger ('Umar b. Abu 'Āfīf al-Azdi) eat the paper on which the epistle was written.

[2] Sura 3, v. 132.

[3] In the theological works on Islam there is no single name which is identified as God's Greatest. Ibn Madja II, 227—28. brings a number of traditions according to which various expressions are styled God's Greatest Name, including a number of prayers offered by simple individuals. Similar traditions are collected by Aḥmad ibn Ḥanbal (Cf. Wensinck, 175—6). Asin Palacios in his work on ibn Massarra (p. 156) states that the *Ism A'tham* according to tradition is the one hundredth name of Allah. Fakhr al-Dīn al-Rāzi in his book *Lawāmi' al-Bayyināt*, on Allah's names, devotes a section to the Greatest (62—73) in which he reports a number of views, among them, that it is *Allah* or حي قيوم; also the Ṣūfic view, that any name may be an *Ism A'tham* if the caller rids himself of human attachments and is absorbed entirely in God. There is also a theory that that name cannot be known.— It is a pretty safe assumption however that we have here a direct influence of the Jewish belief in the Shem Hameforash (שם המפורש). Cf. *Shiites*, II, 82, 87.

[4] *Usul*, 73, adds: and his organs are like human organs. Cf. Shahr. 114.

[5] Sura 28, v 88.

[6] Sura 55, vv. 26—27.

[7] Ed. القشرى. Died 126. Governor of 'Irāḳ during the reign of Walīd and, later, again under Hishām, *EI*, II, s. v.

[8] Ṭab. II, 1620, and IA, V, 154 and others state that he as well as Mughīra (see below)

He said to him: If you can defeat armies with the Name which you know, then repel my men with it away from you.

This sect is excluded from all the sects of Islam because it affirms the divinity of its chief, Bayān, just as idol-worshippers are rejected by the Islamic sects. Those among them who maintain that Bayān was a prophet are comparable to those who believe that Musailima [1] was a prophet and both groups are rejected by the Muslims. It can be argued against the Bayāniyya: If it is possible for part of God to perish what prevents His face from perishing? As for the statement: "Everything will perish save His face" its meaning is, every deed upon which God's face does not look with favor will turn into non-existence [2]. The words: "will endure" mean "your Lord will endure", for He says after it "the Lord of Glory and Honor" in the nominative case in apposition to "face". If "face" were in the construct state to "Lord" he would say "Lord of Glory" in the genitive (dhī), because the qualifying adjective of a genitive is put in the genitive. [3] This is perfectly clear. Praised be Allah for it.

---

were burnt. They also relate that the latter took his punishment like a coward, whereas Bayān grasped the pile in high spirits so that Khālid exclaimed to the sectarians: "Woe to you, you do everything wrong; why did you choose Mughīra as your head?" The same story is told by Ibn Ḥazm, *Shiites*. I, 60.

[1] See above page 38.

[2] This particular explanation of the verse seems to be Baghdādi's original. Ibn Ḥazm (*Shiites*, I, 61) argues that since Allah's face is identical with His essence and since only things on earth can decay it means that everything will perish and God will remain. This is the accepted Orthodox explanation.

[3] See a similar argument, *Usūl*, 76 and especially 110 (IH agrees with this view, II, 166). Al-Ash'ari however, accepts God's face as neither his essence nor not his essence, as he argues about all of God's attributes. See *Ibana*, 8, and 43 f

CHAPTER THREE

THE MUGHĪRIYYA AMONG THE GHULĀT AND THEIR EXCLUSION FROM ALL ISLAMIC SECTS

They are the followers of Mughīra ibn Sa'īd al-'Ijli [1]. In the early years of his career he evinced sympathy for the Imāmiyya,[2] believing that after 'Ali, al-Ḥasan, and al-Ḥusain, the Imāmate belonged to his grandchild Muḥammad ibn 'Abdallah ibn al-Ḥasan [3] ibn 'Ali. He held that this one is the expected Mahdi, and he adduced as evidence for it the tradition which he cited, that the name of the Mahdi will correspond to the name of the Prophet,[4] and his father's name will correspond to that of the Prophet's father.[5] The Rawāfiḍ cursed him for

[1] Mughīra ibn Sa'īd (sometimes Sa'd) al-'Ijli, with the Kunya Abu 'Abdallah, of the Bājila tribe was a resident of Kūfa. The authorities (e. g. Ṭab. II, 1619—20; IA, V, 154—5; *Mīzān al-I'tidāl* III, 191 — *Lisān al-Mīzān* VI, 75—8) emphasize his power as a wizard. They also report that he forbade the use of the waters of the Euphrates because of its uncleanliness; he drank well water. The 'Alids disclaimed any association with him. *Lisān al Mīzān*, ib. 76—7; IA, ib. 155 add that he came to both Muḥammad al-Bāḳir and Ja'far al-Ṣādiḳ to express to them his conviction that they knew the mysteries of the world, but both spurned him. For a similar report regarding his contemporary Bayān, see above, 47.

[2] It is likely that the author meant more specifically the Muḥammadiyya. Ed. 42—45 (Seelye, 62—64).

[3] Ed. has throughout this chapter the reading ibn al-Ḥasan ibn al-Ḥusain ibn al-Ḥasan. Only in the first instance is it supported by MS., but it is obviously a mistake. See genealogy of the 'Alids, *Shiites*, II, 160 and Naubakhti, 115.

[4] Tab. (Zotenberg) I, 70, cites a similar tradition. Friedländer (*Shiites*, II, 53) specifies it more particularly to be Shī'ite.

[5] With Isf. and *Mukhtasar*, 147; MS. and Ed. both read ابن. This reading probably came from a confusion with the transmission of the tradition by the Imāmiyya. See *Vorlesungen*[2], 222 und 365 note 130. We may draw from this another proof of our author's dependence on Imāmite sources. For the corrected version see Naubakhti, 54.

urging them to await Muḥammad ibn 'Abdallah ibn al-Ḥasan ibn 'Ali. Later, after he acquired leadership over them, he announced to them all sorts of extreme heresy, such as his claim of prophecy,[1] and his pretension to know the most exalted Name,[2] with the aid of which, he believed, he could resurrect the dead and rout armies. Another of his heresies was his exaggerated anthropomorphism. He held that the Object of his Worship is a man of light with a crown of light on his head, and that he possesses organs and a heart whence wisdom flows. He also maintained that his limbs have the shape of the letters of the alphabet, that Alif is the counterpart of his leg, and the 'Ain represents the shape of his eye; the Ha he likened to his sexual organ. Still another was that he spoke
230 abusively of the beginning of creation.[3] He held that when God wished to create the universe he uttered His holiest Name. This name flew and placed itself on His head as a crown.[4] He interpreted accordingly God's words: "Glorify the name of your Lord the most High",[5] being of the opinion that the holiest Name was that crown. After the crown had descended on His head He wrote the actions of His creatures on His palm with His finger. Then He contemplated them and was provoked by their acts of disobedience and He perspired[6]. Two seas were formed from His sweat, one dark and briny, the other sweet and lucid.

[1] Ash'ari 7; *Mīzān al-I'tidāl* ib. (*Lisan* 76); Shahr. 134. At-Ash'ari further relates (p. 23) that the Mughīriyya believe that after 'Ali ibn at-Ḥusain, his son Abu Ja'far Muḥammad al-Bāḳir was the Imām and that the latter bequeathed it to Mughīra with the understanding that he was to hold the Imāmate until the appearance of Muḥammad ibn 'Abdallah.

[2] *Ash'ari* 7, (he adds that the earth will burst open for its dead and they will return to life); Ṭab. II, 1619; IA, V, 154. *Bad' wal-Ta'rikh*, V, 130, reports that he made this claim for Muḥammad ibn al-Ḥanafiyya. According to *'Iḳd al-Farīd*, I, 267 he attributed this power to 'Ali ibn Abu Ṭalib. Cf. *Shiites*, II, 83 and n. 1.

[3] The doctrine of Mughīra as exposed in the following passage is annotated adequately by Friedländer, *Shiites* II, 80—85. The account is reproduced by most authorities.

[4] On the identification of the Greatest Name with the crown in other mystic movements see *Shiites*, II, 83.

[5] Sura 87, v. 1. Al-Mughīra no doubt translated it: Glorify the most High Name of your Lord. Grammatically both are possible.

[6] In addition to the parallel sources collected in *Shiites*, II, 83—4, one may cite a similar story of creation out of sweat in Scandinavian and Iranian folk-lore. Cf. Christensen, *Les Types du Premier Homme et Premier Roi*, 35—6.

Afterwards He gazed upon the sea and observed His shadow; He went to seize it, but it flew away. He therefore plucked out the eyes of His shadow and created the sun and the moon from them[1]. The rest of His shadow He destroyed, for He said: It is not proper that there should be with me a God besides me. Then He created mankind from the two seas. The Shīʿa He created out of the sweet and lucid sea; they are the faithful. The infidels, namely, the enemies of the Shīʿa, He formed from the dark and briny sea.

He also believed that God created man before creating his flesh and blood. The first entity among them which He formed was the shadow of Muḥammad[2]. This, he said, is the meaning of His statement: "Say, if the beneficent God has a son then I am the first of those who worship[3]." Then He sent forth the shadow of Muḥammad to the shadows of mankind. He then besought the heaven and mountains to protect ʿAli ibn Abu Ṭālib against his wrong-doers, but they refused.[4] He then made the same request of mankind. ʿOmar bade Abu Bekr

---

[1] Ash'ari, ib., states that He only plucked one eye from which He created the sun. Ibn Ḥazm (*Shiites* I, 59) relates that He made "the sun and another sun"; similarly IA, ib. where السماء should be corrected to الشمس. Shahr., ib, Iji, 344 and *Usul*, 74 agree with our text.

[2] Goldziher in his article on *Neo-Platonic and Gnostic Elements in the Ḥadīth* (*ZA*, XXII [1908] 324—330) discusses the tradition about Muḥammad's pre-existence and on page 326 cites a Shīʿite tradition according to which God first created the persons of Muḥammad, ʿAli, Fāṭima, Ḥasan and Ḥusain in the form of resplendent substances (وخلق الله ارواح شيعتنا قبل ابدانهم بالفى عام). In this traditon we no doubt find the origins of Mughīra's statement. The two-thousand-year period is a usual figure in Jewish and Christian time-divisions. It may be added that in traditions of this kind even among the Sunnites, it is the "light-substance" (نور) rather than his shadow, ib.

[3] Sura 53, v. 81. That Mughīra's interpretation has some foundation is evident from the efforts which Arabic commentators exert to deny the inference of a son in the verse. See Baiḍāwi, Zamakhshari, *ad loc.*

[4] There is obvious confusion in the relation of this as written down by our author. According to Baghdādi who expanded and misunderstood Ash'ari, 8, God seeks somebody to defend ʿAli. Abu Bekr and ʿOmar agree to protect him but decide at the same time to deprive him of the Imāmate. The clause regarding this betrayal is awkwardly introduced and the sense of the passage is strange and unlikely. The correct version has been preserved by Ash'ari, Iji, ib. and Shahr., ib. It is that Muḥammad (he can be the only possible subject of the verb عرض) sought the heavens and earth to prevent ʿAli from procuring the Imāmate but they refused. Abu

to take upon himself to safeguard 'Ali and defend him against his enemies and to betray him in this world. He assured him that he would support him in his betrayal[1] on condition that he bequeath the Caliphate to him after his death.
231 Abu Bekr did so. This is the meaning of his words: Surely, we offered the trust to the heavens and the earth and the mountain and they refused to undertake it and were afraid of it, but man undertook it; verily, he was unjust and ignorant"[2]. He held that the unjust and ignorant one is Abu Bekr[3]. To 'Omar he applied His words: "Like the devil when he says to man, Disbelieve, but when he disbelieves he says, Surely I am clear of you"[4]; according to him the devil is 'Omar.

In addition to his blunders which we have related, Mughīra ordered his adherents to expect Muḥammad ibn 'Abdallah ibn al-Ḥasan ibn al-Ḥasan ibn 'Ali[5]. Khālid ibn 'Abdallah al-Ḳasri heard about him[6] and his heretical views and he impaled him[7]. When Mughīra was executed, his followers nevertheless persisted in their expectation of Muḥammad ibn 'Abdallah ibn al-Ḥasan ibn al-Ḥasan. When this Muḥammad announced his pretensions in al-Medīna, Abu Ja'far al-Manṣūr dispatched 'Īsā ibn Mūsā there as commander of his troops with a large

---

Bekr and 'Omar, however, accepted it with the conditions as stated in the text. This account agrees fully with the Shī'ite views on the usurpation by the first two Khalīfs. That Muḥammad should desire to betray 'Ali is not surprising from the extreme Shī'ite standpoint. — Our author's mistake is that he misunderstood the verb منع assuming it to mean *protect* so that he inserted the expression "against his wrong-doers". See *Mukhtaṣar*, 147.

[1] Reading الغدر به with MS (pro الغدرية); Ed. القدرية.

[2] Sura 59, v. 16.

[3] *Mīzān*, III, 191 remarks that Mughīra was the first to abuse Abu Bekr and 'Omar.

[4] Sura 59, v. 16.

[5] Muḥammad and his brother carried on secret propaganda in behalf of the 'Alids for a number of years during the Caliphate of Abu Ja'far Manṣūr, prior to their appearance in 145. Muḥammad is described as of dark yellow complexion, courageous, pious and a good speaker. His Laḳabs were Mahdi and *Nafs Zākiya* (pure heart) IA, V, 422—3.

[6] With MS. بخبره; Ed. يخبره.

[7] I read فصلبه with *Mukhtasar* instead of فطلبه as MS. and Ed. As in the case of Bayān there is another version according to which he was burnt at the stake. See above 47—8. Since Mughīra was executed in 119, it follows that his partisans adhered to Muḥammad ibn 'Abdallah for twenty-six years, until 145.

army, and they killed Muḥammad, following his capture of Mecca and al-Medīna.[1] His brother Ibrahīm ibn ʻAbdallah had meanwhile conquered the [district[2] of Baṣra and his brother Idrīs ibn ʻAbdallah became master over] the Maghreb. Now Muḥammad ibn ʻAbdallah ibn al-Ḥasan was killed in battle in al-Medīna. Ibrahīm[3] ibn ʻAbdallah ibn al-Ḥasan was misled by Bashīr[4] al-Raḥḥāl and his Muʻtazilite followers who had pledged their assistance to him against the army of al-Manṣūr. When the two cohorts joined battle in Bakhmara[5], which is sixteen farasangs from al-Kūfa, Ibrahīm was killed, and the Muʻtazila took to flight. But ill fate overtook them[6] for the campaign against them was entrusted to ʻĪsā ibn Mūsā and Salm ibn Ḳutaiba, generals of al-Manṣūr. His brother Idrīs[7] died in the Maghreb[8]; 232

---

[1] For the story of his revolt see Muir, *The Caliphate*, Ed. 1915, 453—56; Mueller, *Islam*, I, 491. A detailed account will be found IA, V, 390—401 and 402—424, also Tab. (Zotenberg) IV, 382—421. The date of the uprising is 145 A. H. For the battle and his death see IA, ib. 414—421, esp. 419.

[2] I insert the passage within the brackets from *Mukhtasar*, 149, which assumes rightly that the copyist of our MS. omitted a line.

[3] After a five-year period of wandering from place to place, during which he carried on an active propaganda for his brother Muḥammad and, after the latter's death, for himself, he finally appeared in Baṣra in 145 (IA, ib. 428—30). The inhabitants of the city soon turned their support to him. Abu Jaʻfar Manṣūr's army was operating at the time on three fronts, so that the Khalīf was in a difficult position, *ib.* 432 ff.

[4] With MS., Tab. III, 185, 311. and IA, V, 434; Ed. يسير. Abu Muḥammad Bashīr al-Raḥḥāl was a native of Baṣra who, upon seeing the head of ʻAbdallah ibn al-Ḥasan, Muḥammad's father who was slain by the Khalīf al-Manṣūr, became a partisan of Ibrahīm, Tab. III, 185. But at the time of the encounter he either unwittingly or otherwise foiled several good suggestions made by a Kūfite to Ibrahīm which might have brought him success (Tab. ib. 310—11, IA, V, 434). The great mistake was that the rebel did not march on Kūfa before Manṣūr was prepared to meet him. The remaining events were a series of mistakes. Neither of the two sources identifies Bashīr as a Muʻtazilite.

[5] Ed. Nakhmara; in the MS. the first letter is unpointed. See *ib.*

[6] MS. and Ed. لحقه.

[7] With MS.; Ed. الرئيس

[8] Idrīs and his brother Yaḥya joined the rebellion of al-Ḥusain ibn ʻAli ibn al-Ḥasan ibn ʻAli in 169 (24 years after the uprising of their two older brothers). When Ḥusain was killed at Medīna and the battle lost, Idrīs fled to Egypt and thence to the Maghreb and settled in Walīla in the district of Tanja (IA, VI, 60—63; Yaḳut, IV, 941).

some say he was poisoned[1]. A few historians report that Sulaiman ibn Jarir al-Zaidi[2] poisoned him and fled to 'Irāḳ.

After the death of Muḥammad ibn 'Abdallah ibn al-Ḥasan ibn al-Ḥasan the Mughīriyya split regarding al-Mughīra. One group declared itself free[3] from him, cursed him and proclaimed. Verily he lied in his contention that Muḥammad ibn 'Abdallah ibn al-Ḥasan is the Mahdi who will hold full sway over the world, for he has been slain without ruling the earth or a tenth of it. The other group remained firm in their adherence to al-Mughīra and said: Indeed, he is right in his assertion that Muḥammad ibn 'Abdallah ibn al-Ḥasan is the expected Mahdi; he was not killed but is hiding in one of the mountains of al-Ḥājir[4]; biding his time until he will be ordered to come forth. When he reappears the oath of allegiance to him will be taken in Mecca between the Rukn and the Maḳām[5]. He will restore to life seventeen men and give each of them one of the letters[6] of God's Greatest Name and they will rout armies and possess the earth. These believe that the person slain by al-Manṣur's troops in al-Medīna was Satan who appeared to people in the shape of Muḥammad ibn 'Abdallah ibn al-Ḥasan. They are named the Muḥammadiyya[7] on account of their expectation of Muḥammad ibn 'Abdallah ibn al-Ḥasan ibn al-Ḥasan.

---

[1] This view is supported by most authorities, e. g. Tab. III 561; IA, ib. 69; *Nujum*, I, 542; Ya'ḳūbi, II, 488—9.

[2] Ṭabari, IA, *Nujum* name as his assassinator one Shammakh (شماخ) who was engaged by the Khalīf Harūn al-Rashīd; he was later rewarded and given the rule over Egypt. Strothmann, *Das Staatsrecht der Zaiditen*, 108, supports this view, but he places his death in the 70's, apparently drawing on Yaḳut, ib. who states that he came to Walīla in 172 and lived there until 174.

[3] With MS. فبرئت ; Ed. فهربت.

[4] A place in the vicinity of Najd; by the geographers it is described as a spring, See the indexes to the works in de Goeje's *Bibliotheca Geographum.* Naubakhti, who calls that mountain 'Alamiyya, locates it on the left of the road to Mecca, near Najd al-Hājiz, 54. See Yāḳūt, III, 113 (he calls it 'Alam).

[5] This is part of a tradition relating to the Mahdi. See Blochet, 25.

[6] Their views as those of a distinct sect among the Rawāfiḍ are discussed Ed. 42—45 (Seelye, 62—64). We find there a repetition of Mughīra's views regarding the expected Mahdi. — According to Isf. B, 57, they are identical with the Mughīriyya of his day.

[7] Ash'ari reads: so many letters (كذا وكذا حرفا), which is preferable to our text.

Jābir al-Ju'fi[1] adhered to this doctrine and pretended to be the heir of Mughīra ibn Sa'īd. When Jābir died Bekr al-A'war (the one-eyed) al-Hajari[2] al-Ḳatāt claimed to have been appointed heir by Jābir and he pretended that he would not die. For this reason he lived on the wealth of the Mughiriyya, by making fools of them. But when Bekr died they knew that he had lied in his 233
claim and they cursed him.

'Abd-al-Ḳāhir says: How can a group of people be counted as one of the sects of Islam when they compare the Object of their Worship to the letters of the alphabet and claim the gift of prophecy for their founder? If they form a part of the believing community then the view of those who maintain that people professing the prophetic character of Musailima and Ṭalḥa can be included in the community is equally valid. It may be said to the Mughīriyya; If you disavow the death of Muḥammad ibn 'Abdallah ibn al-Ḥasan ibn 'Ali and hold that the slain one was a Satan who assumed his shape, how are you to be distinguished from those who believe that al-Ḥusain ibn 'Ali and his companions were not killed in Karbela, but hid, and Satans who appeared in their likenesses were killed instead? Wait, therefore, for Ḥusain, for he is higher in rank than his nephew Muḥammad ibn 'Abdallah ibn al-Ḥasan ibn al-Ḥasan; or else wait for 'Ali and do not confirm his death, just as the Sabbābiyya await him. Indeed, 'Ali is nobler than his sons. In this particular there is nothing characteristic about them.

---

[1] Jābir ibn Yezīd al-Ju'fi, the traditionist, is reported to have known fifty thousand (some say seventy thousand) traditions. Despite his Shī'ite views the Sunnites were far from unanimous in questioning his authority. See *Mīzān*, s. v.; *Nujūm*, I, 342 also reports that "some found him weak" (وضعفه بعضهم). From the statement made by our author (Ed. 44, Seelye 64) it may be concluded that Jābir believed in a general Raj'a, so also Sam'āni f. 131 b. where the return of 'Ali is predicted by him. Cf. *Shiites*, II, 23. The difficulty in our text is that Jābir who died 128 or 132 could hardly be said to expect the return of Muḥammad, killed in 145; possibly Madhhab refers to a general partisanship for Muḥammad.

[2] See Ash'ari 8, and *Shiites*, I, 60 (he reads Hijri). No further information about him is available. It may be mentioned in passing that Sam'āni s. v. *Hajari* reports a traditionist named ابو اسحاق ابراهيم ابن مسلم who believed in the Raj'a. He resided in Kūfa.

CHAPTER FOUR

THE ḤARBIYYA AND THEIR EXCLUSION FROM THE SECTS OF THE BELIEVING COMMUNITY

They are adherents of ʿAbdallah ibn ʿAmr[1] ibn Ḥarb al-Kindi[2] who was of the persuasion of the Bayāniyya and their belief that God's spirit passed through
234 the prophets and the Imāms until it reached Abu Hāshim ʿAbdallah ibn Muḥammad ibn al-Ḥanafiyya[3]. Thereupon the Ḥarbiyya claimed that that spirit was transferred from ʿAbdallah ibn Muḥammad ibn al-Ḥanafiyya to ʿAbdallah ibn ʿAmr ibn Ḥarb. The Ḥarbiyya claimed for their founder ʿAbdallah ibn ʿAmr ibn Ḥarb what the Bayāniyya claimed for Bayān ibn Samʿān[4]. Both sects deny their Lord and are not among the Islamic divisions, just as the other Ḥulūliyya are rejected by Islam.

---

[1] With Ms. عمرو; Ed. عمر.

[2] On the variants of the name see *Shiites*, II, 124—5 and notes.

[3] Since Abu Hāshim died in 78, we are right in concluding that ʿAbdallah lived before the end of the first century of the Hijra because of his recognition of Muḥammad ibn al-Ḥanafiyya. Ashʿari lists this sect as one of the Kaisāniyya (p. 22). He also informs us that they believed that Abu Hāshim appointed ʿAbdallah ibn ʿAmr as the Imām in his place.

[4] Ibn Ḥazm (*Shiites* I, 73) relates the very significant fact that the founder of this sect renounced his extreme views and became a pious Muslim. His followers then abandoned him and turned to ʿAbdallah ibn Muʿāwiya (see chapter 6), but retained their original name. Shahr. confirms this fact (113; Haarbrücker misunderstood the passage; cf. *Shiites*, II, 126). It is noteworthy that in *Usul*, 332—3, Baghdādi does not list this sect among the Ghulāt. Ashʿari's remark ثم وقعوا على كذب عبد الله .بن عمرو .بن حرب is a reference to some incident which may have brought on this denial, probably his conversion; cf. the word كذب employed by Shahr. and him.

CHAPTER FIVE

THE MANṢŪRIYYA AND THEIR EXCLUSION FROM ISLAM

These are the followers of Abu Manṣūr al-'Ijli[1] who held that the Imāmate circulated among the descendants of 'Ali until it reached Abu Ja'far Muḥammad ibn 'Ali ibn al-Ḥusain ibn 'Ali, called al-Bāḳir.[2] This al-'Ijli claimed that he was successor to al-Bāḳir;[3] then he forsook this pretension and maintained that he had been taken up to heaven and that God stroked his head with His hand and said[3a]: O son, convey a message from me. Then He sent him down to the world. He believed that he was the Fragment[4] fallen from heaven which is mentioned in God's words: "If they should see a fragment of the heaven coming down they would say: Piled up clouds".[5] This group denies the resurrection and the existence 235
of Paradise and Hell. They interpret paradise to mean the pleasures obtained in this world and hell to be the misfortunes encountered in the world.[6] In addition

---

[1] He is thus a member of the same tribe to which Mughīra belonged as a Mawla. This is important in view of the fact that the practice of strangling opponents mentioned later on is charged by ibn Ḥazm (*Shiites*, I, 62) and Van Vloten in *Worgers in Irak* to Mughīra as well (see note 1, below). Naubakhti informs us that he owned a house in Kūfa; he had been brought up in the desert and was an illiterate, 34.

[2] He died 117 A.H. He is the fifth Imām of the Imāmiyya and, more particularly, the Mahdí of the Bāḳiriyya, one of the groups within the Imāmiyya (Ed. 45—6, Seelye, 64—5).

[3] According to Shahr. 135—6 and Iji, 345 he began to make pretensions for himself only after al-Bāḳir refused to have anything to do with him. Their explanation is accepted by Goldziher (*Streitschrift*, Introd. 4—5).

[3a] Naubakhti *ib.*, adds the curious detail that God's Command was given in Syriac.

[4] Iji and Shahr. *ib.* inform us that Abu Manṣūr at first claimed 'Ali ibn Abu Ṭālib to be the Fragment, but later asserted it about himself. Friedländer is therefore wrong in calling Shahr's account of the change of attitude a "contradiction with himself" (*Shiites*, II, 89).

[5] Sura, 52, v.44.

[6] According to Ash'ari, 9; Shahr. 135—6; Iji ib; *Shiites*, I, 62, Abu Manṣūr argued that Hell and all the prohibitions of the Law refer to men whom Muslims are enjoined to hate,

to this heresy they thought it permissible to strangle their opponents.[1] Their heresy continued in practice among them until Yūsuf ibn 'Omar al-Thaḳafi[2], governor[3] of 'Irāḳ was informed about the ignominies of the Manṣūriyya. He seized Abu Manṣūr al-'Ijli and impaled him. This sect too is not counted Islamic because of its denial of resurrection, paradise and hell.

---

whereas paradise and the precepts are men whom they are bidden to love. The authorities, especially Ash'ari, relate a number of other views entertained by him. Thus he would call the Family of Muḥammad Heaven, and the Shī'ā Earth. His oàth was "No, by the Word" (Cf. *Shiites*, I, 62 and II, 90). He also maintained that 'Īsā ibn Mariam was the first-born and that prophecy will cease. The latter view is also recorded by Shahr. On this Goldziher comments that Abu Manṣūr denied Muḥammad to be the Seal of the Prophets and was thus the forerunner of the Bāṭiniyya who definitely rejected this view and thereby aroused the anger of the Sunnites. *ZA*, XXII (1908) 339, n. 4.

[1] Baghdādi does not emphasize that they employed strangling *only* and did not permit the use of arms, maintaining that only with the appearance of the Mahdi will the right to carry arms be granted to them. See *Shiites*, I, 62—4 and 92 f. In an article on Stranglers (*Worgers in Irak*. Feestbundel......................aan Dr. P. J. Veth), Van Vloten edited and translated a long passage from the Kitāb al-Ḥayawān by Jāḥiẓ, describing a wide-spread movement of strangling which Van Vloten explains as a mixture of religious fanaticism and roguishness. The 'Ijl and Bājila groups figure prominently among them as well as the Kinda tribe. In a poem cited there Mughīra ibn Sa'īd "the blind" is also mentioned as one of the stranglers. Do we not have in this a confused allusion to Mughīra's second successor, Bekr al-A'war? Cf. above, 55.

[2] He was governor of 'Irāḳ 120—126 A.H. Acc. to Naubakhti, *ib.*, punishment was meted out to him by Khālid al-Ḳasri who disabled him ('a'yāhu). He further informs us that 'Omar whom he strangely surnames "the strangler" (al-Khannāḳ) executed al-Ḥusain b, Abu Mansūr, who claimed to have inherited his father's powers.

[3] Reading والى with MS.; Ed. وإلى.

CHAPTER SIX

THE JANĀḤIYYA[1] FROM AMONG THE GHULĀT AND THEIR EXPULSION FROM ISLAM.

They are the followers of 'Abdallah ibn Mu'āwiya[2] ibn 'Abdallah ibn Ja'far ibn Abu Ṭālib. The reason for their allegiance to him is that the Mughīriyya who had declared themselves free from Mughira ibn Sa'id after the death of 'Abdallah ibn al-Ḥasan ibn 'Ali[3], went forth from Kūfa to Medina in search of an Imām. 'Abdallah ibn Mu'āwiya ibn 'Abdallah ibn Ja'far met them and invited them to accept him, declaring that he was the Imām by direct descent after 'Ali and his

---

[1] In *Ghunya*, 99, they are called طيارية after their founder whom it calls *al-Ṭayyār. Bad'wal-Tarikh* misunderstands the meaning of the name طيارة, and confuses the sect bearing this name with the Sabā'iyya, ascribing to the latter the chief characteristics of the sect under discussion, 135 (Arabic, 129).—The name Janāḥiyya is derived from the Kunya of the founder of the family, Ja'far ibn Abu Ṭalib, brother of 'Ali and one of the first Muslims. When he lost both his hands in the battle of Mula, where he also lost his life, God gave him two wings, Ībn Ḳuṭaiba, *K. al-Ma'ārif*, 103, Nawāwi 194 (Cf. *Mukhtaṣar*, 153, note 1). Ibn Sa'd, IV, part 1,25, does not report the loss of his hands, but only that Muḥammed said: I see Ja'far flying about paradise on two wings. Friedländer traces the name to his father Mu'āwiya who was called *Dhu-l-Janāḥain (Shiites*, II, 44), but Ash'ari 6 and Iji 345 give his genealogy as follows: عبد الله .بن معاوية .بن عبد الله .بن جعفر ذى الجناحين so that it is more correct to trace the name to Ja'far.

[2] He appeared in Kūfa in 127 A. H., after having carried on his seditious propaganda secretly. When he was defeated by 'Abdallah ibn 'Omar, the 'Ummayyad general, he fled to the Eastern provinces holding under his control the district of Fars in which Ispahān is situated. He was defeated there once again in 129 and killed in prison by Abu Muslim. See IA, V, 262—4 and 282—5; Wellhausen, *Arab Kingdom and its Fall*, 384—6, 393—5; *EI*, I, 26.

[3] Ed. 232 (above, 54). According to Ash'ari and *Shiites*, I, 71, the people who chose 'Abdallah ibn Mu'āwiya were not former Mughīriyya but Ḥarbiyya who either repudiated, or were abandoned by their master. This is supported by Naubakhti, 29.

236 children[1]. They recognized him as Imâm and returned to al-Kūfa and related to their followers that 'Abdallah ibn Mu'āwiya ibn 'Abdallah ibn Ja'far held himself a God and that the spirit of God was incarnate in Adam, then in Shīt; then it circulated among the prophets and Imāms until it reached 'Ali; then it circulated vamong[2] his three children[3], and finally passed to 'Abdallah ibn Mu'āwiya[4]. They maintained that he said to them: Verily learning sprouts in his heart like mushrooms and green grass. This division denied paradise and hell and allowed the use of wine, the eating of corpses, adultery, sodomy, and the other prohibitions. They did away with obligatory prayer and fasting and alms-giving and the pilgrimage[5]. They interpreted these acts of worship as allegorical ordinances for those members of 'Ali's family to whom it is one's duty to display friendliness, and explained that the prohibitions mentioned in the Ḳur'ān allude to certain people whom one is obliged to hate, such as Abu Bekr, 'Omar, Ṭalḥa, al-Zubair and 'Āisha.

Ibn Kuṭaiba relates in his *Kitāb al-Ma'ārif* that 'Abdallāh ibn Mu'āwiya made his appearance in the districts of Fars and Ispahān at the head of his army[6]. Abu Muslim al-Khurāsāni sent an army against him and they slew him[7], but his

[1] Acc. to Naubakhti, his followers gave the following account of his rise: He received the bequest from Abu Hāshim 'Abdallāh b. Muḥammad b. al-Ḥanafiyya. But as he was still a minor, Ṣāliḥ b. Mudrīk was appointed his regent, and he kept the bequest for him until the latter reached his maturity.

[2] The remainder of this chapter as well as the beginning of the next are missing in both Ed. and MS., and have been supplied from other sources. The rest of this chapter is taken from *Mukhtaṣar*, 153–4.

[3] I. e. Muḥammad ibn al-Ḥanafiyya, al-Ḥasan and al-Ḥusain.

[4] Ghunya, 99, informs us that they believed fully in metempsychosis, describing their views as follows: يقولون بالتناسخ وان روح آدم عم روح الله فنسحت فيه والمتعمقون من الغالية القائلون بالتناسخ يزعمون ان الروح المنقولة الى هذه اديار بعد ان خرجت من الدنيا بالموت اول ما تنتسح في الجمل ثم تنتقل الى ما دون هيكله ابداً حالا بعد حال الى ان تنتقل الى دود العذرة وما شا كل ذلك وهو اخر ما تنتسح فيه...

[5] The person instrumental in introducing these doctrines was the father of 'Abdallāh b. al-Ḥārith (al-Harb). He ascribed these doctrines to the traditionists Jābir b. Abdallāh al-Anṣāri and Jābir b. Yazīd al-Ju'fi. (Naubakhti, 31; see also 35—37 for a lengthy discussion of their views or Tanāsukh.) The latter was a follower of the Mughīriyya, above.

[6] Ibn Ḳuṭaiba, ed. Wüstenfeld, 105.

[7] Ibn Athīr reports that 'Abdallah made overtures to Abu Muslim who was carrying on great activity in behalf of the 'Abbāsids and had already conquered Khurāsān but the name

ollowers deny his death and maintain that he is alive in one of the mountains of spahān[1] until he will reappear. One can argue against this division: If there xists no paradise nor hell nor reward nor punishment, your opponents need have o fear about killing you or seizing your possessions or leading your wives astray

---

Au'āwiya seemed to Abu Muslim and his men to be foreign in the 'Alid family and they there-ore suspected him to be a pretender. IA, V, 284—5.

[1] Naubakhti and Ash'ari explain that his followers broke up into three groups: One ad-mitted his death, another maintained that he is alive in the mountaims of Ispahān where he will sojourn until he will reappear and lead the chief horsemen (?; Naubakhti: its chief men) o a man of the Banu Hāshim (it was through Muḥammad and his son Abu Hāshim that he claimed the divine spirit to have come to him. Yet Naubakhti adds: of the offspring of 'Ali and Fāṭima). The third group also believes that he is alive in Ispahān and expects him to come forth and rule over mankind since he is the expected Mahdi.

CHAPTER SEVEN

THE KHAṬṬĀBIYYA AND THEIR EXCLUSION FROM ISLAM.

They are the adherents of Abu-l-Khaṭṭāb al-Asadi[1], and fall into five subdivisions. They all maintain that the Imāmate belonged to the offspring of 'Ali until it reached Muḥammad ibn Ja'far al-Ṣādiḳ[2]. They assert that the Imāms are Gods. During his lifetime Abu-l-Khaṭṭāb used to say that the children of al-Ḥasan and al-Ḥusain were God's children and favorites[4]. He also believed that Ja'far is a God. When this came to the knowledge of Ja'far he cursed him and banished him[5]. After that Abu-l-Khaṭṭāb claimed divinity for himself[6]. His followers declare that Ja'far is a God, but that Abu-l-Khaṭṭāb is superior to him. The Khaṭṭābiyya permit false testimony by their partisans against their opponents[7].

---

[1] His full name is *Abu-l-Khaṭṭāb Muḥammad ibn Abu Zainab al-Asadi al-Ajda'* (the criple). Ibn Ḥazm *(Shiites, I, 69)* makes him a client of the Banu Asad; Maḳrīzi, 352, gives as his father's name *Abu Thaur ibn Abu Yezīd.* For variants see *Shiites,* II, 111-2.

[2] The sixth Imām of the Twelvers. He is very highly esteemed by both Sunnites and Shī'ites. He was born 80 A. H. and died in 148. Nawāwi, 195; IKhall, I, 300—01.

[3] Ash'ari, 11, specifies more clearly that he at first maintained they were prophets.

[4] The same version occurs in *Shiites,* I, 69 (emended by Friedländer) and most notably Ash'ari, 11, where only Ḥusain's children are mentioned and thus coincides with Shahr. 136 and the original version of Ibn Ḥazm; in Iji 343 the reading is والحسنان ابناء الله similarly Ed. 242 reads الحسن والحسين واولادهما ابناء الله واحباؤه.

[5] Shahr. and Iji ib.; Naubakhti, 37.

[6] The sources which do not report his repudiation by Ja'far attribute this view to his followers. Ibn Ḥazm *(Shiites, I, 69)* and Sam'āni, f. 203 a. ascribe thts view to Abu-l-Khaṭṭāb himself without mention of his banishment. Naubakhti, who does not confirm Baghdādi's statement, relates that Abu-'l-Khaṭṭāb claimed successively to be heir to Ja'far, prophet, apostle, angel, 38.

[7] Naubakhti, 38; Ash'ari, 11; *Mukhtaṣar,* 155; Iji, 346; Goldziher has justly characterized it as a form of Taḳiyya *(ZDMC.* LX, [1906], 222). Massignon, *Studies E. G. Browne,*

Abu-l-Khaṭṭāb sallied forth against the governor of Kūfa in the reign of al-Manṣūr. The latter dispatched an army against him which took him prisoner, and al-Manṣūr ordered his crucifixion in the slums of al-Kūfa[1]. His followers said: It is necessary that in every age there should live one articulate Imām and another silent one[2]. The Imāms are Gods and they know the mysteries. They declare that 'Ali was a silent one during the lifetime of the Prophet, while the Prophet was the articulate one. After him 'Ali became the speaker. They profess the same about the Imāms up to the time of Abu Ja'far. In his time Abu-l-Khaṭṭāb was a silent Imām, but became the articulate one after him.

The followers of Abu-l-Khaṭṭāb broke up after his execution into five groups:

The Mu'ammariyya.[3] — They believe that the Imām who followed Abu-l-Khaṭṭāb was a man by the name of Mu'ammar[4] and they worship him as they had worshipped

330, cites a ruling by a Shāfi'ite according to which a Khaṭṭābi is not to be credited as a Rāwi. Cf. Muslim, I, 33 where Nawāwi relates similarly about Shāfi'i's attitude towards the traditions reported by the Khaṭṭābiyya. In *Lisān al-Mīzān* V, 170, Abu-l-Khaṭṭāb is listed but definitely rejected. See Ed. 351

[1] I have not found the execution recorded by any of the historians. According to Ash'ari, 11, it occurred by order of al-Manṣūr's general, 'Īsā ibn Mūsa, probably while he was governor of Kūfa, 132—147 A. H. (Zambaur, 43.), So also Naubakhti, 59—60, who describes the battle in detail.

[2] Ash'ari reports that Abu-l-Khaṭṭāb himself propounded this theory (See also *Ghunya*, 99). With the authority of al-Ash'ari behind this statement, the "reluctance" of Friedländer, (*Shiites*, II, 112, n. 3) to accept this fact, surprising as it may seem, is obviated. What lends even greater weight to the trustworthiness of this statement is the general opinion of authorities about the relation between Abu-l-Khaṭṭāb and the founder of the Bāṭiniyya. *Naubakhti*, 589; Maḳrīzi, (Fagnan) 47; IA, VIII, 21; *Fihrist*, 186. Massignon, *ib.* lists Abu-l-Khaṭṭāb's book as the first among "textes strictement qarmates." It is also noteworthy that Naubakhti accuses them of allegorizing laws, 38. This, too, they share with the Bāṭiniyya, see below, 135. For the theory of the Speaking and Silent Imāms see below p. 134-5.

[3] Ash'ari, 11, also cites another name for them which cannot be identified nor even correctly read (الموبية sic!).

[4] Called by Ibn Ḥazm "the corn-dealer" and a resident of Kūfa, *Shiites*, I, 64—69. Friedländer's suggestion that our Mu'ammar may possibly be identical with the Mu'tazilite Mu'ammar al-'Abbād al-Sulami (*l. c.* II, 114), can hardly be sustained since the authorities refer to him so indefinitely as above. Moreover, the founder of the Afṭaḥiyya was a Kūfite, 'Abdallah b. Faṭīḥ, acc. to some. Naubakhti, 66—7. The similarity of opinion which he finds

Abu-l-Khaṭṭāb. They assert that the world will not perish [1], and they disavow the Resurrection and profess the Transmigration of Souls.

The Bazīghiyya [2]. — They are followers of Bazīgh [3], who asserted that Ja'far is a god, but is not the person people saw, for what] [4] people saw was an image like him. They maintain that to every believer a revelation will be made, interpreting in accordance with this God's [4a] words: "And a Soul will not die except with the permission of God"; that is, a revelation will be granted him by God. They quote further proof in God's words: "And when I revealed to the disciples" [5], claiming for themselves that they are the disciples. They further cite God's word: "Your Lord revealed to the bee" [6], and say: Since the revelation to the bee is admissible, the revelation to us should be admitted more readily. They are also of the opinion that there are some among them who are superior to Jibrīl and Mīkā'īl and Muḥammad. They also hold that they will not die [7] and that when one of them reaches his appointed [8] end he is raised to the invisible world [9].

---

is not apparent. *Ghunya* lists two Mu'ammariyya sects, both Shī'ite; the founder of the second is 'Abdallah b. Ja'far al-Afṭaḥ (see Shahr., 126), 99-100 and 101.

[1] Al-Ash'ari, *ib.*, in addition ascribes to them views similar to those of Manṣūriyya on Paradise and Hell, and to those of the Janāḥiyya on Precepts and Prohibitions.

[2] On this sect see Ash'ari, 12; Shahr., 137; Iji, 346; Makrīzi, 352.

[3] Ash'ari calls him Ibn Mūsa. In *Shiites*, II, 112, he is described as a weaver and is accused of having claimed divinity for himself. Isf. B, 57b calls him Abu-l-Bazīgh (Isf. P. 76b: Abu-l-Rabī' and the sect Rabī'iyya!). Acc. to Naubakhti, *ib*, he rose during Abu-l-Khaṭṭāb's lifetime. The latter severed relations with him.

[4] The passage from the beginning of the chapter to this word, which is missing in both Ed. and MS., is taken from Isf. B. 57 a—b.

[4a] Sura 3, v. 139.

[5] Sura 5, v, 111.

[6] Sura 16, v, 70.

[7] Ash'ari 11, and Makrīzi 352, inform us that the Mu'ammariyya likewise believed that they will not die but will be lifted bodily to *Malkūt*. Friedländer sees in this view a preservation of the old belief in a general Return. *Shiites*, II, 24, n. 1.

[8] Arabic: ﺩﻧﺐ.

[9] *Bad'wal-Ta'rikh*, V, 137, (Arabic 130—31), relates in the name of the Bazīghiyya that their founder ascended to heaven, that God passed His hand over him and put His saliva in his mouth; he also saw 'Ali sitting to the right of the Lord.

They maintain that they see those who ascended from among them at daybreak and nightfall.[1]

The third division among them is called ʻOmairiyya[2] — followers of ʻOmar Ibn Bayān al-ʻIjli.[3] They give the lie to those among them who claim that they will not die, and declare: Verily we shall die, but our descendants will never cease as Imāms and prophets. They worship Jaʻfar and call him Lord.[4]

The fourth group among them is the Mufaḍḍaliyya, because they trace their origin to a certain man called Mufaḍḍal al-Ṣairafi (the broker). They profess Jaʻfar's divinity but not his prophecy. They repudiate Abu-l-Khaṭṭāb because Jaʻfar repudiated him.[5]

The fifth division among them is simply called Khaṭṭabiyya. — It persists in its partisanship for Abu-l-Khaṭṭāb and all his claims and it does not recognize the 237
Imāmate of anyone after him.

ʻAbd-al-Ḳāhir says: If the Bayāniyya[6] and Manṣūriyya and Janāḥiyya and Khaṭṭābiyya have declared Abu Bekr and ʻOmar and ʻUthmān and most of the Companions to be infidels because of their eliminating ʻAli from the Imāmate in their time, they themselves have wrenched the Imāmate from the children of ʻAli during the age of their chiefs. One can say to them: Since ʻAli in his age had

---

[1] The lack of intelligence with which copyists of MSS. of.en did their work is well illustrated in the parallel passage from Isf. B, رفع الى الملكوت غدوة وعشيا. *Bad' wal-Ta'rikh, ib.* finds a parallel to this belief of the Bazīghiyya among the Hindus.

[2] With Ms. عميرية; Ed. عجرية.

[3] Ibn Ḥazm (*Shiites*, I, 64) names him التبان, the straw-dealer. On the basis of this Friedländer would regard our reading بيان as a corruption of تبان, ii, 96. In view of the agreement among authorities (Ashʻari, 12; Shahr. 137 [بنان]; Iji, 346 [بنان]: Maḳrīzi, ib.; Isf. B, 57 b.) on his father's name, this cannot be accepted. If anything, it is Ibn Ḥazm who is guilty of the corruption. The utterance "If I wanted to turn this straw into gold" (I. 64) is not proof either way. Naubakhti 39 names a certain Ibn Labbān as a Khaṭṭābi, probably our ʻOmar. — His relation to the ʻIjl is noteworthy as Friedländer, *ib.* has already pointed out.

[4] Ashʻari and Maḳrīzi both report that they erected a tent in the slums of Kūfa — possibly on the site where Abu-l-Khaṭṭāb was executed — and convened there to worship Jaʻfar. But Yezīd ibn ʻOmar ibn Hubaira seized and killed ʻOmar, imprisoning some of his men.

[5] Maḳrīzi reports that he was also banished by Jaʻfar for calling him God, ib.

[6] With MS.; Ed. الباضية.

greater claims to the Imâmate than the other companions, his children were more deserving of it in their time than their chiefs. However, these blunderers are not to be wondered at. The wonder is rather that some of the partisans of ‘Ali kill these, yet find themselves alone in their support of others for the Imamate.

CHAPTER EIGHT*.

THE GHURĀBIYYA, MUFAWWIḌA, DHAMMIYYA AND THEIR EXCLUSION FROM THE SECTS OF THE COMMUNITY.

The Ghurābiyya[1] consists of a group of people who are of the opinion that God despatched Jibrīl to ‘Ali, but the angel went astray and came to Muḥammad because the latter resembled ‘Ali[2]. They say: He resembled him more closely than a raven (Ghurāb) does a raven[3] or a fly a fly[4]. They hold that ‘Ali was the Apostle and that his children after him are apostles. This sect greets[5]
its adherents by saying: Curse the feathered one, meaning Jibrīl[6]. The heresy 238
of this sect is viler than that of the Jews, who said to the Apostle of God: Who

---

* Owing to the omission of a folio in the MS. on which a new chapter began, this and the subsequent chapters are all numbered in the Ed. one less than their actual number.

[1] The three sects mentioned in this chapter are, unlike the other sects hitherto treated, not traced to any individual. Ibn Ḳutaiba, 300, has called attention to this in connection with the Ghurābiyya.

[2] It is interesting that Ibn Ḥazm (*Shiites,* I, 56—7) refutes this contention of the Ghurābiyya by a comparison between ‘Ali and Muḥammad, mentioning among other facts that the former was some thirty years older than the latter, and that Muḥammad could be called tall, whereas ‘Ali was rather short.

[3] A curious explanation of the name is quoted by Blochet, 148, from the *Bayān al-Adyān* to the effect that they are called so because they believe that ‘Ali is in heaven in the form of a raven.

[4] The expression "like raven to raven" is part of a standard expression in Arabic, more generally "like date to date and raven to raven". Goldziher, *ZA*, XVII, (1903), 53.

[5] MS. and Ed. تقول. I base my translation on Maḳrīzi, 353; وجعلوا اشعارهم اذا اجتمعوا ان يقولوا, (tr. de Sacy, Introd., 54).

[6] In *Shiites,* I, 56, we read that some of the Ghurābiyya exonerated Jibrīl, since it was an error.

brought you a revelation from God[1]? and added: We do not like Jibrīl because he brings chastisement. If Mīkhā'īl had brought the revelation to you — and he never announces anything but grace — we would believe in you. Now the Jews, despite their denial of the Prophet and despite their hostility to Jibrīl, do not curse Jibrīl, but simply believe that he is one of the angels of punishment and not of grace. But the Ghurābiyya among the Rawāfiḍ damn Jibrīl and Muḥammad. God, however, has said: "Whoever is the enemy of God and His angels and His apostles and Jibrīl and Mīkā'īl, so surely God is an enemy of the unbelievers."[1a] In this we find a confirmation of the name infidel for anyone who bears hate to any of the angels. And it is not admissible to include within Islam anyone whom God has named infidel.

Concerning the Mufawwiḍa among the Rawāfiḍ. — It is made up of a group which maintains that God created Muḥammad, then He committed to him the management of the world and the disposal of its affairs[2]. It is he, and not God, who brought the universe into existence. Then Muḥammad entrusted the rule of the universe to 'Ali ibn Abu Ṭālib[3]. He is thus the third ruler. This sect is more ignominious than the Magians who think that God created Satan and that Satan created all evil things; more shameful indeed than the Christians who call 'Īsa the second ruler. Whoever reckons the Rāfiḍite Mufawwiḍa among the Islamic sects is on one level with those who count the Magians and Christians as Muslims.

Concerning the Dhammiyya. — They are a section which believes that 'Ali
239 is God and they revile Muḥammad, claiming that 'Ali sent him to enlighten[4] the

[1] The following story is related in Aḥmad ibn Ḥanbal's *Musnad*, I, 274, and by Tayalisi, 356—7 (No. 2731; he does not mention Michael but simply غيره). Bukhari, II, 331—2 has the same tradition but relates it of one Jew, 'Abdallah ibn Sallām.

[1a] Sura ii, v. 92.

[2] With MS. وتقديره; Ed. وتدبيره.

[3] According to Ash'ari 16, 'Ali as ruler of the universe is not recognized by the same group which holds that view about Muḥammad but by another section within the Mufawwiḍa. However, it may be that there was a harmonization between these two views at a later date so that Baghdādi's statement may be correct. Makrīzi, 353, counts a sub-sect among the 'Ulyāniyya (see below) which, while recognizing the divinity of both 'Ali and Muḥammad, gave the latter precedence, and it is on that account called Mīmiyya (abbreviated from Muḥammadiyya, see *Shiites*, I, 97, and II, 102—3.

[4] With MS. ليبين; Ed. ليثنى.

world about him, but that he employed the charge in his own interest[1]. This sect is excluded from Islam because it denies that Muḥammad's prophecy was derived from God.

---

[1] This sect whose name is derived from ذم, to blame, also appears under other names. Ibn Ḥazm, *Shiites*, i, 66, and Maḳrīzi, 353 call them 'Ulyāniyya, the latter tracing the name to 'Ulyān ibn Ḍhirā' al-Sadūsi or al-Asadi. Shahr. 134, names him 'Ilba or 'Ulba. Ash'ari, 14, in speaking of them does not call them by any name. — The groups cited in this chapter persisted for a good many centuries. The Ghurābiyya are cited in Ḳumm in the fourth century A.H. (*EI*, II, 177). Ibn Jubair (Italian trans. by Schiaparelli, 272) found them in Damascus, 1184. The Dhammiyya exist to the present day under the name of 'Ali-'Ilāhi. See *Mukhtaṣar*, 158, n.3. and esp. Minorski's article on this sect in *Monde Musulman*, XLIV—XLV (1921), 205-302.

CHAPTER NINE.

THE SHURAI'IYYA AND THE NAMĪRIYYA[1] AMONG THE RAWĀFIḌ[2].

The Shurai'iyya are followers of a man who was known as al-Shurai'i. It is he who held that God was embodied in five corporeal beings, to wit: the Prophet, 'Ali, Fātima,[3] al-Ḥasan and al-Ḥusain. They believe that these five are Gods and there exist five who are their converses[4]. But they differ regarding their opposites, some maintaining that they are praiseworthy because the excellence of a person in whom God inheres would not be known except through his opposite. Others maintain that the converses are to be condemned. It has been related of al-Shurai'i that he claimed once that God dwelt in him.

After him came one of his followers called al-Namiri. Of him it is related that he asserted God abides in his person. These eight Ghulāt sects of the Rawāfiḍ are all excluded from the category of Islamic sects for recognizing gods[5] other than Allah. One of the most astonishing facts is that the al-Khaṭṭābiyya

[1] I read the name of this sect Namīriyya, instead of Numairiyya, guided by MS. Cf. also Massignon, *EI*, II, 333.

[2] Ibn Ḥazm mentions both men as tricksters with a mule, IH, I, 110 (trans. Asin Palacios, II, 226). The translator disclaims any further knowledge of them. According to Naubakhti, 78, the founder of this sect was called Muḥammad b. Nuṣair al-Namīri. He claimed prophecy, and asserted that he was sent by 'Ali al-Hādi, the tenth Imām (Middle of 3rd century, A. H.), and not his son al Ḥasan al-'Askari (*Shiites*, ii, 127). He attributed divinity to 'Ali, and was himself a believer in Tanāsukh. He abolished all prescriptions and prohibitions. His partisans had been supporters of 'Ali.

[3] According to Maḳrīzi, 353, who deals with the same group under the Dhammiyya they called Fāṭima by a masculine name, Fāṭim. He cites a poem in support of this, also quoted by Blochet, 51. N. 5.

[4] Al-Ash'ari enumerates them: Abu Bekr, 'Omar, 'Uthmān, Mu'āwiya and 'Amr ibn al-'Āṣ.

[5] With MS. الٰه for الهة; Ed. الى.

believe that Ja'far al-Ṣādiḳ entrusted to them a volume in which information can be obtained regarding any knowledge[1] of the Occult which they should seek. They call this volume Jafr[2]. They are of the opinion that only he who professes their views can read what is in it. Hārūn ibn Sa'd al-'Ijli[3] treats this in his song as follows: 240

Do you not see the Rawāfiḍ split among themselves
And each of them making a shocking statement regarding Ja'far?
Some say a God,[4] while other groups
Among them name him the Immaculate Prophet.
But what causes my inexpressible astonishment is a volume Jafr[5].
I declare myself free before God from all the followers of the Jafr[6];
I declare myself free before God from every Rāfiḍite
Well-informed[7] in matters of heresy, but ignorant of true faith.

---

[1] Inserting علم with Goldziher; missing in Ed.

[2] With MS. جفرا; Ed جعفرا. See on this book Macdonald's article in EI, I, 1037. The meaning of this word and its etymology are not definitely established. Goldziher, *(Literaturgesch. d. Schi'a*, 456, n. 5.), and Friedländer, *Shiites*, II, 106, n. 2, derive it from Ja'far. Our line ممن "بجعفرا" seems to support this assumption. The Jafr is said to be a work dealing with all past and future events. Guyard, 292, n. 3, who claims to have examined a Jafr with ibn al-'Arabi's commentary asserts that it is nothing but the alphabet explained Ḳabbalistically. Cf. de Goeje 116—17. - Ja'far's capacities as a magician are well known in Islamic literature. He is also credited with the composition of a work on the magic qualities of Ḳur'ānic verses. See Christensen *Khavas-i-ayat*, Notices, 4.

[3] Ikhall, II, 154 ff. In the *Mizan al-I'tidal*, iii, s, v, هارون, he is described as an extreme Rāfiḍite and his traditions are, of course, discredited. Friedländer, *Shiites*, II, 106, has justly raised the problem of the authorship of this poem. It may however, be that Hārūn as a moderate Zaidite will allow himself to talk in this "orthodox" manner of extreme Shī'ites. The poem, with the same authorship is also to be found in *Mukhtalif al-Hadith*, 85.

[4] Ikhall, ib. reads the Imām and so also the oriental Ed. I, 558 and *Mukhtalif al-Ḥadīth*. There is no doubt, however, that our text is the more correct one, since there is nothing extravagant in his being called Imām, unless the stress is on the second half of the line.

[5] With MS. جفر; Ed. جعفر.

[6] Ikhall Isf. and *Mukhtalif al-Ḥadīth* read تجفر; I prefer our reading.

[7] With MS. يصر, for بصير; Ed. بصير.

When the adherents of truth abstain from an innovation they incite[1] [people]
[To accept] it, and if they should follow truth it would fail.
If they were told that the elephant is a lizard they would accept it,
Or if they were told that the Ethiopian's complexion has turned fair.
They are more stupid than the urinating[2] camel for he,
If he faces you, will turn his back.
May abomination overtake the people who involve Him in impostures[3]
Of the kind of falsehoods which the Christians spread about ʻĪsa.

---

[1] With MS. حضوا ; Ed. مضوا.

[2] With MS. بول ; Ed. يوم.

[3] With MS. بفرية, for بفريه: and in the next hemistich الفرا: Ed. بعزبة and القرا.

CHAPTER TEN.

THE ḤULŪLIYYA AND THEIR EXCLUSION FROM ISLAMIC SECTS.

The Ḥulūliyya,[1] as a whole, consist of ten sects all of which have arisen since the institution of Islam. Their common aim is the endeavor to undermine the tenet of the unity of the Maker. The distinct sects among them go back in the main to the Ghulāt of the Rawāfiḍ, since the Sabbābiyya, the Bayāniyya, the Janāḥiyya, the Khaṭṭābiyya, the Shurai'iyya[2] and the Namīriyya are all members of the Ḥulūliyya. In addition to these, the Mukanna'iyya appeared in the district beyond the river Jaiḥūn[3]; a group called the Ruzāmiyya,[4] and another called the Berkūkiyya arose in Merw[5]. Besides these, a section sprang up among the Ḥulūliyya known as the Ḥulmāniyya, another by the name of Ḥallājiyya, which is to be traced to al-Ḥusain ibn Manṣūr, known as al-Ḥallāj, and a third group, called the 'Azāḳira[6], originating with ibn Abu-l-'Azāḳiri. These Ḥulūliyya groups were followed by a division from the Khurramiyya who joined them in allowing

---

[1] *Hulūl,* which has several technical meanings, is used here especially in the sense of incarnation which the orthodox reject unconditionally. See *EI,* II, 333. The Sunnite-Ṣūfic point of view on Ḥulūl together with a polemical discussion of incarnation is found in al-Hujwiri, *Kashf al-Mahjub* (tr. Nicholson) 260-6. The name Hulūliyya, referring to an abstract idea rather than a person, is not applied to the same sects or people by all historians alike. See below, esp. on al-Ḥallāj.

[2] Missing in Ed.

[3] Transoxania called in Arabic *Ma-wara-l-Nahr.* Baghdādi regularly adds Jaiḥūn (the name of a river coursing through Khurāsān, Yaḳūt, s. v.), which indicates that he did not regard it as a proper noun.

[4] Most authorities (Shahr, [Haarbrücker,] I, 173; *Shiites,* II, 110; Iji, 347) name it Rizāmiyya and its founder Rizām. I follow MS. which carefully inserts a *Ḍamma* over the *Ra.*

[5] With MS. مرو; Ed. مرق.

[6] With MS. عزاقرة; Ed. عذاقرة, and similarly for the name immediately following.

the forbidden and in abolishing precepts. We shall briefly mention their several distinctions.

The Sabbābiyya are included within the category of the Ḥulūliyya because of their view that 'Ali became a God through the embodiment of God's spirit in him. Similarly the Bayāniyya maintain that the spirit of God circulated among the
242 prophets and Imāms until it reached 'Ali. From him it went on to Muḥammad ibn al-Ḥanafiyya, then it passed into his son Abu Hāshim, and was embodied after him in Bayān ibn Sam'ān. They therefore acknowledge the divine character of Bayān ibn Sam'ān. By the same token, the Janāḥiyya are Ḥulūliyya because they declare that the spirit of God circulated among 'Ali and his offspring and passed thence to 'Abdallah ibn Mu'āwiya ibn 'Abdallah ibn Ja'far. They are infidels because of their claim that God's spirit inheres in their chief, and, moreover, because they deny the Resurrection and Paradise and Hell. The Khaṭṭābiyya are all Ḥulūliyya because they assert that the spirit of God was incarnated in Ja'far al-Ṣādiḳ and, after him, in Abu-l-Khaṭṭāb al-Asadi. This sect is guilty of heresy from this aspect and because they contend that al-Ḥasan and al-Ḥusain and their offspring are children and favorites of God. Anyone who pretends that he is of God's children is a greater heretic than the rest of the Khaṭṭābiyya. The Shurai'iyya and the Namīriyya belong to the Ḥulūliyya because they declare that the spirit of God was embodied in five persons, to wit: The Prophet, 'Ali, Fāṭima, al-Ḥasan and al-Ḥusain, and because they claim that these five persons are gods.

The Ruzāmiyya[1] are a division in Merw who went to extremes in aligning themselves with Abu Muslim, the supporter of the 'Abbāsid rule[2]. They transferred the Imāmate from Abu Hāshim to the 'Abbāsids. Then they transferred it from Muḥammad ibn 'Ali to his brother 'Abdallah ibn 'Ali al-Saffāḥ[3]. Following

---

[1] This sect is named after its founder Ruzām (Ruzām ibn Sābiḳ, Maḳrīzi, 353.).

[2] On the history of the period see the last chapter in Wellhausen's *Das Arabische Reich*, and Van Vloten, *La Domination arabe, le Chiitisme et les Croyances Messianiques*. Abu Muslim is frequently known as Ṣāḥib al-Da'wa (master of the mission, Friedlander, JQR, NS. I, 202). Possibly orthodoxy prevented our author and the other historians from employing for the 'Abbāsid Khalīfs the term Da'wa, generally accepted as heretical.

[3] The transfer is traced by Maḳrīzi, ib. through 'Ali ibn Abu Ṭālib, his son Muḥammad, his son Abu Hāshim, 'Ali ibn 'Abdallah ibn al-'Abbās by bequest, his son Muḥammad,

Following al-Saffāḥ, they held, the Imāmate passed to Abu Muslim[1], admitting, nevertheless, the execution and death of Abu Muslim. But one section among them, called the Abu Muslimiyya[2], are absurdly extravagant about Abu Muslim believing that he became a God through the embodiment of God's spirit in him. They hold that he is better than Jibrīl and Mīkā'īl and the other angels. They 243
also hold that he is alive and did not die, and they persist in expecting him. Those in Merw and Herāt are called Barkūkiyya[3]. When they are asked whom al-Manṣūr killed they say: It was Satan who assumed the likeness of Abu Muslim in the eyes of the people.

The Muḳanna'iyya are the same as the Mubayyiḍa[4] in Ma-wara-l-Nahr beyond the Jaiḥūn. Their chief, known as al-Muḳanna'[5], was a blind fuller[6] in Merw, native of a village called Kaza Kaimun Dat[7]. He had acquired a smattering of engineering and mechanics and the art of incantations, and was of the persuasion of the Ruzāmiyya in Merw. Subsequently he claimed divinity for himself and concealed himself from people behind a silk veil. The people of Jabal

---

al-Saffāḥ by bequest and, from him, to Abu Muslim. Naubakhti correctly says of this party: واصلهم مذهب الكيسانية, 42.

[1] According to Iji, *ib*, it went from Abu Ja'far al-Manṣūr to Abu Muslim. Ash'ari, 21-22 calls the Ruzāmiyya a branch of the Rawandiyya and similarly the Abu Muslimiyya. Maḳrīzi is, therefore, right in his classification of the Baslamiyya (see next note) for which he is criticized. *Shiites, ii, 119.*

[2] Friedländer's contention, *ib*, is no doubt correct, that Maḳrīzi's Baslamiyya are worshippers of Abu Muslim, and not Abu Salma, and are, therefore, identical with the sect under discussion.

[3] I am tempted to identify this group with the Isḥāḳiyya who, according to *Fihrist*, 344-5, arose in Ma-wara-l-Nahr as a result of Isḥāk the Turk's activities.

[4] Lane, *s. v.*, on the authority of the *TA*, identifies this group with the followers of al-Muḳanna' who chose this color in contradiction to the 'Abbāsids who wore black. It was probably done in protest, because of Abu Muslim's execution. See also the note on p. 533 of Wellhausen's *Arab Kingdom and Its Fall* (Eng. Tr.).

[5] "The veiled one", - so called from the fact that he wore a veil of silk (according to others a mask of gold) see Ikhall, II, 105-6; IA, VI, 26; Albiruni, 194; Maḳrīzi, 354.

[6] With MS. قصاروا (read قصارا); Ed. فصاروا.

[7] Yaḳut IV, 226 who calls it Kaza, describes it as a village near Merw. Albiruni *ib.* writes Kawaklmardan.

Īlāḳ [1], and also some people from al-Sughd [2] were deceived by him. His sedition against the Muslims endured for a period of fourteen years [3]. He was aided against the Muslims by the infidel Turks of al-Khalj [4] who sought to make a raid upon them. They routed many Muslim armies during the reign of al-Mahdi ibn Manṣūr. Al-Muḳanna' had allowed unto his followers that which was prohibited and forbade them to believe in prohibitions. He abolished prayer, fasting, and the other acts of worship. He asserted before his followers that he was a God and that he had once appeared in the shape of Adam [5], another time in the shape of Ibrahīm. He then continued to manifest himself in the likeness of prophets down to the time of Muḥammad. After him he assumed the form of 'Ali. After that he was transmitted in the likeness of his children, then he assumed the shape of Abu Muslim. He asserted finally that in the age in which
244 he himself lived he appeared in the shape of Hāshim [6] ibn Ḥakīm, for his own

---

[1] With MS.; Ed. ايلاق. It is a city not far from Shash in the territory of Mawara-l Nahr. Yakūt speaks of it as being one of the pleasantest cities; its mountains contain deposits of gold and silver. I, 241.

[2] The correct reading is الصغد; MS and Ed. الصعد. IA, *ib.* relates that the Mubayyiḍa came to help him from Bukhāra and al-Sughd. Cf. Yaḳūt, III, 394.

[3] The agreed date for his downfall is 163 A. H. According to some it lasted from 149 to 161 (IA, *ib;* although he dates the defeat in 161, he adds that al-Muḳanna's head, according to the version that he was poisoned, first reached the Khalīf in 163); according to others it started in 160 or 161 (*Tab.* III, 484) Cf. also *Nujūm* II, 430; Abu-l-Feda, Oriental Ed., II, 10. The number in our text, also copied by Isf. 59b, includes perhaps the early years of his rebellion before it assumed such large proportions.

[4] A town near Ghazna, Yaḳūt, *s. v.*

[5] The theory of God's revelations successively in various persons is declared by Goldziher, who attributes it to Christian influence, to have been first proposed by Muḳanna'. According to this theory all prophets are really identical. This, of course, is also the point of view of the Bāṭiniyya, *ZA,* XXII, (1908), 337 ff. The Mubayyiḍa are indeed counted as one of the sub-sects of the Bāṭiniyya. See below 107. IA, VI, 26, relates that their war-cry was: O Hishām help us! To this Goldziher, *ib,* adds that in his epistles his views of himself as a God are apparent.

[6] With MS; Ed. هشام. Isf. 59b (هشام, read هاشم); Aibirūni, *ib.* agree with our author. Tab. *ib,* and IA, *ib,* as well as Ya'ḳūbi *Bibliot. Geogr.,* VII, 304) and Ḳazwīni (cited by Browne, *Lit. History of Persia,* I, 319. all call him Hakīm. Ikhall, II, 205 calls him

name was Hāshim ibn Ḥakīm. He said: Verily I am embodied in shapes because my worshippers cannot bear to see me in the form which is properly mine. Whoever sees me is consumed by my light[1]. He had a strong firm fortress in the vicinity of Kashsh[2] and Nakhshab[3] in a mountain called Siyām[4]. The width of the wall of its rampart was more than one hundred baked bricks and below it there was a wide fosse[5]. He had with him the inhabitants of Sughd and the Turks from Khalj. Al-Mahdi dispatched against him Mu'ādh ibn Muslim, general of his army, with seventy thousand of his warriors and he put them under the command of Sa'īd ibn 'Amr al-Ḥarashi[6]. Then he singled out Sa'īd to attack and conduct the battle[7]. He fought him for a number of years. Then Sa'īd prepared two hundred steps of iron and timber in order to set them across the width of Muḳanna''s

---

'Aṭa (عطا) but disclaims knowledge of his father's name (Oriental Ed. I, 573 adds وقيل اسمه حكيم; cf. *Nujum, ib*). It is noteworthy that in discussing the transmission of God's spirit, IA, *ib.* credits him with making the statement that "Hāshim, according to his doctrine, is al-Muḳanna'".

[1] In further illustration of the claim by al-Muḳanna', it is worth citing the incident related in Isf, 59 B. His devotees pressed him to reveal himself to them. Despite his warnings they insisted. He therefore placed a concave brass mirror against the sun on his mimbar so that it would reflect against the door of the Mosque. He called them to prayer at midday where he said he would reveal himself to them. But as the first people stepped into the Mosque the sunlight reflected by the mirror burnt them and they were convinced of the truth of his claim (see also, Maḳrizi, *ib*). He is also said to have manipulated a scheme by which he could bring the moon up whenever he wanted. Ikhall, *ib; Siasset Nameh*, 290.

[2] Ed. and MS. كثير; Isf. B. and P. correctly كش. That the town Kashsh is meant is attested by the various sources.

[3] MS. and Ed. بخشب; Ist. B. نخشب. It is the Persian name for Nasaf, a city right near Kashsh.

[4] IKhall ib. reads سنام (Oriental Ed., *ib.*) Yaḳūt, III, 155 mentions it specifically as the town where Muḳanna' had his fortress. Muḳaddasi, 376; IA, ib., Abu-l-Feda all agree with our reading.

[5] With Ed. خندق; MS. خنادق.

[6] With MS. الحرشى; Ed. الحرش.

[7] "In that year (161) Mu'ādh ibn Muslim and a number of generals and armies marched against Muḳanna' and Sa'īd al-Ḥarashi as his superior (على مقدمته).... Then jealousy developed between him (Mu'ādh) and al-Ḥarashi. The latter wrote to al-Mahdi slandering Mu'ādh and guaranteeing him victory if he should entrust the conduct of the war entirely to him. Al-Mahdi yielded, and al-Ḥarashi became the only commander". IA, VI, 34. Cf. also Ṭab, iii, 484.

fosse, so that his men could pass over it. He ordered ten thousand buffalo skins from Multān[1] in India, stuffed them with sand, and levelled with them the fosse of al-Mukanna'. He then fought al-Mukanna''s army beyond his fosse. He compelled thirty thousand of them to capitulate and he killed the rest. Al-Mukanna' set himself on fire in a furnace in his fortress in which he had dissolved copper with wines, so that he dissolved within it[2]. His associates were seduced by this afterwards since they did not find either his body or his ashes and they thought that he had ascended to heaven. His followers at the present day in the mountain of Īlāk are the most detestable among the inhabitants. In everyone of their villages they have a Mosque, in which they do not pray, but hire[3] a Muezzin who calls to prayers. They permit themselves to eat carcasses
245 and pork. Everyone of them enjoys intercourse with other men's wives. If they get hold of a Muslim whom the Muezzin in their Mosque did not notice they kill him and hide him, yet they are not generally maltreated by the Muslims in their district. Praised be Allah for it.

The Ḥulmāniyya among the Ḥulūliyya originated with Abu Ḥulmān al-Dimishḳi[4], a native of Fars, whose place of upbringing was Aleppo[5]. But he promulgated his innovation in Damascus and for that reason is named after it. He is guilty of heresy for two reasons. In the first place, he believed in God's

---

[1] Yaḳūt IV, 688. None of the geographers in de Goeje's *Bibliot.* save Muḳaddasi, devote much space to the town. Even Muḳaddasi, however, mentions nothing about the presence of buffaloes in it, 480-1.

[2] Most authorities, e. g. Ṭab., III, 494; *Nujum*, I, 438: IKhall, *ib.*; Ya'ḳubi, *ib.*; Abu-l-Feda, *ib.* agree that he poisoned himself and his adherents. IA, VI, 34 reports both versions.

[3] Friedländer's remark on this word that "it gives no sense" (*Shiites*, II, 120, n. 2) is surprising, as the VIII. form of كرى makes very good sense indeed being synonymous with يستأجرون employed by Isf. which Friedländer prefers; cf. Ed., 197.

[4] Massignon, *al-Halladj*, 362, puts his death at about 340 A. H. By his two heresies (see text below) he recognizes him as an adherent of al-Ḥallāj but adds: «C'est là un résumé perfide de deux thèses connues d'al-Hallādj». Hujwīri, *Kashf al-Mahjūb* (tr. Nicholson) 260, regards this sect as well as the Ḥallājiyya as condemned by the Ṣūfis. But he adds that many consider Abu Ḥulmān a worthy Ṣūfi. Ṭūsi in the كتاب اللمع (ed. Nicholson, 289) calls him Abu Ḥulmān al-Ṣūfi.

[5] Massignon, *EI*, II, 333 calls him a disciple of Sālim of Baṣra (see below on the Sālimiyya).

embodiment in handsome beings. Whenever he and his followers saw a pretty face they prostrated themselves before it, taking it into their heads that God abides in it[1]. The second aspect of his disbelief was his advocacy of licentiousness, and his assertion that whoever knows God, in the way in which he (i. e. Abu Ḥulmān) believes him to be, is relieved of all interdictions and prohibitions, and can allow himself all that he delights in and craves.

'Abd-al-Ḳāhir says: I found one of these Ḥulmāniyya citing, in proof of the possibility of God's incarnation in bodies, God's word to the angels regarding Adam: "So that when I have made him complete and breathed into him of my spirit, fall down making obeisance to him"[2]. He held that God commanded the angels to bow down before Adam only because He had embodied Himsef in him and really abode in him because He created him in the most beautiful form. Therefore, He said: "We have created man in the finest form"[3]. I said to him: Tell me about this verse from which you bring proof that God commanded the angels to bow down before Adam, and about the eloquent verse that man is created in the finest form. Is all mankind meant by these two verses? Or one
particular individual? He inquired: What will follow from either of the two 246
interpretations which I may offer? I answered: If you state that what is meant by them is mankind in general, you are obliged to kneel before every man, even if he is ugly, since you assert that God abides in all men. But if you say that the allusion is to a particular person, then it is Adam and no one else. Why then do you bow before others who are blessed with beautiful faces, yet do not bow before a horse of noble breed,[4] or a fruit-bearing tree, or handsome birds and beasts? Sometimes it is the flame of hell-fire[5] which gleams in a face. If you admit bowing to the flame then you have combined the error of the Ḥulūliyya with that of the fire-worshippers. But since you do not kneel before fire, water, air or the heavens, despite their fairness of form under certain circumstances, do not prostrate yourself before persons of fair appearance. I further said to him:

---

[1] Cf. Ash'ari, 214.

[2] Sura 15, v. 29.

[3] Sura 95, v. 4.

[4] Reading رائع with MS; Ed. الرابع.

[5] Reading النار with Goldziher; Ed. and MS: الناس.

Verily the fair forms in this world are numerous, and with respect to God's incarnation in them no single one is more deserving than the other. If you maintain that God abides in all fair forms, is this embodiment like the existence of a property in a body, or like the existence of a body within a body? However, the location of an accident in many subjects is absurd and the location of one being in many places is impossible. Since that is absurd, then that to which it leads is also absurd.

Concerning the Ḥallājiyya[1]. — They trace their origin to Abu-l-Mughīth al-Ḥusain ibn Manṣūr, known as al-Ḥallāj[2]. He was a native of the province of Fars,
247 of a city called al-Baiḍā'[3]. In the early days[4] of his career he was engrossed in the philosophy of the Ṣūfis. His manner of expression at that time was of the kind which the Ṣūfis call Shaṭḥ[5]. It is the kind that lends itself to two interpretations: one, noble and commendable, the other vicious[6] and blameworthy[7]. He pretended to possess both a detailed and a general knowledge of the several sciences. Some of the inhabitants of Baghdād and numbers of people from Ṭalikān in Khurāsān

---

[1] A very exhaustive study of the founder of this sect is contained in the large work by Massignon, *La Passion d'al Hosain ibn Mansour al-Halladj*, Paris, 1922.

[2] The name means a carder. But whether it refers to an actual profession of wool-carding in which his father may have been engaged, or to some miracle, or is some metaphorical name is discussed by Massignon, l. c., 18-20 and 69. (al-Ḥallāj was born in 244).

[3] A city on the right bank of Kūr, eight farasangs from Shīraz, l. c., 14.

[4] These early days probably include the period from his adolescence to his fiftieth year, l. c. 20-62.

[5] Ecstatic, enigmatic phrases. l. c. 375. Nicholson, ***Kashf***, 168 translates it simply as *"ecstatic phrases"*. On its importance in Ṣūfic literature see Massignon l. c. 923.

[6] With MS. قبيح ; Ed. قبح.

[7] This characterization is no doubt the prejudiced view of a rational Sunnite. A more objective and more sympathetic definition is one which Massignon gives in his *Lexique technique de la Mystique Musulmane*, 99: that it is the recognition of "a divine element" in the "slightest action or phrases". It comes in a state of ecstasy where every word is realized in its fullness, so that the divine speech is heard in it, "au seuil de l'union mystique, intervient le phénomène de Shaṭḥ, l'offre de l'échange, l'interversion amoureuse des rôles est proposée; l'âme soumise est invitée a vouloir, a exprimer, sans s'en douter, «a la premiere personne», le point de vue même de son Bien-aimé; c'est l'épreuve suprême de son humilité, le sceau de son élection".

were seduced by him[1]. The theologians, the jurists and the Ṣūfis entertain various views regarding him[2]. The majority of the theologians are inclined to condemn him as an infidel and to believe that he was of the persuasion of the Ḥulūliyya[3]. But several of the Sālimiyya Mutakallims of Baṣra[4] accept him and class him with the mystical theorists of the Ṣūfis[5]. The Ḳāḍi Abu Bekr ibn al-Ṭaib al-Ash'ari[6] ranked him with those who are endowed with perspicacity and capacities for the preternatural[7]. In his work, in which he demonstrates the incapacity of the Mu'tazila to establish the distinctive features of prophecy on the basis of their principle, he mentions the supernatural deeds of al-Ḥallāj and the manner of his miracles.

The jurists have also been divided in their attitude to al-Ḥallāj. Abu-l-'Abbās ibn Suraij[8] abstained from pronouncing an opinion when he was asked for one

---

[1] On his work and preaching in Baghdād see Massignon, *al-Ḥalladj*, 132 and 338-9. On Ṭaliḳān see l. c., 77-80 and 337-8.

[2] IKhall says: "....and people are still at variance respecting his true character, some extolling him to the utmost whilst others treat him as an infidel", I, 423.

[3] This contention is refuted by 'Omar al-'Ordi (d. 1024 A. H.) Massignon, l. c. 395. In the discussion of his Ṣūfiism, he takes up this question several times, 464-532.

[4] According to Hujwīri, *Kashf*, 131, the Sālimiyya is one of the Ḥulūliyya sects. Isf., 60b identifies them with the Ḥashwiyya (see on them Houtsma's article, *ZA*, XXVI, 196-202 and my article, *JAOS*, liv (1934), 1-28). The fullest description of the sect is given in *Ghunya*, p. 61, upon which Goldziher based his sketch, *ZDMG*, LXI, 73-78. Among the heretical views are. 1) that in the resurrection God will be seen by everybody, including infidels and animals; 2) that Muḥammad knew the Ḳur'ān even before it was revealed to him; 3) that Īmān (faith) is one of God's names.

[5] Massignon, l. c. 361, translates "to have realized the ideal set by Ṣūfiism". On Ḥaḳīḳa in the sense of mysticism or inner reality see *Kashf*, 383-4, and Massignon l. c., 565-6. I owe my translation of the phrase to Nicholson, *Kashf*, 119.

[6] Died, 403. He is generally surnamed al-Bāḳilāni (IKhall, II, 672), and he is called Ash'ari because of his adherence to the Ash'arite doctrine or because he is a descendant of Abu Mūsa al-Ash'ari (so Sam'ani, *s. v.* Ash'ari). On his attitude to al-Ḥallāj see Massignon, l. c., 364-5.

[7] l. c., 136-8.

[8] Ed. and MS. سريج. He died 306. For his biography see IKhall, II, 46 ff. and for his views Massignon l. c. 165-7.

regarding the forfeiture of his life[1]. Abu Bekr ibn Dāud[2] pronounced himself in favor of his execution. The religious leaders among the Ṣūfis have also disagreed about him. 'Amr ibn 'Uthmān al-Mekki[3] and Abu Ya'ḳūb al-Aḳṭa' (one-handed)[4] and a number of others declared themselves free from him. 'Amr ibn 'Uthmān said: I was walking with him one day and recited something from the Ḳur'ān. Thereupon he remarked: I can write compositions like it. It is reported that al-Ḥallāj one day passed al-Junaid[5] and said to him: I am the Truth. Al-Junaid answered: You exist by the Truth. What a gibbet you will smear with your blood[6]. What al-Junaid remarked about him came true, for he was afterwards impaled.
248 Another group of Ṣūfis have accepted him. Among them are included Abu-l-'Abbās ibn 'Aṭā'[7] in Baghdād, Abu 'Abdallah ibn Khafīf[8] in Fars, Abu-l-Ḳāsim al Naṣrabādi[9] in Nīshāpūr, and Fāris al-Dīnawari[10] in his province. Those who ascribe heresy

---

[1] Massignon, l. c. 164, correctly explains that this abstention is in accordance with the Murjite tradition. His Fatwa read: It is a man whose inspiration I cannot discern; therefore, I shall say nothing about him.

[2] Died 296, IKhall, II, 662-5 and Massignon, l. c. 167-82. He was a Zāhirite (see on his father Goldziher's *Zahiriten*, p. 27-40). He was often consulted together with ibn Suraij on legal matters.

[3] Died, 297, Massignon l. c., 32-3; on his clash with al-Ḥallāj l. c., 56-9.

[4] Al-Ḥallāj's father-in-law and secretary to al-Junaid (see following note); on his rupture with his son-in-law, ib. 62.

[5] Called by Massignon Hallāj's "spiritual director", 59 and elsewhere (for a definition of the term see *Kashf*, 55-7). He is a very prominent Ṣūfi. See *Kashf*, 126-30 and 188-99 and Massignon l. c., 33-6. The clash between the two is related, *ib*, 59-62.

[6] A curious anecdote is told *ib*, 52, that during their first meeting al-Junaid already predicted al-Ḥallāj's end employing the same expression. On al-Junaid's capacity for presaging see *Kashf*, ib.

[7] Died, 309. He was a devoted orthodox who died from stripes he received for defending al-Hallāj, Massignon, l. c, 260-61.

[8] Died 371. He was a Zāhirite mystic, *ib*, 563-4. For a fuller description of him and his views see *Kashf* 247-51.

[9] *Ib*. 159-60. He is the same as Ibrahīm Naṣrabādi cited in Massignon, l. c. 407. He died 372.

[10] Died 342. He was an active adherent of al-Hallāj after the latter's death *ib*, 334 and 337, n. 7.

and the beliefs of the Ḥulūliyya to him relate that he said[1]: He who mends his state by obedience, and restrains himself from[2] pleasures and lust, ascends to the sphere of the favorites of God. He shall then not cease to keep pure and he will mount on the steps of the purified until he will be freed from fleshly bonds. When there will not remain in him a particle of his material qualities, the spirit of God which was embodied in 'Isa ibn Mariam will become incarnate in him. In that state he will no sooner desire anything but it will be fulfilled as he desired it, and all his acts will be divine. They are of the opinion that al-Ḥallāj claimed to have attained this rank.. They relate[3] that some letters of his to his followers were seized, and in them the salutation read: "From Him who is Lord of Lords, who takes on any form, to His worshipper So-and-so". They also obtained possession of some letters which his followers sent to him and in them the superscription is: O Essence of pleasure and Object of the most Extreme Delights[4]. We testify that you are the One assuming some likeness at all times and in our time the likeness of al-Ḥusain ibn Manṣūr. We seek your protection and hope for your grace[5], O knower of secrets". They tell that in Baghdād he gained influence over a group of the Khalīf's retinue and harem[6], so that the Khalīf Ja'far al-Muktadir Billāhi[7], fearing the shame of his sedition, imprisoned him and consulted doctors of the Law for their opinion on the inviolability of his person. He lent a ready ear to the Fatwa of Abu Bekr ibn Dāud authorizing his execution. He ordered

[1] The following alleged statement by al-Hallāj agrees very closely with the passage in IḤauḳ, 209-10.

[2] Reading عن with Isf.; MS. and Ed. على.

[3] Reading وذكروا with MS; Ed. وذكر.

[4] Reading With Isf. 61 a, يا ذات الذات ومنتهى غاية اللذات; Ed. and MS. ومنتهى غاية الشهوات

[5] In this accusation against al-Ḥallāj, called in Arabic دعوة الربوبية, Massignon sees Shī'ite and not Sunnite influence. He even goes so far as to claim that Baghdādi's list of the Ghulāt sects is nothing but a copy of Imāmite heresiography, l. c, 138 ff.

[6] The rather clumsy expression of our author is elucidated by the phrase in Isf. 61b; جماعة من خواص المقتدر. But see the same expression in IḤauḳ, 210. — Even the Khalīf's mother was impressed with him. See al-Tanūkhi, *Nishwār al-Muḥāḍara*, ed. Margoliouth, 83.

[7] Khalīf from 295 to 320 A. H. See a vivid portrayal of him and his relation to the 'Abbāsid rule, Massignon, l. c. 199-206.

Ḥāmid ibn al-ʿAbbās[1] to flay him a thousand strokes[2], and to amputate his arms
249 and legs, and to impale[3] him after that near the bridge[4] of Baghdād. This order was executed on Tuesday at three o'clock, six days before the end of Dhū-l-Ḳaʿda in the year three hundred and nine. He was lowered from the scaffold to which he had been pinned and was committed to the flames. His ashes were thrown into the Tigris. Some of his devotees believe that he is alive and was not killed, but instead one on whom he stamped his likeness was executed. Those Ṣūfis who cherish his memory hold that the states of divine grace were bestowed upon him, but he made them public. He was punished, in that mastery over him was granted to those who disavow miracles in order that his state might continue to be concealed. These believe that the essence of Ṣūfiism is a state in which the exoteric is merely a disguise and the esoteric is sanctification. They cite in evidence of the sanctification of al-Ḥallāj's inner life what has been told regarding him, that while his arms and legs were being cut, he pronounced: It is the aim of the ecstatic to recognize the divine essence in its purity[5]. When he was asked one day about his creed[6], he began to say: It consists of three letters which have no diacritical points and two which have, and his remark was cut short. But he meant Unity (Tawḥīd)[7].

Concerning the ʿAzāḳira[8]. — They are a faction in Baghdād, adherents of a

---

[1] Abu Muḥammad Ḥāmid ibn al-ʿAbbās (223-311) was the vizier of al-Muḳtadir. For his character see *ib*, 211-13 and for his machinations in bringing about al-Hallāj's end, 274-90, esp. 287 f.

[2] With MS. سوط ; Ed. صوت.

[3] Massignon points out, *ib*, 293, n. 4. that the story of his crucifixion is of Ṣūfic origin.

[4] Over the Tigris, *ib*, 293, n. 5.

[5] Ed. MS. and Isf. 61a use الواحد in both clauses, so that it reads حسب الواحد, افراد الواحد. I follow Massignon, l. c., 324-28 and Nicholson, *Kashf*, 311 in reading الواجد for the first. The translation is also Massignon's; see *ib.*, and for his criticism of Nicholson's translation, 327.

[6] Reading with Isf. *ib.*, دينه; our reading ذنبه, if correct, may perhaps be a bit of dry humor.

[7] See Massignon, *ib.*, 127 for an explanation of the letters along the lines of Ḳabbalistic interpretation. He also completes the statement.

[8] It is hard to determine whether MS. reads عزاقرة, or عذاقرة with Ed. But several lines below the copyist definitely changed a doubtful reading into *Z.* and towards the end the *Z* is unquestionable.

man who made his appearance there in the time of al-Rāḍi[1] ibn al-Muḳtadir, in the year three hundred and twenty two. He was known as ibn Abu-l-'Azāḳir, but his real name was Muḥammad ibn 'Ali al-Shalmaghāni[2]. He pretended that God's spirit was embodied in him and he named himself the Holy Ghost. He left a book to his followers which he called "On the Sixth Sense". He advocated explicitly the abrogation of the Law, and permitted sodomy[3], maintaining that it was the communication of light from the superior one to the inferior. His followers allowed him to enjoy their wives, because of a craving for a communication of his light to them. Al-Rāḍi Billahi seized him[4] as well as a group of his followers, among them al-Ḥusain ibn al-Ḳāsim ibn 'Ubaidallah ibn Sulaimān ibn Wahb[5] and Abu 'Imrān Ibrahīm ibn Muḥammad ibn Aḥmad ibn al-Munajjim[6]. He discovered their 250
letters in which they addressed him as Lord and Master, and described him by his attributes of power over what he wished[7]. They admitted writing them. They confessed in the presence of the jurists, among whom were Abu-l-'Abbās Aḥmad

---

[1] Khalīf, 322-329.

[2] This is the correct reading for the name which was given him after his town Shalmaghān, near Wāsit (IA, VIII, 215). Our text reads السلقانى. On the variants see *Shiites* II, 115.

[3] IA, viii, 219-20.

[4] He was actually seized by ibn Muklah, the vizier of al-Rāḍi, IA, VIII, 217 and Yaḳūt, *Irshād,* III, *s. v.* Shalmaghān. On ibn Muklah, who was vizier under Muḳtadir, Ḳāhir and al-Rāḍi see Miskawaih, *Eclipse of the 'Abbāsid Khalifate* (Tr. D. S. Margoliouth,) I, 209-28, 272-300, 328-379.

[5] Vizier under Muḳtadir, 319-30. His Kunya is Abu 'Ali (*Nujum* II, 286). IA, *ib.* calls his grandfather 'Abdallah.

[6] Yaḳūt, l. c., 206 calls him ابن هلال ابى النجم; Isf., 61 b, المسبح; He was a writer of note and the composer of a number of works. Yaḳūt's discussion of ibn Abu-l-'Azākir is given in connection with his biography of this author.

[7] Two very interesting and curious tenets in the philosophy of ibn Abu-l-'Azāḳir are: first, that everyone in whom God is incarnate has a Satan who is his converse, so that his excellency may be more definitely demonstrated (*Shiites,* II, 116), and secondly, that everyone is a lord over the one below him in rank. A fine characterization of his views is given, IA, VIII, 218-20 and Yaḳūt, ib An extract of the latter is translated in Miskawaih, l. c. part I. of translation at the beginning of the book (unpaginated).

ibn 'Omar ibn Suraij[1] and Abu-l-Faraḥ al-Māliki and a number of Imāms. The one called al-Ḥusain ibn al-Ḳāsim ibn 'Ubaidallah was ordered to disavow ibn Abu-l-Azāḳir and[2] to slap him[3]. He did so and repented publicly. Ibn Suraij ruled in accordance with the code of al-Shāfi'i, that the acceptance of his repentance was admissible[4]. But the Mālikite[5] issued a decision rejecting the repentance of the Zendik since he was seized against his will. Al-Rāḍi had him imprisoned until his case would be investigated[6]. He ordered the execution of ibn Abu-l-'Azāḳir and his companion ibn Abu 'Aun. Ibn Abu-l-'Azāḳir pleaded with him: Give me a three day respite, so that my guiltlessness may be demonstrated from heaven, or vengeance visited on my enemies. But jurists directed al-Rāḍi to hasten their execution. Thereupon he crucified them, burnt them, and threw their ashes into the Tigris.

---

[1] He is the same jurist who withheld from pronouncing an opinion in the case of al-Ḥallāj. See above, 81.

[2] With MS. وبأن; Ed. بان .

[3] IA, VIII, 217-18 tells that this was required of Aḥmad ibn Muḥammad ibn 'Abdūs and of ibn Abu 'Aun. Ibn 'Abdūs did it, but Ibn Abu 'Aun's hand trembled, so he kissed Shalmaghāni's head and called him "my lord" and "my bestower". This will explain why he was killed together with his master.

[4] *Umm*, I. 227.

[5] Mālik is stricter with the Zendik than with the other apostates because the former apostasize secretly so that they cannot be trusted even when they repent unless the confession is voluntary. See Goldziher, *Muh. Stud.* II, 215-16.

[6] Both Yaḳūt and IA, *ib.* report that an offer similar to the one made to the vizier was also extended to ibn Abu 'Aun, but that he refused (see note 2). They further relate that ibn Abu 'Azāḳir tried to disavow any connections with the letters in which he was called by divine names, but his testimony was proved false. - Friedländer, *Shiites,* I, 70, cites an edition of IH, which tells of the vizier's execution, but it is not substantiated. See l. *c.* II, 117.

THE ADVOCATES OF LICENSE AMONG THE KHURRAMIYYA[1] AND THE REASON FOR THEIR EXCLUSION FROM THE CATEGORY OF ISLAMIC SECTS.

These consist of two divisions. One of them was active before the Islamic Era. This was the Mazdakiyya[2] who permitted forbidden practices, holding that men are partners in property and women. The faction endured until Anūshirvān killed them during his reign.[3] The second division[4] consists of the Khurramdīniyya[5]

---

[1] The significance of this term is not unanimously accepted. Van Vloten, in his work *La domination arabe, le Chiitisme,* mentions that the Arabic scholars derive it from Persian خرام which signifies pleasure. L. H. Gray connects the name with Mazdak's wife *Khurrama,* who fled to Rai after her husband's execution and carried on her teachings under the name *Khurram-dīn* (*ERE,* VIII, s. v. Mazandaran; Justi, *Iran. Namb. s. v.* Khurrama, see below). The most probable explanation is that it is derived from the city name Khurrām, for Yaḳūt, II, 427, informs us that Bābāk probably hails from there, although he himself also cites the interpretation from the Persian.

[2] Either founded or propagated (Noeldeke, *Perser u. Araber,* 456—7) by Mazdak. It is, of course, not surprising that our author stresses only what are to him the abominations of Mazdak's doctrine. But it was deeply religious and had some noble motives. See Noeldeke *l. c.,* 458—61; Mirkhond, tr. by de Sacy, *Antiquités de la Perse,* 354; Shahr., 192—4.

[3] Chosrau, a great Persian emperor who reigned 531—79 was called Anūshirvān (the blessed one) as a result, so the Arabic sources state, of his vigorous campaign in which he destroyed the Mazdakite heresy. Whether he did it as prince or as king is discussed by Noeldeke, *l. c.,* 463—67. Our author, like the other Arabic historians, is of the opinion that he accomplished it after ascending the throne.

[4] The association between these two divisions rests merely on the common characteristics of communism of property and wives. See Noeldeke, *l. c.,* 461, against Blochet, ch. 5.

[5] This name is used as an appellation for the sect interchangeably with Khurramiyya. Cf. for example, Muḳaddasi, 398, in which he identifies a mountain called Khurramdīniyya as the home of the Khurramiyya, adding, curiously enough, that they are Murjites. See also Blochet, 44—6 and *Uṣūl,* 323; *Siasset Nameh,* 298 and Ash'ari 438.

who appeared since the institution of Islam. It split into two sects, the Bābākiyya and Māzyāriyya, both of which are known as the Muḥammira[1].

The Bābākiyya are followers of Bābāk[2] al-Khurrami[3] who appeared in Jabal al-Badain[4] in the district of Adherbaijān, and gained many followers. They considered all the prohibitions permissible and slew many Muslims. The 'Abbāsid Khalīfs[5] equipped many armies against them under Alfishīn[6] the Chamberlain, Muḥammad ibn Yūsuf al-Thughri[7], Abu Dulaf al-'Ijli[8] and their associates[9]. The armies continued to face him for a period of twenty years[10], until Bābāḳ and his brother Isḥāḳ ibn

---

[1] Lit. those apparelled in red dress. See Ṭab., Index, *s. v.*, and Wellhausen, *Arabisches Reich* (Eng. trans.), 533. *Fihrist*, 324, calls the Muḥammira the earlier of the two Ḫurramiya (sic!). Iji explains the name as coming from the red dress which they wore during the time of Bābāk, 349.

[2] The following biographical note is taken from Flügel's article in *ZDMG*, XXIII (1869), 537—42. His father, whose name was 'Abdallah, lived in Badain and was an oil dealer. He also travelled to Adherbaijān. Bābāk was the child of an illegitimate union. A story is told that when he was ten years old his mother noticed a blood spot on his body and realized that he was destined to do great things. He was found by Jāwidān b. Sahrūk, a tribal leader in the mountains of al-Badain who enlisted him as one of his followers. When Jāwidān died as a result of a battle with his opponent Abu 'Imrān, Bābāk was induced by Jāwidān's wife to claim that the latter's spirit became incarnate in him. Bābāk did so and became his successor.

[3] With MS.; Ed. الخزى.

[4] With MS. Ed. البدين. This may be his native city. See *Murūj*, VII, 123.

[5] They were al-Ma'mūn and al-Mu'taṣim. There was an attempt made to crush the rebels in 204 (Tab. III, 1038). In 205 'Īsa ibn Muḥammad ibn 'Ali was sent against him but was defeated the following year (*ib.*).

[6] So vocalized in MS. See *Muruj*, VII, 132. It is the famous general al-Afshīn whose real name was Ḥaidar ibn Ḳāus. IA, VI, 182.

[7] Abu Sa'īd Muḥammad b. Yūsuf had been sent previously against Bābāk and even dealt him a defeat (called the first one). *Ib.*

[8] De Goeje suggests that this general is perhaps the same as that mentioned Ṭab. III, 798, who was urged by Muḥammad b. 'Īsa to join him in the revolt against Ma'mūn.

[9] They are Muḥammad ibn al-Ba'īth and Bugha al-Ḳatīn. IA, *ib.* and *Nujūm*, I, 656.

[10] It need not be gathered that fighting was carried on during all this time. Al-Afshīn was first entrusted with the task in 220 (IA, *ib.*) but, as stated above, Bābāk's revolt commenced as early as 204.

Ibrahīm[1] were seized and crucified in Surra-man-raa[2] in the reign of al-Mu'taṣim. Alfishīn, the Chamberlain, was accused of lending assistance to Bābāk during the war and was, therefore, executed[3].

The Māzyāriya are the followers of Māzyār[4] who proclaimed the rite of the 252
Muhammira [among the Bābākiyya in one of the mountains of Ṭabaristān. After them the Ḳanṭarat al-Muḥammira][5] in Jurjān is named. In their mountain retreat the Bābākiyya[6] celebrate a festival-night when they gather over wine and song, and their men and women carry on promiscuously. When their torches and brands go

---

[1] This is the name, not of his brother, who was called 'Abdallah (*Murūj*, VII, 131), but of the governor of Baghdād who executed him. Ṭab. (Zotenberg) IV, 523 tells that he fought the Khurramiyya and defeated them previously and also participated in later attacks. It may be of course that a line fell out from our MS. but what argues against it is that Isf. B., 62a has مع اخيه اسحق بن ارهيم and that the same error reappears Ed. 268. It is surprising to find that *Mukhtaṣar*, 173 not only repeats this mistake but even traces the *Isḥākiyya* to him. For Isḥāḳ ibn Ibrahīm see *Shiites* II, 32 where the genealogy of the Muṣ'ab family is outlined. It is curious that Maḳrīzī (Fagnan) 48, speaks of this Isḥāḳ ibn Ibrahīm as participating in a rebellion with 'Abdallah ibn Maimūn al-Ḳaddāḥ in the days of al-Ma'mūn. See Fagnan's note *ad loc.*

[2] Originally Samarra but called by this name when Mu'taṣim rebuilt it. (Lit. everyone who sees it rejoices). Muir, *Califate*, 513, n. 2. See also Maṣ'ūdi, *Tanbīh*, 457.

[3] History relates that al-Afshīn was executed after the defeat of Māzyār whom he incited to rebel against 'Abdallah ibn Ṭāhir, governor of Khurāsān, whose position he coveted. Al-Afshīn had already been provoked against the governor because the latter had revealed some dishonest deals by Al-Afshīn with moneys which he received. See IA, VI, 209 ff. and Browne, *Lit. Hist. of Persia, I,* 330ff. Our author, however, consistently links al-Afshīn's act of treason with the Bābākiyya so as to give it a religious motive. See Ed. 268 (below). He was executed 266 A.H. IA, vi, 212.

[4] His real name was Muḥammad ibn Kāren. *Muruj*, VII, 137 and 414 n. See also IA, VI, 202. His sedition occurred in 225.

[5] The passage in brackets is omitted in Ed. The Arabic reads as follows: دين المحمرة البابكية في بعض جبال طبرستان واليهم تنسب قنطرة المحمرة.

[6] *Mukhtasar*, 163, ascribes this celebration to the Māzyāriyya, which is more reasonable, in view of their adoration of Sharwīn, (see below). Perhaps this is also the intention of our author who regards the Bābākiyya as the mother sect of the Māzyāriyya.

out[1] the men deflower the women, contending that it is a necessary practice[2]. The Bābākiyya[3] trace the origin of their cult to a king of theirs of pre-Islamic times by the name of Sharwīn[4]. They believe that his father was Ethiopian and his mother a Persian Princess. They maintain that Sharwīn was superior to Muḥammad and to the other prophets. They have built mosques for the Muslims in their mountain[5] and in them the Muslims are called to prayer. They teach their children the Ḳur'ān, but they do not pray privately nor do they fast in the month of Ramaḍan, nor do they concede the duty of making holy war on the infidels.

The sedition of Māzyār took on large proportions in his district[6] until he, too, was captured in the days of al-Mu'taṣim[7], and he was crucified in Surra-man-raa next[8] to Bābāk al-Khurrami[9]. At present the followers of Māzyār in their mountain are composed of the peasantry which borders on the mountain from Sawād al-Jurjān. They feign Islam but secretly practise the opposite. But it is God whose help is to be sought against people of error and disobedience.

---

[1] Reading طفئت with MS.; Ed. اطفئت. Since this sect is no doubt derived from the Zoroastrians it is hardly likely that they would intentionally extinguish a light as Ed. implies. Isf. reads يطفؤون السرج, 62 a. An identical charge, it is alleged by Justin Martyr, was made against the early Christians. *Dialogue with Trypho*, in *Ante-Nicene Fathers* (Amer. Ed.), I, 199.

[2] Arabic على تقدير من عزيز.

[3] As pointed out in a preceding note it would be more correct to read Māzyāriyya here.

[4] Justi. *l. c.*, 290 identifies him with Sharwīn b. Shurkhat, Ispehbed of Ṭabaristān, 772-97, who defeated the Arabs in 783 with the assistance of Vendad Hormuzd, IA, VI, 131. (He is named there as Māzyār's grandfather). But see Albiruni, 48.

[5] This notice is very curious. Any friendly relations between them and the Muslims should be excluded a priori. We have in addition even better testimony of their enmity in a statement by abu-l-Faraj who relates that Bābāk's adherents, whenever they caught a man, woman or child who was a Muslim, would cripple and kill him. (cited *ZDMG*, XXIII, 541 n. 2). *Fihrist* adds والمسلمون غريبهم ومواليهم, 344.

[6] Ṭabaristān in Khurāsān, IA, VI, 202. His trouble started as early as 201. Ṭab. III, 1015.

[7] He was caught by 'Abdallah ibn Ṭāhir, governor of Khurāsān against whom he had waged war in 224 A. H.

[8] *Muruj*, VII, 138-9; Isf., *ib.*

[9] With MS.; Ed. الخزى.

CHAPTER TWELVE. 253

THE FOLLOWERS OF THE DOCTRINE OF METEMPSYCHOSIS AMONG THE PEOPLE OF FANCY AND THE REASON FOR THEIR EXCLUSION FROM ISLAM.

Those who believe in metempsychosis consist of several divisions. One includes the philosophers, and another the Sumaniyya[1]. These two divisions existed before the rise of Islam. The two other divisions made their appearance since the institution of Islam: one from the Ḳadariyya and the other from the Ghulāt Rawāfiḍ.

The believers in transmigration among the Sumaniyya assert the pre-existence of the world and also reject deductive and inductive speculation[2]. They hold that nothing can be known save through the five senses. Most of them dispute the existence of the world to come and the resurrection after death. One faction among them believes in transmigration in diverse forms. They regard it as possible for the soul of a man to be transferred into a dog and the spirit of a dog into a man. Plutarch tells of a doctrine similar to this held by some philosophers. They maintain that whenever anyone commits a sin while in one body, punishment for it will place him in another body. They entertain a similar doctrine regarding reward. One of the most astonishing facts is that the Sumaniyya profess metempsychosis, which cannot be perceived with the senses, despite their thesis that nothing 254
can be known except through the five senses.

The Mānawiyya also adhered to the doctrine of metempsychosis[3], for

[1] Horten, *Systeme*, 93-6, classifies them as a Hindu group. See their views there. He identifies the name with Shraman (a Buddhist Monk). *Arch. f. Gesch. d. Philos.*, XXIV, (1910) 144, n. 1. The article pp. 141-66 gives a detailed study of their views.

[2] See Horten's article referred to above. Uṣūl, 320 describes them as sceptics.

[3] A. V. W. Jackson's article on the doctrine of metempsychosis in Manichaeism, *JAOS*, XLV (1925), 246-68 proves conclusively that the doubts expressed by some authorities hitherto, as for example, Bevan in his article *ERE*, VIII, 399 and Kessler in the *PRE*, XII, 215 are not valid, particularly since there is no statement which must be necessarily interpreted as op-

Māni says in one of his works that the souls which leave their bodies are of two classes: the souls of the righteous, and the souls of those involved in error. When the souls of the righteous leave their bodies they travel with the Pillar of Dawn[1] to the light which is above the heavenly sphere and remain in that world in eternal bliss. The souls of the sinful people, when they leave their bodies and wish to reach the Supreme Light, are turned back the other way to the lower world and are transferred into the bodies of animals until they are purged of the spots caused by unrighteousness[2]. Then they attain the Supreme Light.

The historians relate that Socrates and Plato and their disciples in philosophy professed meṭempsychosis[3] along the lines which we have explained in the Book on Religions and Dogmas[4]. Some Jews profess transmigration. They claim to have found in the book of Daniel that God transferred Bukhtanaṣar into seven animal forms and beasts of prey, and thus punished him, until finally He transformed him into a believer in one God[5].

As for the adherents of the Doctrine of Metempsychosis since the era of Islam, the Bayāniyya, the Janāḥiyya, the Khaṭṭābiyya, the Rawandiyya[6] among the Rawāfiḍ who profess incarnation, all accept the doctrine of the transfusion of God's

---

posed to the doctrine. Prof. Jackson has certainly combed all the extant literature and recently discovered Chinese, Turkish and Pehlevi fragments. See *l. c.* 249, 261-8.

[1] Perhaps we should read عمود السبح (pillar of praise) with *Fihrist*, 335; Cf. Jackson, *l. c.*, 246 and 251, note 1.

[2] Same references as above.

[3] Cf. *Murūj*, IV, 65-7.

[4] Arabic Kitāb al-Milal wal-Niḥal. The statement in Seelye, 9, that the book is preserved in a Constantinople library, which she took from Goldziher, ZDMG, LXV (1911) 350, has been denied by Goldziher himself and the error blamed on a careless reading of the title of the MS. by the cataloguer in the library. L. c., LXVI (1912), 165-6.

[5] Daniel, III. That this information was also known to the Arabs is apparent from the fact that Ṭab. (Zotenberg), I, 571-2, relates that as a punishment for throwing Daniel into the Lion's den he was changed into a beast and lived among animals for seven years.

[6] It is surprising that Baghdādi always mentions this sect casually and indirectly, although it is of such great importance. Ash'ari, 22-3, describes it as a mother sect from which both the Ruzāmiyya and Abu Muslimiyya branched out. For a full discussion of this sect see Van Vloten, *La :omination Arabe, le Chiitisme,* and *Shiites,* II, 121-4.

spirit in the Imāms. The first to teach this error were the Sabbābiyya among the Rawāfiḍ, claiming that 'Ali became a God ever since God's spirit was incarnate in him. The Bayāniyya hold that the spirit of God was transmitted through the 255
Imāms[1] until it came to Bayān ibn Sam'ān. The Janāḥiyya make a similar claim regarding 'Abdallah ibn Mu'āwiya ibn 'Abdallah ibn Ja'far. The assertion of the Khaṭṭābiyya regarding Abu-l-Khaṭṭāb is similar to theirs and so also the claim of a group of people among the Rawandiyya concerning Abu Muslim, the supporter of the 'Abbāsid Caliphate. These profess the transmigration of the divine spirit but not of human souls. Far be He from any such extravagance.

Among the Ḳadariyya a number of people accept the doctrine of transmigration. One of them is Aḥmad ibn Ḥā'iṭ who was a Mu'tazilite, a disciple of al-Naẓẓām[2]. He adopted the latter's innovation of the Leap[3], his denial of indivisible particles[4], and the denial of God's power to augment the pleasures of the inhabitants of Paradise or the tortures of the people in Hell. But he exceeded al-Naẓẓām by his blunder about transmigration. Another among them was Aḥmad ibn Ayyūb ibn Yanūsh[5]. He was a disciple of Aḥmad ibn Ḥā'iṭ in the subject of metempsychosis but the two of them differed later as to its manner. There was also Muḥammad ibn Aḥmad al-Ḳaḥṭabi[6]. [He was a contemporary of al-Jubba'i and adhered to Mu'tazilism, but added to it his innovation of metempsychosis, and wrote a treatise in proof of it. Another was Abu Muslim al-Ḥarrāni[7] who cites al-Ḳaḥṭabi[8]] and glories in the fact

[1] Ed. reads "through the Prophets and the Imāms". My reading follows MS.

[2] For al-Naẓẓām's views see Ed. 113-32 (Seelye 135-157). The doctrine of metempsychosis is really a corollary to al-Naẓẓām's thesis of *Kumūn* (hiding) which our author does not recall here. Cf. Horten's article in *ZDMG*, LXIII (1909), 780.

[3] Reading الطفرة with MS.; Ed. الفطرة. See Ed. 124—5.

[4] Ed. and MS. read «divisible particles», but this is an obvious mistake.

[5] See on the variants of his name *Shiites*, II, 10 ff.

[6] Fd. القحطى; Isf., 63 a, calls him Aḥmad ibn Muḥammad, *Fihrist*, 342 adds no further information about him. But see text towards end of chapter. See MS. passage in the next note.

[7] According to ibn Ḥazm as quoted by Schreiner, *Der Kalam in der jüd. Phil.*, 62—63. (see also *Shiites*, ii, 64) his name Is Abu Muslim al-Khurāsāni; but this reading is unacceptable in view of the fact that our author calls him Ḥarrāni both here and below. Further, Abu Muslim al-Khurāsāni is probably the famous general of the early 'Abbāsids and he was doubtless a Shī'ite and not a Ḳadarite.

[8] The passage in brackets is omitted in Ed. In Arabic it is as follows: وكان في زمان

that he shared their view on both problems of Mu‘tazilism and Tanāsukh (metempsychosis). Finally there was ‘Abd-al-Karīm ibn Abu-l-‘Awjā’[1], an uncle of Ma‘an ibn Zā’ida[2] He reconciled four kinds of heresies. In the first place he secretly preferred the tenets of the Manicheans among the Dualists[3]. Secondly, he believed in Tanāsukh; thirdly, he favored the Rawāfiḍ on the question of the Imāms; and, fourthly, he held Ḳadarite views on the problems of justice and injustice[4]. He had invented
256 numerous traditions bearing Sanads with which he deceived those who had no knowledge of the method of deciding between the false and true[5]. The traditions which he left are all blunders in anthropomorphism and divesting. In some of them he aims to contradict the precepts of the Law. It is he who led the Rawāfiḍ to abandon the inauguration of the fast of Ramaḍān with the coming of the new moon by means of a calculation which he provided for them. He ascribed this calculation to Ja‘far al-Ṣādiḳ. The story of this heretic was related to Abu Ja‘far Muḥammad ibn Sulaimān, al-Manṣur's governor at al-Kūfa[6], and he ordered him

---

الجباي وكان على مذهب الاعتزال وزاد على الاعتزال بدعته في التناسخ وله كتاب في اثبات التناسخ ومنهم ابو مسلم الحراني ذكر القحطبى.

[1] See on him below.

[2] A well known general and governor who served under the 'Umayyads and went into hiding under the ‘Abbāsids. But when he saved the Khalīf al-Manṣūr from the attacks of the Rawandiyya he was restored to their graces. He served respectively in Yemen and Khurāsān where he slew many Khārijites until he was finally assassinated by them deceitfully. *EI*, III, 225

[3] *Fihrist*, 338; Albirūni, 80.

[4] Reading والتجوير with MS.; Ed. والتحوير.

[5] *Mīzān al-I‘tidāl*, II, 144 calls him a Zendīḳ and a deceiver. He erroneously locates him at Baṣra.

[6] There is confusion about the name of this governor. Ṭab., IA, *Nujum*, do not mention the Kunya Abu Ja‘far. Our author and Albiruni who seem to have used the same source call him Abu Ja‘far. (The person mentioned by this name IKhall, V, 85 lived much later). The confusion comes no doubt from the fact that the Khalīf al-Manṣur's name was Abu Ja‘far. Perhaps the translation should read: Muḥammad ibn Abu Sulaimān brought the report to Abu Ja‘far, but the construction does not allow it. Isf. has Abu Ja‘far ibn Sulaimān al-Hāshimi who was Muḥammad's brother. (Ṭab. III, 304, sqq.; *Nujum*, I, 471). Copying from al-Baghdādi, Isf. *ib.* carried the confusion still further in an attempt to straighten it out his own way.

to be executed[1]. But 'Abd-al-Karīm said: Even if[2] you kill me I have already composed four thousand Ḥadīths in which I allow the forbidden and prohibit the allowed. I made the Rawāfiḍ break their fast during one of their fast days and made them observe a fast on one of the non-fasting days[3].

The following is a detailed exposition of the views of these people on metempsychosis[4]. Aḥmad ibn Ḥā'iṭ maintained that God originally made His creatures pure of heart[5], secure from evil, intelligent and mature, placing them in an abode other than the world in which they dwell at the present time. He endowed them with perfect reason and created within them a consciousness and knowledge of Him, and bestowed His grace upon them in abundance. He held that the person who was bidden and forbidden, the object of God's grace, is the soul which resides in the body; the bodies are frames for the souls. He was of the opinion that it is the soul which is endowed with life, power, knowledge and that all living beings are of one genus. He also held that all species of

---

[1] The circumstances in connection with this statement are reported more fully in both Tab. III, 375-7 and IA, VI, 3. Both of these authorities relate that the Khalīf wrote the governor to wait for his decision in regard to the execution, but that the governor executed him before receiving the Khalīf's approval. In fact he lost the governorship as a result of this step. Al-Manṣūr's special care came from the fact that Abu-l-'Awjā' had influential friends at the court, *ib.*, Albiruni, *ib.*

[2] Reading لئن with MS.; Ed. لن.

[3] Ṭab., *ib.*, does not cite this story. IA, who tells it, does not refer it to the Rāfiḍite, nor does the Mīzān, *l. c.* which is much briefer, making no reference to the fact at all. See, however, Albiruni, 76–80.

[4] The doctrine about to be described in detail is ascribed by Naubakhti, with as much detail as here, to the Khurramiyya, 32–34. In view of the close relationship between the Khurramiyya and the Bāṭiniyya, it must be said that the former seem to have been logically the originators, or at least expounders of this theory. According to IH, I, 91 the believers in Transmigration adduced as proof the verse "and into whatever form He pleased He constituted you", (Sura 82, v. 8) and "He made mates for you from among yourselves and mates for the cattle too, multiplying you". (Sura 42, v. 9). Ibn Ḥazm's explanation of these verses which is the accepted orthodox one will be found on f. 91, bottom. On the whole he dismisses the Muslim believers in this doctrine briefly by saying that Ijmā' declares such people infidels. His argument is devoted in particular to the pagans.

[5] Reading اصحاء with MS.; Ed. اصحابه.

animal life are charged with the duty of observance[1] and upon all of them ordinances and prohibitions have been imposed in accordance with their diverse forms and methods of expression. He asserted that when God bade them, in the abode in which He had originally set them, to feel grateful to Him for
257 the grace which He had bestowed upon them, some heeded Him in all that He had commanded them, while others disobeyed Him in all that He had commanded them. [Still others complied with Him in part of what He had ordained for them and violated the rest[2]]. Whosoever obeyed Him in all that He had enjoined upon him was left undisturbed in the pleasurable abode in which He had placed Him from the first[3]. Whoever disobeyed in everything that He had ordained was banished from the abode of pleasure to the abode of eternal torture, that is, Hell. Whoever fulfilled part of what He had commanded and violated the rest was brought forth to the earthly world and equipped with one of these bodies in the various forms of men, birds, animals, beasts, insects, and so on, which are solid moulds, and are afflicted with suffering and difficulties, hardships and fears[4], passions and pains, in proportion to their sins and disobedience and the former abode in which He had created them. Now, he whose obedience in that abode outbalanced his disobedience, exists in a comelier form in this world, but he whose obedience in that abode was less than his disobedience exists in a homelier mould in this world. He further believed that the living being, which consists essentially of the soul[5], will continue to reappear in various moulds and forms as long as his obedience is adulterated with iniquity. The grades of his mould, whether in the human or in the animal world, will be determined by the relative proportion of his merits and demerits. Moreover,

[1] This doctrine is disputed at length by IH, I 78—87 (part of it tr. in Asin, II, 190—6). According to him, Ibn Ḥā'iṭ proved his thesis by inference from two Ḳur'ānic verses in one of which (Sura 6, v. 38) He calls all beings nations and the other in which He states that He sent messengers to all nations (Sura 35, v. 22).

[2] This passage is missing in Ed. The Arabic reads as follows: واطاعه بعضهم في بعض ما امرهم وعصاه في بعض ما امرهم به.

[2] IH, I, 91, top. (Asin, II, 199).

[4] Reading رخاء with *Mukhtasar*, 165; Ed. and MS. رجاء.

[5] Arabic: الحيوان الذى من الروح. My translation is confirmed by Isf's reading: الحيوان في الحقيقة هو الروح

a messenger from God to every kind of living being will never cease to appear, and God's charge to the living being will always continue[1] until his works become pure obedience. Then he will be restored back to the abode of eternal bliss which is the abode in which he was created. On the other hand his works may become extreme disobedience[2]; then he is to be condemned to Hell and its eternal tortures. These are the teachings of Ibn Ḥā'iṭ on Tanāsukh. 258

Aḥmad ibn Ayyūb ibn Yanūsh[3] teaches that God produced the complete creation with one fiat. Some of his adherents relate in his name that God first created the logical[4] particles, everyone of which is indivisible. He held that those particles possessed intelligence and life, and that God made them uniform in all respects, so that none of them could claim superiority over the others; nor was any of them guilty of evil deeds on account of which it would be reduced to a position inferior to that of the others.

After He had amply bestowed His grace upon them, He offered them the choice between being tested by active obedience so that they might become deserving of reward for them, since the rank of merit is nobler than the rank of grace[5], and between leaving them[6] in this abode as an act of grace to them. Some of them preferred the test[7], while others declined. Those who refused it were left in their first abode as heretofore. But those who preferred to be tested were tried in this world. When He tried those who preferred the trial, some disobeyed Him while others submitted. He reduced those who disobeyed Him to a station which is inferior to the grade in which He had created them. But those who obeyed He raised to a rank higher than the grade in which He had created them. Then He made them pass successively through persons and moulds until

[1] Maḳrīzi, 347, cites verses in support of this contention. Schreiner, *l. c.*, 63. states that Aḥmad ibn Ḥā'iṭ utilized certain verses. See also Goldziher, *Richtungen d. Islamischen Kor'anauslegung*, 309.

[2] Reading يتمحض with MS.; Ed. يمحض.

[3] Ed. and MS. بانوش: IH. VI, 198 states that he claimed a gift of prophecy saying that he was meant by the verse ومبشرا برسول يأتى من بعدى اسمه احمد (Sura 61, v. 6.)

[4] Reading المعدودة with MS; Ed. المقدرة.

[5] Reading تفضل with MS.; Ed. تفصيل.

[6] Reading عليهم MS. and Ed. notwithstanding; they read عليه.

[7] Reading المحنة with MS.; Ed. المحبة.

a number of them became humans while others became animals or beasts in proportion to their sins. Those of them who became animal forms were relieved of the charge of obedience. He was at variance with Ibn Ḥā'iṭ regarding the charge to animals. He said of beasts that they will be continually transformed[1]
259 into ugly forms and that they will suffer affliction such as slaughter and the yoke until they shall have received in full that retribution which they earned for their sins. After that they will be restored to their ancient station. Then God will offer them a second choice of testing. If they select it He will reimpose upon them the task of obedience in the manner which we described. But if they abstain from it they will be abandoned to their actual state unburdened with any charge. He held that if any of those bidden to obey should perform deeds of obedience until he merited becoming a prophet or an angel he would have it granted by God. Al-Ḳaḥṭabi[2], who was one of them, held that God did not propose to them the burden of obedience at first, but that they asked Him for an elevation in their rank and for an opportunity to contend for superiority. He informed them that these characteristics could not be granted to them until after the imposition of obedience and the trial, and that if they accepted the charge and then disobeyed they would incur chastisement upon themselves. They declined the test and this, he said, is the meaning of God's word: "Surely we offered the trust to the heavens and the earth and the mountains, but they refused to be unfaithful to it and feared it. Man took it upon himself; surely he is unjust, ignorant"[3] Abu Muslim al-Ḥarrāni thought that God created souls and charged those among them which he knew would obey Him but not those who would disobey Him. The latter disobeyed him in the beginning and were punished alternately by metempsychosis and transformation into diverse bodies in proportion to their sins. This is an exposition of the beliefs of the adherents of the doctrine of metempsychosis. We have already destroyed their argument sufficiently in the Book of Religions and Dogmas.

---

[1] Reading تتردد with MS.; Ed. تترد.

[2] With MS.; Ed. القحطى. Schreiner, *l. c.*, 66, n. 3, says: "That Dualists adhered to the doctrine of metempsychosis we realize from the case of al-Ḳaḥṭabi". Where did he discover that al-Ḳaḥṭabi was a dualist?

[3] Sura 59, v. 16.

CHAPTER THIRTEEN.

AN EXPOSITION OF THE ERRORS OF THE ḤĀ'IṬIYYA AND THE REASON FOR THEIR EXCLUSION FROM ISLAM.

They are the followers of Aḥmad ibn Ḥā'iṭ [1] the Ḳadarite, a disciple of al-Naẓẓām in Mu'tazilism. We discussed his views on metempsychosis previously. In this chapter we shall relate his blunders about the Unity of the Maker [2]. Ibn Ḥā'iṭ and Faḍl al-Ḥadathi [3] believed that the created universe contains two lords and two creators. One of them, eternal, is God, and the other, brought into existence, is 'Isa ibn Mariam [4]. They believed tha' Christ is the son of God by adoption, [5] and not by birth. They also maintained that it is Christ who will call mankind to reckoning on the Day of Judgment. He it is whom God meant when He said: "Thy Lord and the Angel came in ranks" [6] and it is he who will come "in the shadows of the clouds" [7]. It is he who created Adam in his image. This is the explanation of the tradition which has come down that God created Adam [8] in His image [9]. He [10] believed ..ia. it is he whom the Prophet

[1] On the variants of the name of Aḥmad's father see *Shiites*, II, 10 f.

[2] In addition to his heresies listed in this and the previous chapters he is accused by IH, IV, 197 and by Maḳrīzi, 347, of blaming the Prophet for his numerous marriages, claiming that Abu-Dharr al-Ghifāri (*EI*, I, s. v.) was more abstentious than he.

[3] Isf. الحارثى. *Intisar*, 148, calls him الحذاء (see p. 222).

[4] Makrizi, 347; Shahr. 42.

[5] Reading التبنى with MS.; Ed. النبى. We no doubt have here the traces of the Adoptianist heresy of early Christianity (Cf. *ERE*, I, 103—5, esp. par. 1—4). For the influence which Christianity exerted on these men their doctrine bears evidence. See also *Shiites*, II, 11.

[6] Sura 89, v. 23. The orthodox translation of Malak is as a collective. Baiḍawi, II, 402.

[7] Sura 2, v. 206.

[8] With Goldziher; Ed. and MS. اطا. Maḳrīzi, 347.

[9] With Ed.; MS. صورته. I have not been able to locate this tradition. Its Biblical source is obvious. *Genesis*, I, 27.

[10] I. e. Aḥmad.

referred to when he said: You will see your Lord as you see the moon when it is full[1]. It is he whom he meant when stating that God created the intellect
261 and said to it: Come forward, and it came forward. Then He said: Step back and it turned back. Then He said: I have not produced a nobler creature than you. Through you I shall give and through you I shall take[2]. They asserted that Christ became embodied, but before his embodiment he had been the Intellect.

'Abd-al-Ḳāhir says: These two non-believers have identified themselves with the Dualists and the Magians by affirming the existence of two creators. But their doctrine is more heinous than the doctrines of the latter. The Dualists and Magians ascribe the origin of all good to God and ascribe only the bad to Darkness or Satan. But ibn Ḥā'iṭ and Faḍl al-Ḥadathi trace the production of all good to 'Īsa and even credit to him the reckoning with mankind in the world to come. The surprising point in their doctrine is that 'Īsa created his grandfather Adam. Is there anything more wonderful than a branch producing its root! Whoever includes these two erring sects within Islam is similar to one who counts the Christians among the sects of Islam.

[1] The tradition is found in all the collections. See Wensinck, s. v. *Allah.*

[2] Shahr., 44 gives this tradition in greater detail. Goldziher who quotes this tradition from Ghazāli cites it as a definitely Neo-Platonic element in Islam, *ZA*, XXII, (1908) 318-9.

CHAPTER FOURTEEN.

THE ḤIMĀRIYYA[1] AMONG THE ḲADARIYYA AND THE REASON FOR THEIR EXCLUSION FROM ISLAM.

They form a group among the Mu'tazilites of 'Askar Mukram[2]. They have selected some peculiar errors from the heresies of the various Ḳadarite divisions, adopted from Ibn Ḥā'it his doctrine of transmigration into bodies and frames,
and subscribed to 'Abbād ibn Sulaimān al-Ḍaimari's[3] view that those whom 262
God transforms into monkeys and pigs become human after their transformation but turn infidels[4]. From Ja'd ibn Dirham[5], whom Khālid ibn 'Abdallah

[1] The mystery surrounding this name (our author sheds no light on its origin; cf. *Mukhtasar*, 167 n. 1), can be solved to my mind by tracing it to the last 'Umayyad Khalīf, Merwān ibn Muḥammad, who was nicknamed al-Ḥimār, and who, as *Fihrist*, 338, relates, was a Zendīḳ. See also IA, V, 329. It is noteworthy that this Khalīf was a pupil of Ja'd ibn Dirham (see below) who plays a rcle in the formulation of the doctrine of the Ḥimāriyya. Baghdādi's silence is doubtless due to his orthodoxy which restrained him from linking this heterodox sect to a Khalīf.

[2] This is the reading according to Yakūt, s. v. *'Askar*, Makrīzī (Fagnan) 40, reads *Mukarram*. It is a place near Khuzistān. While Yakūt speaks of it as a place of learned men, Muḳaddasi, 410, calls attention to their heretical teachings; وهم عقلاء فهماء واكثرهم علماء... غير انهم قد بغضوا انفسهم... بعلم الكلام وخالفوا بالاعتزال جميع الاسلام حتى ذمهم المذكرون. Goldziher quotes a passage acc. to which the place was a Mu'tazilite nest in 1156. *Islam*, III (1912) 219. It is significant that 'Abdallah ibn Maimūn al-Ḳaddāḥ, the Ḳarmatian leader, was also a native of this town. Blochet, 67.

[3] With MS. الضيمرى; Ed. الضميرى. 'Abbād (and not Ubād as Seelye, 147, reads or as Nyberg, *Intisar*, 203 allows) was a Mu'tazilite who argued that it is wrong to say of Allah that He created the unbelievers since their unbelief could not have been created by God. *Lisan-al-Mizan*, III, 229—30 (he calls him الضمرى which resembles our reading and not that in Ed. 147 and Nyberg ib.) says that he lived in the days of al-Ma'mūn.

[4] Maḳrīzī, 347.

[5] The following biographical information is recorded about him in *Fihrist*, 337-8: He was a teacher of Merwān ibn Muḥammad whom he converted to Zendikism. But Ḥishām ibn

al-Kasri offered up as a sacrifice, they have adopted the thesis that when deductive proof leads to knowledge, that knowledge becomes an act without an agent. In addition they hold that wine is not a product of God but is the work of the vintner, because God will not produce what will be a cause for disobedience. They believe that man creates several species of animal life. For instance, when a man buries flesh or places it in the sun so that it breeds maggots, they hold that these maggots are man's creation. Similarly the scorpions which appear in straw under baked bricks are believe to have been produced by the one who combined the baked bricks and straw [1]. They are more heretical than the Magians who ascribe the origin of serpents. creeping things and venomous snakes to Satan. Whoever counts them among the sects of the community is like him who counts the Magians among the sects of the community.

'Abd-al-Malik finally executed him after he had kept him in prison for a long time. It is told Ja'd's family brought the story of his imprisonment to Hishām and complained about its lengthiness. Hishām was surprised to hear that he was still alive and ordered Khālid to kill him. The latter executed him on the Sacrifice Day after accusing him of Zendikism from the pulpit. The editor of Ibn Ḳuṭaiba, *Ikhtilāf fil-Lafth,* 56, n. calls him the first one to have asserted the created character of the Ḳur'ān. See also *Nujum,* I, 357 and IA, V, 196-7.

[1] Maḳrīzī, *ib.*

THE YEZĪDIYYA AMONG THE KHAWĀRIJ AND THE REASON FOR THEIR EXCLUSION FROM ISLAM.

They are the followers of Yezīd ibn Abu Unaisa[1] the Khārijite, a native of Baṣra. Later he removed to Tūn[2] in the land of Persia, and followed the docrines of the Ibāḍiyya among the Khawārij. Then he renounced the faith of the entire community[3] by preaching that God will appoint an apostle from among the Persians and will reveal to him a book from heaven, and will abrogate the Law of Muḥammad with his new Law. He held that the disciples of the awaited prophet are the Ṣābians spoken of in the Ḳur'ān. The people of Wāsiṭ and Ḥarrān who go by the name of Ṣābians are not the Ṣābians mentioned in the Ḳur'ān[4]. In addition to his error he befriended anyone among the People of the

[1] The founder of the sect which still exists to this day is one Yezīd whose personality has not been determined. According to some, e. g. Sam'āni s. v. *Yezīd*, he is identical with the 'Umayyad Yazīd ibn Merwān. But our author's statement is the more correct. See Isya Joseph's *Devil Worship*.

[2] Near Ḳuhistān in Persia, between Herat and Nishāpūr, Isf., B. reads حور and Isf. P., جوه (or جور). The probable reading is خور. Both Tun and Khur are towns in this mountainous region and Yezīd may have gone to either of these two. Muḳaddasi, 301 and more fully 321; Yaḳūt, IV, 201 f. s. v. Ḳuhistān.

[3] Ash'ari and Shahr. do not include this group among the Ghulāt but discuss it as a sub-sect of the Ibāḍiyya (Ash'ari 102, ff, and Shahr. 100-02.)

[4] Chwolson, in his study of the Ṣābians, also adopts this distinction between the Ṣābians who are discussed in the Ḳur'ān and those of Ḥarrān, I, 11—22. He states that the latter took this name on the advice of a jurist when the Khalīf al-Manṣūr persecuted those who did not profess a revealed religion (13—14). An exposition of the Ṣābians of the Ḳur'ān will be found *ib.* chapter 5, and of the Ḥarrānians, 139-541, esp. 158—180. Pedersen, who differs with Chwolson regarding the nature of the original Ṣābians does not want to recognize the two types. See his article in *Oriental Studies to E. G. Browne*, 383—91.

Book who confirmed the prophetic character of Muḥammad even if he did not join his Religion, and in view of that called them Believers. According to this theory the ʻĪsawiyya and Raʻyāniyya[1] among the Jews are necessarily believers since they have acknowledged the prophetic character of Muḥammad, but do not join his community. There is nothing which can allow anyone who regards Jews as Muslims to be counted as one of the sects of Islam. How then can he be counted among Islamic sects who predicts the abrogation of the Law of Islam?

---

[1] The reading is unmistakable, but in all probability the Yudghāniyya or Shadghāniyya are meant, see above 37, note 6. Goldziher's remark in his review of this book, in which he argues against the possibility of the appellation to be derived from his name al-Rāʻī may give us the clue to this name. See Friedländer's remarks in support of this reading, *JQR, NS*, III (1912—13) 284-5 and notes. Albīrūni, 18, lists two false prophets one of whom is Abu ʻĪsa al-Isfahāni and the other al-Rāʻi (no doubt Yudghān) see *REJ*, xii (1886), 259—60. Ḳirḳisāni relates that Yudghān was called "The Shepherd" by his followers. — *Hebrew Union College Annual*, vii, 328.

CHAPTER SIXTEEN.

THE MAIMŪNIYYA AMONG THE KHAWĀRIJ AND THE REASON FOR THEIR EXCLUSION FROM ISLAM.

They are the followers of a man among the Khawārij of Shiḥr[1] whose name was Maimūn[2]. He belonged to the school of the 'Ajārida[3] among the Khawārij. Later he contradicted the 'Ajārida in the matter of God's will, human free-will and the power to act, adopting on these three dogmas the doctrines of the Ḳadariyya who deviate from the truth. In addition to this, he held that children of polytheists dwell in paradise. If this Maimūn had satisfied himself with these heresies which we have related and had not added any other errors, we should have classed him with the Khawārij for branding 'Ali, Ṭalḥa, al-Zubair, 'Ā'isha and others as infidels[4], and for calling sinners infidels; [we should have also classed him] with the Ḳadarites for his opinions on the problems of will, free-will and power to act, which conform to those of the Ḳadariyya. But he exceeded the Magians. He permitted men to marry the daughters of the children of common grandparents and the daughters of the children of brothers and sisters[5]. He argued: In the prohibitions against marrying certain women be-

---

[1] This rendering is somewhat doubtful: MS. apparently reads السخرية, which makes no sense. Ed. reads الشخرية. Shiḥr is a town in S. Arabia, Yaḳūt, *s. v.* That there were Khawārij in that district is clear from ibn Ḥauḳal, 32. Yet Ash'ari, 95, locates him in Balkh.

[2] Shahr. 96, transmits his name as Maimūn b. Khālid. Makrīzī, 354, and Iji give his full name as Maimūn b. 'Amrān.

[3] Ed. 72—82 (Seelye 94—104). As in the case of the Yezīdis, our author is more conservative than the other authorities in classing them with the Ghulāt. Ash'ari, 93, 354 and Shahr. 96 enumerate them among the Khārijites.

[4] This is a cardinal dogma with all Khārijite sects. See Seelye, 75.

[5] These are forbidden relations according to the four most important orthodox rites See Syed Amer 'Ali *Mohammedan Law* (1929) II, 277; Ahmad Shakri, *Mohammedan Law of Marriage and Divorce*, 25.

cause of consanguinity, God specified only mothers, daughters, sisters, paternal
265 aunts and brothers' daughters and sisters' daughters [1]. But he did not specify daughters of daughters or sons, nor daughters of brothers' children, nor daughters of sisters' children. If he carried his analogy further to mothers' mothers and fathers' mothers and grandfathers' mothers, he would become a thoroughgoing [2] Magian. But since he does not permit the marriage of grandmothers, for he infers the rule governing grandmothers from the prohibitions against grandmothers' mothers, he is compelled to apply the principle governing children of one's own loins to children of children. If he does not pursue his analogy this way, his argument is destroyed.

Al-Karābisi [3] relates that the Khārijite Maimūniyya disacknowledge the Sūra of Joseph as part of the Ḳur'ān [4]. But to disavow part of it is like disavowing it all. Whoever permits to himself any of the prohibited laws adheres to the cult of the Magians, and Magians are not counted among the sects of Islam.

[1] Sura 4, v. 27.

[2] The Alif of محض which appears in Ed. seems to be erased. I therefore adopt the reading المحض rendering it as above. Brockelmann's emendation لخاض is not borne out by MS.

[3] Al-Ḥusain ibn 'Ali ibn Yezīd al-Karābisi (and Karasi as in IH, IV, 190). He was a famous Shāfi'ite of the third century A. H. He died 244. See IKhall, I. 416 and IA, VII, 34. The information cited above is probably drawn from al-Karābisi's Kitāb fil-Māḳālāt, characterized by Fakhr-al-Dīn al-Rāzi's father as 'معول المتكلمين في معرفة مذاهب الخوارج وسائر اهل الاهوا', Subki, *Ṭabaḳāt*, I, 252.

[4] See Noeldeke-Schwally, *Geschichte des Qorans*, ii, 94.

CHAPTER SEVENTEEN.

CONCERNING THE BĀṬINIYYA[1] AND THE REASON FOR THEIR EXCLUSION FROM ALL THE SECTS OF ISLAM.

Know — may God make you prosper — that the damage caused by the Bāṭiniyya to the Muslim sects is greater than the damage caused them by the Jews, Christians and Magians; nay, graver than the injury inflicted on them by the Materialists and other non-believing sects; nay, graver than the injury resulting to them from the Antichrist who will appear at the end of time. For those 266
who, as a result of the missionary activities of the Bāṭiniyya, have been led astray ever since the inception of the mission up to the present time are more

Although our author is consistent in calling this sect Bāṭiniyya it is, nevertheless, known by many other names, most of which, no doubt, date from the period later than Baghdādī. Some of these names are connected with persons; others, like the Muḥammira, are not usually employed as epithets for this mystical sect. Iji, 348, mentions seven *lakabs*, with explanations: Bāṭiniyya, Ḳarāmiṭa, Ḥuramiyya, Sab'iyya, Bābākiyya, Muḥammira, Isma'īliyya. Goldziher in *Streitschrift*, p. 37, lists the following ten names: Bāṭiniyya, Karāmiṭa, Ḳarmaṭiyya, Khurramiyya, Khurramdīniyya, (the last two are not treated separately by our author; see above p. 87). Isma'īliyya, Sab'iyya, Bābākiyya, Muḥammira, Ta'līmiyya. *Siasset Nameh*, p. 290, however, has the following ten: Isma'ili (Aleppo and Cairo), Karmat, (Bagdad, Ma-wara-l-nahr and Ghazna), Mubareky (Kufa), Rawendi and Burquoy (Basra), Khalefy (Rai), Muhammira, (Jurjan), Mubayyida (Syria), Saidy (Maghreb), Djenneby (Lahsa and Bahrein), Batiny (Ispahan). The Mubareky sect is mentioned by Shahrastani p. 128 and by Baghdādi p. 47 (Seelye p. 66) as an Imamiyya group, (the latter unnecessarily makes them adherents of Muḥammad's children rather than of Muḥammad himself). They are borne out by Naubakhti, 58.

Baghdādi even mentions the Isma'īliyya as a branch of the same main division (p. 39; Seelye p. 60), but in the discussion on page 56 (Seelye p. 65) he relegates them to the Ghulāt. They applied to themselves the term Ta'līmy (on the meaning of this name see *Streitschrift*, p. 5 ff. and page 38.)

numerous than those who will be led astray by the Antichrist when he appears, since the duration of the sedition of the Antichrist will not exceed forty days[1]. But the vices of the Bāṭiniyya are more numerous than the sand-grains or the raindrops.

The heresiographers relate that a number of people laid the foundation for the Bāṭiniyya movement. One of them was ['Abdallah ibn] Maimūn ibn Daiṣān[2], known as al-Ḳaddāḥ, a mawla of Ja'far ibn Muḥammad al-Ṣādiḳ and a native of Ahwāz. Among them was also Muḥammad ibn Ḥusain, surnamed Dhaidhān[3], [and several

---

[1] Isf. 65a adds: And the sedition of these appeared in the days of al-Ma'mūn and it still endures.

[2] Despite the consistent use of the name Maimūn (see his and his son's biography in Massignon's article in *Studies Presented to E. G. Browne*, 330—31) in our text here and elsewhere, which is generally supported by Isf., and despite the skillful calculation of Casanova in *JA*, 1915, pp. 5—17, esp. pp. 13—15, in which he credits this account, the correct reading in the particular instance under consideration is 'Abdallah ibn Maimūn as Isf. reads here. For even if Maimūn, to judge by the account given of him in IA, VIII, 21, may, in a sense, be regarded as the founder of the sect and, according to Casanova (*ibd.*; see below), may, together with his son, have hoped for an overthrow of Arab rule in 194 a. H, the details of the career in the following passage do not at all tally with his biography as we know it from other sources, but agree well with the career of his son. The epithet al-Ḳaddāḥ (the oculist) is applied by some authorities to the father (e. g. *Fihrist*, p. 186, ويعرف ميمون بالقداح and de Goeje p. 13 and p. 15), by others to his son (e. g. IA, *ib.*). Even our author declares (Ed. p. 16. Seelye p. 35) that 'Abdallah was the founder of the sect.

It may also be added that the alternatives upon which we are compelled to fall back, if we should adopt Casanova's conclusions in the said article are far-fetched. For one thing he asks us to recognize two Zaidāns or Dhaidāns or to actually discern two individuals in the two variant readings. It is even more difficult to assume as he does that the Bāṭiniyya movement was made up of a series of attempts rather than a well planned conspiracy which reached its successful climax with the establishment of the Fāṭimid dynasty in 296, as it is described by most historians. But the strongest argument against his view is that Baghdādī whom he calls "Bien informé" (p. 13) tells (Ed. 277 below p. 131 and in Uṣūl p. 329) that the founders of the movement which commenced in the days of al-Ma'mūn (198—218) were Ḥamdan Ḳarmaṭ and 'Abdallah ibn Maimūn al-Ḳaddāḥ, grandfather of the chief of the Bāṭiniyya in Egypt.

[3] Isf. B. 65 a, reads ذيدان. Isf. P, 86 b, دندان, *Fihrist*, 188—222, زيدان, IA, 21, دندان; editor mentions that one of his MSS. reads ديدان, Maḳrīzi (Fagnan p. 45) gives his name

other people called descendants of Hamdan Mukhtar who met the one called Dhaidhān][1] and ['Abdallah ibn] Maimūn ibn Daiṣān in the prison of the ruler of 'Irāḳ. In that prison they formulated the religion of the Bāṭiniyya. Their doctrine appeared in public, after their liberation from prison, through the activities of the one called Dhaidhān. He commenced his missionary work in the district of al-Jabal[2]. Many of the Kurds of al-Jabal as well as the inhabitants of the mountain named el-Badain[3] joined his religion. Then ['Abdallah ibn] Maimūn ibn Daiṣān journeyed to the province of al-Maghreb and there claimed to be descended from 'Aḳīl ibn Abu Ṭalib[4], pretending that he was an offspring of his. After a number of the Ultra-Rawāfiḍ and the Ḥūlūliyya responded to his call, he pretended that he was one of the children of Muḥammad ibn Isma'īl[5] ibn Ja'far al-Ṣādiḳ. The simpletons[6] accepted this from him despite the information[7] possessed by the genealogists that Muḥammad ibn Isma'īl ibn Ja'far died leaving no progeny[8].

---

as Muḥammad ibn al-Ḥusain ibn Djihan Bakhter. According to *Fihrist,* 188 Dhaidhān was secretary to Aḥmad ibn 'Abd-al-'Azīz ibn Abu Dulaf who ruled c. 265. But Massignon in his article on Ḳarmaṭian Bibliography *op. cit.*, p. 331, gives the following biographical notice of "Dindān": Abu Ja'far Aḥmad ibn al-Ḥusain ibn Sa'īd al-Ahwāzi, died at Kumm c. 250. He was not 'Abdallah's accomplice, but his disciple. He was a famous traditionist, and before his conversion belonged to the Khurramiyya. He wrote the *Kitāb al-Ihtijāj.* He may be the same as Aḥmad ibn al-Kayyāl.

[1] The passage in brackets, missing in both Ed. and MS., is taken from *Mukhtasar,* 170. I have not been able to obtain any information regarding the clan of Hamdan Mukhtar.

[2] Isf. B. reads جبل نوذ while P. reads جبل تور. According to Yakut *s. v. al-Jabal,* it is the same district as the one now called Irak. The word Jabal is omitted in Ed.

[3] This is a mountain in Azerbaijan and is the birthplace of Bābak al-Khurrami as well as the scene of his activity. See above p. 88 and note.

[4] See Maḳrīzi (Fagnan), 40. For the genealogy of this family see ibn Ḳutaiba, *Kitāb al-Ma'ārif,* 102–3.

[5] The allegiance to Isma'īl ibn Ja'far accounts for the name Isma'īliyya by which this sect is sometimes known. Although Ja'far divested his eldest son of the Imamate because of the latter's addiction to wine drinking, the Isma'īliyya claimed that Ja'far, being infallible, could not revoke what he once had granted. See Blochet p. 49 and Browne, *Literary History of Persia,* I, p. 393. (Both of them draw from the same source), Cf. especially Naubakhti, 57-8.

[6] Read اغبياء with MS; Ed. اغنياء.

[7] Read مع علم with MS; Ed. على.

[8] Although our author makes the same statement Ed. p. 47 (Seelye p. 66), there are

Later there arose a man known as Ḥamdān Ḳarmaṭ[1] and summoned the people to the faith of the Bāṭiniyya. He was nicknamed thus because his handwriting was crabbed, or perhaps because he minced his step[2]. He had been at

---

no sources for it to my knowledge. Blochet 38, in speaking of Muḥammad says "He had several children who fled to Khorasan". Wüstenfeld in his genealogical tables *(Geschichte der Fatimiden, 13)* also lists several children, and similarly Huart in his article on the *'Alids* in *EI*. I s. v. and de Sacy, Introd. p. 67. De Goeje takes it for granted that Muḥammad ibn Isma'īl had children (p. 50—67, et passim), similarly Naubakhti, e. g., 90, and elsewhere, and Maḳrīzi (Fagnan) pp. 36—37. Perhaps our author was misled by a statement in Tab. III, 2218 (IA, vii, 353), regarding ibn Zikrwaih's spurious genealogy to the effect that وقيل ان لم يكن لمحمد بن اسماعيل ابن يسمى عبد الله. In view of Naubakhti's statement to the contrary, it is improbable that Baghdādi's contention is of Imāmite origin. A similarly curious denial of the existence of the twelfth Imām of the Twelvers is made by Ibn Ḥazm and cannot be traced by Friedländer. See Shiites, I, 48 and ii, 53.

[1] Ḥamdān (*Siasset Nameh*, 269, gives his name as Mubarek doubtless a confusion with Mubārak, Mawla of Isma'īl b. Ja'far, and founder of the Mubārakiyya sect. Naubakhti, 58) Ḳarmaṭ, after whom the Ḳarmaṭians, one of the most important sub-sects in the Bāṭiniyya movement, are called, was converted by Ḥusain al-Ahwāzi (Maḳrīzi, I, 396; Wüstenfeld, 7; Blochet, 63, etc; yet cf. *Fihrist*, 187), a missionary of Aḥmad ibn 'Abdallah ibn Maimūn al-Ḳaddāḥ, and later became active himself as a propagandist in 'Irāḳ, making his first appearance in 274 (de Sacy Introd., 166), or 277, IA, VII, 309 ff. For a full biography of him and of his brother-in-law and associate, 'Abdān, see de Sacy, Introd., 166—200. De Goeje, who, on the authority of ibn Ḥauḳal, believes with de Sacy that Ḥamdān and 'Abdān finally repudiated the secret conspiracy and again became loyal supporters of the 'Abbāsids (p. 210), disagrees with him nevertheless about the cause of this defection, maintaining that it came as a result of the establishment of the Fāṭimid dynasty by 'Ubaidallah, the former chief of the Ḳarmaṭians in Syria. Cf. 57—69.

[2] The meaning of the nickname Ḳarmaṭ is not ascertained. According to Ikhald (*'Ibār*, III, 335,) and IA, VII, 311, it was the name of his Syrian employer who was red-eyed (*Karmita* in Syriac), or of the one who carried him on his donkey when he lay ill on the road (IA, ib. 310). Massignon, *(Bibliogr.* 329) is also inclined to see in it a Syriac word but with the reading *Kurmata,* which would correspond to the Arabic word *Tadlīs,* (concealment), the sixth degree of initiation, see below p. 144. See de Goeje, 199—203. Our author's interpretation finds support in *Siasset Nameh*, 269. Naubakhti, 61, simply relates that it was a nickname given to Ḥamdān, who was a Nabatean. He makes the significant remark that the Mubārakiyya group is earlier than the Ḳarmaṭians.

the beginning of his career one of the farmers of Sawād al-Kūfa[1]. To him the Karmaṭians owe their name. After him, Abu Sa'īd al-Jannābi[2], who was one of the converts that had adhered to Ḥamdān[3] began his missionary activity for this heresy. He subdued the country of Baḥrain[4], and the Banu Sanbar[5] joined his call. Then, after a long time had elapsed, the one called Sa'īd al-Ḥusain ibn Aḥmad ibn 'Abdallah ibn Maimūn ibn Daiṣān al-Kaddāḥ appeared among them. He changed his name and his pedigree; he declared to his followers; I am 'Ubaidallah ibn al-Ḥasan ibn Muḥammad ibn Isma'īl ibn Ja'far al-Ṣādiḳ[6]. Then 267

---

[1] IA, VII, 310, (also reproduced de Sacy, Introd., 172 ff.), tells of his rise to power from the farming profession. According to that report his occupation was only a ruse employed by him to further his missionary activity. But Wüstenfeld, *ib.*, believes him to have been sincere in his extremely religious practices.

[2] For a detailed account of the activities of this powerful leader and the characterization of his personality see de Goeje pp. 31—47 and p. 69 ff.; de Sacy, *Introd.*, 211—216. He was killed by a slave in 301 and was succeeded at first by one son (Abū-l-Ḳāsim Sa'īd) and by his designated successor Abu Ṭāhir Sulaimān, when the latter became mature, in 305 A. H. (217).

[3] He was converted by Yaḥya ibn al-Mahdi (de Sacy, *Introd.* p. 212). De Sacy himself is inclined to the view that Abu Sa'īd was sent directly by Ḥamdān Ḳarmaṭ, whereas de Goeje, p. 31, attributes his appointment to 'Abdān, Ḳarmaṭ's brother-in-law and a leading figure in the plot. (see on 'Abdān, de Sacy, *l. c.* p. 154 ff.).

[4] Whether his first mission was to Baḥrain is fully discussed by de Goeje p. 37 ff.

[5] He married the daughter of al-Ḥasan ibn Sanbar (de Goeje p. 37; IḤauḳ, 210: Sunbur). The Banu Sanbar were an important family in al-Āḥsā'. See IḤauḳ. p. 21.

[6] *Fihrist*, 187, gives the following order for the succession: 'Abdallah, his son Muḥammad, his son or brother Aḥmad (called Abu Shala'la', sometimes Shalaghlagh) and Sa'īd ibn al-Ḥusain ibn 'Abdallah ibn al-Maimūn (al-Ḥusain having died before his father). De Goeje, 21, favors this order: 'Abdallah, his two sons Ḥusain and Aḥmad (Abu Shalaghlagh) and Ḥusain's son Sa'īd-'Ubaidallah. Maḳrīzi, I, 396, lists them as follows: 'Abdallah, Aḥmad, his sons Ḥusain and Muḥammad Abu Sha'la'la'.

The entire problem of the credibility of the Fāṭimid claims to be descendants of 'Ali has not been and probably will never be definitely settled (Cf. ibn Ḥammād's *Rois Obaidites*, tr. Vondenheyden, Arabic II, French 17). While some reject unhesitatingly any and all of their claims, others are equally convinced that they are true descendants of Fāṭima. But just as the former are probably prejudiced for religious reasons (or political, especially among the Shī'ites) the latter may have been influenced by some equally strong considerations. See IA,

his revolt broke out in the Maghreb [1]. His descendants at present are rulers of the Egyptian affairs of State [2].

Then there came forth among them one called Zikrwaih [3] ibn Mihrwaih al-Dandāni, a disciple of Ḥamdān Ḳarmaṭ [4]. Ma'mūn [5], brother of Ḥamdān Ḳarmaṭ, arose in the land of Fars. The Ḳarmaṭians of Persia are, therefore, called Ma'mūniyya [6]. A man from among the Bāṭiniyya known as Abu Ḥātim [7] penetrated into the land of al-Dailam, and a body of Dailamites heeded his call [8], among

---

VIII, 14; Maḳrīzi (Fagnan), 36 ff.; Ikhall. ii, 77; IKhald (Macdonald), 24—30 and among modern scholars de Goeje 4 ff. esp. 8 ff.; Blochet, 77; Zambaur, 95.

[1] He was invited there by Abu 'Abdallah al-Shī'i (called al-Muḥtessib, *Siasset Nameh*, 282) who had made conquests there to appear as the expected Mahdi. 'Ubaidallah later killed him as well as his brother. See Wüstenfeld, 8—10, 15—38 (where the oriental sources are enumerated) and 38—70 for a history of the reign of the first Fāṭimid Khalīf.

[2] The reference is to the F.ṭimid dynasty which held Egypt frnm 358 to 567 A H.

[3] So MS; Ed. ابن كرويه بن مهرويه.

[4] This is "*Zakrouya ibn Mahrouya Salmani*" discussed at great length in de Sacy, *Introd.*, 184 and 198—210. See also de Goeje, 47 ff. According to Nuwairi, who places Ḥamdān's relinquishment of his missionary activity in the period of Aḥmad ibn 'Abdallah, Zikrwaih became the *dā'i* in place of Ḥamdān.

[5] No other source to my knowledge mentions Ma'mūn. Both by his relationship to Ḥamdān and by his field of activity, I believe him to be identical with 'Abdān, Ḳarmaṭ's brother-in-law, and a very important figure in the propagation of the cult of the Isma'īliyya, who, unless my identification is true, is nowhere mentioned by Baghdādi — a very strange omission indeed. Perhaps his real name was Ma'mūn, and 'Abdān only a *kunya.*

[6] Makrīzi (Fagnan, 58) and *Fihrist*, 186 mention a sect Maimuniyya which they relate to Maimūn ibn Daiṣān. Fluegel in his note on page 77 identifies this sect with the Khawārij Maimūniyya (see above, 105; see also Maḳrīzi (Fagnan), *ib*). The summary in IA VIII, 21 of Maimun's views would support Flügel's contention, yet the entire hypothesis seems unlikely. If the Ma'mūniyya are the same as the Maimuniyya, perhaps the man Ma'mūn is a creation of Baghdādi's who for some reason confused him with Maimūn b. Daiṣān.

[7] He was made ruler of Jurjān in 315. IA VIII, 148.

[8] A missionary movement in Dailam carried on by Abu Ḥātim in the year 195, is reported by Blochet, 67. His full name is given there as Ja'far Makhzūm Abu Ḥātim Aḥmad ibn Ḥamdān al-Rāzi. See de Sacy, *Introd*, 210, *Siasset Nameh*, 273—4. Massignon, *l. c.*, 332 calls him "Abou Hatim ('Abd al-Rahman?) al-Warsnani al-Razi". Cf. *Fihrist*, 188; خلفه ابو حاتم الورسنالي وكان ثنويا ثم صار دهريا ثم تزندق وحصل على الشك.

them Asfār ibn Shirwaih[1]. In Nīshāpūr, a missionary of theirs, al-Sha'rāni[2] by name, made his appearance. He was executed while Abu Bekr ibn Muḥtāj[3] was governor there. Al-Sha'rāni summoned al-Ḥusain ibn 'Ali al-Marvrūdi to join him. After him, Muḥammad ibn Aḥmad al-Nasafi continued his mission, preaching to the people of *Ma-wara-n-nahr,* and so-did Abu Ya'ḳūb al-Sijizli who is known as Bandāna[4]. Al-Nasafi wrote for them the "Book of the Sum and Substance"[5]. Abu Ya'ḳūb compiled for them the "Book of the Fundamentals of the Mission" and the "Book of the Interpretation of the Precepts" and the "Book of the Revelation of the Secrets". Al-Nasafi[6] and the one known as Bandāna were killed for their errors. 268

The historians relate that the preaching of the Bāṭiniyya made its first appearance in the days of al-Ma'mūn[7], and spread during the reign of al-Mu'taṣim[8].

---

[1] Conqueror of the district of Rayy by order of Naṣr b. Aḥmad the Samanid, and subsequently an independent r.bel ruler. See *Muruj,* ix, 6—19: IA, viii, 138—144.

[2] Abu Sa'īd al-Sha'rāni is cited in Blochet 67. See also *Fihrist,* 188, which dates him in 337, but this is hardly possible, cf. next note; *Annales Moslemici,* II, p. 295, note N. The *Siasset Nameh,* 211—2, tells that Ḥusain ibn 'Ali al-Mervezy was converted by Ghiath whose activities are described ib. pp. 271—2. See also *Fihrist, ib.* IA who tells of his rebellion and his fate in detail (VIII, 48—9) does not relate his conversion.

[3] Abu Bekr Muhram ibn al-Muzaffar ibn al-Muḥtāj was governor of Nīshāpūr during the years 320—326. Zambaur, 49 and 204.

[4] Massignon, probably drawing his information in part from our author and in part from Albirūni (tr. Sachau, 32) calls him Bandānah Abu Ya'ḳūb al-Sijzi. Sachau (*ib.*) translates the place-name as "of Sijistān". Unfortunately the Laḳab is missing in Albirūni (...الملقب). He may perhaps be the Isḥāḳ Sinjari of Blochet p. 68. His work cited as كشف المحجوب in Albiruni is no doubt our كشف الاسرار.

[5] *Fihrist,* 189, which does not mention this work (Ar: المحصول), ascribes three other works to him: عنوان الدين ، صول الشرع ، المنجية الدعوة. Massignon, *l. c.,* 332, lists the *Mahṣūl* only.

[6] The death of Muḥammad ibn Aḥmad came at the hands of Nūḥ ibn Naṣr ibn Aḥmad the Samanid, Emīr of Khurāsān, whose father had become a devout convert to the cause of the Bāṭiniyya (*Fihrist,* 188). The story of the rebellion against Naṣr, which Blochet (66, note 1) very appropriately compares with Anūshirvān's vengeance on Mazdak, is graphically told in the *Siasset Nameh,* 276—281. See also *Fihrist,* 88, line 4—9.

[7] This is the period of 'Abdallah ibn Maimūn's activities. See above, 108 note 2.

[8] His Caliphate extended from 218 to 232 A. H. Like his brother and predecessor Al-Ma'mūn, he was an intolerant Mu'tazilite.

They tell that al-Afshīn, commander of the army of al-Mu'taṣim, joined their movement, and dissimulated[1] with regard to Bābāk al-Khurrami. Al-Khurrami was the leader of a rebellion in the district of al-Baddein. The people of his mountain were Khurramiyya after the fashion of the Mazdak cult, and the Khurramiyya joined forces with the Bāṭiniyya. A body of three hundred thousand men, made up of the people of al-Baddein and of those of the Dailamites who joined them, gathered around Bābāk. The Khalīf sent al-Afshīn to wage war against them believing him to be genuinely devoted to the cause of the Muslims, whereas he secretly sympathized with Bābāk. He, therefore, procrastinated in his war with him and disclosed the places of concealment of the Muslim forces to him, so that many of them were killed[2]. Then reinforcements reached al-Afshīn, and Muḥammad ibn Yūsuf al-Thughri[3] as well as Abu Dulaf al-Ḳāsim ibn 'Īsa al-'Ijli also joined him. Later on General 'Abdallah ibn Ṭāhir came to his aid, but the valor of the Bābākiyya and the Ḳarmaṭians triumphed over the Muslim armies to such an extent that the latter erected for themselves the city known as Berzend[4] for fear of a night attack[5] by the Bābākiyya. The struggle between the two parties continued for many years until God granted victory to the Muslims over the Bābākiyya. Bābāk was taken prisoner and impaled in Surra-

[1] I have chosen the reading يداهن of Isf. B, f. 65 b, instead of the word مراهنا of Ed. and MS. which does not suit the context.

[2] It goes without saying that the wholesale accusation hurled against al-Afshīn, and, to a certain extent, perhaps even his heretical tendencies are chiefly the result of prejudice and have no historical foundation. All historians are unanimous in lavishing the highest praise on Afshīn's campaign against Bābāk. Even the charge made at the trial about an attempt to save the Khurrami from execution was directed against Afshīn's brother and not against the general himself. As for the suspicions about Afshīn's concealed sympathies with his former faith, it is probably true that they were based on fact. But it is equally clear that his fall came not on account of his religious views, but much more probably for "purely political reasons" (Browne, *Lit. Hist.* I, p. 334). See the full description of the trial in Tab. III, page 138, sqq. (trans. Browne, *l. c.*, pp. 331—36).

[3] On these leaders of war see above, 88.

[4] MS.: برزند; Ed.: بيرزند. Berzend is a city near Tiflīs where al-Afshīn made his encampment. It had been a deserted place prior to that. Yaḳūt, *s. v.* and IA, VI, 316.

[5] Reading بيات with *Mukhtaṣar*, 173 and apparently MS. See also Brockelmann, *Monde Oriental*, XIX (1925), 88. Ed. بيان.

man-ra'a in the year two hundred and twenty three. Then his brother Ishāk[1] was seized and crucified in Baghdād together with al-Māzyār[2], commander of the al-Muḥammira in Ṭabaristān and Jurjān. After Bābāk was killed the perfidy of al-Afshīn and his treacherous behavior towards the Muslims during his wars with 269
Bābāk became known to the Khalīf. He therefore ordered him executed and impaled, and he was duly crucified.

The historians tell that those who laid the foundation of the cult of the Bāṭiniyya were descendants of the Magians who were still attached to the religion of their ancestors, but did not dare to make a public avowal of it, dreading the Muslim swords. The ignorant among them used to appoint an Asās[3] who was entrusted by them with the teachings of their faith and who secretly preferred[4] the precepts of the Magians. They interpreted the verses of the Ḳur'ān and the traditions of the Prophet allegorically in accordance with their fundamentals.

The proof of this contention is that the Dualists maintain that Light and Darkness are pre-existent Makers, Light being the creator of the good and useful and Darkness the creator of the evil and harmful. Bodies are blended of Light and Darkness. Each of the two includes four humors, namely: heat, cold, moisture and dryness. The two primary sources together with the four humors regulate this world.

The Magians share with them the belief in two makers, but they maintain that one of the two Makers is pre-existent; he is God, the author of the Good. The other, Satan, a created being, is the author of Evil. Now, the spokesmen for the Bāṭiniyya state in their books that God created the Soul; God is, therefore, the First Cause and the Soul is the Second[5]. These two regulate this world.

---

[1] His brother's name was not Isḥāḳ but 'Abdallah. See a discussion of this above, 89, note 1.

[2] See above, 89.

[3] The Asās is a man whose task it is to instruct the members of his sect in the fundamentals of the sectarian beliefs. Although the term properly belongs to the beliefs of the Bāṭiniyya, Baghdādi has extended its meaning as in this case. On the Asās see below, 134. Perhaps the reading in *Mukhtasar*, 174, ought to be preferred: ووضعوا للأغمار.

[4] Reading تفضيل with *Mukhtasar, ib.* and Goldziher; Ed. تفصيل.

[5] Shahr.. 147-8 (Haarbr., 222) explains that both the intellect and the soul are God's creations, He Himself being transcendental. But see *Streitschrift*, 44 where Ghazāli speaks of

They call these two the First and the Second, but generally they name them 'Aḳl (Intellect) and Nafs (Soul)[1]. They declare, in addition, that these two regulate this world through the regulatory powers of the Seven Planets and the Primary matter[2]. [But[3] this is an acceptance of the teaching of the Dualists, that Light and Darkness govern the world by the emanation of the primary matter[4]]. Their view that the First and Second Causes regulate the world is exactly like the view of the Magians about attributing all created substances to[5] two Makers, one of whom is pre-
270 existent and the other generated[6]. Only the Bāṭiniyya designate the two Makers

---

السابق (*Universalintellekt*) and التالى (*Universalseele*) See also Guyard 185-6, 286, 295 note 13 etc. Cf. esp. the long note below.

[1] Ivanow, *Ismailitica*, 25 and note 6, recommends the translation "Living Powers" instead of our translation "Soul".

[2] The recurrence of the word اول below induces me to accept the reading of Ed. and MS. as the correct one (perhaps more probably الاول) and to translate it as primary matter, one of the five emanations of God. The seven planets may be interpreted as Space and the fifth emanation—Time—, which is ordinarily included, should be regarded as eliminated here, just as it is in the Salisbury Fragment (*JAOS*, II, 1849-50, pp. 299, 306). It is also possible, however, to read الاربع with *Mukhtasar*, 175 and Isf., f. 66 a, instead of الاول, rendering it "the four elements", and to consider all these as metaphorically employed for the primary matter from which they have developed. See, indeed, Guyard, *ib.* and Shahr, *ib.*

[3] The sentence in brackets is missing in Ed; MS.: وهذا تحقيق قول الثنوية ان النور والظلمة يدبران العالم بترتيب الطبائع الاول.

[4] Ivanow, *l. c.*, relates Baghdādi's exposition of the Bāṭinite belief in two makers to their belief in the Imām who is an incarnation of the Godhead. P. 11 note 37 and also p. 25.

[5] MS. الى; missing in Ed.

[6] It seems to me that Strothmann, after quoting this statement by Baghdādi, raises an unnecessary difficulty in attempting to solve the question as to who the two Makers could be (*EI* IV, p. 738, s. v. *Thanawīya*). Massignon, in the article *Ḳarmaṭian* (*EI*, II, p. 767 ff.), to which Strothmann refers, speaks of an *'Akl* and *Nafs*, both of which are begotten. But, as already pointed out above, Baghdādi, unlike Shahr., fails to make this distinction and calls the *'Akl* God and the *Nafs* His creation, although it always remains an open question whether the more elementry Baghdādi or the more philosophic Shahr. is nearer to the actual teaching of the sectarians. Of course, in order to make Baghdādi's statement sound more profound, it may be possible to identify the *'Akl* with the *nur sha'sha'ani* as Strothmann does (*ib.*), but we have no grounds for calling the *Nafs* with him the *nūr zulami*. Besides, Baghdādi's charge does not necessarily compel us to recognise a principle of light and darkness in the doctrine

as First and Second, whereas the Magians speak of them as Yazdān[1] and Ahramān.

This is the intrigue concealed[2] in the hearts of the Bāṭiniyya. They have appointed an Asās who is to initiate people into it. They could not practise the worship of Fire[3] openly, so they resorted to artifice by instructing the Muslims: It is proper that all Mosques be fumigated with incense and that an incense-burner be introduced into every mosque in which at least ambergris and aloe-wood be placed. The Barāmika made a suggestion to al-Rashīd in an enticing manner that he set an incense-burner in the interior of the Ka'ba in which aloe-wood should continually be burnt. Al-Rashīd realized that with this they aimed at the worship of fire in the Ka'ba, desiring that the Ka'ba become a fire-temple. This was one of the reasons for al-Rashīd's arrest of the Barāmika[4].

---

of the Bāṭiniyya, but merely two makers. However, it is interesting that Browne in following the idea of God as distinct from the 'Aḳl later comes across a difficulty in that "in the correspondence between the Grades of Being and the Isma'īli hierarchy there seems to be a lacuna, since God, the prime unknowable Essence, is represented by no class in the latter" *Lit. Hist.*, I, 409). Certainly, on the basis of Baghdādi's presentation the lacuna would not occur. See also Guyard, 185-6 where Baghdādi's standpoint is adequately explained. For, although the *'Akl* is really begotten, it, nevertheless, "Primitivement se confondait avec lui (God). Aussi peut on considérer la Raison Universelle comme la véritable Divinité des Ismaélis...", 186. Cf. also 293 note 10.

Curiously, an emanation of the *'Akl* from God is also reported in a tradition in Ghazāli, *Ihya'* and also above p. 100. See Goldziher, *ZA*, XXII (1908) p. 319-20.

[1] Yazdān is the name for Ahuramazda. Shahr., 181 (Haarbr., 275).

[2] The rendition of يدور as above is somewhat unusual; Bevan, in *Studies to E. G. Browne*, p. 66, cites a verse from the *Kitab al-Aghani* where the phrase دار لى occurs in the sense of "suggested itself to me".

[3] MS. نيران ; Ed. ثيران.

[4] The religious factor is nowhere put forth so definitely as by our author as a major cause of the fall (187 A. H.) of the Barmecids, a powerful Persian family that occupied a most important position in the government from the rise of the 'Abbasids on (they were already court favorites under the 'Omayyads, Bouvat, 36-7). On the contrary, owing to the lustre of their wealth and position (see, e. g., the life of Ja'far ibn Yaḥya al Barmaki in IKhall [tr. de Slane, I, 301—315], himself a descendent of the Barmecids [Bouvat, 9]), a Sunnite even as orthodox as Ṭabari is very obviously displeased with their assassination by the command of al-Rashīd (Ṭab. [Zotenberg] IV., Ch. 100; see also Bouvat, 94 ff.). However, there is no doubt that their religious views were not in conformity with Islam (Bouvat, 81 and 83, note 1). Their ancestor

After the Bāṭiniyya had interpreted the fundamentals of religion in polytheistic fashion[1], they also employed artifice in interpreting the precepts of the Law in such a manner as would entail the abolition of Muslim law or lead to the adoption of tenets similar to those of the Magians. What corroborates the fact that this was their intention in their allegorical exposition of the Law is that they allowed their adherents to marry daughters and sisters and they allowed wine-bibbing and all other sorts of dissipation. This is confirmed with even greater certainty by the fact that the fellow who appeared in their midst in the Baḥrein and in al-'Aḥsā' after[2] Sulaiman ibn al-Ḥasan[3] al-Ḳarmaṭi instituted the practice of sodomy among his followers and prescribed a death-sentence for the boy who refused to yield to one that wished to have sexual relations with him. He decreed that a man's hand be amputated if he extinguished a fire with it and that his tongue be cut out if he extinguished it with a puff. This youth is the one called ibn Abu
271 Zakaria al-Ṭammāmi[4] who appeared in the year three hundred and nineteen. His

---

Barmak's services in a Buddhist temple (mistaken by Arab authorities as Zoroastrian, e. g., *Bad'wal-Tarikh* VI, 102) is generally attested (*Muruj* VI, 414. See Barthold in *EI*. I, s. v. *Barmakides*, 691 and also *EI, ib*. 693). IA, VI, 119, who offers several explanations for the fall of the Barmecides does not mention their Zendikism. Tab., III, 572 and 669 reports a charge of heresy against the Barmecids, but by no means so explicit as that of our author, a parallel to which I have not been able to discover elsewhere. Their ruin is probably due primarily to the jealousy which the Khalīf conceived on account of the tremendous power which they gained in his day (Bouvat, 75 ff.). On the story of al-Rashīd's love for his sister 'Abbāsa and her marriage to Ja'far al-Barmaki in conformity with the Khalīf but with the express command not to live with him conjugally, said by many to be the cause of the family's fall, cf. Bouvat, 113 ff. He himself does not lend much credence to the story.

[1] MS. على معنى; معنى missing in Ed.

[2] The chronology here is wrong, although it is in accordance with our author's view that Sulaimān was killed in 318 A. H., see below, 126 and note 9. The accepted view is that he died in 332, de Goeje, 142. Indeed, according to accounts reported *l. c.*, 130 and 132, it was Abu Ṭāhir Sulaimān who was misled by him first. Massignon, *EI*, II, p. 769 also says of ibn Abu Zakaria that he was "enthroned by Abu Ṭāhir". On Sulaimān son of Abu Sa'īd al-Jannābi see below p. 120 ff.

[3] With MS., Ed. Ḥusain.

[4] With MS., Ed. الطامى. The depravities of ibn Abu Zakaria or Abu-'l-Faḍl al-Zakari al-Ṭammāmi as he is called by Massignon who characterizes him (*EI, ib*) as "a madman", "a

uprising lasted until God granted mastery over him to the person who slew him in bed[1]. What confirms even more positively all that we have asserted regarding the inclination of the Bāṭiniyya to the religion of the Magians is that we cannot discover on the face of the earth any Magian who does not sympathize with them, and does not hope for their conquest of the country, believing that the government will thereby be restored to them. The ignorant among them generally adduce proof for this belief from what the Magians tell in the name of Zaradusht, who predicted to Kushtāshp[2] that the rule would pass from the Persians to the Romans and Greeks; then it would be restored to Persia. Afterwards it would pass from the Persians to the Arabs and would finally be restored to Persia. Jāmāsp[3], the astrologer, sustained him in this prediction, holding that the kingdom would return to the Persians upon the completion of one thousand five hundred years from the time of the appearance of Zārādusht[4]. Among the Bāṭiniyya there lived a man called Abu 'Abdallāh al-'Aradi[5] who boasted a knowledge of astronomy[6] and was

kind of Heliogabulus" are reported in virtually the same words by Albirūni in his *Chronology* (Tr. Sachau), 196 who also adds that "he called upon people to recognise him as lord, and they followed him". De Goeje also cites other reports, 129 (His attempt to connect other accounts of a false Mahdi with this strange individual is rejected by himself in his article in *JA*, 1895, 27.). Cf. Mas'ūdi, *Tanbih* (tr. de Vaux), 497.

[1] He was slain by order of Abu Ṭāhir, see Albirūni, ib., and de Goeje who quotes him, 131, and gives a fuller account, 132-3. His uprising endured for eighty days, (*ib.*).

[2] With MS., Ed. كشتاسب. I. e Vishtaspa, a Persian "king or princely ruler" who was the first convert to Zoroaster's faith in, what is generally agreed upon, the city of Balkh. See A. V. W. Jackson, *Zoroaster* Ch. 5, 56—68.

[3] Jāmāsp, said to be a son-in-law of Zoroaster (Jackson, *l. c.*, 21), was a counsellor to the king and an ardent disciple of the Prophet, *ib.*, 76.

[4] According to Albirūni, *l. c.*, 196, the end of the period as predicted by Jāmāsp fell in 1242, Seleucid Era (930-31).

[5] Albirūni, *ib.*, calls him al-'Adi. He is followed by Casanova, in *JA*, 1915, 10. Sachau's conjecture that he is to be identified with *Abu 'Abdallah al-dā'i* can hardly be maintained in view of the reading in our text. Sam'āni lists both *nisbas*, but it is noteworthy that 'Adi is definitely Persian as can be judged by the several proper names in the article under this heading and the city of Nasaf (Nakhsheb) cited there.

[6] For the important role which astronomy and astrology play in Mohammedan life as well as for the interpretation of the conjunctions, cf. de Goeje, 117—122. See also the very important discussion by Casanova, *l. c.*, 8 ff.

a fanatical Magian. He has written a work in which he states that the eighteenth conjunction[1] after the birth of Muḥammad corresponds with the tenth millenium[2], which is also the period of the return of Jupiter[3] and Sagittarius. He says[4]: Simultaneously with that phenomenon a man will arise who will restore the Magian regime and will gain control over the entire land. He believes that that man will reign for a period of seven conjunctions[5]. They say; the truth of the prediction of Zārādusht and Jāmāsp has been demonstrated by the transfer of the kingdom of the Persians to the Romans and Greeks in the days of Alexander; then it returned to the Persians at the expiration of three hundred years[6]. Afterwards the rule of the Persians was again transferred to the Arabs, but it will certainly revert to the Persians at the end of the epoch which Jāmāsp forecast. The time which they set coincided with the reigns of al-Muktafi and al-Muktadir[7], but the event foretold by
272 them failed of realization and the government did not then come back to the Magians.

The Ḳarmaṭians had before this fixed date agreed among other things that the expected Mahdi would come forth in the seventh conjunction in the fiery trigon[8]. Sulaimān ibn al-Ḥasan from al-'Aḥsā'[9] came forth[10] relying on this as-

---

[1] The eighteenth conjunction (the sixth in the fiery trigon) came in the year 298-9, A. H. Casanova *l. c.*, 10.

[2] The tenth Millenium is doubtless an echo of the Persian belief in the world-ages, see *ERE*, v. 376. Albīrūni's statement disagrees to some extent with that in *ERE*. See Albīrūni, 17 and esp. the section on the chronology of the Persians, 107 ff.

[3] Acc. to Albīrūni, 197, the reading should be *Saturn*.

[4] See this passage almost verbatim, though a little more fully *ib.*, 197 (cited by Casanova *l. c.*, 10).

[5] Albīrūni reads seven and a half *ib.*, line 8.

[6] The Persian Empire fell in 312 B. C. at the hands of the Seleucids, and was restored by the Sassānids in 226 A. D. so that 538 and not 300 years passed. See Huart, *Ancient Persia*, 219 ff. Albīrūni, 121, also arrives at the same results, but he adds on line 31 that most authorities believe it to have been an epoch of some 300 years.

[7] Al-Muktafi reigned 289—295, and al-Muktadir 295—320 A. H.

[8] See Casanova, *l. c.*, 10 at the bottom. Brockelmann who changes نارية to ثانية (*Monde Oriental*, XIX [1925] 198), and translates it "im zweiten Drittel", has misunderstood the passage.

[9] With Goldziher and *Mukhtasar* 177 against Ed. and MS. which read الاحياء.

[10] Abu-Ṭāhir probably became chief of the Ḳarmatians in 310 or 311 A. H. See a full account of his activity in de Goeje, 75—142.

sumption, and he attacked the pilgrims to Mecca and he slew them nefariously. Later he entered Mecca, killed all those who were performing the circuit (Ṭawāf), seized the veils of the Ka'ba, and cast the slain into the Zemzem well. He crushed many Muslim armies, but in one of his battles he was forced to flee to Hajar[1]. He then addressed a poem (Ḳaṣīda)[2] to the Muslims in which he declared:

If my retreat to Hajar has deceived you regarding me,
Then[3] shortly news will indeed reach you.
When Mars rises over the land of Babylon[4],
And the two stars[5] will be in conjunction with him, then beware, beware!
Am I not the one mentioned in all the Scriptures?
Am I not the one announced in the Sūra of the Companies[6]?
Verily, I shall rule over the people of the earth East and West.
As far as Ḳairuān of the Greeks, Turkey and the Khazars.

By the two stars he meant Saturn and Jupiter[7]. This conjunction took place during the years of his activity, yet he did not hold sway over any part of the
world save the town from which he hailed. He coveted a reign lasting for a 273
period of seven conjunctions, but he did not reign seven years, for, indeed, he was killed in Hīt[8] when from her roof a woman hurled a brick on his head

[1] The capital of Baḥrain, which province is also often called Hajar. See below, 123 and de Goeje, 36 ff. and 43 ff.

[2] The verses below constitute only a part of the poem. *Nujum*, II, 239 contains a longer version, although it lacks our third couplet. But even there we do not obtain the complete text as is apparent from the word ومنها, which interrupts the sequence of the quotation twice. De Goeje in his translation combines the stanzas of both Nujūm and Albirūni.

[3] MS. فعما; Ed. فما.

[4] Both de Goeje's translation, 114, and Sachau's, 197, are based on a reading in Albirūni which I do not have before me. Judging from note 1. de Goeje, *ib.*, Albirūni's variant reads like Ed., but is declared by the Dutch scholar to be "absolument fausse". Instead he renders it "Et que son influence ne sera pas affaiblie par celle des deux astres". See his argument against our reading on p. 123.

[5] MS. النجمان; Ed. النجمات.

[6] Sūra 39. De Goeje conjectures that the allusion may be to v. 38. 114.

[7] A conjunction of these two planets is especially disastrous for the 'Abbāsids, since it announces the victory of the Ḳarmaṭians. De Goeje, 123.

[8] A town near Baghdād, Yaḳut, IV, *s.v.* See below, 126 and note 8. Hīt was stormed in 315 A.H.

and brained him. A man slain by a woman is the most contemptible among the slain and the most despicable among those lost. At the end of the year one thousand two hundred and forty of the Alexandrian Era, one thousand five hundred years had elapsed since the age of Zarādusht[1]. Yet in that year the domination of the world was not restored to the Mag'ans. On the contrary, the belt of Islam was extended over the earth after that year, and God conquered for the Muslims the land of Belāsāghūn[2] and the land of Tibet[3] and most of the provinces of China. Then He further conquered for them all of the land of India, from Lamghān[4] to Kannawj[5]. The land of India down to Tatar(?)[6] by its seashore all became part of the expanse of Islam in the days of Yamīn[7]-al-Dawla Amīn-al-Milla Maḥmūd ibn Subuktekin[8]. This sums up the aspirations of the chiefs of the Bāṭiniyya, and

---

[1] The same fact is indicated by Albirūni, 196-7, though he places the completion of the 1500 years in 1242 Alexandrian Era and relates it to the death of Abu Zakaria.

[2] More correctly Balsaghūn (see Yaḳūt, I, 708 and de Goeje, *Bibl. Geogr.* index Vols. 1—3, *s. v.*). It is in Central Asia (its location cannot be defined exactly, see Barthold, *EI.*, I, 614). The latter, *l. c.*, 615, does not fix a definite date for its conquest, but in c. 340 A. H. a Mohammedan prince occupied its throne. In the 10th and 11th centuries of the Christian Era it served as the capital of the Khans of Turkestan. Arnold, *Preaching of Islam*², 216, note 2.

[3] With Goldziher and probably MS. Ed. اتبب.

[4] With MS.; a city in the Ghazna district, Yaḳūt, IV, 343. Lamghān was captured by his father Subuktekin in 366 A. H., IA. VII, 505. Ed. reads: لمغات.

[5] With Ms. and Goldziher. A large town in Central India, west of the Ganges River. Albirūni, (India, tr. Sachau, 199) speaks of it as being mostly in ruins, but possessing an illustrious history during the period when the capital was situated there. On the other hand, Istakhri, 9, and ibn Ḥauḳal, 16, declare it to be still the capital city. Muḳaddasi, 480, also describes it as a thriving town and summer resort. The conquest of India, resembling, to a large extent, the perilous expedition of Alexander the Great is narrated in Utbi, *Kitab-i-Yamini,* (tr. Reynolds), 449—62.

[6] See Goldziher's note *ad loc.* His reference to Yaḳūt is unfortunately misprinted. Ed: سيتر سيقا.

[7] With MS. Ed. امين. In accordance with a custom instituted since the appearance of the Buwaihid Dynasty, Maḥmūd received these honorific titles from the Khalīf al-Ḳādir in 999 A. D. (Yamīn al-Dawla was bestowed on him later). *EI,* iii, 133.

[8] With MS. Mahmūd of Ghazna's career and deeds as well as his court are well portrayed in Müller, *Der Islam im Morgen-und Abendlande,* Vol. II, 48—70. A very

of the Magians who believe that Jāmāsp predicted the restoration of that kingdom to them. But they suffered the evils of their enterprise, and the outcome of their desires brought extinction upon them with the glory of God and His providence.

Then 'Ubaidallah ibn al-Ḥasan arose among the Bāṭiniyya in the province of Ḳairuān and beguiled a group among the Kutama, and a number of people among the Maṣāmida, and masses of dull-heads[1] among the Berbers, with magic[2] and necromancy by which he, concealed under an upper and lower garments, conjured up apparitions of images before them at night. The ignorant thought that they were miracles performed by him. In consequence of this they followed him in his heresy and he gained mastery over them in the land of Maghreb[3]. Then the one called Abu Sa'īd al-Ḥusain ibn Bahram issued from their midst against the inhabitants of al-Aḥsā' and al-Ḳaṭīf and Mesopotamia. He led an attack by his
followers against his enemies, took their women and children captive, and burnt 274
copies of the Ḳur'ān as well as mosques. Then he captured Hajar, killed its men and enslaved their children and women. Then the one known as al-Ṣanādīḳi[4] appeared in al-Yaman and slew many inhabitants, killing even children and women. Another one, ibn al-Faḍl[5] by name, joined him together with his followers but God

---

detailed biography of him will be found in Utbi, *l. c.*, his official biographer. See also the article in *EI*, iii, 132—35.

[1] With MS. اغتام here and passim where Ed. reads اغنام. Goldziher has pointed out that this word has no sectarian sting, being applied to Sunnites as well. *ZDMG*, xxxvi (1882), 281—2.

[2] Reading بحيل with MS: Ed. بجبل. This accusation has been hurled against the entire family of Maimūn, from whom 'Ubaidallah is believed to be descended. IA. VIII, 21.

[3] See above, 112.

[4] Under the year 207 A. H., *Nujūm*, I, 595, mentions Ṣanādīḳi who appeared in Yemen, led people astray from Islam and finally perished in a plague, but he says nothing about his affiliations with the Ḳarmaṭians. In the light of this information it will be surprising that our author passes in silence over the man who figured most prominently in the Ḳarmaṭian movement in Yemen — Abu-l-Ḳāsim al-Ḥasan ibn Faraj ibn Ḥawshab ibn Zādān Al-Manṣūr. However, van Arendonk, *Opkomst van het zaiditische Imamat in Yemen*, 110, n. 8, reports that al-Manṣūr is called al-Ṣanādīḳi by several authorities, and terms *Nujūm's* statement an anachronism. See a short account of al-Ṣanādīḳī's activities in Maḳrīzi's *Itti'āz al-ḥunafā' bi-Akhbār al-A'imma al-Khulafā'* (ed. Bunz), 113—4.

[5] Tab. III., p. 2256, relates a victory over the defenders of Ṣan'a by a missionary whom marginal glosses in two MSS. name على ابن الفضل. According to Janadi's story of the

turned them and their followers over to the destructive power of gangrene and the bubonic plague, and they died[1]. Then there came forth in Syria a grandchild of Maimūn ibn Đaiṣān, called Abu-l-Ḳāsim ibn Mihrwaih[2], and these two[3] said to whomever followed them: This is the time appointed for our rule. This occurred in the year two hundred and eighty nine. Subuk[4], al-Mu'taḍid's general, set out against them. They slew Subuk in the field of battle, entered the city of al-Ruṣāfa[5] and burnt its general mosque[6]. Afterwards they directed their course to Damascus. Al-Ḥamāmi[7], a slave of ibn Ṭūlūn[8] faced them aud drove them to Raḳḳa[9]. Then Muḥammad ibn Sulaimān, the secretary of al-Muktafi, sallied forth against them with one of al-Muktafi's armies[10] and routed them and killed thousands of them. Al-Ḥusain[11] ibn Zikrwaih ibn Mihrwaih was forced to flee to al-Ramlah[12], but the

---

Ḳarmaṭians in Yemen as told in Kay, *Omarah, Hist. of Yaman,* 191—212, 'Ali ibn Faḍl, an associate of al-Manṣūr, was a depraved individual who, after becoming powerful, renounced his allegiance to the Mahdi and was finally poisoned by a doctor in 303 A. H. In a recent work on the history of Yemen by 'Abd-al-Waṣi' ibn Yaḥya al-Yamani, ibn-Faḍl is said to have proclaimed himself a prophet and to have abrogated the law. IA who tells his story VIII, 22, calls him Muḥammad.

[1] Maḳrīzi, *op. cit., ib.*

[2] This Abu-l-Ḳāsim ibn Mihrwaih is Yahya ibn Zikrwaih (Ṭab. III, 2218 and IA, VII, 353) whose genealogy Nowairi traces to al-Ḳaddāḥ (de Goeje, 60).

[3] The two spoken of in this passage are probably Yaḥya and his brother Ḥusain. IA, VII, 362 sqq.

[4] Ṭab. III, 2219, reads سبك الديلمى; IA, VII, 353 reads شبل although he cites several MSS. with the reading سبك.

[5] A city in Syria near Raḳḳa, built as a summer home by the 'Omayyads, but some believe that it is pre-Islamic. Yaḳūt II, 784.

[6] Ṭab., ib.; IA, *ib.* For the history of this uprising see de Goeje, 47—50.

[7] Badr al-Ḥamāmi was one of the generals of the Egyptian Army which was sent to reinforce Ṭughj ibn Juff, governor of Damascus. IA, VII, 362. Ṭab. III, 2219 calls him Badr al-Ḳahīr.

[8] He was the slave of Abu Mūsa Hārūn ibn Khumārawaih, died 292 A. H. Zambaur, 93. Ms. reads طيلون; Ed. طيون.

[9] A town on the Euphrates, three days from Ḥarrān, Yaḳūt, II, 802.

[10] 291 A. H., Ṭab. III, 2137 sqq.

[11] MS. and Ed: الحسن بن زكريا. He was known as "the fellow with the Mole" صاحب الشامة. Ṭab. iii, 2224, passim.

[12] Al-Ḥusain was captured not at Ramlah but in Dāliah, a town not far from Kūfa,

governor of al-Ramlah seized him and conveyed him together with a troop of his followers[1] to al-Muktafi. He executed them in Baghdād on the highway after torturing them severely[2]. With their death, the power of the Ḳarmatians was broken down until the year three hundred and ten. Afterwards the uprising of Sulaimān ibn al-Ḥasan[3] took place in the year three hundred and eleven. It was then that he captured al-Baṣra[4], killed its chief Subuk al-Muflihi[5] and carried off its booty into Mesopotamia. In the year three hundred and twelve, on the tenth day before the end of the month of al-Muḥarram, he attacked the pilgrim caravan at al-Habīr[6], slew most of the pilgrims, and led their wives and children in captivity. He next 275
entered Kūfa[7] in the year three hundred and thirteen, put its inhabitants to death, and pillaged their possessions.

In the year three hundred and fifteen he fought with ibn Abu Sāj[8], took him prisoner, and routed his men. In the year three hundred and seventeen, he entered

---

whither he had hoped to escape unnoticed But the prefect of the town recognized him and delivered him to the Khalīf in Raḳḳa. See Ṭab. III, 2237—46 and IA, VII, 366—7.

[1] Acc. to Ṭab, Ḳarmaṭians resident in Baghdād were also included in this *auto-da-fe*. Altogether their number amounted to 320 odd, or 360. 2245.

[2] The cruel manner in which they were executed is described fully Tab., *ib.*; IA, *ib.*

[3] For a detailed story of Abu Ṭāhir Sulaimān ibn Abu Sa'īd al-Ḥasan ibn Bahrām al-Jannābi, see de Goeje, 73—143.

[4] De Goeje, 79.

[5] A freedman of Mufliḥ (a favorite of Muḳtadir, cf. ibn Miskawaihi, *Eclipse of the Abbasids*, index, *s. v.*) and governor of al-Baṣra. The incident of his death is described *l. c.*, I, 105 and IV, (Engl. transl. 116—17.). The correct pronounciation of the governor's name is not established. Carra de Vaux in his translation of Mas'ūdi's *Tanbīh*, reads Soubk (the original has no vowel). Similarly the father of Maḥmūd of Ghazna is called Subuktekin. (see Barthold's article on Maḥmūd, *EI*, III, *s. v.*).

[6] With Goldziher and probably MS. Ed. الهبير. Cf. de Goeje, 84—86.

[7] De Goeje, 86.

[8] Abu-l-Ḳasim Yūsuf ibn Diwdād ibn abi Sāj, born about 250 A. H., was called by the vizier al-Khasībi to conduct the war against Abu Ṭāhir. He had been governor of Azerbaijan. For his early relations with the Abbāsids see Harold Bowen, *'Ali ibn 'Isa*, 154—156. His general attitude and his more than suspicious behavior in preparation for the war with Abu Ṭāhir are described by de Goeje, 88—95, esp. 91 ff. (cf. Bowen, *l. c.*, 263). See also Maḳrīzi (Fagnan), 82, on the homage paid by him to 'Ubaidallah. He was killed by the Ḳarmaṭian leader in 315 A. H. See Zambaur, 179, note 3.

Mecca and smote whomever he found performing the Ṭawāf[1]. It is reported that he put three thousand to death, led away seven hundred maidens, abducted the Black Stone and carried it to al-Baḥrain[2]. It was returned thence[3] to Kūfa and later sent back from al-Kūfa to Mecca with Abu Isḥāḳ Ibrahīm ibn Muḥammad ibn Yaḥya al-Muzakki [the sheikh[4] of] Nīshāpūr[5] in the year three hundred and twenty nine[6]. Sulaimān ibn al-Ḥasan marched against Baghdād in the year three hundred and eighteen[7], but when he reached Hīt[8] a woman hurled a brick at him from her roof and killed him[9]. Then the power of the Ḳarmatians was

---

[1] See the detailed report about the ravaging of Mecca in de Goeje, 100—111. It goes without saying that the event aroused hot blood in all the Arab historians, very obviously manifested in their accounts of it which abound in maledictions and bristle with passionate hatred.

[2] The abduction of the Black Stone aroused the anger of even the Fāṭimids. But de Goeje, 83, argues with good reason that it was only feigned anger, and that, in all probability the act was perpetrated in the first place by order of the Fāṭimid ruler.

[3] MS. رد منها; Ed. ردوها.

[4] This phrase is supplied from Sam'āni, f. 526 b.

[5] A well known Rawi, died 362 A. H. *Nujum*, II, 439; Yaḳūt I, 465. See esp. Sam'āni f. 526 a—b. None of the authorities consulted mentions this traditionist in connection with the restoration of the Black Stone to Mecca, all of them attributing it to Sanbar (e. g. de Goeje, 145). He may perhaps have been merely an adviser in the matter. At any rate we can hardly reject the statement of Baghdādi who was born shortly after that event.

[6] According to de Goeje, 145, and other sources, this event took place in 339, by order of the Fāṭimid Khalīf al-Manṣūr. On page 146, note 1, he quotes Hamza Ispahāni in support of our author's date, but rejects that statement.

[7] Bagdad was threatened by him in 315 A. H. before his pillage of Mecca. Mas'ūdi *Tanbīh* (tr. de Vaux), 469, de Goeje 97, Bowen, 268 ff. The attack on Hīt also occurred in 315. Miskawaih, IV, 198 ff., Mas'ūdi, *l. c.*, 490. The confusion in our book may be due to the second capture of Kūfa in 319, (de Goeje, 113), since it was the capture of Kūfa which in 315 had preceded his threat to Bagdad.

[8] From this statement one would be inclined to believe that he never reached Bagdad having been killed at Hīt before that. As a matter of fact he made his attack on Hīt after Bagdad. (see note above).

[9] The grounds for this unsubstantiated story of Abu Tāhir's death which really happened in 332 is the defeat suffered by him at Hīt, as related by Mas'ūdi, who was an eye-witness, *l. c.*, 488.

broken. Following the death of Sulaimān ibn-al-Ḥasan, they extorted money from the pilgrims travelling to Mecca from al-Kūfa and al-Baṣra[1] by collecting escorts' fee[2] and guaranteed tribute[3], until al-Aṣfar al-'Uḳaili[4] captured one of their towns.

The control of Egypt and its affairs had fallen into the hands of the Ikhshīdiyya[5]. Some of them joined the son of 'Ubaidallah al-Bāṭini[6] who already held sway over Ḳairuān and penetrated into Egypt in the year three hundred and sixty three[7]. They built there a city which they named Cairo[8], and which the adherents to his heresy inhabit. But the population of Egypt clings firmly to the orthodox faith unto the present day[9], although they demomonstrate their loyalty to the governor of Cairo by remitting to him the tax levied upon them.

---

[1] This refers to the treaty which the Ḳarmaṭians concluded with the 'Abbāsids in 327 A. H. the terms of which guaranteed to them a fixed tribute and toll fee for escorting the pilgrims. De Goeje, 140 ff.

[2] With MS. بخفارة . Ed. لخطاة.

[3] Arabic مال مضمون ;

[4] With MS; Ed. الاصغر. See on him de Sacy, Introd. 223, de Goeje, 193, IA, IX, 40. Cf. also Kay's remarks on the 'Uḳaili tribute in *JRAS*, 1886, pp. 504—05. He was prompted by selfish motives in his defeat of the Ḳarmaṭians and not by piety, for he himself now collected the tribute which had previously fallen into the pockets of the heretics, (and let it be remembered that the Banu 'Uḳail had themselves been adherents of the Ḳarmaṭian heresy). Indeed, IA, IX, 221, in recording his death, characterizes him as the one الذي كان يودي الحاج في طريقهم (who used to heavily tax the pilgrims on their journeys). The town he conquered was al-Ḳaṭīf.

[5] Ed., MS. الخشادية. A family which ruled Egypt (nominally in the name of the 'Abbāsid Khalīfs) from 323 to 338 A. H. Ikhshīd is a title and goes back to Farghāna in Persia where their forefathers were said to have been rulers (EI, II, 458). See also Lane-Poole, *Hist. of Egypt*, 101—2.

[6] The son, or rather, the grandson of 'Ubaidallah is Abu Tamīm Ma'add al-Mu'izz, fourth Fāṭimid Khalīf, who ruled 341 to 365 A. H. See Wüstenfeld, *l. c.* (1881) 3—37.

[7] Egypt was conquered by the Fāṭimids in 358 A. H. Wüstenfeld, *l. c.* 7—13; IA, VIII, 435. The date in our text probably refers to Mu'izz's arrival in Egypt in 362. IA, 457, *Nujum*, II, 436.

[8] See on the name Maḳrīzi, I, 377. The building of the city was commenced in 356 and completed in 363. It was named after Mars which was then in the ascendant and called قاهر الفلك. See also Lane-Poole, *l. c.*, 103.

[9] This fact, besides demonstrating the steadfastness of the Sunnites during that period, testifies equally to the spirit of tolerance which generally distinguished the Fāṭimids. See Gold-

Abu Shujā' Fanākhusraw[1] ibn Buweih had made preparations to march[2]
276 against Egypt and wrench[3] it from the hand of the Bāṭiniyya[4]. He enjoined his chiefs in al-Sawād in writing: In the name of Allah the Merciful, the Compassionate. Praised be Allah, Lord of the universe and may the Lord pray for Muḥammad, Seal of the Prophets, Obedient to God, Prince of the Faithful. Enter Egypt safely, God Willing. He then composed a Ḳaṣīda, the beginning of which is:

Do you not see the fates obeying me
And clearly communicating to me as though it were ascertained information?
And mankind bears witness to me that I am
The one who is hoped for, and the one who is expected
To aid Islam, and the summoner to
The Khalīf of Allah, the Glorious Imām[5].

---

ziher, *Streitschrift (Introd)*, 7 and note 4: *Fihrist*, 189; and Gottheil, *ZA*, XXVI (1911), 203.

[1] Generally called 'Aḍud-al-Dawla (the support of the government), a title conferred on him in 351 A. H. by the nominal ruler, the Khalīf Muṭī' in accordance with a custom introduced at the time of the capture of Bagdad by the Buwaihis in 334 A. H. Fanākhusrau ruled over 'Irāḳ and almost the entire extent of Asiatic Islām from 367 to 373 A. H., and, before that, since 335 over other parts of the Persian Empire. Müller, *l. c.* ii, 43 ff.

[2] MS. wrongly. لقصة or لفضة; Ed; لقصد.

[3] MS. wrongly, والتزعاها; Ed: وانتزاعها.

[4] The only reference I find to this planned attack is Wüstenfeld, *Fatimiden*, (1881), 47—48, who relates that 'Aḍud-al-Dawla must have been angered by the theft of a lion from the entrance to his palace, perpetrated by order of the Fatimid al-'Azīz, but he "war indess damals schon zu kränklich... als er sich ernstlich darum hätte bekümmern können" (45). Perhaps the story finds its origin in 'Aḍud-al-Dawla's demand of al-'Azīz that he produce his genealogy in order to confirm his claim of relationship to Muḥammad ibn Isma'īl. Still another conjecture is that our author developed this tale on the basis of an encounter between the Turkish general, al-Aftakin and al-'Azīz in 365 A. H. during which the general was urged by the Fāṭimid Khalīf to recognize his sovereignty (IA, VIII, 483—87). Ikhall, II, 483, adds that Aftakin turned to the Buwaihid ruler for help. Cf. Wüstenfeld, *l. c.*, 40—46.

[5] In view of the fact that the Buwaihids were of Shī'ite confession, it is likely that the allusion is to the twelfth Imām, particularly since the Sunnite Khalīf would hardly be called *al-Imām al-muftakhar*. This in no way conflicts with Fanākhusraw's allegiance to the 'Abbāsids. Nor should we wonder at the readiness with which Baghdādi cites the sectarian poem. We have already seen that he utilizes Imamite sources. See above, 102 n. 1. Indeed, the entire story of the campaign may be of Imāmite origin.

When his warriors went forth with the purpose of proceeding to Egypt, death claimed him and he went the way of all flesh. After Fanākhusraw departed this life, the chief of Egypt cast a covetous glance upon the kingdoms of the Eastern provinces. He communicated with them, exhorting them to pledge allegiance to him. Ḳabūs [1] ibn Washmkīr made the following reply to his letter: I shall not mention you save in repose. Nāṣir al-Dawla abu-l-Ḥasan Muḥammad ibn Ibrahīm ibn Sīmjūr [2] gave his answer by writing on the back of his letter to him: O, you infidels! I shall not worship that which you worship [3], down to the end of the Sura. Nūḥ [4] ibn Manṣūr, governor of Ḳhurāsān, answered by killing the missionaries of his heresy. One of the rulers of al-Jurjān in the land of Khwarezm responded to his call. His conversion to his religion became for him a cause of adversity in that his kingdom vanished and his men were annihilated [5]. Later Yamīn al-Dawla and Amīn al-Milla Maḥmūd ibn Subuktekin became master of their land and killed all of the Bāṭinite propagandists who were active there. Abu 'Ali ibn Sīmjūr [6] sympathized secretly with their views, so he attempted rebellion [7], but his efforts in this undertaking miscarried. Nūḥ ibn Manṣūr,

---

[1] With the surname Shams-al-Ma'āli, of the Ziarid dynasty; ruled over Jurjān and Ṭabaristān from 366 to 403 A. H., except for a period of 17 years (371—388) on account of a revolution during which his son reigned in his place. Ikhall, II, pp. 507—10; Ibn Isfandiyar, *Hist. of Tabaristān*, (tr. Browne), 225—233. Yaḳūt who gives a full biography of him in *Irshād*, VI, 6, 143—152, mentions nothing about his correspondence with the Fāṭimids Ed. has وشمكين as his father's name. Ms. correctly وشمكير.

[2] Commander of the armies in Khurāsān; removed in 371, (IA, IX, 7), but reinstated in 372, *ib*, 17—18.

[3] Sura 109, vv. 1—2.

[4] Surnamed al-Riḍa; one of the Samanid rulers, 366—387 A. H.

[5] I have not been able to discover whom our author refers to. It may possibly be one of the Ziarid rulers who held sway over Jurjān, although they were nominally dependent on the Samanids and later the Ghaznavids, Hartmann, *EI*, I, 1065. Or perhaps it is one of the rebels whom Ḳābūs finally crushed.

[6] The full account of Abu 'Ali's activity and struggle with Nūḥ are recorded in 'Utbi, *l. c.*, pp. 108—178. Also Ḳazwīni, *Tarikh Guzida* (tr. Gantin) I, 43—53.

[7] None of the sources dealing with the rebellion of Abu 'Ali mentions his Bāṭinite sympathies. But it should be remembered that Baghdādi, who lived in Nīshāpūr, Nūḥ's center

277 governor of Khurāsān, seized him and sent him to Subuktekin; he was executed in the province of Ghazna [1].

Abu-l-Ḳāsim al-Ḥasan ibn 'Ali [2], surnamed Dazsamand [3], became the missionary of the Bāṭiniyya doctrine by appointment of Abu 'Ali ibn Sīmjūr, but Baktūzūn [4], commander of a Samanid army, overcame him in Nīshāpūr and killed him [5]. He was buried in an unknown place. Amīrak al-Ṭūsi, governor of the district Tharwaih [6] had joined the mission of the Bāṭiniyya. He was taken captive, carried to Ghazna and killed there on the same night as Abu 'Ali ibn Sīmjūr [7]. The inhabitants of Multān in the land of India, had enrolled in the movement of the Bāṭiniyya. Maḥmūd set out against them with his army, killed thousands of them [8], and chopped off the arms of thousands of them. Thus the successes [9] of the Bāṭiniyya vanished from their midst. In this we find clear proof of the ill-fortune which the rite of the Bāṭiniyya brings upon its imitators; let those who will take heed.

The theologians differ in their opinions regarding the ultimate aim sought by the Bāṭiniyya in the missionary activity in behalf of their heresy. Most of them lean to the view that the object of the Bāṭiniyya was to convert [the Muslims] to the religion of the Magians with the aid of the method of allegorization

of activities, for a number of years, may have collected some unrecorded data which circulated among the inhabitants of that city.

[1] According to Ḳazwīni, *l. c.*, 53, and 'Utbi, *l. c.*, Abu 'Ali was killed by order of Nūḥ, either while being sent to his protector, al-Ma'mun (Ḳazwīni) or in prison ('Utbi). IA, however, agrees with Baghdādi's report, except that according to him he died in prison instead of being executed. IX, 76.

[2] The brother of Abu 'Ali who took up the latter's efforts after his death. For his history see 'Utbi, l. c. 189—95, 218—24. His fall came in 388 A. H.

[3] Casanova's correction; Ed. and MS. دالشمند.

[4] Ed. بكفوزن MS. بكتوزن. He was the general of the army under Manṣūr, successor to Nūḥ. 'Utbi, *l. c.*, 206, calls him Lord Chamberlain. Cf. IA, IX, 91.

[5] According to Ḳazwīni, *Tarikh Guzida* (tr. Gantin) I, 59—61, he met his final defeat at the hands of Naṣr ibn Subuktekin, Maḥmūd's brother.

[6] I have not been able to identify this name.

[7] 'Utbi, *l. c.*, 196.

[8] *Ib.*, 326—329.

[9] With MS. غضراء; Ed. نصراء.

›y which they interpret the Ḳur'ān and the Sunna. In proof of this they cite he charge that their founder Maimūn ibn Daiṣān was a Magian taken captive (?) t al-Ahwāz. His son, 'Abdallah ibn Maimūn[1] invited people to adhere to the eligion of his father. They find further support in the fact that their missionary, l-Bazdahi[2] by name, states in his book entitled *al-Maḥsūl* (Sum and Substance) hat the first Author originated the Soul *(al-Nafs)*. Since then the First and Second regulate the world by regulating the seven stars and the four elements[3]. 278
This indeed is the essence of the teachings of the Magians, that al-Yazdān reated Ahriman, and that He together with Ahriman manage the universe, except hat al-Yazdān is the author of good deeds and Ahriman the author of evil. Others have linked the Bāṭiniyya to the Ṣābians who live in Ḥarrān. They also find confirmation of their view in this, that the Ṣābians keep their doctrines secret[4], nd reveal them only to their adherents. Like them, the Bāṭiniyya do not reveal heir doctrines save to one who becomes one of them after they administer[5] an oath to him that he will not relate their mysteries to any one outside their group.

'Abd-al-Ḳāhir says: The most plausible explanation to my mind is that hey are Zendik Materialists who profess a belief in the eternity of the universe, nd disacknowledge the apostles and all the precepts of the Law, because they re disposed to permit everything to which one's natural desires incline[6]. Proof hat they are as we have described them will be forthcoming from what I have read in an Epistle of theirs entitled: *Conduct, the Most Exalted[7] Communica-*

---

[1] With the exception of a historically correct statement Ed. 16, (Seelye, 35), this is the only time that our author mentions 'Abdallah, the man who played a far greater role in the organization of the Bāṭiniyya than his frequently cited father. In *Usul*, 329, he gives the same nformation as in the citations above.

[2] Abu 'Abdallah Muḥammad ibn Aḥmad al-Nasafi mentioned above, 113, and called there Bandāna. Massignon, *Bibliogr. Qarmate*, 332, calls him Baradha'i making him a native of Baradha'a, a town on the borders of Azerbaijan (Yaḳūt, *s. v.*).

[3] See above, 115-7, and notes.

[4] Chwolson, *Die Ssabier*, 161.

[5] MS. has the unused VIII. form: احتلافهم.

[6] The same accusation is hurled against them by Nowairy in de Sacy, *Introd.* 127. Cf. also *Streitschrift, Introd.*, 38.

[7] With MS. الاكبر; Ed. الاكيد.

tion, and the Most Authoritative Law. It is a writing sent by ‘Ubaidallah ibn al-Ḥasan al-Ḳairuāni [1] to Sulaimān ibn al-Ḥasan Abu [2] Sa‘īd al-Jannābi in which he enjoins him as follows: Carry on your activity among the people by ingratiating yourself with them by way of showing sympathy with whatever they are inclined to, and put the false idea into the heads of all of them that you are one of them. Any one of whose sincerity you are satisfied, — draw the veil aside for him. If you gain influence over a philosopher, hold on to him, for in the philosophers our trust resides. We and they are agreed [3] with respect to the law-books of the prophets, and the belief in the eternity of the world. Only [4]
279 some of them differ with us, believing that the world has a governing agent whom they do not acknowledge. He treats in this letter of the denial of the belief in the world-to-come and in retribution, and he declares in it that Paradise consists of the pleasures enjoyed in this world, and that torture is simply the engagement of observers of the Law in prayer, fasting, pilgrimages and holy wars. [5] He also states in that epistle: Verily, the followers of the Revealed Law worship a God whom they do not know and whom they attain only in name, not in substance. Further on he writes: The most renowned materialists are of the same cast as we, and we as they. [6]

Herein we find proof of the relation between the Bāṭiniyya and the Materialists. What lends greater strength to this view is that the Magians profess the prophetic character of Zaradusht and the descent of a revelation to him from

---

[1] Massignon who characterizes the following epistle as being “d'un cynisme rare” apparently doubts its authenticity, *l. c.*, 332. It is, judging from the similarity to the extracts found in de Sacy, *Introd.* 148 ff., the same letter as the one called السياسة by Nowairi.

[2] Casanova's correction, contra “ibn” of Ed. and MS.

[3] I omit the word أن, since our text seems to follow almost verbally the paragraph on p. 152 of de Sacy's *Introd.*, so far as can be gathered from the translation.

[4] Reading with MS. لولا; Ed. لوما.

[5] For a more objective statement of the Bāṭiniyya views on Paradise and Hell see Guyard, 191.

[6] It is in itself very doubtful whether the adherents of the Bāṭiniyya movement would readily identify their views with any existing. That it accommodated itself to any and every creed is true only of its preliminary stages.

God. The Ṣābians claim prophecy for Hermes[1], Wālīs[2], Dūr[3], Taiyūs[4], Aflāṭūn and a number of philosophers. The believers in a Revealed Law, all communities alike, affirm the descent of a revelation from heaven upon those, respectively, whose prophetic character they maintain, and they assert that that revelation comprises commands and prohibitions and information regarding life after death, reward and punishment, and paradise and hell, in which retribution will be received for[5] past deeds[6]. The Bāṭiniyya, however, reject miracles, disavow the appearance of angels from heaven with a revelation and with commands and prohibitions; nay, they deny that there is an angel to be found in heaven. Instead, they explain angels allegorically as the missionaries for their innovation; they interpret the Satans to be their antagonists, and the Iblīses[7], the learned among their antagonists[8]. They contend that the prophets are men who aspire to supremacy, and that they govern the general public by laws and artifice, seeking lordship by claiming for themselves prophecy and the Imāmate[9].

---

[1] The list in Albīrūni, 187, differs quite substantially from ours, mentioning of those in our text only Hermes and Walis. Hermes whom Albīrūni, 198, identifies with Idrīs, the Arabic for Enoch (but see Noeldeke. *ZA*. XVII, 83-4) is merely a means on the part of the Ṣābians to claim a prophet whom the Muḥammadans will recognize. Chwolson *l. c.*, I, 627–37, and for a characterization of both Hermes and Idrīs, 783—92.

[2] He may perhaps be ايلاوس mentioned by al-Ḳifṭi as quoted by Asin Palacios, *Abenhazam*, II, 235, note 120. Chwolson, *l. c.*, 800, prefers the reading ايلون in ibn Ḥazm's text and identifies him with Hellen.

[3] I have not been able to identify him.

[4] He is probably Tatius (Tat), son of Hermes. a Syro-Egyptian God, inventor of writing. *ib.* 794-5.

[5] With MS. على ; Ed. عن .

[6] These to a Muslim are the pre-requisites for any religion before it is tolerated. Chwolson, *l. c.*, 627 ff.

[7] From this statement it appears that Iblīs is a higher type of demonic spirit than the Satans. While Wensinck and Gaudefroy-Demombynes (*EI, s. v. Iblīs* and *Shaiṭān*, respectively) and the latter also in *ERE*, s. v. *Demons and Spirits in Islam*, all testify that the Satans are sometimes identifiable with Jinn, and G.-D. also states that al-Shaiṭān or Iblīs is their head, it is a little astonishing to find our author talking of a number of Iblīses.

[8] With MS. علماء مخالفهم ; Ed. على مخالفيهم . The same expressions are employed *Uṣūl*, 330.

[9] *Streitschrift, Introd.*, 38.

280 Each one[1] of them is the master[2] of a sevenfold cycle[3]. When the seven in their cycle[4] are terminated they are followed by another cycle[5]. When they speak of the prophet and his heir[6] they declare: Verily, the prophet is the *Nāṭik* (speaker) and the heir, his *Asās*, is the *Fātiḳ*[7] (possessor of command). On the Fātiḳ devolves the task of interpreting esoterically the speech of the Nāṭiḳ[8] in

---

[1] The following, which sounds like an exposition of the views of the Bāṭiniyya on the prophetic cycles, is hardly in place here among Baghdādi's deprecatory arguments.

[2] The صاحب دور is also known as the صاحب الزمان or قائم الزمان. For the Ḳarmaṭians, Muḥammad ibn Isma'īl is the master of the cycle since it is his teachings that hold sway at present, de Sacy, *Introd.*, 108, and n. 2. For other sectarians, e. g. the Druses, Nuṣairis, etc., the incumbent is another person.

[3] The wide extent to which they utilize the numeral seven which has given them the name Sab'iyya (*Streitschrift, Introd.*, 37, n. 7; Iji, 348) is well illustrated in Sam'āni, f. 229 b. Although the group under discussion there is not excluded from Islam by the Sunnites since they recognize Mūsa al-Ḳāthim as the seventh Imam, there can be no doubt that many of the seven-groups listed there were adopted by the Bāṭiniyya.

[4] With MS. من دوره: Ed. omits من.

[5] The meaning behind this laconic statement is as follows: Since the world consists of a series of emanations, each less perfect than its progenitor, there is a constant urge to attain the perfection of the Universal Intellect. This urge is already shared by the Universal Soul. But in her effort the Soul must be aided by an agent sent by Reason which is the Active Intellect. But the Reason and the Soul, in order to guide the world to salvation, must be incarnated in two beings, the Nāṭiḳ and his Asās. However, since man is mortal, the incarnation, although always the same, is externally different, being represented by seven Nāṭiḳs and, between each pair, by seven Imāms who carry on while the Law of the Nāṭiḳ is diffused, and the world is being prepared for the next speaker .Guyard, 187—9; de Goeje, 166 f., Shahr., 148, (Haarbrücker, 222-3).

[6] Reading with MS. والوصى: Ed. والوحى. The theory of the prophet and his heir is not altogether foreign to Shī'ite circles. Even the more moderate Imamiyya consider the Imāms to be the heirs of the prophets and destined to maintain God's proof on earth. See ibn Babuye, *Zur Mahdi-Lehre des Islams*, Ed. Ernst Moeller, 24.

[7] Baghdādi is, to my knowledge, the only authority who employs this term for the *Asās*, the first of the seven who form the cycle of a *Nāṭik* and who are called *Ṣāmits* (Silent). The seven Nāṭiḳs are Adam, Noah, Abraham, Moses, Jesus, Muḥammad and Muḥammad ibn Isma'īl. The seven Asās are Seth, Sem, Ishmael, Aaron, Peter, 'Ali and 'Abdallah ibn al-Ḳaddāḥ. See e. g. Guyard, 291. There was still another scheme of twelve Nāḳibs (heads) comparable to the twelve signs of the Zodiac, *ib.* 306 & 321, n. 20.

[8] It is the duty of the Asās to promulgate the Law newly revealed by the Speaker, and

accordance with the way he sees his desire tending. Whoever is converted to his esoteric interpretation is one of the pure angels [1], but he who acts in accordance with the exoteric sense is one of the unbelieving Satans. Furthermore, they allegorize every fundamental of the revealed law in such wise as will entail heresy. They maintain that the meaning of prayer is the patronage of their Imām, and that the pilgrimage is the visit to him and perseverance in his service [2]. By fasting the abstention from revealing the secret of the Imām is intended, and not abstinence from food. Harlotry according to them is the divulgence of their secrets contrary to the covenant and bond [3]. They hold that whoever knows the meaning of worship is thereby freed of the duty of performing it. They interpreted in this sense His words: "Serve your Lord until you attain absolute certainty" [4]. They stretched the words "absolute certainty" to mean knowledge of the esoteric.

In fact, Al-Ḳairuāni states in his epistle to Sulaimān ibn al-Ḥasan: Behold, I enjoin you to instil doubt into peoples' hearts regarding the Ḳur'ān, the Torah, the Psalms and the Gospels, and to urge them to relinquish the precepts [5] of the Law, to reject the dogmas of an after-life and resurrection [6], to reject the belief in angels in heaven, and to reject the belief in Jinn on earth. I bid you further to urge them to accept the view that a multitude of people existed before Adam; this will be of assistance to you in teaching the pre-existence of the world. In

in this sense he is the possessor of it. Perhaps we could also interpret the word (*Fātik*) in its meaning of slitter, since he cuts open the secret, that is, he expounds the inner meaning of the Nāṭiḳ's words. Guyard, 303 and 319, n. 5.

[1] The proof is apparently in the story of God's command to the angels to bow before Adam, the first Nāṭiḳ, and the curse pronounced on Satan, Sura 38, vv. 71-6. Cf. Guyard, 288-9 and 299 n. 26.

[2] The importance of the Imām grows in the system of the Bāṭiniyya as time passes. See Ivanow, *Ismailitica,* Passim. It is with this later view that Ghazāli has his main quarrel in the *Streitschrift,* e. g. "The Sharī'a of the Prophet" is a veil of the Imām (p. 26).

[3] The great stress laid on keeping the secret is emphasized in the severe oath administered to the novitiate, see below.

[4] Sūra 15, v. 99.

[5] *Streitschrift, Introd.*, 38, lines 13-14.

[6] *Ib.* line 21, Cf. also *ib.*, 46, last line f.

this we find a corroboration of our claim that the Bāṭiniyya are materialists who teach the eternity of the world and disacknowledge the Maker[1]. What substan-
281 tiates our charge that they favor the abrogation of the Law is that al-Ḳairuāni also writes in his letter to Sulaimān ibn al-Ḥasan: It is urgent that you thoroughly comprehend the tricks and contradictions of the prophets in their various declarations. For example, 'Isā son of Mariam said to the Jews: I shall not abolish the law of Moses[2]. Then he abolished it by consecrating Sunday in place of the Sabbath. And he permitted work on the Sabbath, and he reversed the Ḳibla of Moses in the opposite direction. For this reason the Jews[3] killed him, as his words were contradictory.

Then he writes to him: Do not be like the chief of the down-trodden nation[4], who, when asked regarding the spirit, replied: "The spirit comes by the command of my Lord[5]," because the answer to the question did not occur to him. Be not like Moses in his claim for which he had no evidence save lying supported by the most magnificent artifices and juggling. As the Law-giver in his time [Pharaoh] did not find any testimony to confirm his claim, he said to him: "Verily thou shalt not take to thyself a God other than me[6]. He [Pharaoh] said to his people: "I am your most exalted Lord[7]," because he was the master of the time in his cycle[8]. At the end of his letter he declares: There is no wonder so great as the wonder over a person who pretends to be intelligent, yet, if he has a beautiful sister or daughter, does not make one of them his wife by virtue of her beauty, but declares her unlawful to himself and marries her to an outsider.

---

[1] *Ib.*, 38, line 20.

[2] Matthew, 5, 18; Luke, 16, 17.

[3] Reading with MS. أليهود; Ed. البلاد.

[4] An epithet for the Arabs well in line with the Persian origin of the movement. (Cf. Goldziher's article on the Shu'ūbiyya *Muh. St.* Vol. I.). It is an even more appropriate term from the pen of one who regarded Islām as a means for enslaving the people to the advantage of a few. If the epistle is a pure invention, the choice of the adjective is nevertheless a happy one.

[5] Sura 17, 87. Orthodox Islām also regards this reply as a confession of ignorance. See Baiḍ. *ad loc.*

[6] Sura 26, v. 28. [7] Sura 79, v. 24.

[8] MS. دوه for دوره: Ed. وقته. Isf. reads here: ودلك الحق في زمانه قال انا ربكم الاعلى واعا سماه محقاً على مذهبه على معنى انه كان صاحب زمانه في دوره.

But if the stupid one possessed sense he would understand that he has better title to his sister or his daughter than the stranger. The true aspect of this is simply that their master[1] forbade to them the enjoyment of the good and inspired into their hearts fear of a Hidden Being who cannot be apprehended. This is the God in whose existence they believe. He related traditions to them about the existence of what they will never witness, such as resurrection from the graves, retribution, paradise and hell. Thus he soon subjugated them and reduced them to slavery to himself during his lifetime, and to his offspring after his 282
death. In this way he arrogated to himself the right to enjoy their wealth, for he says: "I ask you no reward for it except friendliness to my relatives[2]." His dealings with them were on a cash basis, but their dealings with him were on credit. He required of them an immediate exchange of their lives and property for a future promise which would never be realized. Is Paradise aught[3] save this world and its enjoyment? Or are hell and its torture any thing but the state to which the observers of the Law are reduced, namely: weariness and exertion in prayer, fasting, the holy war and the pilgrimage?

Finally he declares to Sulaimān ibn al-Ḥasan in this epistle: You and your brethren are the heirs who will inherit Firdaus[4], and in this world you have acquired its pleasures and luxuries which are forbidden to the ignorant, those held in check by the precepts of the law-givers. Congratulations to you upon the freedom from their power which you have attained. — In what we have related

---

[1] i. e. Muḥammad.

[2] Sura 42. 23. There is no distortion of meaning in this verse on the part of the Bāṭiniyya. Despite the contentions of the modern Arab translators of the Ḳur'ān, Maulvi Muḥammad 'Ali and Hafiz Ghulam Sarwar, *ad loc.*, the old commentators agree with the interpretation as given here. Baiḍāwi, II, 230, even cites a tradition according to which the relations are 'Ali and Fāṭima and their offspring. Cf. de Sacy, *Introd.*, 203, n. 2. See also *Koranauslegung*, 268-9.

[3] Or, there is no paradise etc. See Worrell's article on the Particle هل, *ZA*, XXI (1906), 116—150, especially 131—2 and 149.

[4] Whether the alleged author of this letter meant by *Firdaus* anything other than paradise (which is the meaning given to it by Muḥammad, *E. I.*, *s. v.* Firdaus), it is difficult to say. Among the orthodox the word assumes a more specialized sense, referring to certain portions of Paradise, *ib.*

one finds evidence that the goal of the Bâtiniyya is to teach the doctrine of the Materialists, to allow the things which are forbidden, and to relinquish works.

In luring the dull-heads and converting them to their heresy, the Bāṭiniyya avail themselves of strategic devices according to Degrees which they name:[1] Perception, Familiarization, Instilling doubt, Leaving in Suspense, Intoxication,[2] Concealing, Laying the Foundation, Sealing the Bond by Oath and Covenant, and finally, Ungodliness and Renunciation.

Concerning Tafarrus (Perception). - They say: It is a pre-requisite for a missionary of their heresy that he be skillful in dissembling and well-versed in the methods of interpreting the exoteric so as to give it an esoteric meaning. He must at the same time distinguish[3] between one whose conquest and seduction may[4] be attempted and
283 one who offers no prospect. With this in mind, they make the following recommendations to their missionaries: Hold no discussions in a house where there is a light, meaning by the light one who knows dogmatic theology and the various ways of speculation and analogy. They further instruct their missionaries: Do not cast your seed into saline soil. They understand by this the abstention of their missionaries from disclosing their heresy to people upon whom their evil teachings will produce no effect, just as seed in saline ground will produce nothing. They

[1] Iji's list *Mawakif,* (350—51) is quite the same as ours except that the first degree is called الذوق, and the eighth, instead of the covenant, is الخلع which our author joins with السلخ as the last. Ghazāli agrees with Iji, cf. *Streitschrift, Introd.*, 40—42. Indeed, as will be pointed out later, the oath and covenant which should be discussed as the fifth degree under *Rabt* is detached from its context and given later as a separate stage (Ed. 287, ff.), thus leaving *Rabt* an empty term and forcing our author to identify it with *Ta'lîk.* De Sacy who devotes pages 75—147 of his Introd. to the degrees and the oath differs almost completely from the other authorities in his discussion. While he also counts nine stages, he seems to crowd into the first all that the others spread over the first six, cf. 74—96, specially 94 f. His remaining eight degrees deal actually with a gradual initiation into the inner secrets of the movement. Although the consensus among the three authorities seems to confirm the exposition, it cannot be denied that de Sacy's system is more logical. Maḳrīzi's version, which de Sacy utilized, will be found in the *Khiṭaṭ,* I, 291—95.

[2] See below.

[3] Reading مميزاً with Ms; Ed. مخبراً.

[4] Reading with Ms. ان; Ed. من.

call the hearts of their stupid followers fertile soil, because they are susceptible to their doctrine. But this comparison ought rather to be reversed, since the fertile hearts are those which receive the orthodox religion and walk in the righteous path. They are the ones who do not swerve after the fashion of the blundering people, like pure gold which does not become rusty in water, is not consumed by the earth, and is not diminished by fire. The saline soil is like the hearts of the Bāṭiniyya and the other godless people whom sound sense does not deter, nor do laws restrain. They are the foul and the impure, the dead, not the living[1]. "They[2] are nothing but as cattle, nay, they are furthest astray from the path", and the most easily deceived. He who has provided sustenance for swine in their pasturages and provided food for lizards[3] in their wasteland has apportioned to them their share of sustenance. "He cannot be questioned concerning what He does, and they shall be questioned[4]."

They direct further: It is required of the missionary that he be acquainted with the various methods by which parties can be swayed. For the conversion of the groups is not along one line; nay, every group of people provides its own starting point from which it is to be invited to the doctrine of the Bāṭiniyya. If[5] it is one whom the propagandist sees inclining to acts of worship, he urges 284
him to devote himself to ascetic practices and good works. Then he inquires of him about the meaning of works and the underlying causes of the precepts, and he throws him into doubt with respect to them. Whomever he finds to be impudent and dissolute he tells: Religious acts are foolish and stupid, whereas intelligence manifests itself in the quest for pleasure. He expresses his thoughts to him in the words of the poet[6]:

---

[1] An allusion to Sura 16, verses 20, 21.

[2] Sura 25, V. 44.

[3] Reading with Ms. الضب; Ed. العنب.

[4] Sura 21, v. 23.

[5] The various methods of approach, including those to Jews and Christians are related much more fully in de Sacy, *Introd.*, 148 ff. They probably draw from one source.

[6] The following couplet is from the pen of Salm al-Khāsir (see his biography) *Aghāni*, xxi, 110ff. The anecdote about the line, which also involves his teacher Bashshār b. Burd is related *ib*, 112-13 and *op. cit*, III, 49.

He who is mindful of people dies of solicitude,
But the bold man acquires pleasure.

When he sees one in a troubled state regarding his religion or regarding after-life, reward or punishment, he speaks to him openly about discarding them, and urges him to enjoy the things which are forbidden, and comforts both him and himself with the words of the shameless poet:[1a]

Shall I renounce the joys of the red wine
Because of the meat and wine which they promise?
Life, then death, then resurrection, —
Fictitious tales, O mother of 'Amr.

If it is one whom he identifies as a member of the Ghulāt among the Rawāfiḍ, such as the Sabbābiyya or the Mughīriyya or the Manṣūriyya, or the Khaṭṭābiyya, he does not need[1] in that case to interpret the verses of the Ḳur'ān or the traditions, because all of them alike render them allegorically in harmony with their blunders. When he sees one of the Rawāfiḍ, either Zaidite[2] or Imāmite, disposed to challenge the traditions about the Companions, he makes his overtures to him by way of reviling the Companions, and elaborates on the hatred for the Banu Teim because Abu Bekr belonged to their tribe, and the hatred for the Banu 'Adi because 'Omar ibn al-Khaṭṭāb was a member of their tribe. He exhorts him to hate the Banu 'Umayya because 'Uthmān and Mu'āwia came from them. Generally the Bāṭini of our age finds support in the words of Isma'īl ibn 'Abbād:[3]

To be condemned to hell because of affection for the rightful heir
And because of preferring the family of the Prophet
285 Is more attractive to me than the Garden of Eden
Where I would dwell eternally by recognizing Teim or 'Adi[4].

---

[1] Ms. يحتج. [1a] See Additional Notes.

[2] De Sacy, *Introd.*, 148 ff.

[3] 385—386 A. H. with the honorary title of al-Ṣāḥib. He was vizier to Mu'ayyid-al-Dawla Abu Manṣūr Buwaih ibn Rukn-al-Dawla, and, later, to his brother Fakhr-al-Dawla. He was of Shī'ite persuasion. Yaḳūt, who gives a long account of him and quotes much of his poetry (*Irshad*, II, 273—343) does not cite our verses. See on his Shī'ite leanings, *l. c.*, 328 ff.

[4] The names Teim for Abu Bekr and 'Adi for Omar are terms of insult. Goldziher, *Spottnamen d. ersten Chalifen bei den Schî'iten in WZKM*, XV (1901) 326.

'Abd-al-Ḳāhir says: We have made a reply to this singer in the following verses:

Do you entertain hopes of entering the Garden of Eden
While you are an enemy of Teim and of 'Adi?
Why, they have left you in a worse plight than Thamūd,
They have left you more disgraced than a bastard son.
Verily, you will some future day roast in hell fire,
Since the Friend of the Prophet[1] regards you as an enemy.

When the missionary discovers one who accepts Abu Bekr and 'Omar he eulogizes them in his presence and says: These two played a role in the interpretation of the Law. For this reason the Prophet sought Abu Bekr as his companion in the cave and later in Medina and communicated to him in the cave the true meaning of his law. When the person who is attached to Abu Bekr and 'Omar questions him regarding this above-mentioned interpretation, he engages him by covenants and bonds to keep secret whatever he reveals to him. Then he relates to him by degrees some of the explanations. If he agrees to them he reveals the remainder to him, but if he does not accept the first interpretation from him, he withholds the remainder and conceals it; but as a result of that the deceived one is thrown into doubt regarding the fundamentals of the Law.

Those among whom the doctrine of the Bāṭiniyya makes progress fall into several divisions. First there is the general public whose comprehension of the essentials of knowledge and speculation is trifling[2], like the Nabateans[3], or the Kurds, or the descendants of the Magians. The second group includes the Shu'ūbiyya[4] (Persian nationalists) who believe in the superiority of the Persians to the Arabs,

---

[1] i. e. Abu Bekr, called al-Ṣiddīk (the Friend).

[2] With Ms. قلت; Ed. قتلت.

[3] On the rift between the Nabateans and Arabs see Goldziher, *Muh. St.* I, 156 ff.

[4] See Goldziher's masterly study of this group which he characterizes as "ein Kreis von Schriftstellern und Gelehrten, nicht aber von unzufriedenem Volk und aufrührischem Pöbel" in *Muh. St.*, I, 147 ff. On their utilization by the Bā.iniyya see *ib.*, 175. Cf. *Streitschrift, Introd.*, 42, l. 9. The view was generally prevalent that a gap existed between the Arab and non-Arab elements. See e. g. the account which makes the Fāṭimids descendants of Jews as reported IA, VIII, 20. See also the conversation as cited from *Bayan al-Adyan* in Blochet, 149. Cf. IH, in *Shiites* I, 35; II, 16.

and are eager for the restoration of the kingdom to the Persians. The third group consists of the senseless among the Banu Rabī'a owing to their jealousy of the
28 Muḍar because the Prophet came from them[1]. It is for this reason that 'Abdallah ibn Khāzim al-Sulami[2] said in his inaugural sermon[3] in Khurāsān: The Rabī'a have always been embittered against God ever since He raised His Prophet from the Muḍar. Because of the envy nurtured by the Rabī'a against the Muḍar, the Banu Ḥanīfa invested Musailima[4] the Liar, hoping that there would be a prophet among the Banu Rabī'a as there had been among the Muḍar. When the gullible Persian or the Rabī'ite, envious of the Muḍar[5], becomes more familiarized with the statement[6] of the Bāṭini: Your people have better title to the government than the Muḍar, he inquires of him regarding the occasion when the power will be restored to his people. When he asks him about it he answers him: Verily,

---

[1] The Muḍar and Rabī'a are both sub-divisions of the northern Arabs, known variously as Nizār, Ma'add or Adnān, all three of them ancestors. Besides the general enmity between these latter northern, or Ḳais, and the southern or Yemenite tribes (see Goldziher's article *Der arabische Stammwesen und der Islam* in Muh. St., I, 40 — 100 and particularly 78 ff.), rivalry also existed between the two sub-divisions of the northern group which may well have had other causes than the jealousy over the Prophet's tribe. As O'Leary says about the "marked rivalry, often leading to warfare, between the Rabī'a and Muḍar": "The rivalry of the two may have been developed, if not actually started, by the jealousies bred by the spoil gained by the Muslim armies as they advanced into Asia". *Arabia before Mohammed,* 19. Indeed, in Baṣra we find the Rabī'a and the Azd (a southern tribe) making common cause against the Muḍar. Wellhausen, *Arabisches Reich,* 248.

[2] See ibn Hajar's *Biogr. of Persons who knew Mohammed,* ii, No. 9010. He was governor of Khurāsān in 32 A. H. (it was gained dishonestly, IA, III, 106 and more fully 366–7.) and again 64—73, the second time as a rebel against the 'Omayyads. He was killed in battle in 73, IA, Index, *s. v.* The statement reported here was not made in his Khuṭba in Khurāsān, when he eagerly sought to justify himself (IA, III, 367), but at the time of his siege of the Rabī'a tribe in Herat in 64 A. H. IA, IV, 130. According to Ṭab. III, 1242 these words were spoken by the Khalīf al-Ma'mūn to account for his dislike of the Arabs (cited by Goldziher, *l. c.* 149).

[3] With Ms. خطبته ; Ed. خطيته.

[4] IA, II, 267. In his defense see Caetani, *Annali dell' Islam,* II. (Anno 11) par. 168—9.

[5] Contra Ed. and Ms. الطر, with Brockelmann, *l. c.,* 286.

[6] With Ms. بقول ; Ed. يقول.

the law of Mudar will continue for a fixed limit of time. Its end is drawing nigh and after its termination the government will come back to you. Then he expounds to him the allegorical interpretation of the fundamentals[1] of the Law of Islam step by step. If he accepts this from him, he becomes a godless person and a Khurrami[2], finds works burdensome, and derives pleasure from allowing to himself the things which are forbidden. This is an exposition of the degree of Perception among them.

The stage of familiarization is closely related[3] to the stage of perception. It consists in extolling to the utmost in the presence of the person that in his doctrine to which he is attached[4], and in asking him later[5] on about the interpretation of that to which he adheres and instilling doubt into him about the essentials of his religion. When the novice asks him about that, he says: The knowledge of this rests with the Imām. In this way he attains the degree of Instilling Doubt[6], when the initiate arrives at the conviction that what is aimed at by the apparent explanation (of the Ḳur'ān) and the tradition is not their determined meaning in the language. As a result of that it becomes a light matter for him to transgress the prohibitive laws and to relinquish works. The degree of intoxication is with

[1] Ms. ان كان for اركان; Ed. انكار.

[2] With Ms. خرميا; Ed. حرسا. Brockelmann's emendation ("Hideous Infidel"), ib., is obviously unnecessary.

[3] With Ms. قريبة; Ed. قربية.

[4] Ghazāli in *Streitschrift*, Text No. 2 (Arabic part p. 4) describes in detail the way pursued to win his confidence. Evening meetings are arranged in the house of a neophyte where a man with a good voice reads the Ḳur'ān, discourses and pleasing words are heard, condemnation of present rulers and uninformed scholars is pronounced and blessings promised to the few by the Prophet's Family. All this time the missionary weeps occasionally, utters deep groans, alludes to divine secrets when he hears a verse of the Ḳur'ān recited or a tradition related, which are revealed only to those whom God has chosen. Late in the night he still keeps awake praying, so that the owner of the house finds him in that state when he wakes. But as soon as he is discovered he slinks away so as to create an impression of his eagerness to hide it. In this way he gains the person's confidence and attracts his attention to all he says. According to 'Iji, 350, the second stage comprises most of what our author included under the first.

[5] This part of the sentence is really the third degree as Baghdādi goes right on to say. A full account of the procedure for instilling doubt will be found below 149 ff. Ed 291, ff.

[6] With MS. متى; Ed. حتى.

them the state of leaving the soul of the novice in suspense in its quest for the
287 true meaning of the fundamentals of the law[1]. Now he either accepts its interpretation from them in such wise as will induce him to discard it [the Law], or he remains in a state of doubt and confusion regarding it. The stage of falsification consists in telling the deceived one who is ignorant of the principles of deductive and inductive reasoning that the exterior meanings are chastisement and the hidden meanings are an act of grace[2]. He cites to him His words in the Ḳur'ān: "Then separation would be brought about[3] between them, with a wall having a door in it. The inside of it shall be mercy, and the outside of it, before it shall be chastisement[4]". If the deceived one questions them regarding the meaning of the "inside of the door", they say: God's Sunna abounds in cases of the conclusion of covenants and bonds with his apostles. Therefore He says: "And when we made a covenant with the prophets and with you and with Nūḥ and Ibrahīm and Mūsa and 'Isa son of Mariam and we made with them a strong covenant[5]".

[1] *Streitschrift,* (Text No. 4, p. 5) describes how the missionary is to persist in his refusal to reveal the secrets and in telling him that God's religion is too precious to be disclosed to any but the right people. He even makes a pretense of sending him away. Our author becomes exceedingly vague and confused in the presentation of the following degrees. He is quite alone in identifying *rabt* with the fourth stage of suspense. Both *Streitschrift,* 40—41 and 'Iji 350, describe it as the oath-taking process and so does Baghdādi several lines below although there it follows the sixth stage.

[2] *Streitschrift,* Introd. 41, (Text No. 5. pp. 6—7), which sets forth this stage more fully characterizes it as a procedure in which knowledge by the general public is denied, intellect and tradition and in particular the apparent meanings of the Ḳur'ān as criteria of knowledge are criticized. Persuasion is utilized that in adopting these views the novice will not be alone, and that the very finest people (some names of men who live far away are mentioned: cf. Hebrew saying הרוצה לשקר ירחיק עדותו), entertain the same views. Cf. 'Iji 350 last line.

[3] The correct vocalization of the word is ضرب.

[4] Sure 89, V. 13. The ordinary meaning of this sentence is that the wall will separate between the righteous and the wrongdoers, the former finding grace inside the door within nearer reach of Paradise. See Baiḍ. ad loc. A good specimen of Bāṭinite interpretation of the Ḳur'ān, believed by Guyard (315) to be part of a complete commentary, will be found Guyard, 202—217 (trans. 302—318).

[5] Sura 33, V. 7, The same sentence is cited Iji 350, *Streitschrift,* Text № 4, (p. 6) where the following verses are also quoted; de Sacy, *Introd.* 92-93.

They quote to him His words: "Do not break the oaths after making them fast and you have indeed made Allah a surety for you[1]". Once the beguiled one pledges himself to them by means of strong oaths and by divorce and freeing of the slaves and by the dedication of his property to charity[1a] they bind him with them[2]. They expound to him that side of the interpretation of the external meanings which, they believe, leads to abandoning them[3]. If the fool accepts this from them he joins the religion of the Zendiks secretly[4] and seeks shelter in Islam openly. But if the one engaged by oath shrinks from putting faith in the allegorization of the Zendik Bāṭiniyya he keeps it secret in accordance with the terms because he has sworn to them that he will hide whatever mysteries they reveal to him. If he is heedful they administer an oath to him and strip[5] him of the religion of Islam and say to him at that time: Verily, the exoteric is like the husk and the esoteric like the kernel, and the kernel is better than the husk[6].

'Abd-al-Ḳāhir says: One who had joined the movement of the Bāṭiniyya, but 288
whom God aided to regain His truth and guided him in loosening their bonds, related to me[7] that when they bound him by his pledges they said to him: Behold, those who are called prophets such as Nūḥ, Ibrahīm, Mūsa, 'Isa and Muḥammad and all those who claimed the spirit of prophecy were nomians and necromancers who aspired to chieftaincy over the public, and they deceived them with incantations and enslaved them with their precepts[8]. This narrator told me: Then the one who revealed this secret to me contradicted himself by declaring to me: It is important for you to know that Muḥammad ibn Isma'īl ibn Ja'far is he who called Mūsa son of 'Amrān from the Bush and said to him: "Behold, I am your

---

[1] Sura 16, V. 93. [1a] These are the fines for breaking the oath, see p. 147. The reading of Ed. سبيل ought perhaps to be emended to تسبيل.

[2] The mention of the oath in this particular place is unjustified. See above.

[3] This may be the stage of Ta'sīs, also the definition which he gives above of Tadlīs seems much more to accord with Iji's description of the seventh stage, 451, lines 1-2. From its content this one appears to be the eighth. Cf. Iji, *ib.* If this view should be accepted we should not find it necessary to combine *Khal'* and *Salkh* as Baghdādi is compelled to.

[4] Reading with MS. باطنا; Ed. باطلا. [5] This is the last stage of *Salkh.*

[6] This comparison is met with in all discussions of the Bāṭiniyya, e. g. *Streitschrift,* Iji, Sam'āni, etc. Cf. *REJ,* L (1905), 34-5.

[7] Read لى ; Ed. له. [8] See above 133.

Lord, take off your shoes[1]". Then I said to him: May your eye be inflamed! You asked me to disbelieve in the Eternal Lord, Creator of the universe, urging me, nevertheless, to recognize the divinity of a created human being; and you think that before his birth he was a god who sent Mūsa. Now, if Mūsa, according to you, was a great deceiver[2], then he whom you believe to have sent him is a worse liar. Then he said to me: May you never prosper, and he regretted having bared his secrets to me. I repented from their heresy. — This is an account of their technique with their followers.

Concerning their oaths[3]. — Their missionary says to the one who takes the oath: You have imposed upon yourself a covenant with God and an agreement with Him and a pledge to Him and to His apostles, and any or all covenants or agreements which God made with the prophets that you will conceal whatever you hear from me and whatever you know that concerns me or the Imām who is the master of your age or his partisans and followers in this country and in the other countries
289 or those who obey him, whether male or female[4]. Do not reveal of this either much or little and do not bare anything which may lead to it, whether by writing or allusion, except what the Imām, master of the time, permits you or what the one to whom this permission was given[5] in connection with his missionary activities allows you. You will then act in this matter to whatever limit he extends[6] to you. You have now taken upon yourself the task of fulfilling your promise con-

---

[1] Sura 20, V. 12. What the missionary meant of course is that it is the same incarnation as of the one who called Moses. See Guyard, 193-95, and 275-77 and n. 1. (from the point of view of the later Isma'īliyya or Assassins).

[2] Reading with MS. زرّاقا; Ed. رراقا.

[3] This oath is also repeated de Sacy, Introd. 138 ff., and Maḳrīzi, I, 396-7. Substantially the versions are similar, although the latter is more elaborate.

[4] This extreme secrecy is held by them in common with the Ikhwān al-Ṣafa with whom they are also closely related otherwise. Goldziher, *Koranauslegung*, 191, n. 4. An illustration of it is afforded in the answer given by Abu-l-Fawāris when the Khalīf al-Mu'taḍid inquired about the belief in the incarnation of God's spirit in man: ان حلت روح الله فينا فما يضرك وان حلت روح ابليس فما ينفعك فلا تسئل عما لا يعنيك. IA, VII, 354.

[5] Arabic المأذون. According to Iji, 349, (trans. *JAOS*, II, [1849-50], 280), it is an official title of one of the missionaries whose function it was to act as negotiator with the candidates.

[6] Ed. يؤذن; MS. ياذن.

cerning this, and charge yourself equally in states of good will or anger, desire or fear. Say[1], Amen. When he says Amen, he says to him: You further take upon yourself that you will protect me and those whom I will name to you from whatever you will protect yourself by the covenant with God and your agreement with Him and your pledge to Him and to His apostles; and you will maintain a sincere relationship with them both openly and secretly. You will not act treacherously towards the Imām or his patronizers or the members of his mission with respect to their lives or their property. You will not apply to these oaths any casuistry nor adhere to anything which will make them invalid.

If you should do anything of this you are severed from God and His apostles and His angels and from all the Scriptures which God has revealed. Further, if you should transgress anything of what we imposed upon you, then you owe it to God to make a hundred pilgrimages[2] to His house on foot, regarding it as an obligatory vow. Everything which you possess during the period when you are in this state shall be forfeited as charity to the beggars and needy. Any slave who is in your possession on the day when you have transgressed or thereafter shall be set free. Any wife of yours at present or on the day of your trespass or one whom you should marry afterwards shall be divorced from you by a triple divorce[3], God is an adequate witness to your intention and your hidden beliefs about what you have sworn to. When he says Amen, he says to him: God is an 290
adequate witness between us and between you.

When the victim takes these vows he thinks that he cannot violate them, but the dupe does not know at all that from their standpoint their vow is neither valid nor inviolable. For they see no sin in making it or breaking it, nor blasphemy, nor shame, nor punishment in the world to come. How can an oath by God or by his Scriptures or by his messengers possess sacredness for them when

---

[1] With MS. قل ; Ed. قال .

[2] Maḳrīzi, *ib.;* de Sacy, *Introd.* 145, and *Streitschrift, Introd.*, 41, read thirty.

[3] Sachau, *Muhammedanisches Recht,* 13 (§ 37) and 66—8. The divorce is of the type where the man pronounces the required formula three times or actually divorces her three times. It means that he cannot re-marry her unless she was in the meantime married to someone else, and fulfilled certain other requirements.

they do not confess in an eternal God; nay, they do not[1] acknowledge the creation of the world and do not accept a book revealed from heaven or an apostle to whom a revelation was made from heaven? Or how can the oath of the Muslims have a sacred character for them when it is a tenet of their religion that the merciful, compassionate God is merely their chief in whose behalf they make propaganda? Those among them who incline to the religion of the Magians maintain that God is Light and against Him stands Satan whom He overcame and dismissed from His kingdom. Furthermore, how can the votive pilgrimage or prescribed visit to Mecca possess any meaning for them, when they ascribe no importance to the Ka'ba and ridicule the person who makes a pilgrimage or pays the visit? Finally, what sanctity can a divorce-act have for them when they consider relations with every woman lawful without the marriage contract? This is a clear account of the law of oaths which obtains among them.

As regards the law of oaths which is in force among the Muslims, we teach: Every oath which the swearer takes initially by his own dictates is in accordance with his own intention[2]. Every oath taken by him in the presence of a Ḳāḍi or a Sultan who orders him to take it is to be considered. If it is an oath following a claim made by a plaintiff against him who denies it, in which the plaintiff is acting unjustly towards the defendant, then the oath of a swearer is in accordance with his own intention[3]. But if the plaintiff is right and the repudiator acts
291 wrongly towards the claimant, then the oath of the former is interpreted in accordance with the meaning of the judge or the sultan who administered it to him[4]. The oath-taker thereby becomes perfidious with respect to his oath. Since these premises are true, he who investigates the dogmas of the Bāṭiniyya is absolved of his oath in view of the fact that his purpose is to expose their heresy or he desires to do them harm; his vow is, therefore, at his own discretion. If he makes exception in his heart for the will of God then his vow is not binding upon him and he does not break it by revealing the secrets of the Bāṭiniyya to

---

[1] Supplying لا from MS., missing in Ed.

[2] i. e. he has the right to make some mental reservation. See Sachau, 731, l. 5-6.

[3] i. e. if he swears the truth he may in this case also make a mental reservation. *Ib.*, l. 12—30.

[4] *Ib.*, 730, last line ff.

the public. His wives are not divorced, his slaves not set free and a compulsory act of charity does not become obligatory upon him. The chief of the Bāṭiniyya is not considered an Imām by the Muslims. Whoever, therefore, reveals his secret does not disclose the secret of an Imām but that of an infidel and a Zendik. It has been transmitted in a well-authenticated tradition: speak of the infidel in so far as it will caution people. This is a description of their wiles with those who are ignorant of the faith.

Concerning their method of beguiling the simpletons by instilling doubt. — It is achieved by way of asking them questions about the precepts of the Law, misleading them to believe the opposite of their obvious meaning. Often they question about the physical world, creating the impression that profound learning is involved therein which no one but their chief can comprehend. Some of the queries put forth to the duped one by their missionary are as follows[1]: Why is man endowed with two ears and one tongue? Why does man possess one penis and two testicles? Why are the nerves connected with the brain and the veins with the liver and the arteries with the heart? Why is man distinguished by growth of hair on both his upper and lower eyelids while the other animals have hair grow- 292
ing on their upper eyelids but not the lower? Why are the breasts of the human on his chest and those of other beasts on their bellies? Why does not the horse have nodous lumps or paunches or ankle-bones? What is the difference between living beings which lay eggs and do not bear and between those which bear and do not lay eggs? How can one distinguish between fish from the river and fish from the sea? They ask many similar questions and make believe that the knowledge thereof rests with their chief.

Among their questions on the Ḳur'ān is the query regarding the meanings of the letters at the beginnings of the Suras, as when He says: *Alif-lam-mim*[2] or *Ra-ḥa-mim,*[3] or *Ṭa-sin,*[4] or *Ya-sin,*[5] or *Ṭa-ha,*[6] or *Kaf-ha-ya-ʿain-ṣad,*[7]?

[1] Some of these questions may be found in de Sacy, *Introd.*, 74 ff. Many of those recorded there are not reported by our author.

[2] Suras 2, 3, 29, 30, 31, 32 and some others with additional letters.

[3] Suras 40—45.

[4] Sura 27 and with final mīm, 26 and 28.

[5] Sura 36.

[6] Sura 20.

[7] Sura 19.

Generally they ask: What is the meaning of every single letter in the alphabet? Why does the alphabet consist of twenty nine letters? Why are some of them provided with points and others are wanting in points? Why is the joining of some of them with the following letter allowed? Usually they say to the beguiled ones: What is the meaning of God's word: "And above them eight shall bear on that day the throne of your Lord"? [1] Why did God make the gates of Paradise eight and the gates of Hell seven? What is the meaning of His saying: Over it are nineteen [2]? What is the advantage of this number? Often they inquire about verses between which they allege discrepancies, maintaining that no one knows their explanation save their chief. For example, He says: "So on that day neither man nor jinni shall be asked about his sin [3]." Yet he declares in another
293 place: "So by your Lord we shall certainly question them all [4]." Other questions bear on the precepts, as for example: Why does the morning prayer consist of two *rak'as*, the mid-day prayer of four and the evening prayer of three? Why does every *rak'a* consist of one bow and two kneelings? Why is an ablution of water required for four limbs and of sand for two [5]? Why is washing required after a semenal discharge, although it is clean in the case of most Muslims, whereas no washing is required after urinating despite its uncleanliness in the case of everyone [6]? Why does a menstruating woman make good whatever fast-days she missed but does not make up whatever prayers she missed [7]? Why is the punishment for stealing — amputation of the hand, for adultery — flaying? Why is not the penis cut off with which he committed the act of adultery in the same way as the hand is cut off with which he stole while committing theft? When the deceived one hears these questions from them and turns to them for their

[1] Sura 69, 17. This question finds its echo in Ṣūfic literature. See ibn 'Ārabi's *Futuḥāt*, I, 191 (cited by Asin, *ibn Masarra*, 71). Ibn Ḥazm also takes up this verse admitting frankly his failure to grasp its meaning, although he definitely believes in it, and again lays down the following principle so frequently reiterated by him فقوله الحق نؤمن به يقينا والله اعلم بمراده في هذا القول ولعله عنى... السموات السبع والكرسى فهذه ثمانية اجرام هى يومئذ... نقول ما قال ربنا تعالى ونقطع انه حق يقين على ظاهره وهو اعلم بمعناه ومراده. IH, II, 125-6.

[2] Sura 74, V. 30. [3] Sura 55, v. 39.

[4] Sura 15, v. 92. [5] Juynboll, 73-4.

[6] *Ib.*, 72, note 2.

[7] *Ib.*, 80.

elucidation they tell him: The knowledge of it rests with our Imām[1] and with the one who was authorized to reveal our secrets. When it is established as a certainty in the mind of the duped one that their Imām or the one authorized by him are the individuals who know the explanations, he is convinced that what is meant by the external interpretation of the Ḳur'ān and the Sunna is not the exoteric explanation. With this trickery they make him relinquish the fulfillment of the precepts of the Law. Once he gets habituated to the relinquishment of worship, and allows himself the forbidden things, they lift the veil for him and say to him: If we had an eternal God, free from want of anything, He would have no profit from the bowing and kneeling of mankind, nor from the ceremony of circumambulating a house of stone,[2] nor from running between two mountains. When he accepts this from them, he is stripped by that time of a belief in the unity of his Lord and becomes a renegade and a Zendik.

'Abd-al-Ḳāhir says: The retort to them in answer to the questions which 294
they propose with the aim of instilling doubt into the hearts of the ignorant regarding the fundamental dogmas of religion can be made from two angles. In the first place, it can be said to them: You cannot escape one of two conclusions. Either you admit the creation of the world and confirm to it a Maker eternal, knowing, wise, with the power to impose on mankind whatever charge He pleases in any way He wishes, or you deny this, and profess the eternity of the world and the denial of the Maker. Now, if you believe in the eternity of the world and the non-existence of its Maker, wherefore you do not confess in a God who made anything obligatory or prohibited it, created it or fashioned it, there is no sense in your asking Why did God ordain this, or why did He prohibit that; why did He create this, and why did He create that after that pattern? Therefore, the discussion between us and you becomes like the discussion between us and the Materialists about the problem of the creation of the universe. But if you aver the origination-in-time of the universe and the unity of its Maker and you admit His power to demand whatever obedience He chooses in the form of worship, then this capacity of His is an answer to you

[1] This attitude is called Ta'līm and has given the sect the name Ta'līmiyya. See *Streitschrift, Introd.*, 5 ff.

[2] This and the following rites are ceremonies connected with the pilgrimage.

when you ask: why did He ordain this and why did He forbid that? For you recognize His capacity to do this, once you believe in Him and in the possibility of His demanding obedience from people[1]. Similarly their queries about the sensible properties lose their value if they affirm the existence of a Maker Who caused them to be. But if they deny a Maker then there is no point to their question: Why did God create this? seeing that they deny that it had an eternal Creator.

The second way of replying to them and to their inquiries about riddles of creation is to say to them: In what way are the chiefs of the Bāṭiniyya specially gifted with a knowledge of causes, when the doctors and philosophers have dis-
295 cussed them in their books? Aristotle composed a work on the natures of animals, yet the philosophers have related nothing of this branch of knowledge which is not stolen from the Arab scholars who lived before the period of the wise men[2], such as the Ḳaḥṭāniyya, the Jarhamiyya, the Tasmiyya, and the other Ḥimyarite tribes. In their poems and proverbs the Arabs discuss the various traits of the animals. Yet in their time no Bāṭini lived, nor any Bāṭini leader. However, Aristotle took the distinction between breeding animals and those that lay eggs from the Arabs who state in their proverbs: Every animal with slit ears[3] is a breeder and those hard of hearing lay eggs. For this reason the bat[4] among the birds is a breeder and does not lay eggs, because it has long ears. All those which are hard of hearing lay eggs, like the serpent and lizard and the egg-laying birds.

Abu 'Ubaida Ma'mar ibn al-Muthanna[5] and 'Abd-al-Malik ibn Ḳuraib al-

---

[1] This standpoint is fully in consonance with the theological views of the Ash'arites to which our author adheres almost blindly. See the discussion below on orthodox Islam.

[2] This is a typical medieval claim.

[3] See ibn Ḳuṭaiba, *'Uyūn al-Akhbār* (ed. Brockelmann) 474, l. 12—14. Al Aṣma'i's definition in Haffner, *Abhandlungen z. arab. Lexikographie*, establishes the meaning beyond doubt: والشرق ان يشق شق في الاذن فتسمى شرقاء (135). The same statement occurs *Usul*, 29, but there the reading is شرفاء (long ears). Al-Kazwini's *Nuzhat ul-Qulub* (trans. Stephenson), 2, tells us that "those whose ears project from their heads bring forth their young and those whose ears do not project lay eggs." This definition agrees with *'Uyūn*.

[4] See *'Uyūn*, 477-8.

[5] Born 107 A. H. in Baṣra of Jewish parents, died 210. He was a Khārijite and Shu'ūbite. See Brockelmann, *Gesch. d. arab. Lit.*, I, 103-4; IKhall, III, 388 ff. where numerous works on animals are credited to him. On his erudition see Goldziher, *Muh. St.*, I, 194—6.

Aṣma'i[1] relate that during the Age of Ignorance the Arabs taught on the basis of their experience[2] that all animals have lashes on their upper eyelids but t on the lower, whereas the human has lashes growing on both the upper and the lower lids[3]. They say: All animals will swim when thrown into water, except men, monkeys, and sluggish horses; these will drown, but man can acquire the art of swimming[4]. They tell that if a man's head should be chopped off and he thrown into the water, he will rise to an upright position in the water[5]. They say further: All birds have their palms on their feet, but the palms of the human and the monkey are on their hands. All quadrupeds have their joints in their forelegs[6] (lit. hands), but the joints of men are in the legs. They 296
say further: Horses lack nodous lumps, goitres, spleens, and udders, and the male ostrich has no brain[7]. Seabirds and seafish possess neither tongues nor brains,[8] but the fish of the river possess tongues and brains. They state that all fish are devoid of lungs[9] and consequently[10] do not breathe. The Arabs taught as a result of their experiences that sheep produce once a year[11] and

[1] Born 122 A. H. died 216. Like Abu 'Ubaida he also was a pupil of Abu 'Amr ibn al-'Ala. He was a pure Arab and wrote numerous works. See Brockelmann, *l. c.*, 104; IKhall, II, 121 ff; Goldziher, *Abhandlungen z. arab. Philologie*, II, 136 and *Muh. St.* II, 402; Damīri, II, 295-6.

[2] MS. and Ed. read بتحرعها, but marginal reading is بتحربتها which can be allowed to stand or may be corrected to بتجربتها, a word which is used further on.

[3] *'Uyūn*, 456, l. 17—20.

[4] This sentence occurs verbatim, *ib.* lines 9—11.

[5] *Ib.*, lines 11—12.

[6] *Ib.*, 457, l. 18—19. He adds وكل طائر ركبه في رجليه, which is the same as our كفه في رجليه.

[7] This sentence seems to be part of a statement by Abu-'Ubaida and Abu-Zaid that "the horse has no spleen, the camel has no gall-bladder, and the ostrich has no brain". Damīri, ii, 176. On the same page, top line, it is remarked that the sayings about the horse and the camel are proverbs for their speed and lack of boldness, respectively.

[8] *ib.*, part of the above statement.

[9] *ib.*

[10] Reading لذلك. with Ms; Ed. كذلك.

[11] The following passage on sheep and goats is found *ib.* 491, l. 19—492, l. 2. See also Damīri, ii, 155.

produce one, not two; but goats gestate twice a year and may produce one or two or three; yet quantity, prosperity and blessing are greater among the sheep than they are among the goats [1]. They said: When sheep graze on grass or green wheat they will grow again, but what the goat eats will not grow back because the sheep nibble it with their teeth and the goats root it out [2]. They declared: When the goat gestates, her milk passes down to her udders in the early part of her gestation, but the sheep do not secrete milk until the time of bringing forth [3]. They taught that the cries of males of all species are louder than the sounds of females except in the case of the goats, the voices of their females being louder than those of the males [4].

Among the proverbs of the Arabs on the subject of animals is their statement [5]: Every ox is flat-nosed and every donkey harelipped; and all mouths with molars in them are distended [6]. They said by experience that a lion will not eat anything sour and will not approach fire nor will it come near vinegar [7]. They declared that a bitch's period of bearing her young is sixty days, and that if she should bring forth in less than that they will not be able to survive [8]. They stated that the female of the dog begins to menstruate at seven months
297 and that her menstruation occurs every seven days; the symptoms of her mens-

---

[1] See *Nuzhat,* 7. The goat was generally spoken of disparagingly among the Arabs. See e. g. *'Uyūn,* 461, and at greater length, Damīri, *ib.*

[2] *Ib.*, 492, lines 15–16.

[3] *Ib.*, 462, l. 17—18. He quotes the following verse in this connection رمدت المعزى فرنق رنق ورمد الصأن فربق ربق, which Lane, s. v. رنق and ربق respectively translates: "The she-goats have secreted milk in their udders, but wait thou, wait thou (for the bringing forth, for they show signs but do not bring forth until after some time). The ewes have secreted milk in their udders: therefore, prepare thou the ارباق: prepare thou the ارباق (for they will bring forth soon because they begin to secrete milk in their udders at the time of bringing forth)."

[4] According to *'Uyūn,* 463, l. 2, it is the female of the ox which forms the exception to this rule.

[5] Reading قولهم with Ms; Ed. فهو ظلم.

[6] *Uyūn* gives the same information except for the last, where he reads وكل دباب اقرح (every beast of burden is ulcerous).

[7] *Ib.*, 465, lines 12—13; see also *'Ajā'ib,* ii, 183, 184.

[8] *Ib.*, 467, lines 3–5.

truating are that her vulva[1] is inflamed. They said that the dog does not acquire any of his teeth save the molars[2]. They remarked regarding the wolf that he sleeps with one eye and keeps vigil with the other. In view of this, Ḥumaid ibn Thaur versified regarding him:

He sleeps with one of the apples of his eye, but bewares
Of death with the other, for he is a wakeful sleeper[3].

The hare sleeps with both eyes open[4]. They said there is no animal with its tongue inverted[5] except the elephant. Nor is there among the quadrupeds any with his breasts on his chest[6], except the elephant[7]. They taught that the female elephant produces her young once in seven years, the she-ass once a year; the cow resembles woman in this respect. They said that the penis[8] of the hare and the fox is a bone[9]. They said, every twolegged creature stands on one leg and limps when one of the two is broken, but not the ostrich, for he, when one of his legs is broken, roosts in his place. For this reason the poet sang regarding himself and his brother:

For I and he are like the legs of the ostrich
With regard to what we share with the rich and the poor[10],

meaning by it that neither of them has any more than his fellow. They said of the female ostrich that she lays from thirty to forty eggs, but that she selects

---

[1] Reading اثفارها with Brockelmann; Ed. اثغارها. See *'Uyūn, ib*, l. 5—6.

[2] Ed. الثامن; Ms. التامن. The reading adopted here is النابين. following *'Uyūn, ib.* l. 8.

[3] *'Uyūn*, 469, l. 5, reads هاجع with the same meaning: Ed. and Ms. نائم. Damīri's reading is: ويتقى بأخرى الاعادى فهو يقظان هاجع. I, 312.

[4] *Ib.*, 470, l. 6; *Nuzhat*, 11; *'Ajā'ib*, II, 182; *al-Damīri*, I, 19.

[5] *'Uyūn*, 469, l. 10; *Nuzhat*, 23, trans. crooked; Damīri, ii, 188.

[6] *'Uyūn*, 469, l. 13, reads لذكوره. This guided me in the choice of the pronoun *his*.

[7] *'Uyūn*, 16, adds: الانسان.

[8] Arabic قضيب. which al-Aṣma'i defines as follows: والقضيب من التيس والثور ويجوز القضيب في كل ذي ذكر. *K. al-Farḳ*, ed. Muller, *SBWA*, LXXXIII, 242.

[9] *'Uyūn*, 470, l. 5—6. Damīri, more specifically: وقضيب الذكر من هذا النوع كذكر الثعلب أحد شطريه عظم والاخر عصب, I, 18.

[10] *'Uyūn*, 471, l. 14 reads ذى غنى وفقير. The whole passage about the legs corresponds almost verbatim with ib., lines 11—14. Even the variant in line 12: وتحامل على ظلع غيره appears to be related to our phrase وعرج الا الظليم. May it not be وتحامل عليه غير الظليم? See also Damiri, II, 296, and *'Ajā'ib*, II, 248.

thirty of them and broods over them[1] in a straight line like a stretched thread[2] Often she abandons her eggs and sits on the eggs of another[3]. This is why Ibn Harama sang of her:

> Like to her who leaves her eggs in the refuse
> And covers the eggs of another with her wings[4].

298 They said that chicks and chickens are made from the white of the eggs and that the yolk nourishes them[5]. They said that the sand-grouse lays only single eggs. Concerning the black eagle they told that it lays three eggs and hatches two, throwing one away. But the bird known as the Bone-breaker[6] hatches it For this reason the saying goes: More pious than the Bone-breaker. They said that the lizard lays seventy eggs, but she eats whatever hatch from the eggs except those who speedily flee from her[7]. Because of this the saying is current: More undutiful than a lizard[8]. A lizard does not approach water; that is why the proverb says: More watered than a lizard[9]. They stated that a lizard has

---

[1] *'Uyūn*, 473, lines 5—6, relates that she broods over forty but hatches only thirty. *'Ajā'ib*, II, 248, states that she divides her eggs into three parts; she buries one, exposes the other to the sun and broods over the third. When these hatch, she breaks those in the sun, now liquefied, and nourishes her young with them. When the chicks grow stronger she digs up those she had buried, punctures a hole in them so that the insects gather, and these make food for the young. Damīri, *ib.*, tells the same story.

[2] *'Uyūn*, 473, lines 10—11; Damīri, *ib.*

[3] Damīri, *ib.*; *Nuzhat*, 91.

[4] For the first line of this couplet see Damīri, *ib.*

[5] Read الفرخ والفروج with *'Uyūn*, 477, line 16. Ms. and Ed., الفرج والفروج.

[6] The other sources (*'Uyūn*, 478; Damīri II, 105: *Ajā'ib, II, 234; Nuzhat, 78—9)* relate that she throws away not her third egg but her third chick, because, Damīri adds (although on p. 273 he cites several other reasons), she finds it difficult to feed three, but the bone-breaker (Kāsir-al-'Ithām) raises it. Of the bird the authorities have little to say. *'Ajā'ib* merely mentions it; Damīri, who discusses it under المكلفة (the charged one), has nothing more to tell than to identify it as the bird which takes care of the eagle's third chick.

[7] Damīri, II, 65; *Ajā'ib*, II, 280.

[8] *'Uyūn*, 460, l. 9, where the same explanation is given for the saying; Damīri, *ib.* (ويوصف بالعقوق) and 66, toward the bottom, verbatim.

[9] Damīri, II, 64. The saying اروى من is given with النقاقة (frog) *'Uyun*, 461, l. 6; Damīri, II, 301, reads اعطش من النقاقة. Both authorities quote for the lizard the proverb اخدع من الضب (more deceiving), *'Uyūn*, ib. l. 7; Damīri II, 66.

wo penises and the female lizard has two vaginas in front[1]. They said of the serpent that it has two tongues[2] and that its tongue is black, differing in color from the skin. All serpents hate the odor of rue and violet, but they are infatuated with the scent of the apple, the pumpkin and cucumber, the mustard seed, milk and wine[3]. Of the frogs they related that they do not croak unless they hold water in their mouths[4] and they will not croak in the Tigris at all, but they do croak in the Euphrates and the other rivers[5]. The poet has sung of the frog:

It takes into its mouth whatever it sucks,
So that it croaks, but the croaking makes it perish[6],

meaning that its croaking calls to it the attention of the snake so that he catches it and devours it. They said that the frog has no bones[7]. Regarding the dung- 299
beetle they related that when it is buried amid flowers it becomes as motionless as though dead, but when it is brought back to the dung it moves[8].

Now this and whatever else is correct of the properties of living beings and others were known to the Arabs in the Age of Ignorance through their observations, without recourse to the leaders of the Bāṭiniyya, for they knew them a long, long time before the existence of the Bāṭiniyya. In this manner we have exposed the lie of the Bāṭiniyya in claiming that their heads are distinguished by a knowledge of the mysteries and peculiarities of things.

We have accounted for their exclusion from all sects of Islam to a sufficient degree. Praised be Allah for it.

---

[1] *'Uyūn*, 472, l. 17.

[2] Damīri, I, 239, bottom, explains that its tongue is split so that some think it is doubled.

[3] *'Uyun*, 481, l. 10-11. Brockelmann, (*Monde Oriental*, XIX, 1925, p. 195, is doubtless right in preferring Ed.'s reading التفاح to بالاقاحى in his edition of *'Uyun*. However, his explanation of الجرو as a dittography for الخردل is unnecessary. The existence of the word in the language, even if its meaning is doubtful, cannot be challenged. Furthermore, a marginal gloss in the MS. explains it by خيار (MS. الجروزة) الجروة (cucumbers or watermelons). The snakes' affection for milk is also cited, Damīri, 11, 840.

[4] *'Uyun*, 481. lines 17-18. According to Damīri the frog will croak if its lower jaw is in the water, but if any water should come into its mouth it will utter no sounds, II, 70.

[5] None of the other authorities records this peculiarity.

[6] 'Uyūn, 481. Correct ينطفه there to read like our text (Brockelmann, *Monde Oriental*, *ib.*). Damīri, I, 70, cites these verses from 'Abd-al-Ḳāhir. Can he be possibly referring to our author? His mention of a specific snake comes perhaps from some other work of Baghdādi.

[7] Damīri, *ib.*

[8] *'Uyun*, 482, lines 10—12; Damīri, I, 170; *Nuzhat*, 40.

SECTION FIVE.

AN ENQUIRY INTO THE CHARACTERISTICS OF THE SAVING SECT AND PROOF OF ITS SALVATION AND ITS ATTRACTIVE FEATURES.

This section comprises a number of chapters, with the following titles:

1. An Enquiry into the Groups composing the People of Tradition and Consensus.
2. An Enquiry into the Proof of Salvation for the People of Tradition and Consensus.
3. The Fundamental Dogmas on which the People of Tradition and Consensus are agreed.

300 4. The Doctrine of the People of Tradition on the Pious Ancestry of the Nation.

5. God's Preservation of the People of Tradition from accusing one another of unbelief
6. The Excellences of the People of Tradition, the branches of their Sciences and a list of their Leaders.
7. The continued chain of Tradition of the People of Tradition in matters of Religion and Life, and a statement of their glories in both fields.

These are the chapters of this section. We shall give an account in every one of them of all that is required, with the help of God.

CHAPTER ONE.

Know, may God prosper you, that the orthodox community comprises eight division . One class possesses a thorough knowledge of the problems of Unity, Prophecy, Dogmas of Promises and Warnings, Reward and Retribution and the necessary pre-requisites for *Ijtihād*[1], the Imāmate, and the exercise of Authority. In this theological subject-matter they tread the paths of the Ṣifātiyya among the Mutakallims[2] who declare themselves free from anthropomorphism as well as from divesting God of His attributes, and from the heresies of the Rawāfiḍ, the Khawārij, the Jahmiyya, the Najjāriyya, and the other sects of erring fancies. The second class consists of the chief jurists of both systems: those who apply the method of analogy and those who adhere to tradition[3], people who accept the principles of faith in accordance with the doctrines of the Ṣifātiyya on God and His eternal attributes and steer clear of the Ḳadarite views and of Mu'tazilism. 301
They affirm God's vision[4] with an organ of sight without falling into the error of *Tashbīh* (anthropomorphism) or of *Ta'ṭīl* (divesting.) They acknowledge the resurrection from the grave, affirming at the same time their belief in the examination in the grave[5], and recognize in addition the truth of the Pool (of the Apostle), the Bridge, Intercession, and forgiveness of sins which are not of polytheistic

---

[1] *Ijtihād* is the right to make decisions which are to be followed by the community. Those who have this right are called *Mujtahids*. See Macdonald's article, *EI*, II, 448—9.

[2] Our author doubtless refers to the school founded by al-Ash'ari. However it is inexact to employ the name Ṣifātiyya as a synonym for Ash'ariyya, since it comprises other groups. Shahr., for example, also discusses the Mushabbiha and Karrāmiyya under the Ṣifātiyya. pp. 95—127.

[3] The school of Abu Ḥanīfa is an example of the first type; that of Mālik illustrates the second.

[4] Al-Ash'ari's credo is succinctly stated in his *Ibāna*, 7—13.

[5] For the following beliefs regarding the future life see below, 209.

character. They hope for the eternal bliss of Paradise to its inhabitants an eternal tortures of hell to unbelievers. They recognize the Imāmate of Abu Bek 'Omar, 'Uthmān and 'Ali; and they venerate highly the pious ancestry of th nation. They realize the necessity of congregating for prayer on Fridays unde the leadership of Imāms who cut themselves loose from the people of errin fancies. They realize the urgency of extracting the precepts of the law from th Ḳur'ān, Tradition and consensus of opinion among the Companions. They cced to the lawfulness of rubbing the dust off the footgear[1], and the incumbency o divorce in three sentences. They choose to forbid marriage by trial[2]. They urg obedience to the Sultans in whatever does not involve sinfulness.

In this group are included the adherents of Mālik, al-Shāfi'i, al-Auzā'i[3], al Thauri[4], Abu Ḥanīfa, ibn Abu Laila[5], the adherents of Abu Thaur[6], the follower of Aḥmad ibn Ḥanbal, the Ẓāhirites and the other jurists who adhere to th

---

[1] A practice in place of the footwash before prayer, allowed by the Sunnites under certai circumstances. In consonance with the importance it receives as a cardinal point of differenc between orthodoxy and heterodoxy, Strothmann has made it the subject of a characterization o *Ikhtilāf* between the Sunnites and Shī'ites, more particularly Zaidites. See *Kultus d. Zaiditen*, 21—46, esp. 21—26 and 44—46. See also *Vorlesungen*, 368—70 (note 147). The Shī'ite Naubakhti calls this practice of the Sunnites one of the *Aḥkām Abi Bekr wa-'Umar*, 12.

[2] See Ed., 314 (below, 175).

[3] 'Abd-al-Raḥmān b. 'Amr b. Yuḥmid, one of the earliest jurists of Islām (88—157 A.H.). He was Imām in Syria and lived in Beirut. His code prevailed until it was replaced by the Mālikite. Nawāwi, 382—4; *EI*, s.v. *Auzā'i;* Sam'āni, f. 53a.

[4] Sufyān b. Sa'īd b. Masrūḥ, a very famous *Muḥaddith* of Kūfa (79—161 A.H.). Acc. to Goldziher, *Muh. St.*, II, 12, he was more proficient in the mechanical memorization of the Ḥadīth than in the knowledge of its application in daily life. Yet see, in answer to Goldziher, IKhall., I, 577. Nawawi, 386 ff. sings his praises abundantly. He hid from the Khalīf al-Mahdi (IKhall., *ib.*), *Fihrist*, 225.

[5] Muḥammad b. 'Abd-al-Raḥmān of Kūfa (74—148 A.H.). He is said to have been under strained relations with Abu Ḥanīfa (IKhall., II, 584—5) whose predecessor he was in applying the method of *Ra'i* (*Fihrist*, 203).

[6] Ibrahīm b. Khālid al-Kalbi, a disciple of Shāfi'ī (converted to him after having been a Ḥanīfite) with whom he nevertheless disagreed on many matters and developed his own Madhhab which held sway in Azerbaijān and Armenia. He died 246 A.H. *Fihrist*, 211; IKhall., I, 6.

doctrines of the Ṣifātiyya with respect to the rational fundamentals, and do not adulterate their law with any of the heresies of the people of erring fancies.

The third division is made up of those who possess a comprehensive knowledge of the methods of the Ḥadīth and Sunna which are traced to the Prophet, and can discern the sound from the faulty in them. They recognize the reasons for discrediting certain traditions and for pronouncing others trustworthy, and they do not associate with their knowledge of this science any of the heresies of the people of erring fancies. The fourth division consists of people who are 302
extremely well-versed in almost everything pertaining to rhetoric, grammar and inflection. They follow the course of the outstanding personalities in philology, such as al-Khalīl[1], Abu 'Amr ibn al-'Alā[2], Sibawaihi[3], al-Farrā'[4], al-Akhfash[5], al-Aṣma'i[6], al-Mazīni[7], Abu 'Ubaid[8], and the other scholars in philology, both of the Kufite School and the Baṣrian School, who do not mix their pursuit of this

---

[1] Al-Khalīl b. Aḥmad, founder of the study of Arabic meter. Lived in Baṣra 100—175 a.H. Fluegel, *Schulen*, 37—38, 42; IKha'l, I, 493ff.; Brockelmann, I, 100.

[2] One of the seven readers of the Ḳur'ān, and founder of the school of Philology at Baṣra. Fluegel, 32—34; IKhall, II, 399ff.; Brockelmann, I, 99.

[3] The foremost grammarian of Arabic, though himself a Persian. 'Amr b. 'Uthmān b. Ḳanbar died 180 a.H. and was called امام النحاة. Fluegel, 43—45; IKhall, II, 396—98; Brockelmann, I, 100—02.

[4] Abu Zakariya Yaḥya b. Ziyād b. 'Abdallah b. Manṣūr al-Dailami (d. 207), a pupil of al-Kisā'i of the Kūfic School. He was one of the most famous philologists and some one even expressed the opinion that "without al-Farrā' there would be no Arabic." Fluegel, 129—36; Sam'āni, f. 420a; Brockelmann I, 116.

[5] Al-Akhfash is the name of several noted grammarians. Our author may either have had them all in mind or he referred to al-Akhfash *al-Akbar* whose name is 'Abd-al-Ḥamīd b. 'Abd-al-Majīd Abu-l-Khaṭṭāb, a native of Hajar who died in 177. He collected dialectical expressions among the Arabs. Fluegel, 61; IKhall, II, 244; *Nujūm*, I, 485; *EI*, I, s. v.

[6] See above, 153, note 1.

[7] Jahm b. Khalaf, a contemporary of al-Aṣma'i. He was well-versed in rare expressions and in poetry; he also wrote works on insects and reptiles. Fluegel, 50.

[8] Abu 'Ubaid al-Ḳāsim b. Sallām al-Ḥarawi was born in Herāt about 150 and died in Mecca or Medīna about 227. He studied under al-Aṣma'i; lived in Khurāsān and Tarsus; wrote a long dictionary and other works. Fluegel, 85—6; IKhall II, 486—89; Brockelmann, I, 106—7; *EI*, I, 112.

study with any of the innovations of the Ḳadariyya, the Rawāfiḍ and the Khawārij. Any one of them who inclines towards any of the erring fancies cannot be regarded orthodox and his teaching carries no weight in matters of language and grammar.

The fifth division consists of those who have gathered extensive knowledge about the variant readings in the Ḳur'ān and the manner of expounding and interpreting the verses of the Ḳur'ān in accordance with the dogmas of the orthodox, and not with the interpretations of the people of erring fancies. The sixth group is made up of the Ṣūfi ascetics who indulge in study and abstain from pleasure, are well-informed and deliberate in reasoning, resigned to fate and content with the obtainable. They know that the organs of hearing and seeing and the heart are all to be called to account for even the weight of a grain of sand. They make the most careful preparations for the world to come. Their discourses in the fields of interpretation and guidance pursue the course of the Traditionists and not of those who adopt a mocking attitude to tradition; they do not practise good for appearance's sake nor do they abandon it for shame.

In their religious philosophy they proclaim the Unity of God and divest Him of anthropomorphism; their way of life is that of committing their care to
303 God, entrusting themselves to Him, submitting to His command, feeling satisfied with whatever has been bestowed upon them and abstaining from any rebelliousness against Him. "That is the grace of Allah; He gives it to whom He pleases, and Allah is the Lord of mighty praise"[1].

The seventh division consists of people who defend the Muslim frontiers against the infidels, fight the enemies of the Muslims and protect the Muslims. They repel them from their sacred precincts and their homes and observe the law of Orthodox Islam at the front. It is they concerning whom God has revealed His Word: "And as for those who strive hard for Us, We will most certainly guide them in Our ways"[2]. May God increase their reward in His excellence and benevolence. The eighth is made up of the general population of the cities among whom the practices of the orthodox prevail; but not the

---

[1] Sura 57, v. 21.

[2] Sura 29, v. 69.

population of the provinces among whom the rites of the people of fantasy and error are practised. We understand by this group of the general population only the public which attaches itself to that which is approved by the orthodox learned men in relation to the problems of Justice and Unity, Reward and Punishment; who regard them as guide-posts in their faith and make them examples in the derived laws, in matters of the allowed and the forbidden. They do not attach themselves to any of the innovations of the people of erring fancies. They are the ones whom the Ṣūfis call the padding of Paradise.

These are the divisions of Orthodox Islam. Those included in them are adherents of the true religion and the straight path. May God make them endure with the permanent Word in the life of this world and in the future life. Verily in favorable response He is competent, and of it He is capable.

CHAPTER TWO.

AN ENQUIRY INTO THE PROOF OF SALVATION FOR THE PEOPLE OF TRADITION AND CONSENSUS.

We have already related in the first section of this book[1] that when the Prophet spoke of the schisms among his people to the number of seventy-three sects, and declared that one of these would be saved, he was asked regarding this sect and its characteristics. In reply to this, he pointed to those who followed his path and the path of his Companions. We cannot find in our day among the sects of the nation any which is in agreement with the Companions other than the Orthodox among the jurists of the nation and the Ṣifātite Mutakallims; not the Rawāfiḍ, nor the Ḳadariyya, nor the Khawārij, nor the Jahmiyya, nor the Najjāriyya, nor the Mushabbiha, nor the Ghulāt, nor the Ḥulūliyya.

As for the Ḳadariyya, how can they be said to be in agreement with the Companions when their outstanding man al-Naẓẓām attacked most of the Companions and denied the uprightness of ibn Mas'ūd[2]? He imputed error to him

---

[1] Ed. 4—5 (Seelye, 21—2). The error which gave rise to this tradition has been pointed out by Goldziher in *Revue de l'Histoire des Religions*, XXVI, 129—37, and in his study *Beiträge z. Literaturgeschichte d. Schi'a unt. d. Sunnitischen Polemik* in *SBWA*, LXXVIII, (1874) 445. See also Seelye, *Introd.*, 2—3. It is interesting, in connection with this tradition and the use made of it by our author, to cite its Mu'tazilite version as it is alleged to have been told by Sufyān al-Thauri in the name of Jābir b. 'Abdallah; ستفترق امتي على بعض وسبعين فرقة ابرها واتقاها الفئة المعتزلة وهو تمام الخبر ثم قال سفيان لاصحابه تسموا بهذا الاسم لانكم اعتزلتم الظلمة فقالوا سبقك بها عمرو بن عبيد واصحابه فكان سفيان بعد ذلك يروي واحدة ناجية. Arnold, *Al-Mutazila*, 2—3.

[2] 'Abdallah b. Mas'ūd is one of the most outstanding traditionists and one of Muḥammad's most intimate friends. See his biography in ibn Hajar's *Biogr. of Persons Who Knew Mohammed*, II, 890—893 (‡9302). Baghdādi's statement that in not crediting ibn Mas'ūd al-Naẓẓām is guilty of denying the Prophet's miracles is not clear to me. In Bukhāri, III, 26, the tradition of the cleaving of the moon has several *sanads* in which ibn Mas'ūd does not figure

on account of his traditions in the name of the Prophet that he is prosperous who was destined to be prosperous while in his mother's womb, and he is unhappy for whom unhappiness was decreed in his mother's womb [1], and his tradition regarding the cleaving of the moon [2]. This fs his attitude only because he denies the miracles of the Prophet. He inveighed against the rulings of 'Omar because he inflicted eighty stripes for wine drinking [3] and banished Naṣr ibn al-Ḥajjāj to Baṣra when he feared the disturbance [4] of the women of al-Medīna because of him [5]. 305

---

at all, and one of those in which he figures is not finally dependent on him but on 'Abdallah b. 'Abbās. See also *ib.*, 341—2. The same may be said of the traditions reported in Muslim V, 356 (Nawāwi's defence of the truthfulness of the tradition, ib., is very interesting. Cf. also *Streitschrift*, 65, for Ghazāli's defence in approximately the same vein. Andrae, 107, *Mukhtalif al-Ḥadīth*, 31). In Tirmidhi the tradition is reported without ibn Mas'ūd at all, II, 28. He however, adds: قال ابو عيسى وفي الباب عن ابن مسعود وانس وجبير ابن مطعم وهذا حديث حسن صحيح. Similarly, a variety of sources exists for the tradition about the decree. It is reported ultimately on the authority of Anās b. Mālik (Bukh IV, 251, and Aḥmad b. Ḥanbal, III, 116), of Ḥudhaifa (*ib.*, IV, 6; he, too, was attacked by al-Naẓẓām, *Mukhtalif al-Ḥadīth*, 27), of Jābir b. 'Abdallah (A. b. Ḥ, III, 397), and of others (Tirmidhi, II, 20). On 'Abdallah's caution in reporting Ḥadīths see Goldziher, *ZDMG*, LXI, (1907), 860.

[1] This tradition is reported in a different version in the name of ibn Mas'ūd in Muslim, V. 271: الشقي من شقي في بطن امه والسعيد من وعظ بغيره. The idea of the saying is supported by the tradition under Ḳadar in Bukhāri, IV, 251; Muslim V, 269ff. Cf. *Ibāna*, 86. For other sources see above note.

[2] For al-Naẓẓām's attack on ibn Mas'ūd see Ed. 134 (reading *Aba* should be corrected to *bna*), Seelye, 155. (Her reading is to be corrected as well and her references are irrelevant since they do not concern our traditionists.) For his denial of the splitting of the moon, see Maḳrīzi, II, 346 and Shahr. 40, and Isf. f. 31a. — Al-Naẓẓām's objection to the two traditions is no surprise. His Ḳadarism could not endure either the disturbance of the order of the world predicated by the tradition about the moon, nor the determinism implicit in the other. See *Mukhtalif al-Ḥadīth*, 25—6.

[3] See *Kitab al-Umm*, VI, 130—31; *Mukhtalif al Ḥadith*, 195—6.

[4] With MS. فتنة; Ed. فتنته.

[5] It is related in ibn Sa'd, III, I, 204—5 and IKhall, I, 359, that 'Omar was annoyed with the fact that this handsome Naṣr was "celebrated by young females in the privacy of their apartments" and, deciding to send him away from the city where he lived, he banished him to Baṣra. Shahr. *ib.*, also mentions this incident. None of the major historians report it. Ibn Hajar in his biography of Naṣr's father, al-Ḥajjāj b. 'Ilāṭ, (I, 642), promises us a biography of

But this can be explained on his part simply by the lack of zeal for the sacred cities. He also assailed the ruling on the slave-mothers of children, made by 'Ali, who said: "Verily my opinion is that they may be sold." Al-Naẓẓām demanded: Who is he to pronounce judgments based on his own opinion?[1]. He reprehended 'Uthmān because of his edict regarding al-Kharkā'[2] that property is to be divided equally into three parts among the grandfather, the mother and the sister. He charged Abu Ḥuraira with falsification[3] because many of his traditions contradict the dogmas of the Ḳadariyya. He condemned the rulings by way of *Ijtihād* issued by any one of the Companions. He said that they did this only for two reasons: either because they did not know that they were not permitted to do it, or because they wished to be chiefs and leaders of *madhāhib*[4] which are ascribed to them. He characterized the traditions[5] of the Companions as the result of ignorance or hypocrisy.

In his opinion, any one who is ignorant of the precepts of the law is a non-believer, and he who believes contrariwise with no convincing proof is a hypocritical infidel or a wicked transgressor. He thus deemed eternal hell inevitable for the chief Companions; he himself belongs there more rightfully. He further rejected the validity of *Ijmā'* among the Companions, not considering it[6]

---

the son but he seems to have failed to keep his promise. See a fuller account of Naṣr in Subki, *Ṭabaḳāt*, I, 147—9. Cf. Caetani, *Annali dell'Islam*, Anno 23, § 313—14, esp. note.

[1] In Ed. 134 (Seelye 154—5; the passage is mistranslated) he challenges 'Ali's right to base judgements on his opinion in connection with the question of a cow that killed a donkey this is borne out by Mukhtalif al-Ḥadīth, 25; on the question under discussion here 'Ali is said to have changed his mind, ib, 195. Our passage refers to the case of a mother of a child born of concubinage — the term is Umm-Walad — and whether she can be sold after the death of her child's father. See Juynboll, 206, 236, and Sachau, 127, 168—75, where the law is that she cannot be sold. In defence of 'Ali's ruling cf. *Mukhtalif al-Ḥadīth*, 199—200.

[2] I have not been able to identify the name. For the ruling see Sachau, 248, and 252 sqq.

[3] Abu Huraira, one of the most intimate Companions of the Prophet, is credited with more traditions than any one else. On the ease with which he manufactured traditions see *ZDMG*, L (1896), 487ff. and LXI (1907), 860. See also *Zahiriten*, 78—9, and Kremer, *Orient unter d. Chalifen*, trans. S. Khuda Bukhsh, 56 note.

[4] i. e. rites followed by sections of the community.

[5] With MS. اخبار; Ed اجهار.

[6] Reading يره with MS; Ed. ير.

as convincing proof. He thought it possible for the community to agree on an error[1]. Now, how can he be considered to walk in the path of the Companions and to imitate their ways who believes it a duty to contradict all of them, since his opinion is the converse of theirs?

Their founder Wāṣil ibn 'Aṭā' questioned the integrity of 'Ali and his two sons, of ibn 'Abbās, of Ṭalḥa, of al-Zubair, of 'Āisha and of all members of either party who participated in the Battle of the Camel[2]. Because of this he declared: If 'Ali or Ṭalḥa were to testify before me about a bundle of vegetables, 306
I would not pronounce judgment on the basis of their testimony; for I know that one of them is a sinner but do not know exactly who it is. According to his principle it is likely that 'Ali and his followers are sinners, condemned to eternal hell. It is equally possible that the other party known as the Party of the Camel is tortured in hell eternally. He doubted the rectitude of 'Ali, Ṭalḥa and al-Zubair despite the Prophet's promise of Paradise to the three of them[3] and despite their joining the oath called Bī'at al-Riḍwān[4] and their inclusion within the entire group concerning whom God declared: "Certainly Allah was well pleased with the believers when they swore the oath of allegiance to you under the tree"[5].

'Amr ibn 'Ubaid[6] agreed with the views of Wāṣil on the two parties at the Battle of the Camel and even exceeded him by being convinced of the sinfulness of each of the two parties. For Wāṣil was certain that one of the parties sinned; he would not pronounce judgment on the basis of testimony given by two men one of whom was of 'Ali's party and the other of the Party of the Camel, but he would accept the testimony of two men who were both members

---

[1] Ed. 129 (Seelye 149) *Mukhtalif al-Ḥadīth*, 21—2. Acc. to *Intiṣār*, 51, al-Naẓẓām did not hold this view; al-Khayyāṭ attributes it to al-Jāḥiẓ.

[2] On the Orthodox attitude to the participants in this battle, see below.

[3] Tirmiḍhi, II, 314; Ṭayālisi, ‡236.

[4] The pledge of mutual loyalty by Muḥammad's men taken under the tree at al-Ḥudaibiyya, at which time a truce was arranged with the Ḳuraish (6 a.H.) see Bukhāri, III, (trans. III, 144). The name *Yawm al-Riḍwān* comes from the beginning word of the Ḳur'ānic verse quoted immediately in the text.

[5] Sura 48, v. 18.

[6] See on him Ed. 101—2 (Seelye, 123—5).

of ‘Ali’s party or of two men who were both members of the party of the Camel. But ‘Amr ibn ‘Ubaid declared: I will not accept the testimony of any of them no matter whether they be all of one party or whether some of them are of ‘Ali’s group while others are of the Camel group. He maintained that both parties alike were transgressors. According to his premise, it necessarily follows that ‘Ali and his two sons, ibn ‘Abbās, ‘Ammār, Abu Ayyūb al-Anṣāri, Khuzaima ibn Thābit[1] al-Anṣāri whose testimony the Prophet ranked as highly as that of two
307 upright men, and the remaining associates of ‘Ali, as well as Ṭalha, al-Zubair, ‘Āisha, and the other members of the Camel, with thousands of Companions in their midst, are all sinners doomed to eternal hell. There were with ‘Ali twenty-five heroes of the Battle of Badr and most of the participants in the Battle of Uḥud, six hundred Anṣārs and a number of the first Fugitives.

Abu-l-Hudhail and al-Jāḥiẓ and most of the Ḳadariyya were of the same opinion in this matter as Wāṣil ibn ‘Aṭā’. But how can anyone be said to follow the footsteps of the Companions when he declares most of them to be sinners and regards them as people condemned to hell? How can he who does not regard their testimony valid accept traditions transmitted by them? But whosoever rejects their traditions and rejects their testimony ceases to walk in their path and to follow them. Only he imitates them who acts in accordance with their traditions and accepts their testimony in the manner of the People of Tradition and Consensus.

The Khawārij also declare ‘Ali and his sons, as well as ibn ‘Abbas and Abu Ayyub al-Ansāri to be infidels. They also brand ‘Uthmān, ‘Ā’isha, Ṭalha and al-Zubair as unbelievers, and everyone who did not secede from ‘Ali and Mu‘ā-wiya after the arbitration[2]. They call any sinner in the community an infidel. But he who believes in branding most of the Companions as infidels cannot be on the right path trodden by them.

As for the Ghulāt among the Rawāfiḍ, such as the Sabbābiyya, the Bayāniyya, the Mughīriyya, the Manṣūriyya, the Janāḥiyya, the Khaṭṭābiyya and the

---

[1] See ibn Hajar, *Biography*, I, 875—7, where the same tradition about his trustworthiness is related (876).

[2] See below 213—5.

other Ḥulūliyya, we have already demonstrated their exclusion from Islam, and we have also proved that they are in the ranks of idol-worshippers or among the ranks of the Christian Ḥulūliyya. But neither the idol-worshippers nor Christians nor other infidels can point to a pattern or model among the Companions. 308

Concerning the Zaidiyya. — The Jārūdiyya among them declare Abu Bekr, 'Umar, 'Uthmān and most of the Companions to be infidels. He who declares most of them to be unbelievers cannot copy them. The Sulaimāniyya and the Butriyya[1] condemn 'Uthmān as an infidel or else they maintain a neutral attitude regarding him but condemn his defenders as sinners and brand most of the members of the Camel as heretics.

As for the Imāmiyya, most of them adhere to the view that the Companions, with the exception of 'Ali, his two sons, and about thirteen others, apostasized after the decease of the Prophet. The Kāmiliyya believe that 'Ali also became an apostate and a heretic by refraining from making war upon them[2]. How can he be on the right path of the Companions who asserts that they are infidels? Therefore we say: how can the Rawāfiḍ or the Khawārij or the Ḳadariyya or the Jahmiyya or the Najjāriyya or the Bakriyya or the Ḍirāriyya be in concord with the Companions? All alike they do not accept as authentic anything which has come down by tradition on the authority of the Companions regarding the precepts of the law. For they refrain from accepting traditions of the Ḥadīth and the Lives of the Prophet and the heroic deeds on account of their branding as infidels the authors of the Ḥadīth, who are the transmitters of the reports and the *Athār*-traditions[3], and the narrators of the Histories and Lives, and on account of their condemning the jurists of the community who have preserved the traditions of the Companions and have obtained by analogy the derivative institutions of the law from the opinions of the Companions. There has not arisen, by God's grace and favor, a leading jurist, or a leading traditionist, or an outstanding 309 rhetorician and grammarian, or a person credible in transmitting deeds of heroism or Lives of the Prophet or histories, nor was there an Imām for warning and exhorting, nor an authority in interpretation and exegesis of the Ḳur'ān among

[1] With MS ; Ed البشرية .

[2] Ed., 39 (Seelye 60).

[3] See below.

the Khawārij, the Rawāfiḍ, the Jahmiyya, the Ḳadariyya, the Corporealists or the other people of erring fancies. But the leaders in these sciences, whether specialized or general, have all been from the Orthodox group. Since the people of erring fancies reject the traditions which have come down on the authority of the Companions with respect to their precepts and their lives, imitation of their ways is not possible inasmuch as they do not regard them as witnesses, nor do they accept the traditions of those who trace them to the Companions. It becomes clear from this that those who emulate the Companions are those who act in accordance with what has been proved true by authentic traditions regarding their precepts and their lives. This is the tradition of the Orthodox and not of the Hypocrites[1]. By the truth which we have established it is correct to confirm their salvation in accordance with the ruling of the Prophet regarding the salvation of those who imitate his Companions. Praised be Allah for it.

---

[1] MS., السنية. Literally a two-headed axe. Brockelmann's emendation البدع (*Monde Oriental*, XIX [1925], 198) is not warranted.

CHAPTER THREE.

AN EXPOSITION OF THE FUNDAMENTAL DOGMAS UPON WHICH THE ORTHODOX ARE IN MUTUAL AGREEMENT.

The generality of Orthodox Muslims are agreed about certain principles of the essentials of religion, and a knowledge of the essence of every one of these is binding on every understanding, mature person. Every essential consists of branches and they in turn comprise propositions about which there is a consensus of opinion among the Orthodox. They accuse of error everyone who contradicts them regarding this. The first essential which they regard as one of the funda- 310
mentals of the faith is the confirmation of the realities and of knowledge, particularly and generally[1]. The second essential is knowledge concerning the creation of the universe including its parts, both accidents and bodies. The third is a cognizance of the Maker of the universe and His essential attributes. The fourth is to know His eternal attributes; the fifth is to know His names and qualities. The sixth essential is the knowledge of His justice and wisdom. The seventh is the knowledge of His messengers and Prophets. The eighth concerns itself with the knowledge of the miracles of the Prophets and the wonders of the Saints. The ninth is knowledge of the bases of Islamic law on which the community is agreed. The tenth is knowledge of the laws of bidding and forbidding and charging. The eleventh [is knowledge of the inevitable end of every being and his status in the future world. The twelfth][2] is knowledge concerning the Caliphate and the Imāmate and the requirements for leadership. The thirteenth consists of the principles of Faith and Islam in general. The fourteenth is knowledge of the

[1] i. e. whether they apply in general or to a particular instance. On the distinction, esp. in its bearing on *Fikh*, see *Zahiriten*, 120—2.

[2] The passage enclosed in brackets is missing in both Ed. and MS. but is inserted here from the heading of the section in the text. See below.

status of saints and the grades of the pious Imāms. The fifteenth is knowledge of the laws bearing on the enemies among the non-believers and the people of erring fancies[1]. As for these principles, the Orthodox are agreed about their basic character and they accuse of error anyone who contradicts them. Every essential involves fundamental propositions and derived propositions. They agree on their fundamentals but generally differ regarding some of their derived principles to an extent which does not compel mutual accusations of erring or sinning.

Concerning the first essential: the confirmation of realities and knowledge.—Agreement prevails about recognizing knowledge as inherent ideas in the learned,
311 and they believe those to be in error who deny the reality of knowledge and the other properties. They brand the Sophists[2] as ignorant because they deny knowledge and the reality of all things, and regard them as opposing that which has long been incontrovertibly known. The same is true of the Sophists who maintain a skeptical view about the existence of realities, or of those who assert that the reality of things is based on belief, and who call all beliefs acceptable despite their mutual inconsistency and their incompatibleness[3]. These three groups are all heretics for rejecting the incontrovertible, rational axioms.

The Orthodox declare that the kinds of knowledge possessed by men and those possessed by other living beings are three; intuitive, perceptive, and inductive[4].

[1] The same list will be found in *Uṣūl*, 1—2. Our entire chapter is a concise digest of the other work of the author, whose artificial character has already been pointed out by Josef Schacht in the *OLZ*, XXXII (1929), 566.

[2] In *Uṣūl*, 6—7, Baghdādi gives a fuller, though substantially similar description of the three types of Sophists and also refutes their respective positions. The sophistry to which he himself falls a victim is best illustrated in the following argument which seems to have been a stock-argument with the Muslim scholars, (it is employed by IH, I, 8, and by Murtada; see Horten, *Probleme*, 48): They should be asked: Has the denial of realities a reality? If they should answer yes, they affirm one reality. But if they should say no, they can be told: Since the denial of realities has no reality therefore their denial is not admissible and the affirmative is true. (*Uṣūl*, 6.)

[3] "They are forced to admit that the world is pre-existent and created because some people believe in its creation and others in its eternity", *ib.*, 7.

[4] *Uṣūl*, 8—9. These three sources are also enumerated by the Jewish Philosophers Baḥya b. Paḳūda in his *Farā'id-al-Ḳulūb* (ed. Yahuda) 79, (Heb. trans., ed. Zifroni, 48), and Sa'adia in *Emūnōth We-dēōth* (Yusafof ed.), 43, ff. Cf. *Creencia*, 52ff.

They declare: He who disacknowledges intuitive knowledge or perceptive knowledge acquired through the five senses is an Oppositionist; he who denies speculative knowledge established by deductive or inductive proof is to be more closely observed. If he is one of the Sumaniyya[1] who reject speculative reasoning in rational knowledge, then he is a godless infidel. His status is like the status of the Materialists since he, like them, professes the eternity of the world and denies the existence of the Maker, while he goes beyond them in his demand for the abrogation of all religions. If he is of those who credit speculative reasoning in matters intellectual but reject analogy in the derived institutions of the law like the Zāhiriyya[2], he is not an infidel as a result of his rejection of analogy in legal matters.

They believe that the senses with which the phenomena are perceived are five[3]: vision, for perceiving visible sensations[4]; hearing, for perceiving audible 312
sensations; taste, for feeling tastes; smell, for detecting odors; and touch, for sensing hot and cold, wet and dry, soft and hard. They say that the perceptions coming from these senses are inherent in the organs which are called senses. They accuse Abu Hāshim ibn al-Jubbai of error because of his contention that the act of perceiving is neither an idea nor an accident nor anything else but the thing perceived[5].

They teach that indirect information which is handed down without interruption serves as a necessary recognition of the truth of what has been transmitted uninterruptedly, if that information is of the kind which can be attested or perceived either with the senses or axiomatically. Such, for example, is the conviction of the real existence of any country which one who obtains the knowledge[6] by

---

[1] See above 91 note 1; *Uṣūl*, 10—11.

[2] Goldziher points out clearly in his work *Zahiriten* that that school is distinct only in its legalistic views (مذهب فقهي) and not in its theological dogmas (مذهب كلامي), 131—3. It may be added that ibn Ḥazm is one notable exception in this respect.

[3] *Uṣūl*, 9—10.

[4] Vision, and not hearing, as the philosophers think, is the most excellent sense of all the five acc. to the Mutakallims, *ib.* 10.

[5] Ed., 183 (Seelye 204).

[6] With MS. السامع للخبر; Ed. السامع المخبر.

information has never visited, such knowledge having been transmitted unbroken; or our knowledge of the existence of prophets and kings who lived before us. As for the veracity of the claims of prophets regarding prophecy it is known to us by logical arguments. They declare as infidels those of the Sumaniyya who deny the admissibility of acquiring knowledge by way of unbroken traditions.

They say: The reports which oblige us to act in accordance with them are of three kinds[1]: a report transmitted without interruption (*Tawātur*), information reported by a few *(Āḥād)*, and the mean between these two — news which spreads (*Mustafīḍ*). A report transmitted without interruption, which it would be absurd to agree to manufacture, necessarily obliges us to recognize the truth of its contents. By this sort of communication we learn about the countries which we have not visited; by it we become acquainted with the kings and prophets and generations that existed before our time. By it a man knows his parents to whom he is linked. Information transmitted by a few, provided its *Isnād* is
313 trustworthy and its contents do not seem absurd to the mind, compels action in accordance with it but not acceptance of it[2]. It has the same standing as the testimony of honest witnesses before the judge, in that it compels him outwardly to decide in accordance with it although he may not know their credibility with respect to the testimony. By this kind of information the jurists have established most of[3] the derived precepts of the law bearing on works and deeds and the other classes of the allowed and the forbidden. They accuse of error anyone who repudiates the duty of acting in accordance with that type of information as a whole, such as the Rawāfiḍ, Khawārij and the other people of fancies. News which circulates, the mean between *Tawātur* and *Āḥād*, shares a characteristic in common with *Tawātur* in that it imposes both recognition and action in accordance with it, but is distinguished from *Tawātur* in that knowledge resulting from it is acquired logical knowledge, whereas knowledge based on *Tawātur* is necessary, not acquired. This source of information falls into several classes: one, the accounts of prophets about themselves and the account [about them] told by a person of whose trustworthiness the Prophet has told us; the recogni-

[1] *Uṣūl,* 12—14.

[2] This distinction is commonly accepted as orthodox. See *Islām,* III (1912), 230—33.

[3] MS. adds من, which Ed. has omitted.

tion of its truth[1] is acquired. Another is the report which is spread by one
person. When he relates it in the presence of a group of people who cannot
be believed to have agreed on a lie, and demands from them acceptance of that
which he related in their presence, then if no one contradicts him we recognize
his veracity regarding it. Through this type of report we learn of the miracles
of the Prophet, such as the cleaving of the moon, his making pebbles utter
praises in his hand[2], the longing of the tree for him when he departed from it[3],
his filling many people with little food[4] and similarly other miracles of his. But
the Ḳur'ān, whose composition is in the nature of a miracle [does not fall in this
category]; for the confirmation of the Ḳur'ān and its revelation to him, and the 314
failure of Arabs and heathens to emulate it[5], are known by *Tawātur* which
obliges men to necessary knowledge. To this division belong the traditions current among the Imāms of the Ḥadīth and the Fiḳh about the truth of which they
are of unanimous opinion as, for example, the traditions about Intercession, the
Reckoning, the Pool, the Bridge, the Balance, the Tortures in the Grave, and the
Questioning by the two angels in the Grave. Similarly the traditions which cir-
culate among many doctors of the law, such as the fixing[6] of a minimum wealth
from which alms-giving is required and the traditions bearing on it[7], the punish-

---

[1] With MS. بصدقه ; Ed. لصدقه .

[2] This tradition does not appear in any of the collections examined by Wensinck, so that it is of a later date. It is cited in the Shī'ite biography of Muḥammad, *Ḥayat-ul-Ḳulūb*, 161. It is also cited *Uṣūl*, 182, with the additional comment: حتى التزمه .

[3] Of this tradition no mention is made by Wensinck. Nawāwi, 42, mentions حنين الجذع and تسليم الحجر . Cf. also IH, V, 7.

[4] There are many versions of this tradition. For reference see Wensinck, s. v. *Muḥammad*, 166 b. and 167 a. The stories agreeing most closely with the wording in our text will be found Bukhāri, III, 95, 493, 508 (trans. III, 124, 656, 675). Cf. Andrae, 46—7. For a biblical parallel, see II Kings IV, 42—44.

[5] See below 204; Andrae, 94ff.

[6] The reading *nuṣub* is attested by the MS., and it is not necessary to change it to *niṣāb* as Brockelmann suggests.

[7] The words in the text واخبار الهوا are difficult to interpret. Brockelmann's suggestion (ib. 199) that we read اخبار الهدو, "Zwang zum Verzicht auf die Talio" seems too far-fetched. Goldziher's emendation واخبارها is the one adopted here.

ment for wine-drinking, the tradition about rubbing the foot-gear, stoning[1], and others among the traditions which the jurists have agreed to credit and to act in accordance with the contents thereof. They have accused of error any of the people of erring fancies who contradict them: the Khawārij for their denial of stoning; those among the Najadāt who deny the punishment for wine-drinking; those who deny the rubbing of the foot-gear. They accuse of heresy anyone who denies God's visibility, the Pool, Intercession, and the Tortures of the Grave. By the same token, they ascribe error to the Khawārij who cut off the hand[2] of the thief for petty and grand larceny, regardless of whether the stolen goods were well guarded or unguarded articles[3], because[4] they reject the trustworthy traditions regarding the establishment of a minimum value and of protection, for punishment by amputation. Just as they declare anyone to be mistaken who rejects the correct traditions, so they accuse of error anyone who persists in lending credence to a traditional precept about whose disavowal the jurists of the two schools of analogy and tradition are unanimous. Thus they ascribe error to the Rawāfiḍ for maintaining the *Mut'a*[5], whose permissibility has been annulled.

---

[1] It is one of the punishments for adultery, see below.

[2] The word يد is missing in MS.

[3] Acc. to the Orthodox law the stolen object must comply with the following two requirements before the thief's hand is to be cut off. It must have a minimum value and must have been stolen from a well-guarded storage-place. See Sachau, 810—11, 825—31, and Arabic, 26.

[4] With MS. لردهم; Ed. كردهم.

[5] *Mut'a* refers to two practices both of which have been abolished by the Sunnites, while the Shī'ites adhere to them. One is concerned with the Pilgrimage; in that case *Mut'a* means the utilization of the *'Umra* for the *Ḥajj*.

'Umra is a pious visit which a Muslim can make to Mecca during any part of the year. The *Ḥajj* or Pilgrimage is preferably to be made in the month of *Dhu-l-Ḥijja* and entails many more observances and prescriptions. Utilization (Ar. *Tamattu'*) is defined by Snouck Hurgronje in *Het Mekkaansche Fest* (*Verspreide Geschriften*, I, 57) as follows: In that case (i. e. utilization), although intending to perform the *Ḥajj*, the *Iḥrām* is taken on before an *'Umra* which is accomplished during the *Ḥajj*-months. The person afterwards remains in Mecca, enjoys the same freedom as the Meccan inhabitants, and takes on the *Iḥrām* again on the first *Ḥajj*-day (the 8th of *Dhu-l-Ḥijja*). Although traditions agree in reporting that Muḥammad himself utilized this arrangement and allowed others to do so, 'Omar nevertheless forbade it. See *ib.* 57ff. See also Wensinck's article in *EI*, II, s. v. *Hadjdj*, esp. 456b; Juynboll,

The Orthodox are agreed that God imposed upon mankind the duty of knowing Him, and enjoined them regarding it and that He bade them know His Messenger and His Book and perform whatever the Book and Tradition guide them to do. They declare as infidels any of the Ḳadariyya or the Rawāfiḍ who 315
maintain that no one was charged by God with the duty of knowing Him, as Thumāma[1], al-Jāḥiẓ[2], and a group of the Rawāfiḍ believe. They agree that as regards any acquired speculative knowledge, it is possible for God to turn us into possessors of a necessary knowledge of the fact known. They declare as Kāfirs any of the Mu'tazila who maintain that our knowledge of God in the Future World will be acquired and not necessary. They agree that the sources of the precepts of the Law are the Ḳur'ān, the Sunna and consensus of opinion among the Ancients[3]. They call a heretic anyone of the Rawāfiḍ who believes that the Ḳur'ān and Sunna possess no validity at the present time, owing to their charge that the Companions altered parts of the Ḳur'ān and mistranscribed others[4]. They declare as infidels the Khawārij, who reject all the traditions which the transmitters have handed down, because they contend that those who transmitted them are infidels. They declare al-Naẓẓām a Kāfir because he denies the validity of consensus and of unbroken tradition, and because of his opinion that it is possible for the community to agree on an error, and that it is possible that the members of a *Tawātur*-tradition have agreed to establish a falsehood.

This is an exposition of the theses of the first essential on which the Orthodox are agreed.

146—8. For the Shi'ites the *Mut'a* is not only allowed but even prescribed. Ḥilli in his *Mukhtalaf*, 90, top, says: التمتع فرض من ليس من اهل مكة . He also quotes a tradition which states: اهل مكة ليس عليهم متعة . وكل من كان اهله وراء ذلك (40 miles) فعليه المتعة . Cf. Strothmann, *Kultus d. Zaiditen*, 69—70. The other case of *Mut'a* is in marriage where a man takes a woman for a specified period, and the union is automatically dissolved when the period is over. This practice was also abrogated by 'Omar. *Vorlesungen*[2], 228—9.

[1] Ed., 157 (Seelye, 177).

[2] He teaches that all knowledge "is an activity in which man has no choice", Ed., 160, (Seelye, 181). Therefore he also argues that only those who have God's knowledge as a necessary part of their nature will believe in Him while the others are not required to do so.

[3] *Uṣūl*, 17—20. In that work, *Ḳiyās* is also included as a source.

[4] Cf. *Koranauslegung*, 270 sqq.

Regarding the second essential, which is the proposition relating to the creation of the Universe, it has been agreed that by Universe we mean everything which is not God [1]. Everything which is other than God and His eternal attributes is created and made; but its Maker is neither created nor made, nor is He of the species of the Universe or of the species of any part in the Universe. They
316 are also agreed that the component parts of the Universe fall into two divisions: substances and accidents [2], contrary to the teachings of those who deny accidents [3]. They agree that every substance consists of an indivisible atom, and declare al-Naẓẓām and the philosophers to be infidels because they teach the divisibility of every atom into parts ad infinitum [4]. This would force us to conclude that its parts are not limited in God's knowledge. But this conclusion involves a rejection of His Word: "and He records the number of all things" [5]. They declare themselves for a firm belief in the existence of angels, jinns and devils as part of the various kinds of living beings in the Universe [6]. They condemn as infidels the philosophers or Bāṭiniyya [7] who disavow them. They teach the homogeneity of substances and bodies [8] and explain: Verily their differences in form, color, and odor are due only to the diversity of the accidents which exist in them. They accuse of error all those whe say that bodies differ because of the differences in their elements [9]. Similarly they ascribe error to those philosophers who profess that there are five elements, maintaining, as Aristotle did, that the heaven is a

---

[1] *Uṣūl*, 33; *Creencia*, 59.

[2] See Maimonides, *Guide*, part I, Ch. 73, prop. VIII, (Munk, I, 398).

[3] *Uṣūl*, 36—7. Among those who deny the existence of accidents it lists Abu Bekr al-Aṣamm and the Materialists. It also offers the Kalamistic proofs for their existence.

[4] Ed., 123—4 (Seelye, 144—5); *Uṣūl*, 36 with a logical refutation of al-Naẓẓam's theory; Ash'ari, 314—8.

[5] Sura 72, v. 28.

[6] Acc. to *Uṣūl*, 38 there are two classes of living beings, one which we perceive in our present life and another which we may see in the future world. Besides the three mentioned here he counts the "black-eyed maidens" (Sura 55, v. 72).

[7] Ed., 280 (above 135).

[8] For the various views on this problem see *Usul*, 52—4. The proof of the Orthodox point of view will be found 54. See also Rāzi, 5 top; Ash'ari 308.

[9] This is the view of the اصحاب الطبائع, *Uṣūl*, 53.

fifth element which is not susceptible of becoming and perishing[1]. They accuse of error all the Dualists who assert: Verily, bodies are of two kinds, light and darkness. The source of all good is the light and the source of all evil is the dark. The Maker of the good and the true cannot make the evil and the false; nor can the Author of the evil and false produce the good and true[2]. We questioned them[3] regarding the status of a person who says: I am evil and darkness. Who is the one who makes this statement? If they say he is light, then he told a lie; and if they say he is darkness, then he told the truth. In this we find the destruction of their thesis that light does not tell a lie nor does darkness 317
tell the truth, which is a necessary conclusion for them in view of their principle. We, however, do not establish light and darkness as two primary Makers. For we say: Verily both of them are created and are not agents.

The Orthodox are unanimous regarding the diversity of accidents, and they declare al-Naẓẓām an infidel for his view that all accidents are of one type[4], all, in fact, being motion. This would compel him to admit that belief is in one class with non-belief, knowledge with ignorance, and speech with silence, and that deeds of the Prophet are of the same species as the actions of the accursed devil. It behooves him, in consequence ol this principle, not to be angry with anyone who curses or reviles him, because the word of him who says: May God curse al-Naẓẓām, is in his opinion in the same class with the wish: May God be gracious to him[5].

They agree that the accidents are brought into existence in the bodies, and condemn as infidels the Materialists who believe that they are concealed in the bodies and that anyone of them appears only when its opposite becomes concealed

---

[1] *Shahr.*, 318.

[2] See *Uṣūl,* 53—4 where he subdivides the Dualists into three groups: Manicheans, Daiṣanites, and Marcionites. Cf. Shahr. 188—96, where, in addition to the three listed by *Uṣūl,* he discusses the Mazdakiyya (see above 87, note 2,3); IH, I, 35—6 (Asin, *l. c.*, 130—1) enumerates the three as in Uṣūl.

[3] The following question is ascribed to al-Naẓẓām in his discussion with the Manicheans, *Intiṣār,* 30.

[4] Ed., 121—2, (Seelye, 143); for a list of the errors inherent in this view see *Uṣūl,* 48.

[5] This refutation is repeated almost verbatim Ed., *ib.*, and *Uṣūl,* 48.

in its subject[1]. They all share the opinion that every property is created in a bearer and that the property does not exist independently[2]. They declare as infidels the Mu'tazila of Baṣra who believe in the creation of the Will of God not in a bearer, far be it from Him[3]! And those who believe in the creation of the act-of-extinction of bodies independently of its subject. They declare Abu Hudhail a Kāfir because of his teaching that God's saying to a thing, Be! is an accident created not in the subject[4]. They consent commonly that bodies are not devoid, and never were devoid, of the accidents which follow one another in them[5]. They declare as Kāfirs the upholders of the Hylic hypothesis who maintain that
318 the hylic matter existed primordially stripped of accidents; then the accidents came to be, with the result that it assumed the present form of the Universe[6]. This view is the apex of absurdity, because the inherence of a property in a substance brings about a change in its quality but does not cause an increase in its quantity. If then the hylic matter of the world had been one substance it would not have been converted into many substances as a result of the inherence of the accidents in it.

They are agreed that the earth is stationary and still[7] and that its motion really results from an occurrence which befalls it, such as a quake or something similar. This runs counter to the view of the Materialists who maintain that the earth swoops downward[8] through the air perpetually, for, if it were so, it would

[1] The extent to which al-Naẓẓām in his philosophy is a disciple of the pre-Socratic philosophers and their views on *Kumūn* are well described by Horten in his study in *ZDMG*, LXIII (1909), 774—92. For a refutation of al-Naẓẓām see *Uṣūl*, 55—6.

[2] See Maimonides, *ib.*, Prop. V; IH, I, 14 bottom.

[3] *Uṣūl*, 103; Ash'ari, 189—91 (he lists five views of the Mu'tazila on Will); *Creencia*, 168 and 171—2, where the Mu'tazilite theory is combated. See below under the fourth essential.

[4] Ed., 108—9 (Seelye, 131; her trans. fails to render the original correctly); Ash'ari, *ib.*, and 363.

[5] *Uṣūl*, 56. The expression "that follow one another" is in accordance with the Kalamistic view that all accidents have a momentary existence and are constantly replaced by new ones. See Maimonides, *ib.*, Prop. VI.

[6] *Uṣūl*, 57, where the contention is refuted as in our text; *Creencia*, 63 ff.

[7] *Uṣūl*, 60 ff. where several attempts to account for the earth's firmness are listed. Cf. Ash'ari, 326.

[8] *Uṣūl*, 319—20; Albīrūni, 189.

necessarily follow that a stone which we hurl with our hands should never overtake the earth, because a light object cannot overtake a heavier one in its descent. They agree that the limits of the earth are finite in all directions[1] and similarly the periphery of the skies is finite in its six directions. This is in contradiction to the opinion of the Materialists who think that the earth is not limited below, on the right, on the left, behind, or in front, and that it is finite only in the direction where it is contiguous to the air above it[2]. They also think that the sky is finite only in its downward direction but is infinite on its five sides other than the lower one. The refutation of their contention is obvious in view of the return of the sun to its rising point every day and its circuit of the orb of the sky and what is above the earth in the course of a day and a night. But the crossing of limitless distances, through set places, in a limited time is not possible.

They agree that the heavens are seven in number and are superimposed on each other, contrary to the opinion of those among the philosophers and astronomers who think that they are nine in number[3]. They also agree that they 319
are not spherical bodies revolving about the earth, contrary to the contention of those who maintain that they are spheres, one within the hollow of the other, and that the earth is in their midst as the center of the sphere is in its inside. Whoever professes this belief cannot recognize a throne above the heavens, nor angels nor anything of that which the Monotheists[4] recognize as existing above the heavens. They further agree that the annihilation of the entire world, considered as something within His ability[5] and capacity, is admissible. But they believe in the eternal[6] existence of Paradise and its pleasures and in the perpetuation of Hell and its tortures as in a divine ordinance[7]. They also regard the annihilation of certain bodies and not others as possible. They declare Abu Hudhail

[1] *Uṣūl,* 61—2 and 66.

[2] This opinion is refuted *Uṣūl,* 62 lines 10—15.

[3] *Uṣūl,* 64—5. Cf. the long discussion regarding the sphericity of the earth, the heavens, God's throne, etc. in IH, II, 97—105, esp. to 101.

[4] With MS. الموحدون; Ed., الموجودون.

[5] With MS. القدرة; Ed., القدر.

[6] With MS., تابيد and below; Ed., تاييد.

[7] IH, IV, 83 ff., esp. 85—6; *Uṣūl,* 238; Ash'ari, 164.

an infidel for his belief in the interruptions of the pleasure of Paradise and the tortures of Hell[1]. They declare those of the Jahmiyya as Kāfirs who predict the extinction of Paradise and Hell[2]. They declare al-Jubbāi and his son Abu Hāshim to be Kāfirs because of their assertion that God cannot decree the extinction of some bodies while allowing others to survive, but that He can decree the destruction of all of them by an act-of-destruction which he may create not in a subject[3].

Regarding the third essential, which is the doctrine dealing with the Maker of the Universe and His essential attributes which it views as compatible with His essence, they teach that all things created have undoubtedly a Creator and Maker[4] They declare Thumāma and his followers among the Ḳadariyya to be heretics because of their view that generated acts have no Author[5]. They state that the Maker of the Universe is the Creator of bodies and accidents, declaring Muʿammar and his followers among the Ḳadariyya infidels because of their contention
320 that God created no accidents, for He created only the bodies and it is the bodies which generate the properties in themselves[6]. They profess that the originated things were before their beginning neither entities nor ideas nor substances nor accidents, contrary to the view of the Ḳadariyya that the non-existents are entities during their state of non-existence[7]. The disciples of the Baṣra School among them maintain that substances and accidents were substances and accidents

[1] Ed., 104—5 (Seelye, 127—8); IH, *ib.*; Ash'ari, 163.

[2] Ed., 199 (above, 13); IH, *ib.*; *Uṣūl, ib.*

[3] Ed., 183—4 (Seelye, 204—5).

[4] The starting point of the Mutakallims for all proofs of the existence of God, — later criticized by the Aristotelians, — is that the world is created, as has been established by our author in the second essential. (For more detailed proofs see IH, I, 9—21, esp. 14 ff. (Asin Palacios, II, 94—109); cf. also the proofs of the Jewish Mutakallims, as e. g. Saʿadia and the adequate summary in Maimonides, *Guide,* I, chap. 74). Once tho world is proved to be existent in time the demonstration of the existence of a Maker generally follows the same line as in our text, see *Uṣūl,* 68—9; IH, I, 21—3 (Asin, 109—113). The most philosophic proof, still contingent on "a world which comes into being", will be found *Creencia,* 59—73.

[5] Ed., 157—8 (Seelye, 178); Ash'ari, 407. Cf. IH, V, 59—60.

[6] Ed., 96 (Seelye, 118); Ash'ari, 303; Shahr., 46.

[7] *Uṣūl,* 70—1. This view is discussed and refuted by IH, V, 42 ff.

before their beginning. The view of these people leads to a belief in the eternity of the World[1], and a view which leads to non-belief constitutes non-belief.

They state that the Maker of the Universe is eternal and pre-existent[2], contrary to the assertion and belief of the Magians in two Makers, one of whom, Satan, is created; and contrary to the opinion of Ghulāt among the Rawāfiḍ who teach that 'Ali, a created and originated body, became a God and an originator, thanks to the dwelling of the spirit of God within him[3], far be God from their assertion. They affirm the denial of any limit or definition to the Maker of the universe[4], contrary to the opinion of Hishām ibn al-Ḥakam al-Rāfiḍi that the Object of his Worship measures seven spans by his own spans[5], and contrary to the view of the Karrāmiyya who think that he is limited in the direction which is contiguous to the throne, but has no limit in the five other directions[6]. They agree that it is absurd to describe Him as possessing form and limbs[7], contrary to the opinion of those of the Ghulāt among the Rawāfiḍ and of the followers of Daūd al-Jawāribi[8] who maintain that He has a human form. Hishām ibn Sālim al-Jawāliḳi and his followers among the Rawāfiḍ even thought that the Object of
their Worship is formed in the image of a human, that He has black hair on 321
His head and He is a black light; His upper half is hollow but His lower half is solid[9]. [Their view] also contradicts the claim of the Mughīriyya among the Rawāfiḍ that the organs of their Worshipped One resemble in shape the letters of the alphabet. Far be God from this!

They are also agreed that no place can contain Him and that He is not

---

[1] A variant in *Uṣūl,* 71 reads: As though they secretly believed in the pre-existence of the Universe but did not dare to publish it; so they professed what leads to it.

[2] *Uṣūl,* 71—2; Creencia, 74.

[3] See the chapter on the Ḥulūliyya, Ed., 241—50 (above, 73—86); Rāzi, 18—20.

[4] *Uṣūl,* 73; *Creencia,* 85—96; Razi, 20—1 and Tusi's note, *ib.* 21—2; Iji, 12—3.

[5] Ed., 215—6 (above 32—4).

[6] Ed., 203 (above 19).

[7] *Uṣūl,* 73—6.

[8] Ed. and MS. Ḥawāri; see above 34 note 1. Acc. to Ash'ari, 153, al-Jawāribi is the one who divided God's body into an upper hollow half and a lower solid one.

[9] Ed., 216 (above 33).

subject to time[1], contrary to the opinion of the Hishāmiyya[2] and the Karrāmiyya who think that He is contiguous to His Throne. Indeed 'Ali, the Prince of the Faithful, has explained: God created His Throne as a manifestation of His power, not as a place for His essence. He said further: He already existed while no place existed yet, and He persists at present the same as He existed formerly[3]. They are unanimous in disavowing His experience of misfortunes and grievances, sufferings and pleasures[4] and in denying to Him motion or rest[5]; contrary to the statement of the Hishāmiyya among the Rawāfiḍ regarding the admissibility of motion to Him and their claim that His place is an act of creation resulting from His motion; contrary to the opinion of anyone who allows to Him the possibility of fatigue and repose, sorrow, joy and boredom as is reported in the name of Abu Shu'aib the Pious[6], far be God from this! They are agreed that God is independent of His creatures and does not obtain through His creatures any benefit for Himself nor does He repel through them any harm away from Himself. This is contrary to the contention of the Magians that God created the angels in order to defend Himself, with their aid[7], against the molestation of Satan and his assistants.

They also agree that the Maker of the World is one[8] contrary to the belief

---

[1] *Uṣūl,* 76—8; IH, II, 172—3; Ḥilli, sect. 88—90.

[2] With MS.; Ed., الشهامية; see Ed., 47 ff. (Seelye, 67 ff.).

[3] This "tradition" is cited in Browne, *A Year Amongst the Persians* (1893), p. 124.

[4] *Uṣūl,* 79—81, where he explains an array of Ḳur'ānic passages as well as traditions which seem to support the claim that He is subject to these. For the proof of the Orthodox standpoint see Rāzi, 25—7 and Ḥilli, 32—3 (sect. 91—3).

[5] IH, II, 119—20; *Creencia*, 79.

[6] "He was an anthropomorphist who taught that his Lord has a human form, flesh and blood, and that He rejoices and grieves, ails and recovers". *Lisān al-Mīzān,* VI, 394 on the authority of Ibn Ḥazm. He calls him *al-Ballal.* Cf. in answer to Abu Shu'aib's teachings, *Creencia,* 180—1.

[7] *Uṣūl*, 82. Our author also includes the Ḳadarites there as opposed to the Orthodox view, since they claim that God created mem in order that they express their thanks to Him.

[8] *Usul,* 83—7, esp. 85—6; *Creencia,* 126—34 (133—4 are in answer to those who believe in a good and evil God); IH, I, 34—48 (Asin Palacios, II, 127—49) who polemicizes with all the proponents of another God; Rāzi, 73—4. Ḥilli, sect. 103—5. The classical proof employed by all the authorities cited, as well as by Jewish and Christian philosophers, is that

of the Dualists in two pre-existent Makers, one of whom is Light and the other Darkness; contrary to the belief of the Magians in two Makers one of whom, God, 322 pre-existent, is called Yazdān[1] and the other, Satan, accursed, is called Ahramān; contrary to the opinion of the Mufawwiḍa among the Ghulāt Rawāfiḍ that God committed the management of the Universe to 'Ali so that he is the second creator[2]; contrary finally to the opinion of the Ḥā'iṭiyya among the Ḳadariyya, followers of Aḥmad ibn Ḥā'iṭ, who assert that God committed the management of the Universe to 'Īsa ibn Maryam and now he is the second creator[3]. We have discussed at great length the various proofs of the Unitarians about the unity of the Maker in the *Book on Religions and Dogmas.*

Regarding the fourth essential, which is the doctrine bearing on the attributes which are of God's essence, they teach that God's Knowledge, Power, Life, Will, Hearing, Seeing and Word are eternal attributes and everlasting qualities in Him[4]. The Mu'tazila have indeed divested Him of all the eternal attributes[5], saying: He possesses neither Power nor Knowledge nor Life, nor Vision, nor means of perceiv-

---

of mutual obstruction: if they are identical, unity is implicit; if one is inferior to the other, the doctrine becomes absurd.

[1] Ed. and MS. بزدان..

[2] Ed., 2?8 (above 68). There is a disagreement between the statement here and above see *ib.*, note.

[3] Ed., 2 0—1 (above 99—100).

[4] These seven are the constant number to which all Ash'arites have bound themselves on the basis of their master's classifications; even Ghazāli and Rāzi adhere to it. It is interesting how in respect to attributes the Jewish Mutakallims part very definitely from the Arabs. Sa'adia lists only three: Life, Knowledge and Power, and Baḥya counts Existence, Unity, Eternity. For the proofs adduced by the Orthodox, see *Ibāna*, 54—9 (based almost entirely on final references to the Ḳur'ānic text); *Creencia*, 201—13 (more philosophic); see IH's attack on the Ash'arite point of view, III, 135 ff. For his own view see *ib.*, 130—4 (a summary in *Zahiriten*, 142 ff.). It is interesting that IH does not for a moment deny that he stands on Text and not Reason, adding on page 131: "Our words are addressed to members of our religion who accept the Ḳur'ān. As for the other religions, we do not address them because they (the proofs) are the consequences of certain traditions, and the consequence is valid only after accepting the premises".

[5] Ed., 93—4 (Seelye 116—7); Horten, *Probleme*, 118 ff.; Galland, *Mo'tazelites*, 51—67, esp. 54 ff. Cf. *Vorlesungen*, 106 ff.

ing the audible. They even confirm created speech in Him[1]. The Mu'tazila of Baghdād have denied Will to Him. But those of Baṣra have recognized in Him a Will created in time, not in a substratum[2]. But we reply: A denial of the attributes implies a denial of the Possessor[3] of the attributes, just as in denying action the author is denied, and in denying speech a denial of the speaker is involved[4]. The Orthodox theologians agree that God's Power is one over all its objects and by means of it He exerts His Power over all its objects in the way of an absolutely new creation not of something acquired[5]. This is contrary to the declaration by the Karrāmiyya that God's Power extends only over the originated
323 existences which belong to His essence[6], but the creatures which exist in the Universe God created only by means of His Words and not by His Power. This is also contrary to what Ḳadarites of the School of Baṣra say that God — far be it from Him — exercises no control over the acts which are the objects of the free will of mankind or of the other living beings[7]. The Sunnites are agreed that the objects of God's Power will not perish, contrary to the opinion of Abu Hudhail

---

[1] The various Mu'tazilite views on the Kur'ān are collected in Ash'ari, 191—3. Cf. Galland, *l. c.*, 67—75.

[2] Ash'ari, 181—91 (the Baghdādian view, 190, line 12 ff.); *Usul*, 90—1. — — The statement about the Mu'tazilite view of God's attributes is not entirely correct. What they denied was the existence of attributes as differing from His essence but not His actual Power or Life. That is, they denied that He possesses life as something with which His essence is qualified but they granted for the most part that His essence means Life, Knowledge, etc. See Ash'ari, 164 ff. and Rāzi, 61. One may of course deduce from this that they actually deny attributes, so in *Ibāna*, 54—5.

[3] Reading الموصوف with MS.; Ed., الموصون.

[4] *Uṣūl*, 90—3; Ash'ari ib.

[5] What he means is that every act performed by man is directly created by God and not indirectly by virtue of the fact that God created man. See *Creencia*, 152, note 1.

[6] Ibn Karrām's views on God's Power are explained Ed., 208 (above 24). Acc. to *Uṣūl*, 93, he classified all the possible accidents which God can create in Himself into five categories: His contiguity to the Throne, His Word, His Will, His perception of Hearing and His perception of Vision. See Ed., 208 (above 24).

[7] This thesis, the chief bone of contention between Mu'tazilism and Orthodoxy, is fully developed from the Orthodox point of view and defended against Mu'tazilite criticism in *Creencia*, 144—56.

and his followers among the Ḳadariyya that the Power of God will reach a state in which it will perish with all its objects[1] and after that He will exercise no Power over anything, nor will He at that time be Master over anyone for evil or for good. He maintained that those who dwell in Paradise and those who inhabit Hell at that moment will remain paralyzed because of the absolute immobility of their essence[2]. Far be God from their opinion! Al-Aswāri and his followers among the Mu'tazila maintain that God possesses Power to do only that which He knew He would do, but that which He knew He would not do or which it was announced in His name that He would not do, He possesses no Power to do[3]. Far be God from this[4]!

The orthodox are agreed that God's attribute of knowledge is one, and with it He knows all its objects in detail, unaided by perception, intuition or inference[5]. Mu'ammar and his followers among the Ḳadariyya hold that it cannot be said of

---

[1] Ed., 102—3 (Seelye, 125—6); *Uṣūl*, 94; Ash'ari, 163. *Intiṣār*, 8—9, denies this to have been Abu Hudhail's teaching and also disavows the charge that he believed in a stagnation of Paradise (page 127; he attributes this belief to Jahm), adding the rather significant and telling remark: "he repented of this doctrine and its proof before his death".

[2] See above 181; *Uṣūl, ib.*

[3] See the interesting report of a discussion on this matter among the leading Mu'tazilites, Ed., 185 ff. (Seelye, 206 ff.); Ash'ari, 2—3. Cf. also Horten, *Systeme*, 245 ff.

[4] The contention of Aswāri which is really difficult to set aside Ghazāli answers in a highly philosophic manner by distinguishing between God's Power as unrelated to His Knowledge which is, of course, not weakened by His Knowledge that the thing cannot happen, and between His Power in relation to His Knowledge which are mutually exclusive and hence impossible. *Creencia*, 141—4. The same reconciliation is made *Intiṣār*, 20—1. Acc. to Ash'ari, 203, 'Ali al-Aswāri himself admitted that when unrelated to each other the two were possible. IH, II, 183—4, also feels that either al-Aswāri's view is to be accepted, which he opposes, or only his own: that God is capable of doing everything. His proof of it is that since the question which is raised about God's ability to do the absurd is itself a creation by God, He no doubt endowed that question with a meaning.

[5] *Uṣūl*, 95; *Creencia*, 162—3; Rāzi, 54—8. Al-Ash'ari takes this subject of God's Knowledge as an occasion to disprove the view of those who deny attributes, *Ibāna*, 54—9. See, however, IH's criticism of his stand, II, 135—40.

God that He knows Himself[1]. It is a marvel indeed that One who knows others should not know Himself. Some of the Rawāfid think that God does not know the object before it comes into being[2]. Zurāra ibn A'yun and his followers among
324 the Rawāfiḍ maintain that God's knowledge, Power, Life and other attributes are created in time[3] and that He was neither living, nor powerful, nor knowing until He created for Himself Life, Power, Knowledge, Will, Hearing and Seeing.

They agree that his Hearing and Seeing encompass all things visible and audible and that God has beheld Himself and heard His own speech eternally[4]. This is contrary to the opinion of the Ḳadariyya of Baghdad that God is not a Seer nor a Hearer in the real sense of the Word, and that the expression "He sees" and "He Hears" are employed merely in the sense that He knows the visible and the audible[5]; contrary also to the declaration of the Mu'tazila that God beholds objects other than Himself but does not behold Himself; It also contradicts the statement of al-Jubbāi regarding the distinction between the hearer (السميع) and the hearing[6] (السامع), between the beholder (البصير) and the beholding (المبصر), so that he could declare that He has eternally been a hearer and a beholder (سميعاً بصيراً) but He has not eternally been hearing and beholding (سامعاً ولا مبصراً). But he may reverse this distinction and yet not discover any difference as a result of its reversal[7]. The orthodox are agreed that God will be visible to the

---

[1] Ed., 141 (Seelye, 161); *Creencia*, 162; *Uṣūl*, *ib.* Cf. *Intiṣār*, 53, where al-Khayyāṭ attempts to deny this.

[2] Rāzi, 56; Cf. Ash'ari, 158 ff. Ibn Rawendi accused the Mu'tazilite Hishām al-Fuwaṭi of maintaining the same attitude, but al-Khayyāṭ in denying this accusation claims that he confused him with Hishām b. al-Ḥakam, *Intiṣār*, 60.

[3] Ed., 52 (Seelye, 71—2); Ash'ari, 36; Shahr., 142. Cf. *Intiṣār*, 5—6 and 8.

[4] *Creencia*, 176—81; *Uṣūl*, 96—8; Rāzi, 48—9; *Ibāna*, 47—54. In answer to al-Ash'ari, cf. IH, II, 140 ff., esp. 141—2.

[5] Ash'ari, 173—4 and 183—5; IH, II, 143.

[6] Meaning that He eternally possessed the attribute of Hearing but was not a Hearer until there were audible things in the world, *Uṣūl*, 96; Ash'ari, 176—7. This view, however, is unorthodox in the light of the Ḳur'ānic verse انني معكما اسمع وارى (Sura 20, v. 48). Cf. IH, II, 144, and *Creencia*, 177 (Ghazāli's adherence to text and tradition is much more evident in his discussion of these attributes than elsewhere).

[7] The same criticism is leveled against him, *Uṣūl*, 96—7.

faithful in the world to come. They declare: That He may be[1] visible in any state and to every living being can be rationally proved; and His appearance that He will certainly appear to the faithful in particular in the world to come is established by Tradition[2]. This is contrary to the opinion of those of the Ḳadariyya and Jahmiyya who consider His visibility impossible[3]; contrary to the opinion of those who maintain that He will be discerned in the world to come with a sixth sense, as Ḍirār ibn ʻAmr was inclined to think[4]; and contrary to the opinion of those who maintain that the non-believers will also see Him as Ibn Sālim al-Baṣri believed[5]. We have already discussed the propositions regarding vision in detail in a special work[6].

The orthodox are agreed that the will of God is His Desire and free choice[7] and that His desire for something means His aversion for the lack of it, just as they believe that when He prescribes something he prohibits the neglect of it. They say further: Verily His Will realizes all its objects in accordance with His knowledge of them[8]. He wills the coming-into-existence of things simultaneously with the time when He knows they will come into being. Whatever He knows

---

1 Reading جواز with MS; Ed. بجواز.

2 See both the rational and the traditional proofs, *Uṣūl*, 98—102, *Creencia*, 110—26, where substantially the same arguments, although more philosophically, as in *Uṣūl* are employed. (Ghazāli utilizes the example of the mirror to prove that a definite direction or place is not required for vision). See *Ibāna*, 13—23 with the Ḳur'ānic verses as the starting point (Cf. Suyūṭi, *Durar al-Ḥisān*, 25). It is interesting that the authorities (*Uṣūl*, 99; *Creencia*, 122 ff.; *Ibāna*, 15) all employ as an example Moses who asked for a vision of God, arguing that Moses would not have made the request if he knew that it could not be. Cf. *Vorlesungen*, 105.

3 Ash'ari, 153 and 213—7.

4 Ed., 201 (Above 16—17); Ash'ari, 216 and 282.

5 See on him *ZDMG*, LXI, (1907), 77—8.

6 Perhaps it is his *Kitāb al-Ṣifāt*, Subki, iii, 239.

7 It is surprising that, in discussing the attribute of Will, Baghdādi does not list the dissenting opinions. For a discussion and a refutation of them, see *Uṣūl*, 102—5; *Creencia*, 165—75; *Ibāna*, 60—7; Rāzi, 42—8; Ḥilli, 22—4. IH, following his literalism and principle that names of God cannot be derived, grants that God wills because there is textual proof for it, but sees no place for attributing a will to Him or for calling Him Willing, II, 176—7.

8 The Will thus becomes a determining principle, which cannot be said of Power or Knowledge. See *Creencia*, 173; Rāzi, 42 ff.

will not come into existence, He wills that it should not become. They say: Nothing is created in the Universe save through the mediation of His Will; what He wishes comes into being and what he does not wish is not originated[1]. The Ḳadariyya of Baṣra believe that God wishes what does not come and that existences have come which He has not wished. But this opinion leads to the belief that God is coerced and compelled to create what He loathes to create[2]. Far be God from this!

The Sunnites are agreed that the Life of God is without the medium of a soul[3] or of nourishment, and that all spirits are created, contrary to the assertion of the Christians about the pre-existence of a Father, a Son and a Holy Ghost. They are further agreed that Life is a pre-requisite to His Knowledge, Power, Will, Vision and Hearing, and that if one is not alive one cannot credibly be knowing, powerful, willing, hearing and seeing[4], contrary to the opinion of al-Ṣāliḥi and his followers among the Ḳadariyya that the existence of knowledge, power, vision and will in a dead person is possible[5].

They agree that God's Speech is an eternal attribute of His[6], and that it is neither created-in-time nor brought-into-being, contrary to the contention of the Ḳadarites that God created His Speech in some body[7]; contrary to the opinion of

---

[1] This tenet is directed against the Mu'tazilites who deny that God wills evil. The discussion is developed *Ibāna*, 63—4; *Creencia*, 174—5.

[2] *Ibāna*, 61—2.

[3] *Uṣūl*, 105, explains that life is an eternal attribute and soul a substance.

[4] *Uṣūl*, 105—6; *Creencia*, 164; Rāzi, 41; Ḥilli, 21—2. IH attacks the Ash'arite view, II, 153 ff., esp. 155 ff.

[5] Horten, *Systeme*, 306, who attributes this view to Ṣālihi, uses our author as his source.

[6] *Uṣūl*, 106—8. Ghazāli, agreeing with the Ash'arite doctrine, solves all the difficulties connected with it by distinguishing between the actual sounds and letters which, of course, are temporal and between what he calls "verbum mentis", (Ar. كلام معنى), a something intermediate between the sounds and the ideas in the sounds. It should not therefore be confused with the Will or the Knowledge or the Power behind the words. *Creencia*, 182—99. IH, III, 4—15, repudiates both the Mu'tazilite and the Ash'arite view, (the latter for the same reason as all the other attributes), and maintains the literal interpretation of the uncreated character of the Ḳur'ān, granting only that the voice which pronounced the words to Muḥammad was created. The Ash'arite view is also rejected Ḥilli, 26—8. Cf. *Vorlesungen*, 109—13.

[7] *Creencia*, 184. Acc. to *Ibāna*, 26 passim (except 32 where he attributes the view to Ḳadarites as well) this is Jahm's doctrine and he accuses him of aping the Christian theory

the Karrāmiyya that His Speech is an originated entity in His Essence[1]; contrary 326
to the assertion of Abu Hudhail that His saying to something: Be! has no substratum but that the remainder of His Speech is created in bodies[2]. We maintain that it cannot be admitted that His Speech originated in Him in time because He is not the subject of created objects; nor that it originated outside of His Essence because that would force us to the conclusion that one other than He speaks, bids, and forbids[3] with it; nor that it originated independently because an attribute cannot exist in itself. The creation-in-time therefore becomes untenable aud it is true that His attribute is eternal in Him.

They say regarding the fifth essential, which is the doctrine bearing on God's names and qualities[4], that the way to find God's names is to determine them from the Ḳur'ān, reliable traditions, or by consensus of thc community. But it is not allowed to apply a name to Him from inference[5]. This is contrary to the view of the Mu'tazila of Baṣra about sanctioning the application of names to Him by inference[6]. Indeed, al Jubbāi went so far in this matter that he named

---

about the Logos in Mary's womb. But in Ash'ari, 191—3, he correctly attributes the teachings about a created Ḳur'ān — — whether as an accident or a substance — — to Mu'tazilites in general. Cf. also 582—92 esp. 589 ff. and IH, III, 5. See a discussion of the Mu'tazilite view in Goldziher's article, *Islam*, iii (1912), 245—7.

[1] Ed., 206f. (above 23f).

[2] Ed.. 108—9 (Seelye, 131—2); *Islam*, *ib.*, 246.

[3] *Uṣūl*, 106—7; *Ibāna*, 26—33 where he at the same time proves his own doctrine. See Ḥilli's attack on the Ash'arites and his defence of the Mu'tazilite attitude, 27—8.

[4] Arab.: واوصافه. Although Ash'ari identifies the significance of this word with *Ṣifāt*, Baghdādi explains the latter as the attribute of any object from the standpoint of the object, and a *Waṣf* as the attribute from the standpoint of the speaker, *Uṣūl*, 115.

[5] Acc. to *Uṣūl*, 115—6, the reason is that a slave cannot confer a name on his master, nor a son on his father. *Lawāmi' al-Bayyināt*, 52, quotes Abu Khalaf ibn 'Abd-al-Malik-al-Sulami's work on God's names to the effect that God fixed the names at ninety-nine instead of hundred in order to show that they must be determined and not inferred.

[6] *Uṣūl*, 116; Fakhr-al-Dīn Rāzi, *Lawāmi' al-Bayyināt*, 18. Abu Bekr al-Bāḳilāni also agrees with this view, *ib.* See also Rāzi, 81—2. (Ṭūsi, *ib.*, points out that that is not the Orthodox attitude). Ghazāli distinguishes between attributes and names, restricting the latter only to those mentioned in the text, while permitting a free use of qualifying attributes. *Cre-*

God Obedient-to-His-creature when He grants Him what he seeks, and he named Him Impregnator-of-women since He causes pregnancy in them[1]. But the community declared him in error for this impudence, which will bring suffering to him[2]. The Orthodox say: True tradition has it that God is known by ninety-nine names and that he who comprehends[3] them enters Paradise. By comprehending them we do not mean the count of their number and an explanation of them. The non-believer, too, may recite them by way of giving an account of them, yet he is not among those destined to enter Paradise. By comprehending them are meant a realization of what is contained in them and a belief in their implicit meaning[4]. This is confirmed by the usage: "So-and-so is a man of comprehension and self-
327 possession", if he is a person of knowledge and understanding[5]. They say: God's names fall into three divisions[6]. One refers to His Essence such as the One, the Self-sufficient, the first and the last, the Great, the Perfect, and the other descriptions of His Essence which are rightfully proper to Him. The second division

---

encia, 449—50. Even al-Shāfi'i agrees that we are allowed to apply to Him names of created acts, but our author rejects this view, *Uṣūl*, *ib.*

[1] Ed., 168 (Seelye, 188); Ash'ari, 194—5.

[2] A *Saj'* in Arabic : هذه الجسارة التي تورثه الحسارة.

[3] This tradition is reported in the name of Abu Huraira, Bukhari, IV, 450 (trans. Houdas, IV, 585); Muslim, V, 289—90. It is neither universally accepted nor unanimously interpreted. Cf. *Lawāmi' al-Bayyināt,* 49 who reports that Abu Zaid al-Balkhi doubted its authenticity, Ghazāli, in reporting that Ibn Ḥazm only listed some eighty names, explains it on the ground that the latter either did not know the tradition or held it apocryphal, *Creencia, ib.* Nawāwi, in his commentary to Muslim, *ib.*, raises no doubt as to its authenticity but explains that the number ninety-nine is not exclusive and others may be added; but it is these ninety-nine which bring one to Paradise. This interpretation is the one that *Lawāmi'*, 50, also accepts. — The number ninety-nine instead of one hundred is generally explained on the ground that God prefers the odd to the even, *Creencia*, *ib.*; *Lawāmi'*, 53.

[4] Bukhari, *ib.,* interprets the Arab. verb: احصيناه حفظناه. Nawāwi, *ib.,* who cites several interpretations also agrees with Bukhāri. *Lawāmi'*, 56—7, cites four interpretations: counting, fixing it in the mind, ability to preserve the sacredness of the names, and, finally, tracing the source and implication of the names.

[5] Reading أصاة with Brockelmann, *Monde Oriental*, XIX (1925), 199. MS. and Ed., اطاة. Lisan al-Arab, s. v. أصا explains: ويقال انه لذو حصاة وأصاة أي ذو عقل وراي.

[6] *Uṣūl*, 121—6; *Lawāmi'*, 22 bottom ff., esp. 24 bottom f.; *Crcencia*, 447—8.

gives an idea of His eternal attributes which are inherent in His Essence. Such are: the Living, the Powerful, the Knowing, the Willing, the Hearing, the Seeing, and the other descriptions derived from the attributes which are inherent in His Essence. God is eternally qualified both by this group of names and by the group discussed above. Both of them are of His eternal attributes. The third division is derived from His acts, such as the Creator, the Bestower, the[1] Just, etc. By all names derived from His acts He is not qualified before the coming-into-existence of His acts[2]. There are some among His names which have a double meaning[3]: one of them an eternal attribute and the other an act of His. For example, the Wise; if we apply it in the sense of wisdom which is identical with His Knowledge it is one of His eternal names. But if we apply it because of the wisdom and stability of His acts, it is derived from His acts and is not one of His eternal descriptions.

They teach regarding the sixth essential, which is the thesis of God's justice and Wisdom — far be He from any imperfection, — that God is the creator of bodies and accidents, the good and the evil alike. He is the creator of the acquired acts[4] of mankind and there is no creator other than God[5]. This is contrary to the belief of those Ḳadarites who hold that God created none of

---

[1] MS. has an illegible word here beg. ...وال. Cf. *Uṣūl*, 126, top.

[2] This is contrary to the view of the Karrāmiyya that God was eternally a Creator and Bestower. Ed., 206 (above 23); *Uṣūl*, 122.

[3] *Uṣūl*, 126—7.

[4] Arab. اكساب. In *Uṣūl*, 133—4, Baghdādi gives the following definition of *Aksāb:* Let us suppose a heavy rock which one man is not capable of carrying while another is. If both should carry it jointly, the achievement is due to the more powerful one, yet at the same time the weaker one is not excluded from being a carrier. In the same way man alone cannot perform his acts; if God should choose to be alone in executing what will be man's act, He possesses power to do it, so that it would be the object of His Power. Its existence is therefore due to God's Power, yet at the same time the acquirer (*Muktasib*) is not excluded from being author of the act.

[5] *Uṣūl*, 134—7; *Creencia*, 144—56 for a discussion and refutation of the Mu'tazilite view. (It is significant that he has no quarrel here with the Jabarites; cf. indeed Rāzi's evaluation of Ash'ari's view, 74); *Ibana*, 67—71 For the discussion of the subject see *Vorlesungen*, 82—92, 98—100; Rāzi, 74—7.

the acquired deeds of humanity [1]; and contrary to the view of the Jahmiyya that
328 man neither acquires, nor has he power over, his deeds [2]. Whoever maintains that man creates his own works is a Ḳadarite entertaining polytheistic notions of his Lord in view of his assertion that in the spheres of knowledge, will, voices and sounds, men create accidents, such as movements and rests, similar to God's creation. In condemnation of the adherents to this view God has made the statement: "Or have they set up with Allah associates who have created creations like His so that what is created became confused to them? Say: Allah is the creator of all things and He is the One, the Supreme" [3]. But if one maintains that man has no control over his acts and that he is neither a doer [4] nor an acquirer, then he is a Jabarite. Balanced Justice [5] excludes both the principle of Jabar [6] and the principle of Ḳadar. He, therefore, who asserts that man acquires his acts, yet God is the creator of his acquired act, is a Sunnite with a balanced sense of justice, keeping away from both Jabar and Ḳadar.

The Orthodox concur in rejecting the views of those who uphold the theory that man performs a certain act in himself from which an effect results in something other than himself [7]. This is contrary to the view of the majority of the

---

[1] Ash'ari, 199 ff. and 227—42; *Uṣūl, ib.*; *Creencia, ib.*; Ḥilli, 42—4; IH, III, 25—6. IH assumes an intermediate position between the various views by recognizing for every act a double "*Istiṭā'a*": one which is a sort of pre-disposition, e. g., sanity of organs and removal of hindrances, which precedes the act, and another, the power from God to effect the act, which is simultaneous with the act, 26—35.

[2] See the refutation of the Jabarites, IH, III, 22 bottom—25 bottom; Ed., 199 (above 13); *Uṣūl, ib.*

[3] Sura 13, v. 17.

[4] Reading بعامل with MS.; Ed., معامل.

[5] Arab. 'Adl, doubtless chosen by Baghdādi because of the fondness of the Mu'tazila for the term and the latter's use of the name اهل الجور (people who assert wrong-doing) as a nick-name for their opponents. Matūridi, 4.

[6] Both Ed. and MS. read الخبر, which is meaningless.

[7] *Uṣūl*, 137—9; Maimonides, *Guide*, I, ch. 73, Prop. VI. This, of course, is a denial of cause and effect. IH, in line with his views on *Iktisāb*, contends in connection with this problem that both views are right. The effect is God's creation, but since man has volition, the apparent relation of an act to a living being is true. In the case of an inanimate agent without choice there is of course no performance of the act by him, V, 59—60.

Kadariyya that man performs deeds effecting other things which result from causes which he generated within himself [1], and contrary to the opinion of those of the Kadariyya who think that the secondary actions are effects which have no author, as Thumāma was inclined to think [2]. They agree that the performance by acquisition of acts of motion, rest, will, speech, knowledge, thought and whatever else follows the line of these accidents which we have mentioned, may be predicated of man, but that the production of colors, tastes, smells, and auditory percepts cannot be predicated of him. This is contrary to the opinion of Bishr ibn al-Mu'tamar and his followers among the Mu'tazila that man produces colors, tastes and 329
smells in the manner of effects [3]. They [i. e. Bishr and his adherents] also hold that even the inducing of vision in the eye and of auditory perception in the organ of hearing is predicable of man [4]. More abominable than this is the assertion of Mu'ammar [5] the Kadarite that God did not create any of the accidents and that they are all effects produced by the bodies. There is shame in plenty for him in this error.

The Orthodox say: God's guidance manifests itself in two ways [6]: one, by giving clear expression to the truth, summoning people to it and establishing proofs for it. From this standpoint, it is right to associate guidance with the apostles and with everyone who calls people to the religion of God, because they point out to people, who are bidden to obey God, the right path to Him. This

---

[1] For the various Mu'tazilite doctrines see Ash'ari, 400—15. Baghdādi taunts them that in accordance with their doctrine it cannot even be proved that God formed the heavens or that He moves the stars: These occurences may be due to the action of angels or jinns, *Uṣūl*, 140.

[2] Ash'ari, 407; Ed , 157—8 (Seelye, 178).

[3] *Uṣūl*, 139—40; Ash'ari, 403; Ed., 143 (Seelye, 163).

[4] *Uṣūl*, *ib.*

[5] Ed., 136—7 (Seelye, 157—8); Ash'ari, 405—6.

[6] For the following discussion of the types of guidance, see *Uṣūl*, 140—2; IH, III, 43—6. Al-Ash'ari does not distinguish between the two kinds of *Huda* (guidance), insisting instead that the Kur'ān is for believers only, *Ibāna*, 78—80; he allows, however, a call or *du'a* to the general public, *ib.* 81. For his interpretation of Sura 41, v. 16 which is one of the chief reasons for the Orthodox predication of a general *Huda* (cf. Baiḍāwi, II, 221), see *ib.* 83 - 4. For IH's refutation, see III, 45—6.

is the meaning of the word of God to His Messenger: "And most surely you show the way to the right path"[1], that is, you summon people to it. The second way in which God's guidance of His worshippers is manifested is by inducing in their hearts a willingness to be guided, as He has expressed it in His Word: "Therefore whomsoever Allah intends that He should guide him aright, He expands his breast for Islām, and whomsoever He intends that He should cause him to err, He makes his breast strait and narrow"[2]. Over this sort of guidance no one has any power except God. The first guidance which comes from God is extended to all who have been bidden to obey, but the second guidance which is sent by Him is limited[3] to those who have been predisposed to it. To confirm this, the Word of God has been revealed: "and Allah invites to the abode
330 of peace and guides whom He pleases into the right path"[4]. Misguiding, according to the doctrine of the Orthodox, comes from God in the sense that error is injected into the hearts of those who fall into it[5], as He says: "And of whomsoever He pleases that He should cause him to err, He makes his breast strait and narrow". They say: Whenever God causes one to err, He does it as an act of justice, and whenever He guides one, he does it as an act of grace. This is contrary to the view of the Ḳadariyya that guidance comes from God in the sense that He points out the right way and calls to truth but that no guidance of heart can be attributed to Him[6]. They [the Ḳadariyya] hold that leading astray is attributable to Him in two ways: one is in naming, that is, by calling the error misguidance, and the other in the sense of punishing people who err for their error. Now, if what they said were true, it would necessarily follow that the Prophet[7] led non-believers astray because he called them misguided; it would

---

[1] Sura 42, v. 52.

[2] Sura 6, v. 125.

[3] Reading with MS. منه خاصة; Ed., من خاصته. Cf. *Usul*, 140, lines 14—5.

[4] Sura 10, v. 26. "In the generalization of the Call, and the limitation of guidance by desire, lies the proof that the matter is not dependent on man's will, and that he who perseveres in error does so because God does not will his going on the right path." Baiḍāwi, I, 413, line 6—7; cf. *Ibāna*, 81.

[5] For the discussion of misleading *(Iḍlāl)*, see *Uṣūl, ib.*; IH, III, 46—51; *Ibāna*, 81.

[6] Ash'ari, 259—62; *Uṣūl, ib.*; *Ibāna*, *ib.* IH, *ib.*

[7] Add النبي and read ان with MS. Ed. انه اضل; see *Uṣūl*, 141, last line.

similarly follow that Iblīs led the believing prophets astray because he named them erring[1]. They would also be compelled to admit that one who inflicts punishment on adulterers, thieves and apostates misguides them because he has punished them for their error. This is wrong and what leads to it is like it.

The Orthodox teach regarding the ordained span of life (Ājāl) that everyone who dies, whether naturally or by slaying, dies at the appointed time which God designated as the end of his life. God has the power to prolong his life for a certain period of time, but if he has not prolonged it that period by which his life has not been prolonged is not his appointed end. In the same way, the woman whom he does not[2] marry before his death does not become his wife even though God has the power to allow him to marry her before his death. 331
This is contrary to the opinion of those among the Ḳadariyya who maintain that when a person is slain his life has been cut, and contrary to the opinion of those among them who hold that he who is killed cannot be called dead[3]; these deny the import of God's word: "Every soul shall taste of death"[4]. This is an innovation which al-Ka'bi followed, and there is enough shame for him in it.

The orthodox explain the problem of the means of sustenance on the basis of the actual state[5]. Everyone who eats or drinks something receives his sustenance, be it lawfully or unlawfully, contrary to the opinion of those of the Ḳadariyya who

---

[1] See al-Ash'ari's refutation from the linguistic angle, *Ibāna,* 80—1.

[2] This word is missing in both Ed. and MS., but see *Uṣūl,* 142, lines 14—5 where the analogy with God's power to add life is expressed more clearly: "and as the woman whom he does not marry before his death does not become his wife although she could have become his wife had he not died". The example is taken from the Mu'tazilite argument that a man's span of life if he dies prematurely is to be measured by God's knowledge of who would be his wife. *Ibāna*, 76.

[3] *Usul*, 143. The view is said to be al-Ka'bi's and so also Ed., 167 (Seelye, 187). But see Ash'ari, 421—4 where the Mu'tazilite views of slaying are recorded anonymously. The explanation of this thesis is that death comes from God whereas slaying is the effect of a human act. The Orthodox who deny cause and effect reply that man dies by God's act and the slaying is an accident in the slayer.

[4] Sura 3, v. 182.

[5] i. e. considering merely whom it is sustaining, regardless of where it comes from or by what method it was procured.

maintain that man may sometimes enjoy the sustenance provided for another person [1].

They say concerning the inception of the charge imposed on man *(Taklīf)* that if God had not bidden His creatures to obey Him in any way it would still be an act of justice by Him [2], contrary to the opinion of those among the Ḳadariyya who maintain that if He had not charged them He would not have been just [3]. They assert that if He added to the task of His creatures over what He had imposed upon them, or if He reduced from the charge laid upon them, — both of these could be possible, contrary to the opinion of those among the Ḳadariyya who reject it [4]. Similarly if He had not produced creation, it could not be concluded that He therefore committed an outrage against justice [5]. The preferable state in accordance with His knowledge in that case would be that He should not create. They declare: If God had created the inanimate objects and not animal life, that too would be admissible, contrary to the opinion among those of the Ḳadariyya who say that if He had not created the living world He would not be wise. They say: If God had brought all of His creatures forth in Paradise, that would be an act of grace on His part, contrary to the opinion of those among

---

[1] The discussion hinges on the question of a person who steals food or marries a forbidden relation. According to the Mu'tazilite doctrine that God can do no wrong, the food procured in this way, or the wife taken against the law, cannot be the gift of God. The Orthodox, denying cause and effect, see no relation between the illegal act — which is a sin, — and the growth of the body or the happiness which are boons from God. See *Uṣūl*, 144—5; Ash'ari, 257; and esp. *Ibāna*, 76—8 where he polemicizes with the Ḳadarites and wards off their attacks. IH, III, 86—7 cannot agree with the Ash'arites to the full extent: God has nowhere said that He gives man the illegal wife. Nor can the Mu'tazilite view be accepted. He therefore argues that while God is the source of the acts, man is the real author of sin and that we are tested by these facts which are illegal.

[2] The pivot of the problem is whether God is free to do as He pleases or not. To the Orthodox who affirm God's freedom above all, it is therefore necessary to preface the discussion of Taklīf with a clear statement of God's will and freedom. Cf. *Uṣūl*, 145—9; *Creencia*, 264—8; Rāzi, 79.

[3] Ash'ari, 252—3; Ḥilli 45—50; IH, I, 69 (Asin, 183).

[4] *Uṣūl*, 149—50; Ash'ari, 246—8 esp. 247 and 249—50.

[5] *Uṣūl*, 150—1.

the Ḳadariyya who maintain that if He had done it, He would not be wise[1]. This according to them is forbidden to God. But we cannot see anything unlawful to 332
Him; nay, we say: To Him belongs the right to order and forbid and to Him belongs the Judgment. He does what He desires and rules as He wishes[2].

Regarding the seventh essential, — the regulations bearing on prophecy and apostolism, — they aver the veracity of messengers from God to His creatures[3], contrary to the opinion of the Barāhima who disacknowledge them despite their belief in the Unity of the Maker[4]. Concerning the distinction between messenger and prophet, they teach that every one on whom a revelation has descended from God, spoken by one of His angels[5] and who is confirmed by some miracles which run counter to the ordinary course of affairs is a prophet. He in whom this attribute has been realized and who is further distinguished by a new dispensation or by the abrogation[6] of part of the precepts of a law which existed before him is a messenger[7]. They say that there were numerous prophets[8] but the messengers are three hundred and thirteen in number. The first is the Father of all flesh, Adam, and the last one is Muḥammad, contrary to the assertion of the Magians that the father of all mankind is Gayōmart[9] who is surnamed

---

[1] Ash'ari, 248–9.

[2] Baghdādi's list of questions coming under 'Adl is much abridged. For a fuller discussion, see *Creencia*, 245—302; IH, III, 97—142 and, from the Mu'tazilite point of view, Ḥilli, 40—53.

[3] To the Ash'árites prophecy is a favor from God being "merely possible, neither necessary nor impossible". *Creencia*, 293 f. Acc. to the Mu'tazilites God is obliged to send prophets since it is His duty to guide men for their advantage. Cf. Ḥilli, 54–6.

[4] They believe that a man is led by his sense and intellect to obey laws. See *Uṣūl*, 154–5. In refutation of the Brahman view see, IH, I, 69—70 (Asin, II, 182—5); *Creencia*, 293—300.

[5] Acc. to Maṭurīdi, 26, it means an angel other than Gabriel; the latter reveals to apostles.

[6] Reading بنسخ with MS.; E., بفسخ.

[7] *Uṣūl*, 154.

[8] Acc. to *Uṣūl*, 157, true tradition records 124,000. On the manner of their creation, see *Ḥayyāt ul-Ḳulūb*, 5.

[9] With Brockelmann, *l. c.*, 199. MS. and Ed. كيكومرت. For the Iranian legend of this first man, possibly conceived (definitely in later literature) as a prototype of man, see Christensen, *Les Types du Premier Homme et Premier Roi*, 11—63. The Islamic sources are collected and discussed *ib.*, 64—101. Cf. also *Uṣūl*, 159 and Justi, *Iran. Namenb.*, 108 b.

Gīlshāh[1], and contrary to their belief that the last[2] of the messengers is Zarādusht; contrary also the opinion of the Khurramiyya who think that messengers will succeed one another endlessly[3].

They profess a belief in the prophecy of Moses in his age, contrary to those of the Barāhima and the Mānawiyya who disbelieve in Him, the latter nevertheless accepting ʻĪsa[4]. They recognize the prophetic character of ʻĪsa, contrary to the opinion of the Barāhima and Jews who deny him[5]. But they deny the
333 crucifixion of ʻĪsa and affirm his ascension to heaven. They say that he will come down to earth after the appearance of the Antichrist, slay the Antichrist, kill the swine, and pour out all intoxicating drink[6]; in his prayer he will face the Kaʻba and will confirm the law of Muḥammad. He will bring to life those to whom the Ḳur'ān granted life and he will kill everyone for whom the Ḳur'ān decreed death. They approve of considering a heretic everyone who falsely claims to be a prophet, whether he lived before the days of Islām, like Zarādusht, Yudāsaf[7],

---

[1] Meaning clay-king. Christensen, *l. c.*, 27, 72 et passim. Among Muḥammadans his *laḳab* is sometimes Garsha (king of the mountain). Cf. *ib.* 68—75. *Uṣūl*, 159 translates it into Arabic.

[2] With Goldziher and *Uṣūl*, 159 line 7; MS. and Ed. اجزاء. *Uṣūl* does not accuse the Magians of this.

[3] *Uṣūl*, 158; Ash'ari, 438.

[4] *Uṣūl*, 160; Jesus plays a very important role in the Manichean doctrine. See Burkitt, *Manichees*, 37—43.

[5] See his polemic with the Jews, *Uṣūl*, 150—1.

[6] This last detail is not mentioned in the traditions regarding Jesus' appearance, collected in Wensinck, 113. The most common version is that "he will appear as a righteous judge, break the cross, kill the swine, dispense with the tax on infidels; wealth will be so abundant that no one will seek it (e. g. Bukhāri, II, 40; Houdas, II, 51). Ibn Maja, *Sunan*, II, 269 who lists all that Jesus will do on that day, citing especially his new function as a Muslim, does not mention the incident of the wine. A detailed description of the sedition of the antichrist is found in Suyūṭi, *al-Durar al-Ḥisān*, 12.

[7] A name very early perverted from Budāsaf (cf. Hommel, *VII. Oriental Congress, Semitic Section*, 116—7), hero of the very famous collection of stories entitled *Barlaam and Joasaph*. Our author no doubt means Buddha described in Arabic sources as a Ṣābian prophet. See Murūj, II, 111—2 and IV, 44—5; Albirūni, 186—9.

Māni[1], Daiṣān[2], Marcion[3], and Mazdak[4], or like Musailima[5], Sajāḥ[6], al-Aswad al-'Ansi[7], and later Yezīd[8] and the others after them who falsely claimed prophecy. They condemn as an infidel anyone who claims divinity for the prophets, and prophetic or divine character for the Imāms of the succession[9] such as the Sabbābiyya, the Bayāniyya, the Mughīriyya, the Khaṭṭābiyya and everyone who pursues their path. They think it right to attribute greater excellence to the prophets than to the angels[10], contrary to the teachings of al-Ḥusain ibn al-Faḍl as well as of the majority of the Ḳadariyya that the angels are of greater excellence than the prophets[11]. They believe that the prophets rank higher than the saints in the communities[12] of the prophets, contrary to the opinion of those who maintain that among the saints there are some of higher excellence than the prophets[13]. They teach the immunity of prophets from sin[14] and account for those lapses which tradition re-

---

1 Shahr., 188—192.

2 *ib.*, 194—5.

3 Contra Ed. and MS. مرقيور. *Ib.*, 195—6.

4 *ib.*, 192—4; above 87.

5 The following prophets all arose during the period of apostasy following Muḥammad's death. On Musailima see IA, II, 274—81; Ṭab. (Zotenberg) II, 276—98; Wellhausen, *Skizzen*, VI, 16—19.

6 Daughter of Ḥārith, of the Tamimites, IA, II, 268—72; Ṭab. (Zotenberg) II, 257—69; Wellhausen, *l. c.*, 12—15.

7 His real name was 'Aihala b. Ka'b, IA, II, 254—9; Ṭab. (Zotenberg), II, 230—7; *EI*, I, 502—3; Wellhausen, *l. c.*, 31—7. MS. and Ed. read والاسود ثم يزيد العنسي; al-'Ansi is misplaced probably through confusion with Unaisa, father of Yezīd.

8 That the reference is to b. Unaisa (Ed., 263 above 103—4) becomes apparent from *Usul*, 162, line 9 ff.

9 Referring to the Shī'ite Imāms who are alleged by them to be the Khalīfs of Islam.

10 *Uṣūl*, 295—6; Ash'ari, 439—40; Rāzi, 89—90.

11 Ash'ari, 48; IH agrees with them. The order according to him is: angels, apostles, prophets, and Companions of the Prophet, V, 20—2. Other groups also ranked angels above Prophets, Andrae, *Person Muhammeds*, 360—61.

12 Arab. reads here من امم which is not clear to me. The translation is conjectural.

13 *Uṣūl*, 167, states definitely that the Karrāmiyya took this stand; Ash'ari, 47 ascribes the view to the Rawāfiḍ. See *Shiites*, I, 34, where the reference is probably to Ṣūfis; cf. II, 13 line 10 ff.

14 *Uṣūl*, 167—9; Rāzi 88—9; Ḥilli, 58—9. The latter states that the Ash'arites allowed minor sins; this is also the standpoint of Maṭurīdi, 26, who holds the view himself and main-

ports about them by explaining that those were committed before they were elevated to prophecy[1]. This is contrary to the opinion of those who consider minor sins admissible to them[2] and contrary to the opinion of the Hishāmiyya among the Rawāfid who consider sinning possible to them although they profess the Imām's immunity from sin[3].

Regarding the eighth essential relating to prophetic miracles and saintly wonders, they teach that a miracle[4] is a state of things which breaks in upon the ordinary course, brought about by a claimant of prophecy and coupled with
334 a challange[5] to his people to emulate him and with failure on their part to compete with him[6], so that it will testify to his veracity during the period when God's charge to man is in force[7]. They say: The prophet doubtless performs one miracle which will indicate his truthfulness. When one miracle which points to his veracity has been manifested to him and they are incapable of vying with him, the proof which obligates them to believe and to obey him becomes binding upon them. If they demand another miracle of him, the matter is up to God[8]: if He wills, He aids him in it, and if He desires, He chastises those who

---

tains that the distinction made by some between a minor sin and a lapse is merely verbal but that essentially they mean the same. Abu Ḥanīfa also agrees with our author, 22, and so also IH, IV, 2—3. Indeed he goes into a lengthy investigation in the following sections to prove that wherever the Ḳur'ān or tradition report anything in blame of the prophets it is not within the category of sin. Contrary to his usual literalism, ibn Ḥazm is obliged to employ some hair-splitting distinctions not easily separable from the *Ta'wīl* to which he is always so averse.

[1] *Uṣūl*, 168; against this view Ḥilli, 59—60. Cf. Goldziher's article in *Islam*, III (1912), 238—45.

[2] The Mu'tazilites allow minor sins, Ash'ari, 226—7; Maṭurīdi ib. But see Andrae, *Person Muhammeds*, 140 ff.

[3] Ash'ari, 48.

[4] For the definition see *Uṣūl*, 170—1; Ḥilli, 56—7 and especially Iji 175—78. Cf. Andrae, *Person Muhammeds*, 101—3.

[5] *Creencia*, 296—7; IH, who says that he read this requirement as a distinction between prophet and saint or magician in Bāḳilāni's work, rejects it summarily, V, 2—3 and 7—8, and IV, 317. See Andrae, *l. c.*, 115.

[6] *Uṣūl*, 171.

[7] This statement is meant to exclude the miracle on the Day of the Resurrection, *Uṣūl*, 170.

[8] *Uṣūl*, 173.

demanded the miracle of him, since they failed to put faith in one, tho proof of whose truthfulness had already been made manifest[1]. This is contrary to the opinion of the Ḳadariyya who think that the prophet requires no greater miracles than the soundness of his law[2], as Thumāma believed[3]. They declare: When one makes honest claims to being a prophet, it is possible for him to perform a confirmatory miracle[4], but the appearance of a miracle in confirmation of a claimant who falsely[5] arrogates prophecy to himself is not admissible. But it is possible for a miracle to occur which will demonstrate his falsehood[6], like the speech of the tree or of one of his limbs, giving him the lie[7].

They say: the appearance of wonders to saints is possible, and they establish them as proofs of their veracity with respect to their states just as the miracles of the prophets are evidence for the justness of their claim[8]. They assert that the duty rests on the performer of the miracle to make it manifest and to challenge others, but the performer of wonders challenges no one else and generally keeps them secret. The miracle worker is assured of the outcome, but the wonder-man is not secure against a reversal of the event[9]. Thus the outcome to Balaam[10] son of Bā'ūra was reversed after the manifestation of his

---

[1] Traditions from the life of Muḥammad illustrating this principle are collected in *Ḥayyāt-ul-Ḳulūb,* 112–20.

[2] See our author's objections to it, *Uṣūl,* 176; cf. *Creencia,* 295.

[3] *Uṣūl,* 175—6 where he also lists the Ibāḍiyya and Karrāmiyya among those who deny the pre-requisite of a miracle (cf. *Kashf al-Maḥjub,* 219) In the several accounts of Thumāma's heresies this one is not recorded.

[4] For the distinctions of where and when prophecy may occur, see *Uṣūl,* 173—4; *Creencia,* 297–9. For the Mu'tazilite denial of it see, Ḥilli, 58.

[5] Reading الكاذب with MS., missing in Ed.

[6] See 'Ali Ṭabari, *Al-Din wal-Dawla* (ed. Mingana), 14 (trans. 11 bottom). Ghazāli denies the possibilities of any miracle occurring through the mediation of a liar. *Creencia,* 301-2.

[7] These incidents are probably culled from the experiences of some false prophet, but I have not been able to trace them.

[8] *Uṣūl,* 174–5; *Creencia,* 300–1. IH denies the possibility of working wonders since the time of the Companions for whom there is written evidence, V, 10—1.

[9] *Uṣūl,* 175; *Kashf al-Maḥjūb,* 220 sqq.

[10] Cf. the Biblical account, Numbers, XXXII—XXXIV.

335 wonders. The Ḳadariyya disacknowledge the wonders of saints because they have not found anyone in their sect worthy of showing a wonder[1].

They profess the miraculous character of the Ḳur'ān manifest in its composition[2], contrary to the view of those of the Ḳadariyya who think that there is no inimitable excellence in the poetic style of the Ḳur'ān, as al-Naẓẓām was inclined to believe[3]. As regards Muḥammad's miracles, they confess their belief in the cleaving of the moon, making the pebbles utter praises in his hand, the flowing of water from between his fingers, his feeding many people with little food, and many others similar to them. But al-Naẓẓām and his followers among the Ḳadariyya dissent from this.

Regarding the ninth essential, relating to the pillars of the law of Islam, they teach: Verily, Islam is erected on five fundamentals: the confession that there is no God except Allah and that Muḥammad is the Apostle of Allah; the recitation of prayers; the contribution of alms; the fast of Ramaḍān; and the pilgrimage to the Holy House. They rule that anyone who rejects the obligatoriness of any of these five fundamentals or allegorizes them to mean a patronization of certain people, as the Manṣūriyya and the Janāḥiyya among the Ghulāt Rawāfiḍ interpret them, is an infidel. They teach that the prescribed prayers are five in number[4]. They declare anyone who abandons the obligation of any of them to be a heretic. Musailima the Liar cancelled the need of the morning and evening prayers, making of their cancellation a wedding-gift to his wife Sajāḥ who put forth a false claim to prophecy; he thus became an infidel and a de

---

[1] *Uṣūl*, 175. The bite in this statement is all too obvious. The Ḳadarites deny these miracles because in their view it would impugn the claim of the Prophet.

[2] *Uṣūl*, 183—4; Ḥilli, 57; *Greencia*, 309—13. *Uṣūl*, *ib.*, and Bāḳilāni, *I'jāz al-Ḳur'ān*, 18—27 esp. 18—20 add to this inimitability also the content of many mysteries in the Book which none can equal, and the perfect knowledge of history since the beginning of time displayed in this Book which was revealed by a man who did not know how to write and who read only with difficulty.

[3] *Uṣūl*, 184; Ash'ari, 225—6. Most Mu'tazilites agree with the Orthodox. The accusation against al-Naẓẓām is also found in *Intiṣar*, 27—8; al-Khayyāṭ denies it.

[4] *Umm*, I, 59—60; *Mudawwana*, I, 55—7; Juynboll, 66—71.

famator[1]. They recognize the obligatory character of the Friday prayer[2] and condemn as Kāfirs those among the Khawārij and the Rawāfiḍ who rule that there is no Friday gathering at present until the re-appearance of the Imām whom they are expecting[3]. 336

They recognize the duty of the poor-rate from the choicest items, such as gold and silver, camels, kine and sheep[4], provided these three species of domestic animals graze at large[5]. They require it from nutritive soil-products which people sow and later use for food[6]. They require it from palm-dates and grapes. Whoever maintains that there is no compulsory poor-rate on these listed products is a Kāfir. But one who confirms the general principle of the compulsory poor-rate, and whose disapproval of the rates is in line with the differences of opinion among jurists, is not a heretic. They accept the compulsory nature of the fast of Ramaḍān and forbid breaking it during that period except for reasons of minority of age, or being possessed, or sickness, or traveling, or a similar reason[7]. They declare that the observance of the month of fasting commences with the observation of the new moon of Ramaḍān or with the completion of thirty days in Sha'bān[8]. They cannot break it at the end of the month except upon observation of the new moon of Shawwāl or the expiration of thirty days in the month of Ramaḍān. They accuse of error those among the Rawāfid who commence their fast one day before the appearance of the new moon and break it one day before the right time[9].

---

1 The account of the wedding-gift is found in Ṭab. I, 1917—19, repeated almost verbatim IA, II, 270—1.

2 The evidence from the Ḳur'ān and the traditions is cited in *Umm*, I, 167. Cf. Juynboll, 85—9, and *Uṣūl*, 190.

3 Querry, Droit Musulman, I, 85; *Uṣūl*, *ib.*

4 *Uṣul*, 191.

5 i. e., if they were not sent to work and grazed on free land which did not cost the owner anything. Juynboll, 100—2.

6 *ib*, 99—100.

7 *ib.*, 121—2.

8 *ib.*, 117—9.

9 Querry, *l. c.*, I, 195.

They affirm the obligation of the pilgrimage and[1] the pious visit at least once upon everyone who is able to perform it[2]. They condemn those among the Bāṭiniyya who reject the obligatory nature of both[3] as infidels, but they do not declare him a heretic who denies the need of making a pious visit, owing to the differences of opinion in the Community regarding its compulsory character[4].

They teach that among the conditions required in order to make prayer valid, are to be reckoned the purification, the covering of the pudenda, the arrival of the right time, and facing the Ḳibla wherever possible[5]. Whoever fails to comply with these requirements or part of them, despite his ability to fulfill them, is an infidel.

They recognize the obligation of the Holy War against the enemies of Islām
337 until they become Muslims or until the poll-tax is paid by those among them from whom the acceptance of tribute is permitted[6]. They affirm the legality of trade[7] and the illegality of usury[8]. They declare everyone who legalizes usury generally to be in error[9]. They rule that sexual intercourse is not allowed save by lawful marriage or rightful concubinage. They condemn the Mubayyiḍa[10], the Muḥammira and the Khurramiyya as infidels because they rule adultery lawful. They also declare those people Kāfirs who interpret the forbidden relations to refer to persons whom they think it forbidden to befriend[11]. They confirm the obligation to inflict punishment for adultery, theft[12], wine and libelling[13] and they

---

[1] Reading والعمرة with Casanova; MS. and Ed. في العمرة.

[2] Sura 3, v. 91.

[3] Reading بهما; MS. and Ed. بها.

[4] Ed., 280.

[5] *Uṣūl*, 193 where the general requirements for the other fundamentals are also listed. Cf. Juynboll, 61—4, 68, 75.

[6] *Uṣūl*, 194; Juynboll, 336—44, and below, under the fifteenth essential.

[7] *Uṣūl*, *ib.*; Juynboll, 261—3; Sachau, 271 and 275—9.

[8] *Uṣūl*, 195; Juynboll, 270—6; Sachau, 271 and 279—81.

[9] Acc. to *Uṣūl*, *ib.*, he is a Kāfir. Cf. Juynboll, 270 and Sachau 279.

[10] With Goldziher; Ed. and MS. المبعضية. On the group see above.

[11] Referring to the Bāṭiniyya and some ultra-Shī'ite sects.

[12] These crimes, to which may also be added highway-robbery, are discussed fully in Juynboll, 300—6; Sachau, 809—12 and 815—37; *Uṣūl*, 197—9.

[13] It is limited to false charges of adultery. Juynboll, 303—4.

declare those among the Khawārij who reject the punishment for wine[1] and stoning[2] to be heretics. They state that the sources of the precepts of the law are the Book, Tradition, and consensus among the ancients[3]. They declare anyone a heretic who does not regard the consensus of opinion among the Companions as evidence. They condemn the Khawārij as Kāfirs for their rejection of the authority of consensus and tradition, and they declare anyone among the Rawāfiḍ a Kāfir who says that none of this serves as evidence because authority rests with the Imām whom they are expecting. These people are at present bewildered in their straying, and there is sufficient shame for them in this.

Regarding the tenth essential which is devoted to what is allowed and forbidden, they teach that the acts of the *Mukallafs* (those bidden to obey) fall under five categories: the obligatory, the forbidden, the commendable, the improper, and the allowed[4]. The obligatory is that which the Lord has commanded as a binding necessity. Whoever neglects it, incurs just punishment on himself for neglecting it. The forbidden is that which God has interdicted and its doer brings due punishment upon himself for doing it. The commendable is that for the performance of which one is rewarded but for whose neglect one is not punished. The improper is that for the avoidance of which one is rewarded but for whose performance one is not punished. The allowed is that for the performance of which one is neither rewarded nor punished, nor does one suffer punishment or earn reward for neglecting it. All this concerns the acts of the *Mukallafs*. As for the acts of the animals, the insane, or children, they cannot 338
be defined at all in terms of legitimate, obligatory or prohibited[5]. They assert that everything, such as knowledge of God, confession, or works, which are binding on the *Mukallaf* are binding only because God enjoined them upon him. Everything which it is forbidden to do is so because of God's prohibition. But if

---

[1] It is the Najadāt who annul this punishment, Ed., 68 (Seelye, 90).

[2] A punishment inflicted in certain cases of adultery, Juynboll, 301—2; Sachau, 809. Among the Khawārij, the Azāriḳa oppose stoning (Ed., 64, Seelye, 84).

[3] *Uṣūl*, 204—5; Juynboll, 39—54. It is to be noted that our author fails to include the fourth source, *Ḳiyās* (analogy). *Uṣūl*, 205, discusses it.

[4] *Uṣūl*, 199—200; Ḥilli, 40—1; Juynboll, 58—61.

[5] IH, I, 78—81 (Asin, II, 190—4).

the command or the interdiction had not come from God to His worshippers, nothing would be obligatory on them and nothing would be forbidden to them[1]. This is contrary to the opinion of those among the Barāhima and Ḳadariyya who maintain that the charge is imparted to the intelligent person by two inclinations which stir in his heart[2]. One of them emanates from God Who exhorts him by means of it to apply reasoning and logic; the other comes from Satan who urges him through it to disobey, and prevents him thereby from following the first inclination. This forces them to the conclusion that Satan was also a *Mukallaf* by two inclinations[3] one of which emanated from God and the other from another Satan. Thereupon the argument regarding the second Satan will be like that about the first, so that an infinite series of Satans will be premised. But this is absurd, and what leads to absurdity is in itself absurd.

Regarding the eleventh essential, which deals with the extinction of mankind and their judgments in the world to come, they teach that God can annihilate the entire world summarily or destroy part of the bodies and allow the others to endure[4]. This is contrary to the opinion of those among the Ḳadariyya of Baṣra who hold that He is capable of destroying all bodies with an accident-of-perishing
339 not in a substratum which He will create[5], but that He is unable to destroy some of the bodies while others continue to exist.

They assert that God will finally resurrect all mankind and the other living beings who died in the world[6], contrary to the view of those who maintain that He will resurrect only people but not the remaining living beings. They affirm the creation of Paradise and Hell contrary to the belief of those who think that

---

[1] *Uṣūl*, 202—3; *Creencia*, 284—92; IH, I, 72—73 (Asin, I, 161—4).

[2] *Uṣūl*, 203—4; *Creencia*, ib. and 295; IH, I, 69—70 (Asin, II, 182—5). The two inclinations are of course very similar to the יצר טוב and יצר רע in Rabbinic theology.

[3] Satan in Arabic theology is a rebel angel who disobeyed, therefore the argument is applied here. *Uṣūl*, 204, adds that if they do not think him a rebel against orders he is not to be condemned.

[4] *Uṣūl*, 229—30; for further information see above 232—3 and notes.

[5] See the protests of our author as an orthodox Muslim against this view, *Uṣūl*, 231—2.

[6] *Uṣūl*, 236—7; *Creencia*, 320—3; Ḥilli, 82—3; Rāzi, 100—2; IH, IV, 79—81, where the problem is raised whether only the soul will be resurrected or the body as well. He decides in favor of the latter. Cf. *Uṣūl*, 235—6.

they were not created[1]. They believe in the perpetual enjoyment of Paradise by its inhabitants and the perpetual sufferings in Hell of the polytheists and the hypocrites, contrary to the opinion of those like Jahm who believe that they will both perish, and to the opinion of Abu-l-Hudhail the Ḳadarite that all the objects of God's power, both within these two places and elsewhere, will perish[2]. They say that only infidels are destined to Hell eternally, contrary to the teachings of the Ḳadariyya and the Khawārij that all who enter Hell will remain there eternally[3]. They assert that the Ḳadariyya and the Khawārij will be condemned to Hell eternally and will not escape from it; how can God forgive those who declare that it is not up to God to forgive and deliver from Hell those who enter it?

They declare that they confirm the examination in the grave[4] and the tortures in the grave for those who deserve them[5]. They have decided that those who deny tortures in the grave will be tortured there. They believe in the Apostle's Pool[6], the Bridge[7] and the Balance[8]. Whoever disacknowledges them

---

[1] *Uṣūl*, 237—8; Ash'ari, 475; Abu Hanīfa, 41—2; Maṭurīdi, 28—9; IH, IV, 81—3.

[2] *Uṣūl*, 238; Ash'ari, 474—5; Abu Ḥanīfa, ib.; ibn Iskander, 24; IH, IV, 83—6. The latter mentions a Shī'ite sect which believes that the people of Paradise and Hell will be created with their destinies.

[3] A full summary of the various views held on eternal Hell etc., will be found IH, IV, 44—6. He himself agrees with our author. See *Uṣūl*, 242; Ash'ari, 274; ibn Iskander, 22; Rāzi, 102—3.

[4] This examination will be conducted by the two angels Nākir and Munkar. For traditions and details, see Wolff, *Muh. Eschatologie*, 71—3 (Arab. 40—1); Ghazāli, *al-Durra*, 20—3 (Arab. 23—7); Abu Ḥanīfa, 43.

[5] Wolff, *l. c.*, 162—71 (Arab. 94—8); *al-Durra*, 24—8 (Arab. 27—32). Ghazāli argues that punishment is possible in the grave but IH, IV, 67 asserts that the examination and torture will take place on the Day of Resurrection and that until then there is no contact between the body and soul of a dead person. See also *Ibāna*, 91—2.

[6] *Uṣūl*, 246; Ḥilli, 83—4; IH, IV, 66; *al-Durra*, 70; *Ibāna*, 90—1; Ash'ari, 473.

[7] Same sources as above. For a description see Wolff. *l. c.* 147—54 (Arab. 82—6).

[8] *Creencia*, 326—8, giving us a good insight into the realistic belief in it by a rational philosopher; Ḥilli, *ib.*; IH, IV, 65—6. The idea of the Balance, and probably the Bridge, is borrowed from the Persians who share it with the Hindus. See Goldziher, *Islamisme et Parsisme, RHR*, XLIII (1901), 11—2. For the Persian doctrines see A. V. W. Jackson's article on the Persian belief in the future life in Sneath, *Religion and the Future Life*, 126—199.

will be forbidden to drink from the Pool and his foot will slip from the Bridge to the fire of Gehenna. They affirm the Intercession[1] of the Prophet and the pious people of the community in behalf of Muslim sinners and of whosoever had in his heart a speck of faith. But those who deny Intercession will have it denied to them[2].

340 Regarding the twelfth essential relating to the Caliphate and the Imāmate[3], they teach that the Imāmate is a duty incumbent on the community, because the appointment of an Imām establishes[4] judges and executives. He guards their frontiers, leads their armies in raids, apportions the booty among them, and vindicates the one wronged against the wrong-doer[5]. They say that the method of conferring the Imāmate on the Imām in this community is selection, by seeking the most qualified person[6]. They say there was no indication from the Prophet regarding the appointment of anyone in particular to the Imāmate[7], contrary to

---

1 *Uṣūl*, 244—5; IH, IV, 63—5; Wolf, *l.c.* 177—85 (Arab. 100—4); *al-Durra*, 56—8 (Arab. 66—9).

2 The reference is to the Ḳadariyya and the Khawārij who believed that Intercession would not prevail. IH, *ib.*, agrees with our author in charging them with denial of it and so also Ash'ari, 474, where it is stated that some Mu'tazila denied it while others limited its efficacy only to believers. In *Ibāna*, 89—90, al-Ash'ari, however, argues with them not about its existence as he does in the case of the Pool and the tortures, but about whom it will be applied to.

3 In *Uṣūl*, Baghdādi counts this as the thirteenth essential and lists Faith (our thirteenth) as the twelfth.

4 Both this word "establishes" (ينصب) and the word "guards" (يضبط) have a damma over the *ya* in the MS. to indicate either the passive or the IV form. Yet neither suits here. The entire phrase is doubtful and unfortunately *Uṣūl's* readings are also uncertain here, 271.

5 *Uṣūl*, *ib.*; IH, IV, 87; Rāzi, 105—6 (Ṭūsi's commentary as a Shī'ite is interesting, 110); Ḥilli, 62—4, maintaining the view in common with the Mu'tazila that reason as well as revelation dictate the appointment of an Imām; Creencia, 348—52; Ikhald, I, 388—91.

6 *Creencia*, 352—5; *Uṣūl*, 279.

7 This question of *naṣṣ* (indication) is the pivot of the entire conflict between Sunnites and Shī'ites. From the Orthodox point of view see *Uṣūl*, 279—81; *Ibāna*, 94 (Ash'ari maintains that there is a naṣṣ but it obviously points to Abu Bekr; the Khalīfs named their successors); IH, IV, 96—105, esp. 96—8 and 102 (he also recognizes a naṣṣ but merely in the Ḳuraish); *Creencia*, 352—9, and finally *Streitschrift*, 63—6 (Arab. 36—9). The Shī'ite

the opinion of the Rawāfid that he definitely indicated the Imāmate of 'Ali, in a way which is absolutely trustworthy. But if it were, as they allege, on the basis of a tradition which has been transmitted [1], others similar to it have been handed down [2]. Whoever makes this claim regarding 'Ali in face of the want of a continuous chain of authority in its transmission, cannot be distinguished from anyone who makes a similar claim for Abu Bekr or for someone else despite the lack of traditions to support it [3].

They teach that it is a condition of the Imāmate that the incumbent be a son of the Ḳuraish [4], descendants of the Banu Naḍr ibn Kināna ibn Khuzaima ibn Mudrika ibn Alyās ibn Mudar ibn Nizār ibn Ma'add ibn 'Adnān [5]. This is contrary to the opinion of the Ḍirāriyya that the Imāmate may be held by all Arabs, or by freed slaves, or by Persians [6], and is also contrary to the belief of the Khawārij

---

claims are recorded in Ḥilli, 64—78 a very full exposition; a refutation of most of it will be found IH, *ib.*: Strothmann, *Staatsrecht d. Zaiditen*, 11—25; a refutation of the Sunnite argument, *ib.*, 13—4.

[1] See two traditions (both characterized as "*Mutawātir*"— transmitted by a continuous chain—in Ḥilli, 75—7; *Hayyāt-ul-Kulub*, *335—47*.

[2] Cf. *Streitschrift*, 64 (Arab. 37—8); *Strothmann*, *l. c.*, 29 and note two; IH, IV, 91. I read the second word "nḳl" as a verb and not an accusative noun as Ed. does.

[3] *Uṣūl*, 280. The same argument is employed *Streitschrift*, 64—5 (Arab. 37—8). Ghazāli answers the charge made by the Shī'ites that the Companions suppressed the tradition because of personal interests. The Shī'ite answer to the question why 'Ali swore loyalty to the other Khalīfs (*Ibāna*, 95), that he did it because he feared to disclose his real feelings, is repudiated by ibn Ḥazm as an insult to 'Ali's courage, IV, 97.

[4] *Uṣūl*, 275—6 and 7; Ash'ari, 461; *Creencia*, 353; IH, IV, 89; Ikha'd, I 394—400. It is interesting to note that according to him the famous theologian al-Bāḳilāni dissented from this opinion.

[5] *Uṣūl* relates that some wanted to trace the Ḳuraishitic branch to an earlier ancestor than Naḍr so as to include themselves, 276—7. IH, *ib.*, claims that the Sunnites are agreed that the Ḳuraish are offspring of Fihr ibn Mālik, two generations later than Naḍr. He has this on the authority of Hishām b. Muḥammad. Cf. Ṭab., I, 1106; IA, II, 18—9. Baghdādi probably carries the genealogy no further because there is a tradition that the Prophet forbade searching beyond Ma'add *Murūj*, IV, 118 and 119. IA, *ib.*, does not record this tradition, but also closes his account because of the great confusion beyond 'Adnān, 23—4.

[6] Ḍirār said that a Persian was even to be preferred to an Arab and a Mawla to a free man. *Uṣūl*, 275. Ash'ari, 462, explains that it is because they have less family protection

in the Imāmate of their chiefs who sprang from the Rabī'a and other clans, such as Nāfi' ibn al-Azraḳ[1] al-Ḥanafi, Najda ibn 'Āmir[2] al-Ḥanafi, 'Abdallah ibn Wahab al-Rāsibi[3], Ḥurḳūṣ ibn Zubair al-Bajali[4], Shabīb ibn Yezīd al-Shaibāni[5] and their
341 like, who deviate from the saying of the Prophet: The Imāms are from the Ḳuraish[6]. They assert that learning, uprightness and statesmanship are pre-requisites to the Imāmate[7]. They require learning of him to the extent of qualifying as one of those who can develop legal rulings[8] in the precepts of the law. They stipulate that he possess enough probity so that he can be included among those on the basis of whose testimony a judge may issue a decision; that is, he should be of a pious religious attitude, kindly disposed to his possessions and affairs, above committing any deadly sin, nor addicted to minor sins, and above failing in manliness under the most trying circumstances. But it is not one of the requirements that he be altogether immune from sin[9], contrary to the opinion of the Imāmiyya who maintain that the Imām is immune from all sins[10]. Yet they have believed it right for him to say in case of fear[11]: I am not an Imām, when in reality he is

---

and IH. explains that it is because these are easier to remove. Naubakhti, 10, cites both reasons. Acc. to him, Mu'tazilites, other things being equal, preferred a Ḳuraishite. We no doubt find here echoes of the resentment felt against the 'Umayyads. But most probably, it is due to Shu'ūbiyya views. See *Muh.* St. I, 157. For an echo of this controversy in tradition see *Mukhtalif al-Ḥadīth*, 149—51.

[1] Ed, 62—6 (Seelye, 83—7).

[2] *ib.*, 66—70 (87—91).

[3] *ib.* 71— (92).

[4] *ib*; I read البجلى with MS.; Ed., النحلى.

[5] *ib.*, 89—92 (111—5).

[6] The tradition in this version is reported Ṭayālisi, ‡926 and 2133, See also Bukhāri, IV, 407; Tirmidhi, II, 36 top; *Uṣūl*, 276; IH, IV, 89—90.

[7] *Uṣūl*, 277; *Creencia*, 353; *Streitschrift*, 82—9; Strothmann, *l.* c., 67—82; Ikhald, I, 392—3. All of these include Ḳuraishitic origin as one of the necessary qualifications.

[8] *Uṣūl, ib.*; Strothmann, *l. c.*, 70; *Streitschrift*, 86—9. For a full discussion of *Ijtihād* see *EI*, II, 448—9.

[9] *Uṣūl*, 278; *Streitschrift*, 66 (Arab. 39—41).

[10] Ḥilli, 64—8; IH, IV, 95.

[11] Arab. *Takiyya* (with Goldziher; Ed. and MS. البقية). It is a principle, granting one the right, and in Shī'ite circles the duty, to dissimulate, conceal one's true belief and feign

the Imām. In this way they have permitted him to lie despite their belief in his freedom from lying[1].

They assert that the Imāmate is bestowed by the act of one who confers it upon a person who is eligible for it, provided the person conferring it is a qualified jurist and an upright individual[2]. They rule that the Imāmate can rightly belong to only one person throughout the entire land of Islam[3], unless a barrier lies between the provinces, such as an ocean, an enemy that cannot be coped with, when the people of the two districts are not able to lend each other aid. In that case it is legal for the people of one province to confer the Imāmate on one of their men who is qualified for it[4].

They recognize the Imāmate of Abu Bekr the Righteous after the Prophet, contrary to the Rawāfiḍ who confirm it only for 'Ali[5], and contrary to the opinion
of the Rawendiyya who confirm the Imāmate of 'Abbās after him[6]. They approve of 342
grading Abu Bekr and 'Omar first in rank, respectively, and after them 'Ali, but

---

adherence to the views of the ruling party in order to avoid dangers. See *EI*, IV, 628—9, and Goldziher's article in the *ZDMG*, LX (1906), 213—26. Although sometimes utilized by Sunnites, and more frequently by the Khawārij, it is essentially a Shī'ite characteristic.

1 The Shī'ite answer will be that according to this reasoning prophets cannot be regarded immune either, since even Muḥammad dissembled. Cf. *EI*, *ib*.

2 Our author follows al-Ash'ari's ruling that the choice by one qualified individual is adequate, *Uṣūl*, 280—1. But there are a number of other views ranging from two people to the entire Muslim community. *Uṣūl*, *ib*.; Ash'ari, 460; IH, IV, 167—71; the latter agrees with al-Ash'ari, *ib*. 169. In this ruling we no doubt have another example of accommodation to circumstances which characterizes the Sunnites, confronted as they were with a phenomenon of dynasties that bequeathed the Caliphate from father to son.

3 *Uṣūl*, 274—5; Ash'ari, 460—1 (he makes no exception for the emergency); IH, IV, 88—9 (He also does not specify any cases where the ruling may be overstepped); IKhald, I, 391—2.

4 IKhald, *ib*., specifies that this view was held by Abu Isḥāḳ al-Isfaraini.

5 One is tempted to believe that unlike his customary application of the term Rawāfiḍ as synonymous with Shī'a, Baghdādi discusses in this case the Imāmiyya more particularly who, unlike the Zaidiyya, took a hostile stand to the "two Sheikhs" (i. e. Abu Bekr and 'Omar). See Friedländer's Appendix on the Rawāfiḍ, *Shiites*, II, 137—59.

6 *Uṣūl*, 281 and 284—5; they are refuted by IH, IV, 91—2.

they diverge about the relative positions of 'Ali and 'Uthmān[1]. They affirm their loyalty to 'Uthmān and they steer clear of anyone who calls him an infidel[2]. They recognize the Imāmate of 'Ali in its time[3]. They judge 'Ali rightful in his wars in Baṣra[4], in Ṣiffīn[5] and in Nahrawān[6], and they assert that Ṭalḥa and al-Zubair repented and withdrew from warfare against 'Ali[7] but that al-Zubair was slain by 'Amr ibn Jurmūz[8] in Wādi Sibā' after his withdrawal from the battle. When Ṭalḥa was about to leave, Merwān ibn al-Ḥakam, who was with the Party of the Camel, shot him with an arrow and killed him[9]. They say that '..'isha was aiming to set

---

[4] *Ibāna*, 94—5; *Creencia*, 363—4 (his explanation that the ranking is beyond the human reason and that it is entirely within the ken of God is the struggle of an intellectual Muslim to put up with the evident lack of justice in 'Uthmān's reign, whom he ranks before 'Ali): Ash'ari, 458—9; Maṭurīdi, 27; Abu Ḥanīfa, 25—6. IH, IV, 112 ranks Muḥammad's wives after the Prophet and then Abu Bekr, 'Omar, 'Uthmān, 'Ali. But he determines the rank only in accordance with what the Muslims have been told of their relative position in Paradise, *l. c.* 111 ff. On the question of the relative rank of 'Ali and 'Uthmān cf. *Bad' wal-Ta'rīkh*, V, 149 and ibn al-Jauzi, *Manākib Aḥmad b. Ḥanbal*, 160—61.

[1] Ash'ari, 454 and sources as above; *Uṣūl*, 286.

[2] The controversy here is with the Kāmiliyya and the Khawārij. *Uṣūl*, 286—7; Ash'ari, 455, and sources as above.

[3] Against the Party of the Camel, i. e. 'Āisha, Ṭalḥa and al-Zubair. Tab. (Zotenberg) III, 632—64.

[4] Against Mu'āwiya, *l. c.*, 670—83.

[5] Aganist the Secessionist Khawārij, *l. c.*, 687—91.

[6] This account is supported by the authorities. See *Muruj*, IV, 316—21; IA, III, 196—7 and 199—201; Ṭab. (Zotenberg) III, 655—60; Ya'ḳūbi, II, 212—3.

[7] Ed. and MS. حرموز. But most scholars agree on the reading جرموز: Ya'kubi II, 213; *Murūj*, IV, 319; IA, III, 200—1; Tab. I, 3218 (although de Goeje adds the note "Cod ut solet حرموز"). Tab. (Zotenberg), III, 660 reads Hormouz and so also *Uṣūl*, 289.

[8] *Murūj*, IV, 321—2; IA, III, 196—7 and 199—200 (Acc. to him it is not certain that Merwān killed him); Ṭab. (Zotenberg), III, 655—60. The authorities tell nothing about Ṭalḥa's intention to leave the battle. Only pseudo-ibn Ḳuṭaiba, *al-Siyāsa wal-Imāma*, 129 (On the authorship see Brockelmann, *Gesch. d. arab. Lit.*, I, 122 and de Goeje in *Rivista degli Studi Orientali*, I (1907—08), 415—21) embellishes our author's account by adding that Ṭalḥa exhorted God to punish the Party of the Camel in whatever way He would choose and that no sooner were the words spoken than Ṭalḥa was shot by Merwān. Cf. Ibn Sa'd, v. 25, 2).

affairs right between[1] the two parties but the Banu Ḍabba and al-Azd overruled her opinion and fought against ʻAli without her permission, so that the succeeding events occurred[2]. Regarding al-Ṣiffīn they rule that right was on the side of ʻAli, while Muʻāwiya and his supporters wronged him by means of an interpretation[3] as a result of which they became sinners but not heretics[4]. They declare that right was with ʻAli in the arbitration, yet the two judges did not sin by depriving him of his office, which necessitated his dismissal, and by the deception which one of the two arbiters practised against the other[5]. They assert that the party of Nahrawān deviated from true religion. The Prophet named them deviators[6] because they condemned ʻAli, ʻUthmān, ʻĀʼisha, ibn ʻAbbās, Ṭalḥa, al-Zubair, and the others who followed ʻAli, after the arbitration, as infidels. They also call everyone among the Muslims who commits a sin an infidel. But whoever makes the

---

1 MS. and Ed. read بعد which is meaningless. The reading here is based on *Uṣūl*, 289, line 11 (بين)

2 The role ʻĀʼisha played in fomenting the rebellion against ʻAli, whom she hated ever since he had urged the Prophet who suspected her chastity to divorce her, under the pretext of avenging ʻUthmān, whom she had likewise opposed, as well as her central position throughout the Battle of the Camel,—actually so called because it was concentrated around her beast,—are too well-known to allow anyone to swallow our author's statement unquestioningly. It is true that on the way to Baṣra, when she passed the place called al-Ḥawb and heard dogs barking, which recalled to her an ominous tradition of the Prophet connected with the barking of the dogs at al-Ḥawb, she wavered for a time wishing to return (but cf. *Muh. St.* II, 126). But she overcame that fear very soon and led the battle. Our author's plea that she went to make peace, told in different versions by pseudo-ibn Ḳutaiba, *l. c.*, 125—6 and *Murūj*, IV, 335, is no doubt a fabrication by Sunnites. We find a sad example of her hostile tendencies in her first words to ʻAli after the battle, Tab. I, 3225. Our author's standpoint is also taken by *Creencia*, 361: IH, IV, 158 and *Uṣūl*, 289.

3 Referring to the pinning of the Ḳurʼān on the swords and the arrangement for the arbitration. *Uṣūl*, 290; IH, IV, 159—61.

4 *ib.*

5 Referring to the decision reached by the two judges to call for the election of a new Khalīf. But when Abu Mūsa al-Ashʻari, ʻAli's representative, openly disavowed his allegiance to ʻAli and demanded a new election, ʻAmr ibn al-ʻĀṣi contrary to his previous agreement, reasserted the Caliphate of Muʻāwiya and carried the victory. Tab (Zotenberg), III, 684—7.

6 Bukhari, II, 337.

343 Muslims Kāfirs and calls the choicest Companions Kāfirs is the one infidel among them.

Regarding the thirteenth essential relating to faith and Islām they teach: Verily the fundamental of faith is knowledge of God and an affirmation of this truth in the heart[1], but they differ regarding whether to term the confession faith, as well as the external acts of obedience, performed by the external organs, despite their unanimity as to the obligatory nature of all the prescribed commandments and the merits of performing the ordained, unwritten works[2]. This is contrary to the doctrine of the Karrāmiyya that faith is confession only, regardless of whether it is sincere or feigned[3]; contrary also to the opinion of those among the Ḳadariyya and the Khawārij who hold that the name Believer is not applicable to sinners[4]. They (the Orthodox) teach that the term faith is not dropped as a result of any sin except heresy. He whose sin is milder than non-belief is therefore a believer even though he transgresses by his disobedience.

They say that the death-sentence on a Muslim is not legal except for one of three crimes: apostasy[5], adultery after marriage[6] and reprisal for a murdered person when he is his equal[7]. This is contrary to the view of the Khawārij re-

---

[1] *Uṣūl*, 248—51. The liberal attitude of our author is surprising in view of the fact that even Abu Ḥanīfa required confession as a condition of faith. But he probably stands on the same platform as al-Ash'ari. His statement in *Uṣūl*, 248, that al-Ash'ari defined faith as "an affirmation of God and His Messengers and their traditions, and this affirmation is valid only if accompanied by a knowledge of Him" is contradicted by *Ibāna* 10, where al-Ash'ari says: "faith consists of words and deeds: it can be increased and diminished". IH, II, 111 and III, 188—9, confirms *Uṣūl, ib.* But the editor takes exception there to this statement, maintaining that Abu-l-Ḥasan identified faith with Islām so that any word or deed which would exclude one from Islām, automatically makes him an infidel. That this defence is weak becomes apparent from *Ibana*, *ib.*: Islām is more inclusive than faith and not every tenet in Islām is part of faith.

[2] For these differences, see *Uṣūl*, 248—9; IH, *ib.*

[3] Ed., 211—2; Ash'ari, 141; IH, *ib.*; *Uṣūl*, 250—1.

[4] *Uṣūl*, 249—50; IH, III, 229—34; Ash'ari, 266—70.

[5] Sachau, 812 and 843—6; see under the fifteenth essential.

[6] Sachau, 809 and 815—7; Juynboll, 301—3.

[7] Reading كفوه with Goldziher; Ed. and MS. كفره. The law is that reprisal *(Kiṣāṣ)* is allowed only on certain conditions among which is that the murdered one must be a Muslim if the murderer is. Juynboll, 294—6; Sachau, 762 and 774—6.

garding the legitimacy of slaying everyone who is disobedient to God. If all the sinners were infidels they would become apostates from Islam. But if they had this status, it would become an obligation to kill them without inflicting any punishment on them. There would thus be no purpose in requiring the amputation of the thief's hand, or the flogging of the libeller or the stoning of a person committing adultery after marriage. The apostate receives no other punishment than execution.

Regarding the fourteenth essential, relating to Saints and Imāms, they assert that angels are immune from sin[1] by the Word of God: "They (the angels) do not disobey Allah in what He commands and do as they are commanded[2]. The majority of them affirm that the excellence of the prophets is greater than that of the angels, contrary to the opinion of those who attribute superiority to the angels over the prophets[3]. From this standpoint it would necessarily follow that the Zabāniya[4] are superior in rank to those of the apostles who possess constancy, earnestness and patience. They believe in the superiority of the prophets to the saints of all nations contrary to the opinion of those among the Karrāmiyya who rank some of the saints higher than some of the prophets[5]. 344

The Orthodox differ regarding the legitimacy of the tenure of the Imāmate by the less qualified of two contestants. Our Sheikh Abu-l-Ḥasan al-Ash'ari denied it, but al-Ḳalānisi granted it[6]. They profess love for ten of the Prophet's Companions and they rule that they are among those who have entered Paradise[7].

---

[1] See IH, IV, 32—5 and his denial of the angelic nature of Hārūt and Mārūt or even Iblīs, see also *Uṣūl*, 296—7.

[2] Sura 66, v. 6.

[3] Ed., 333 (above 201 and notes).

[4] These are the angels who torment the dead in Hell.

[5] *Ib.*; *Uṣūl*, 298.

[6] *Uṣūl*, 304; *Ibāna*, 11 and 95. The Zaidiyya and many Mu'tazilites shared his opinion, Ash'ari, 461.

[7] The tradition whtch lists the ten who are admitted to Paradise is recorded by Aḥmad b. Ḥanbal, I, 193. In another version, also on the authority of Sa'īd b. Zaid, and recorded *ib.*, 187, and Ṭayālisi, 236, the Prophet is one of the ten, Abu 'Ubaida is eliminated and Sa'd ibn Mālik replaces ibn Abu Waḳḳāṣ.

These include the four Ḳhalīfs, Ṭalḥa, al-Zubair, Sa'd ibn Abu Waḳḳāṣ[1], Sa'īd ibn Zaid ibn 'Amr ibn Nufail[2], 'Abd-al-Raḥmān[3], Abu 'Ubaida ibn al-Jarrāḥ[4]. They profess their love for all who were present with the Prophet at the battle of Badr, and are convinced that they are among the people who dwell in Paradise[5]. They maintain a similar attitude to all who witnesssed with him the battle of Uḥud, with the exception of one man whose name is Ḳuzmān. He slew a number of the polytheists at Uḥud, but then killed himself and was therefore classed with the hypocrites[6]. Similarly all who were present at the Pledge of Good Will in al-Ḥudaibiya are among the people who have entered Paradise without a reckoning and everyone of them will intercede for seventy thousand[7]. In this group
345 'Ukkāsha ibn Miḥṣan is also included. They also teach us to love all who died while defending the religion of Islām, provided they were not, before their death, partisans of any heresy of the heresies of the people of erring fancies[8].

Regarding the fifteenth essential, relative to the status of the enemies of the faith, they teach that the enemies of the faith fall under two categories. One existed before the rise of the reign of Islām, and the other sprang up since the institution of Islām. These take shelter in Islām outwardly, but they deceive the Muslims and pursue their own wickedness. Those which existed before Islām comprise a number of groups with diverse characteristics[9]. One consists of the worshippers of idols and images. Another worships particular individuals like those

---

[1] A general who participated in many of the wars of expansion of Islām. EI, IV, 29—30.

[2] Contra Ed. and MS. which read ثقيل. He was a very early convert to Islām and exceedingly pious, *l.* c. 66—7.

[3] Ibn 'Awf, a Ḳuraishite and early convert to Islām, *l. c.* I, 54.

[4] A close Companion of the Prophet, *l. c.* I, 112.

[5] *Uṣūl*, 302.

[6] Ḳuzmān is the man about whom the Prophet had previously remarked that he would go to Hell. After displaying great valor on the battlefield he took his own life when his wound pained him. As the Prophet heard it, he exclaimed: I testify that I am in truth the apostle of God. Ṭab., I 1423—4; IA, II, 125; *Uṣūl*, 302 (the reading قتل is hardly correct).

[7] Tirmidhi, II, 71; cf. Wensinck, 182 a and 112 a.

[8] *Uṣūl*, 317.

[9] See a similar list, with several divergencies, Maḳrīzī, 344—5; *Uṣūl*, 318—24.

who adore Jamshīd[1] or those who invoke Nimrūd ibn Kana'ān[2] or Fir'aun and their like. Another worships all forms which it considers beautiful, in accordance with the doctrines of the Ḥulūliyya and their claim that the Spirit of God is embodied in beautiful forms, Still another worships the sun, or the moon, or the stars as a whole, or some one star in particular[3]. There is one which worships the angels and calls them Daughters of God. With respect to these people God's Word was revealed: "Most surely they who do not believe in the hereafter name the angels with female names"[4]. Another worships the rebellious Satan. Another serves the cow; others worship fire. The law relative to these worshippers of idols, people, angels, and fire is to prohibit to Muslims the eating of their meats[5] and 347
marriage of their women[6]. But they differ regarding the acceptance of the poll-tax from them. Al-Shāfi'i rules: No poll-tax may be accepted from them; it may be taken only from the People of the Book or from those who possess what resembles a Book[7]. But Mālik and Abu Ḥanīfa declare it lawful to take tribute from them, except that Mālik excluded the Ḳuraishites[8] from among those whereas Abu Ḥanīfa made an exception for all Arabs[9].

Among the divisions which were infidels before the days of Islām are also included the Sūfusṭā'iyya who deny realities; the Sumaniyya who teach the pre-existence of the world and reject inductive and deductive speculation, contending that nothing can be known except through the five senses; the Dahriyya who believe in the eternity of the world; those who recognize an eternal hylic matter

---

[1] (Or Jimshīd) one of the earliest Persian kings. IA, I, 46—7, who reports that he also claimed divinity; Albirūni, 200—3; Justi, *Iran. Namenb.*, 144.

[2] Called by other authorities *ibn Kush.* The stories about him are collected IA, I, 67—72 and 81—4.

[3] The reference is to those who worshipped Saturn because he is the highest of the seven planets. *Uṣūl*, 321.

[4] Sura 53, v. 28.

[5] *Umm*, II, 211; cf. Juynboll, 178.

[6] Sura 2 v. 220—1; ibn al-Humam, II, 506—9; Juynboll, 221.

[7] *Umm*, IV, 155—6 and 158; Heffening, *Islamisches Fremdenrecht*, 44. In note three he fails to include the Mālikites with the Ḥanīfites.

[8] Muwaṭṭa (ed. Kazān) 146 and commentary.

[9] ibn Humam, IV, 371; Abu Yūsuf, *Kitab al-Kharāj* (Cairo ed.), 153—4.

in the Universe, while admitting the creation of the accidents; the philosophers who profess the eternity of the Universe and disacknowledge the Maker. This is the view of Pythagoras and Cadmus[1]. Among them are also the philosophers who confess in an eternal Maker, but who maintain that His acts are co-eternal with Him, and teach the co-eternity of the Maker and His Universe. This was the doctrine of Empedocles[2]. They also include the philosophers who profess the eternity of the four elments and the four bases[3], earth, water, fire and air; those who believe in the eternity of these four, as well as of the heavens and stars, maintaining that the heavens are made from a fifth element and that it is not subject to creation and annihilation either in its entirety or in part. The Muslims
347 are agreed that they are not allowed to eat the meats and marry the women of the above groups; but they disagree as to whether to accept the poll-tax from them. Those who would take it from the idol-worshippers will also take it from them. But those who do not take it from the idol-worshippers will not accept it from them. It is this latter view which al-Shāfi'i and his followers support[4].

Regarding the Magians they tell us that they are divided into four sects: Zarwāniyya[5], Massīkhiyya[6] Khurramdīniyya[7] and Bihāfirīdhiyya[8]. The meats pre-

---

[1] Ed. and MS. قاوذروس. But cf. *Fihrist*, 239 and note.

[2] With Goldziher; MS. and Ed. ابن قلس.

[3] With Ed. والعناصر; MS. والعاصى.

[4] *Umm*, IV, 158 f.; ibn Humam, IV, 371; *Uṣūl*, 323—4.

[5] A sect believing in *Zarwān* (lit., time), at first probably an abstract idea, but later a divinity from whom Ahura Mazda and Ahriman are saîd to have sprung. See their account in Shahr., 183—5; *ERE*, XI, 346; Dhalla, *Zoroastrian Theology*, 203—5. A longer study of them has been published by Irvin Blue in *Studies in honor of Dastur Darab Pechotan Sanjana*, (1925), 61—81.

[6] Ed., مسخية; MS. مسخيه for مسخيه; Shahr., 185, مسخية These are the transformers, a sect which believed that "Light alone existed, pure light, then part of it was transformed and became Darkness"., *ib.*

[7] Ed., 251—2 (above 87—8). Dhalla, *l. c.*, 218—9 counts this sect as a heresy within Zoroastrianism.

[8] Also called Sassāniyya, followers of Bihāfirīdh b. Mahfurūdhīn, a reformer who was a contemporary of Abu Muslim. He at first accepted Islām under pressure from the general and became an 'Abbāsid (Arab. اسود), but later apostasized and was killed by him. Albīrūni reports nothing about this previous conversion. See an account of him Albīrūni, 193—4;

pared by all of them are forbidden and likewise marriage with their women. Al-Shāfi'i, Mālik, Abu Ḥanīfa, al-Auzā'i and al-Thauri are unanimous in ruling that it is right to take tribute from the Zarwāniyya and the Massīkhiyya[1]. But they disagree about the ratio of their blood-money. Al-Shāfi'i said: The bloodwit for a Magian equals a fifth of the bloodwit for a Jew or a Christian[2] and the blood-money for a Jew or a Christian equals a third of the blood-money for a Muslim, so that the blood-money for the Magian amounts to a fifteenth[3] of the blood-money for a Muslim. But Abu Ḥanīfa rules that the bloodwit for the Magian, the Jew and the Christian is equal to the bloodwit for the Muslim[4].

From the Mazdakiyya among the Magians the acceptance of tribute is not allowed because they have dissociated themselves from the religion of the original Magians by permitting all the forbidden practices and by teaching that all men have an equal share in goods and women, and because of the other licentious practices. Similarly. the poll-tax may not be accepted from the Bihāfirīdhiyya, although their teachings are superior to the teachings of the original Magians[5], because their religion was promulgated by their chief Bihāfirīdh during the era of Islām, and the acceptance of tribute from the adherent to any form of unbelief which has arisen since the institution of Islām is not permissible.

The jurists differ regarding the Ṣābians among the infidels[6]. Most of them 348
rule that their status with respect to their meats, marriage of their women, and the poll-tax is like the status of the Christians; they are all permitted[7]. But others

---

Shahr., 187—88. The name of the native district of Bihāfirīdh is *Khawwāf*, near Nīshāpūr. *Fihrist*, 344 places him in Rawa near Nīshāpūr (*Abrashahr* in Persian). See Houtsma's article *WZKM*, III (1889), 30—37.

1 *Umm*, IV, 158; *Muwaṭṭa*, 146.

2 *Uṣūl*, 319; *Umm*, VII, 291 and 294. The *diya* (bloodwit) for Jews and Christians is 4000 dirhems, for a Magian 800, and for a Muslim 12000. Cf. Juynboll, 296, note two. Mālik sets the *diya* of the Jew and Christian at 6000, ibn Humam, VIII, 307.

3 Ed. and MS. خمس (fifth).

4 *Uṣūl*, 327; *Umm*, VII; ibn Humam, *ib.*

5 Their practices according to Muslim authorities are nearer to Islām. They drink no wine and forbid illicit relationships. See Shahr. and Albīrūni, *ib.*

6 *Uṣūl*, 324—5. See also Ed., 263 (above 103).

7 *Umm*, IV, 158; V. 6.

differentiate as follows: those among the Ṣābians who profess the eternity of the Hylic substance are subject to the same rulings as the supporters of the Hylic hypothesis whom we have discussed previously. However, anyone among them who believes in the creation of the Universe but disputes us on the attributes of the Maker enjoys the same status as the Christians[1]. This is our view. As regards the Barāhima, who disacknowledge all the prophets and apostles, the followers of al-Shāfi'i are agreed that, although they conform to the Muslims in their belief in the creation of the Universe and the unity of its Maker, their meats may not be eaten nor may their women be taken as wives. The controversy about taking tribute from them follows the same lines as in the case of idol-worshippers.

The jurists of Islam are unanimous in declaring the meats prepared by Jews, Samaritans and Christians to be lawful[2], in permitting the marriage of their women[3], and in regarding the taking of tribute from them as lawful[4]. But they disagree on the rate of the poll-tax. Al-Shāfi'i said; Verily the contribution by every mature[5] person amounts to one dīnār as a ransom for his blood[6]. But Abu Ḥanīfa ruled that the rich one is taxed forty-eight dirhems, the middle-class person twenty-four, and the poor twelve[7]. They also differ regarding the infliction of punishment on them. Al-Shāfi'i says that their punishments are the same as those for the Muslims, and the adulterer among them is to be stoned if he is a married man[8]. But Abu Ḥanīfa ruled that they are not subject to stoning[9]. They also differ regarding their blood-money. Al-Shāfi'i said that the bloodwit for a Muslim, and the compensation for one of their women is a third of the blood-money of a Muslim

---

[1] A geographical distinction between the Ṣābians of Ḥarrān and those of Baṭīḥa is made by the Ḥanīfite school. See *ZDMG*, xxxii (1878), 391—2.

[2] Sura 5, v. 7; *Umm*, II, 196 and IV, 187; ibn Humam, VIII, 52.

[3] Sura, 5, v. 7; *Umm*, v, 5—6 and IV, 187; ibn Humam, II, 509.

[4] Sura 9, v. 29; ibn Humam, IV, 370 and commentaries.

[5] Arab. حالم; al-Shāfi'i relates that the Dhimmis of Yemen employed this term for بالغ. *Umm*, IV, 101.

[6] *Umm*. IV, 101; ibn Humam IV, 368; Juynboll, 351.

[7] Ibn Humam, *ib.*; *Kitāb al-Kharāj*, 146.

[8] *Umm*. VI, 164 ff.; ibn Humam, IV, 132—3; Mālik agrees with Abu Ḥanīfa see *Muwatta*, 283 and commentary.

[9] Ibn Humam, *ib.*

woman[1]. Mālik ruled that the bloodwit for one of the People of the Book is half the blood-money of the Muslim. Abu Ḥanīfa ruled that it is exactly the same as the compensation for a Muslim[2]. They differ regarding the application of the law of retaliation to them. Al-Shāfi'i said that no believer is to be killed for an infidel under any circumstances[3], but Abu Ḥanīfa said that a Muslim is to be killed for murdering a *Dhimmi* but not for the murder of a *Musta'min*[4]. They also differ regarding the exaction of the poll-tax from their aged Sheikh. Al-Shāfi'i required it[5], but Abu Ḥanīfa did not impose it save on one who is capable of leading in war[6]. 349

They disagree about the Thanawiyya, the Daiṣāniyya, the Markiūniyya among the Mānawiyya, who believe in the eternity of light and darkness and maintain that the world is composed of these two; the good and the beneficial come from light, and the evil and harmful come from darkness. Some of the legislators maintain that their status is like that of the Magians and they permit the acceptance of tribute from them although they forbid their meats and their women. But the approved view among us is that their position as regards marriage, meats and tribute is like that of the idol and image-worshippers which we have already explained.

As regards the infidels who have arisen since the institution of Islām, who take shelter in the external practices of Islām but slay the Muslims secretly, such as the Ghulāt among the Rawāfiḍ: the Sabbābiyya, the Bayāniyya, the Mughīriyya,

---

[1] *Umm*, VI, 92; ibn Humam, VIII, 307.

[2] For Abu Ḥanīfa's and M lik's views see ibn Humam, *ib.*

[3] *Umm*, VII, 291 f.; 389—99 (margin); ibn Humam, VIII, 255—7.

[4] With MS. بالمستامن; Ed., المستامن. The *Musta'min* is a member of those groups whom Muslims are enjoined to kill, who has procured security from the Muslims by a pledge or treaty. Heffening, *Das Islamische Fremdenrecht*, has made a historical study of the status of the *Musta'min* in Islām.— For Abu Ḥanīfa's ruling, see ibn Humam, *ib.* He bases himself on a tradition according to which the Prophet ordered the execution of a Muslim who had killed a *Dhimmi*. Al-Shāfi'i who also reports this tradition, *Umm*, VI, 259 (margin) and VII, 389—99 refutes Abu Ḥanīfa's standpoint. See also Heffening, *l. c.* 37—42.

[5] *Umm*, IV, 98 bottom.

[6] Ibn Humam, IV, 372—3. For the general question of the taxation of infidels in Islām, see Tritton, *The Khalifs and their non-Muslim Subjects*, 196—228.

the Manṣūriyya, the Janāḥiyya, the Khaṭṭābiyya, the other groups of the Ḥulūliyya, the Mukanna'iyya, the Mubayyiḍa in the country beyond the river Jaiḥūn, the Muḥammira of Azerbaijān and the Muḥammira of Ṭabaristān; those who profess metemphychosis, such as the followers of Ibn Abu-l-'Awjā', and those of the Mu'tazila who accept the views of Aḥmad ibn Ḥā'iṭ; those of the Khawārij who pro-
350 fess the opinion of the Yezīdis, maintaining that the law of Islām will be abrogated by the promulgation of a law by a Persian prophet; those of the Khawārij who accept the views of the Maimuniyya and permit marriage with daughters of one's sons and daughters; those who follow the doctrines of the 'Azāḳira in Baghdād, or profess the views of the Hallājiyya, extremists among the Ḥulūliyya, or share the opinion of the Barkūkiyya and the Ruzāmiyya who hold extravagant beliefs concerning Abu Muslim, the founder of the dynasty of the 'Abbāsids; those who adopt the attitude of the Kāmiliyya who declare the Companions heretics because they failed to pledge allegiance to 'Ali, and condemn 'Ali as an infidel because he refrained from fighting them, — the status of these enumerated groups is that of apostates from religion; their meats are not allowed and the marriage of their women is not permitted[1]. It is not permissible to grant them the right to dwell within the Pale of Islam in exchange for the payment of tribute[2]. It is neceesary to call them to repentance. If they repent, well enough, but if not, it is one's duty to kill them[3] and to seize their property as war spoils[4]. Opinion varies on the enslavement of their wives and children. Abu Ḥanīfa and also a group of Shāfi'ites, including Abu Isḥāḳ al-Merwezi, author of the commentary[5] sanction it[6].

---

[1] *Umm,* VI, 155.

[2] Their status is thus like that of the *Ḥarbis.*

[3] *Muwatta,* 348 and comm.; ibn Humam, IV, 386—7; *Umm,* VI, 148. al-Shāfi'i condemns apostate men and women alike to death (*ib.*, and 149), but Abu Ḥanīfa condemns only men, ibn Humam, 388—9. See al-Shāfi'i's dispute with him, Umm, VI, 150 ff.

[4] This is in accordance with the principle that a Muslim cannot inheriṭ a Kāfir. Mālik and Aḥmad agree with him; Abu Hanīfa dissents, ibn Humam IV, 391.

[5] Abu Isḥāḳ Ibrahīm b. Aḥmad al-Marwazi, d. 340 a. H. He was the greatest Shāfi'ite in his age. The commentary is on Muzāni's *Epitome* of the *Kitab al-Umm,*— the real handbook of Shāfi'ite law,— which appears in the margin of the printed edition. See IKhall, I, 7: Yaḳūt, IV, 512; *Fihrist,* 212.

[6] ibn Humam, IV, 403. *K. al-Kharāj,* 80.

Some of them forbid it[1]. Those who allow it cite in support of their view the fact that Khālid ibn al-Walīd, when he fought the Banu Ḥanīfa and succeeded in slaying Musailima the Liar, made peace with the Banu Ḥanīfa in exchange for the gold and silver[2] and in exchange for a quarter of the prisoners among the women and children[3], and he sent them to al-Medīna. Khawla, the mother of Muḥammad ibn al-Ḥanafiyya[4], was one of them.

Concerning the people of fancy, such as the Jārūdiyya, the Hishāmiyya, the Najjāriyya, and Jahmiyya, the Imāmiyya who condemn the noblest of the Companions as Kāfirs, the Ḳadariyya who deviate from the truth, the Bakriyya who are 251
linked with Bakr ibn Ukht 'Abd-al-Wāhid, the Ḍirāriyya, all the anthropomorphist sects, and the Khawārij, we brand them as heretics just as they declare the Sunnites heretics. Prayer in their behalf or after their death is not allowed. But our scholars differ regarding the problem of inheriting their property. Some of them say, we may inherit from them but they may not inherit from us. They base it on an opinion by Mu'ādh ibn Jabal that the Muslim may inherit from the Kāfir but the Kāfir may not inherit from the Muslim[5]. The approved course among us is that their property is regarded as booty, for inheritance is not allowed between them and between the Sunnites[6]. It has indeed been transmitted that our sage Abu 'Abdallah al-Ḥārith ibn Asad al-Muḥāsibi did not[7] take anything from the bequest of his father because the latter was a Ḳadarite[8]. Al-Shāfi'i has decreed that the

---

[1] MS. and Ed. read واباح, which makes no sense and does not present the view of the Shāfi'ites. I therefore read واحلال. See *Umm*, IV, 137 bottom; Muzāni, v. 165.

[2] Lit. yellow and white. Against al-Balādhuri (ed. de Goeje), 90, on whose authority Brockelmann wants to insert the word half (نصف) before silver and gold, we have the authority of Ṭab. I, 1952—3; IA, II, 279; Ya'ḳūbi, II, 146—7, all of whom confirm our author's account.

[3] Ṭab., *ib.* tells us that Khālid at first asked for half the women as prisoners but by a ruse arranged by Mujjā'a, the Ḥanafite who turned traitor, Khālid agreed to a quarter. Ya'ḳūbi and Balādhuri, *ib.* agree with Ṭab.

[4] With MS.; Ed., الحنيفة. See *Bad' Wal-Ta'rīkh*, v. 76 (Arab. 74).

[5] *Uṣūl*, 341. Mu'āwiya also maintained this rule. See Shāfi'i's objections, *Umm*, IV, 14. On Mu'ādh, see Nawāwi, 539—41.

[6] *Umm*, IV, 13—6.

[7] Adding لم with MS.; missing in Ed.

[8] *Uṣūl*, 341. He was a pious individual, learned in theology and a renowned Ṣūfi, d. 243. See Subki, *l.c.*, II, 37—9, and Sam'āni, 509 b. Both sources assert that his father was

prayers offered for the soul of one who professes the creation of the Ḳur'ān and the denial of the Beatific Vision are to be declared void. Hishām ibn 'Ubaidallah al-Rāzi[1] tells that Muḥammad ibn al-Ḥasan ruled that anyone who prays for the soul of one who professes the creation of the Ḳur'ān is to repeat his prayer[2]. Yaḥya ibn Aktham[3] reports that Abu Yūsuf was asked what he thought of the Mu'tazila and he answered: They are the Zendiḳs. Al-Shāfi'i had indicated in his book on Testimony that the testimony of people of fancy, with the exception of the Khaṭṭābiyya who allow perjury by their followers against their opponents[4], may be accepted. But in the book on Analogy he points out that he has altered his policy of accepting testimony from the Mu'tazila and the other people of fancy[5]. Mālik rejected the testimony of the people of fancy, according to a tradition by Ashhab in the name of ibn al-Ḳāsim and al-Ḥārith ibn Miskīn in the name of Mālik who ruled regarding the Mu'tazila: They are Zendiḳs, they are not to be called to repentance, but are to be killed.

352 As for those who transact business with them, selling and buying, the regulations bearing on it, according to the Orthodox, resemble the laws on the formation of partnership[6] by Muslims who live in the frontier districts with people whom it is a duty to fight, although one is allowed to kill them. But a Muslim may not buy a copy of the Ḳur'ān from them, nor a Muslim slave, according to the correct ruling of al-Shāfi'i's *madhhab*.

The adherents of al-Shāfi'i differ regarding the status of the Ḳadariyya who have departed[7] from the truth. There are some who declare that their status is the same as that of the Magians because of the Prophet's saying about the Ḳada-

---

a Rāfiḍi although the former admits his possible Ḳadarism; *Fihrist*, 184. On his Sūfism see Hujwiri, 176—83.

[1] See *Lisān al-Mīzān*, VI, 195.

[2] *Uṣūl, ib.*

[3] d. 242. He held a very high position at Baṣra under al-Ma'mun and was a highly distinguished Ḳāḍi. See the exceptionally long article on him in IKhall, IV, 33—49.

[4] See above 62, note 7.

[5] *Uṣūl*, 342, informs us that he changed his opinion only with respect to the Ghulāt.

[6] Reading المفاوضة with Ed.; MS. المعاوضة.

[7] Arabic: المعتزلة.

riyya: They are the Magians of the community[1]. According to this view, the acceptance of tribute from them is lawful. But there are others who decide that their status is like that of apostates. Tribute, accordingly, is not to be taken from them but they are to be summoned to repent. If they repent, well enough: but if not, it is a duty upon the Muslims to kill them. We have made a detailed study of the rules governing the people of fancy in our *Book of Religion and Dogmas.* In this book we have gathered tidbits of the rules according to the Orthodox to an adequate degree. But God knows best.

[1] Wensinck, 121 a.

CHAPTER FOUR.

OUR VIEWS ON THE PIOUS ANCESTRY OF THE COMMUNITY.

The Orthodox are agreed that the Emigrants and the Defenders among the Companions were believers[1]. This is contrary to the opinion of those Rawāfiḍ who maintain that the Companions are heretics because of their failure to swear allegiance to ʻAli, and contrary to the opinion of the Kāmiliyya who declare ʻAli a Kāfir because he refused to make war on them. The Orthodox are agreed that those who apostasized after the death of the Prophet, such as the tribes of Kinda, Ḥanifa, Fazāra, the Banu Asad, the Banu Ḳushayr and the Banu Bekr ibn Wail were not among the Defenders nor among the Emigrants before the capture of Mecca. The law has specified the name Emigrants to designate those who emigrated to the Prophet before the capture of Mecca, and they with the grace and kindness of God, trod the road of the righteous law and straight path.

The Orthodox agree that everyone who was present with the Apostle of God at the battle of Badr inhabits Paradise, and similarly those who were present with him at Uḥud, except Ḳuzmān whom tradition has excluded; also everyone who was present with him at the oath of good-will at al-Ḥudaibiya. On the basis of a tradition which has come down they believe that seventy thousand members of the community of Islām will enter Paradise without a reckoning; among them is included ʻUkkāsha ibn Miḥṣan[2]. Everyone of those will intercede in behalf of seventy thousand. They cherish the memory of people whom tradition has assured of a place in Paradise and of the power to intercede for all of the community, and among them they include Uwais al-Ḳarani[3]. The tradition regarding them is

[1] *Usūl*, 298—303.

[2] A fighter for Islām against the apostates in its early history. See his biography including his admission to Paradise, Nawāwi, 427—8.

[3] One of the Followers, said to have been killed at al-Ṣiffīn. Ṭab. III, 2475. He is known as the "*Sayyid al-tābiʻīn*", *Nujūm*, I, 127. Mālik b. Anās doubted his existence, ***Muh. St.*** II, 147.

well known. They have decided to condemn as Kāfirs all those who brand as infidels any of the ten to whom the Prophet has promised Paradise. They cherish the memory of all the wives of the Apostle and they condemn as heretics those who declare them or any of them to be infidels[1]. They love al-Ḥasan and al-Ḥusain and all the well-known cousins of the Apostle of God such as al-Ḥasan ibn al-Ḥasan, 'Abdallah ibn al-Ḥasan, 'Ali ibn al-Ḥusain Zain-al-'Ābidīn, Muḥammad ibn 'Ali ibn al Ḥusain, who was called al-Bāḳir. It is he to whom Jābir ibn 'Abdallah al-Anṣāri brought greetings from the Prophet. They love Ja'far ibn Muḥammad known as al-Ṣādiḳ, Mūsa ibn Ja'far and 'Ali ibn Mūsa al Riḍa[2]. They have the same feelings for the other offspring of 'Ali such as al-'Abbās, 'Omar, Muḥammad ibn al-Ḥanafiyya, and the remainder of those who followed the traditions of their pious forefathers, but not those who leaned to Mu'tazilism or Rāfiḍism, nor those who allied themselves with them, and displayed an extremely tyrannous conduct and oppression like al-Barḳa'i who oppressed the people of Baṣra unjustly and tyrannously. Most genealogists are of the opinion that he made false pretenses to be one of them, but was not really.

They cherish the noblest followers of the Companions in piety. It is they concerning whom God has revealed: "They say: our Lord! forgive us and those of our brethren who have precedence of us in faith and do not allow any spite to remain in our hearts toward those who believe"[3]. They affirm the same regarding those who accept publicly the fundamentals of the Orthodox, but they declare themselves free from the people of fancy who are excluded from Islām, and from the people of erring fancies who allege affiliation with Islām. These are the Ḳadariyya, the Murjiyya, the Rāfiḍa, the Khawārij, the Jahmiyya, the Najjāriyya and the Corporealists. A study of the peculiarities of these groups has already been presented in the chapter preceding this one, and in it there is sufficiency.

---

[1] IH, IV, 117—21.

[2] For the various 'Alids see the genealogical table *Shiites*, II, 160.

[3] Sura 59, v. 10.

ADDITIONAL NOTES.

P. 105, note 1. The attribute سخرية by which the Khawārij are characterized may be related to the root سخر (witchcraft) and rendered "given to the art of witchcraft".

P. 140. The verses cited by Baghdādi from the "words of the shameless poet" belong to the celebrated Abu Nuwās. They are found in ibn Ḳutaiba's *Kitab al-Shi'r wal-Shu'arā'* (ed. de Goeje), p. 510, in a variant version as follows:

تَعَلَّلْ بِـالمُنَى إِذْ أَنْتَ حَيٌّ   وَبَعْدَ المَوْتِ من لَـبَنٍ وخَمْرِ

حَيَـاةٌ ثم مَوْتٌ ثم بَعْثٌ   حَدِيثُ خُرَافَةٍ يا أُمَّ عَمْرِو

Shahrastāni, p. 433, who quotes only the last couplet, agrees in his reading with ibn Ḳutaiba except that he reads نَشْر instead of بَعْث.

P. 155. On Ḥumaid b. Thaur see ibn Ḳutaiba, *l. c.*, pp. 230—33. The line quoted in our text occurs on p. 231, line 12, and reads:

ينـامُ بـإِحْدَى مُقْلَتَيْهِ وَيَتَّـقِي   المنايا بأُخْرَى فَهُوْ يقظان هَاجِعُ

P. 156. On Ibrahīm b. Harama see ibn Ḳutaiba, *l. c.*, pp. 473—474. The line in our text is found on p. 474, line 9, and reads:

كتاركة بيضها بالعَرَاءِ   ومُلحِفَةٍ بَيْضَ أُخْرَى جناحا

P. 184. The declaration attributed in our text to 'Ali sounds very similar to the statement ascribed by Abu-l-Ma'āli 'Abd-al-Mālik to al-Ash'ari:

كان ولا مكان فخلق العرش والكرسي فلم يحتج الى
مكان وهو بعد خلق المكان كما كان قبل خلقه

(Cited in Spitta, *Zur Geschichte al-Ash'aris,* p. 141). The saying in our version is also popular among the Ṣūfis (Browne, *Literary History of Persia,* I, 438).

BIBLIOGRAPHY.

The bibliography is divided into three parts. The first includes titles of books which appear in the notes in abbreviated form; the second comprises the remaining more important bibliography, and the third contains encyclopedias and periodical literature. Works to which reference was made only once or twice are not generally listed. For the lack of correct transcription see the Preface.

'Aja'ib – Zakaria ibn Muhammad ibn Mahmud al-Kazwini: *Kitab 'Aja'ib-al-Makhlukat.* Printed on the margin of Damiri's *Hayat al-Hayawan. See below.*

Albiruni – Albiruni: *Athar-ul-Bakiya.* Chronology of Ancient Nations. Translated by G. Edward Sachau. London, 1879.

Andrae, Muhammad – Tor Andrae: *Die Person Muhammeds.* Stockholm, 1918.

Ash'ari – Abu-l-Hasan 'Ali ibn Isma'il al-Ash'ari: *Makalat al-Islamiyin wa-Ikhtilafi-l-Mudillin.* Edited by Hellmut Ritter. Two volumes. Istanbul, 1930.

Bad'wal-Ta'rikh – Mutahhar ibn Tahir al-Makdisi: *Bad'wal-Ta'rikh.* Edited and Translated by Cl. Huart. Six volumes. Paris, 1899–1919.

Baid., Baidawi – Nasir al-Din Abu Sa'id Abdallah 'Omar al-Baidawi: *Anwar al-Tanzil-Asrar al-Ta'wil* (Commentary on the Kur'an); edited by H. O. Fleischer. Two volumes. Leipzig, 1846–1848.

Blochet – E. Blochet: *Le Messianisme dans l'hétérodoxie musulmane.* Paris, 1903.

Brockelmann – Carl Brockelmann: *Geschichte der arabischen Literatur.* Two volumes. Weimar and Berlin, 1898–1902.

Bukhari – Abu 'Abdallah Muhammad ibn Isma'il al-Bukhari: *Al-Jami' al-Sahih.* Edited by Krehl and Juynboll. Leyden, 1862–1907.

Creencia – Algazel: El justo medio en la creencia. *Compendio de teologia dogmática.*. Traducción española par Miguel Asin Palacios (translation of Abu Hamid al-Ghazali's *Kitab al-Iktisad fil-I'tikad* [Cairo. n. d.]). Madrid, 1929.

Damiri – Kamal-al-Din al-Damiri: *Hayat al-Hayawan al-Kubra.* Two volumes. Cairo, 1311 A. H.

De Goeje – M. J. de Goeje: *Mémoire sur les Carmathes du Bahrain et les Fatimides.* Leyden, 1886.

De Sacy – Silvestre de Sacy: *Exposé de la religion des Druzes.* Two volumes. Paris, 1838.

Al-Durra al-Fakhira – Abu Hamid Muhammad al-Ghazali: *Al-Durra Al-*Fakhira (La perle précieuse), Edited and Translated by Lucien Gautier. Geneva, 1878.

Ed. – The Printed Arabic Text of Baghdadi's *Kitab al-fark baina-l-firak.*

Fihrist – Al-Nadim: *Kitab al-Fihrist,* ed. Flügel, (posthumously published by Johannes Roediger and August Mueller). Two volumes bound in one. Leipzig, 1871.

Fiqh al-Akbar – Abu Hanifa al-Numan ibn Thabit al-Kufi: *Al-Fiqh al-Akbar,* with a commentary by Abu-l-Muntahi Ahmad ibn Muhammad al-Maghnisawi al-Hanafi. Hyderabad, 1321. The authenticity of the authorship of the *Fiqh al-Akbar* has been denied.

Flügel, Schulen – Gustav Flügel: *Die grammatischen Schulen der Araber.* Erste Abteilung. Leipzig, 1862.

Guyard – Stanislas Guyard: *Fragments relatifs a la doctrine des Ismaélis,* texte. . . . . avec une traduction complète et des notes. (Published in *Notes et Extraits des manuscrits de la bibliothèque nationale),* vol. XXII, 177–428. Paris, 1874.

Hamilton's Hedaya – Charles Hamilton: *The Hedaya or Guide.* (Second Edition by Standish Grove Grady). London, 1870.

Hilli – Hasan ibn Yusuf ibn 'Ali ibn al-Mutahhar al-Hilli: *Al-Babu 'l-Hadi 'Ashar* (A treatise on the Principles of Shi'ite Theology) with commentary by Miqdad-Fadil al-Hilli. Translated by William McElivee Miller. London, 1928.

Horten, Probleme — M. Horten : *Die philosophischen Probleme der spekulativen Theologie im Islam.* Bonn, 1910.

Horten, Systeme — M. Horten : *Die philosophischen Systeme der spekulativen Theologie im Islam.* Bonn, 1912.

Hyat-ul-Kuloob — Hyat-ul-Kuloob : *The Life and Religion of Mohammed as contained in the Sheeah Traditions.* Translated from Persian by James L. Merrick. Boston, 1850.

Hitti — Philip K. Hitti, Editor : *Mukhtasar Kitab al-fark baina-l-firak* (English Title : *Al Baghdadi's Characteristics of Muslim Sects, abridged).* Cairo, 1924.

IA — Abu-l-Husain 'Ali ibn Muhammad al-Shaibani ibn al-Athir : *Kitab al-Kamil fil-Tarikh.* Edited by C. J. Tornberg. Fourteen volumes. Leyden, 1867.

Ibana — Abu-l-Hasan 'Ali ibn Isma'il al-Ash'ari : *Kitab al-Ibana 'an Usul al-Diyana.* Hyderabad, 1321 (?).

Ibn Humam — Muhammad ibn 'Abd-al-Wahid ibn al-Humam : *Fath al-Kadir.* With supercommentaries. Eight volumes. Bulak, 1315.

Ibn Iskander — Husain ibn Iskander al-Hanafi : *Kitab al-Jawhara al-Munifa.* Hyderabad, 1321.

Ibn Maja — Muhammad ibn Yazid ibn Maja : *Sunan.* Two volumes. Cairo, 1313.

Ibn Rosteh — Abu 'Ali Ahmad ibn 'Omar ibn Rosteh: *Kitab al-A'lak al-Nafisa,* and Ahmad ibn Abu Ya'kub ibn Wadih al-Ya'kubi : *Kitab al-Buldan.* Edited by M. J. de Goeje (*Bibliotheca Geographorum Arabicorum,* Pars VII). Leyden, 1892.

IH — Abu Muhammad 'Ali ibn Ahmad ibn Hazm al-Zahiri : *Kitab-al-Fisal fi-l-Milal wal-Ahwa' wal-Nihal.* Five volumes. Cairo, 1317—1327 (?) A.H.

IHauk, IHaukal — Abu-l-Kasim ibn Haukal : *Kitab al-Masalik wal-Mamalik.* Edited by M. J. de Goeje (*Bibliotheca Geographorum Arabicorum,* Pars II). Leyden, 1873.

I'jaz — Abu Bekr Ahmad ibn 'Ali ibn-al-Tayib al-Bakilani : *Kitab I'jaz al-Kur'an.* Cairo, 1315 A. H.

IKhald — Abu Zaid 'Abd-Al-Rahman b. Muhammad ibn Khaldun : *Prolégomènes* (Arab : *Mukaddima*), French Translation by Mac Guckin de-Slane.

Published in *Nates et extraits des manuscrits de la bibliotheque imperiale,* vols. XIX–XXI (Part one of each volume is the translation, part two the text). The references are to the Translation. Paris, 1862–68.

IKhall – Abu-l-'Abbas Ahmad ibn Ibrahim ibn Khallikan: *Wafayat al-A'yan* (Biographical Dictionary). Translated by MacGuckin de Slane. Four volumes. Paris, 1843–71.

Intisar – 'Abd al-Rahman ibn Muhammad ibn 'Uthman al-Khayyat: *Kitab al-Intisar wal-Radd 'ala ibn Rawandi.* Edited by H. S. Nyberg. Cairo, 1925.

Isf. B. P. – Shuhfur ibn Tahir ibn Muhammad Al-Isfaraini: *Kitab al-fark baina-l-firak.* Ms. Ahlwardt's Catalogue of Berlin MSS., No. 2801; Bibliotheque Nationale, No. 1400.

Irshad – Abu 'Abdallah Ya'kub ibn 'Abdallah: *Irshad al-Arib ila Ma'rifat al-Adib,* edited by D. S. Margoliouth. Vols. I, II, III, V, VI. Leyden 1907–1913. (E. J. W. Gibb Memorial, VI, 1–3, 5–6).

Istakhri – Abu Ishak Ibrahim ibn Muhammad al-Farisi al-Istakhri: *Kitab Masalik al-Mamalik.* Edited by de Goeje (*Bibliotheca Geographorum Arabicorum,* Pars I). Leyden, 1870.

Koranauslegung – Ignaz Goldziher: *Die Richtungen der islamischen Koranauslegung.* Leiden, 1920.

Kashf – 'Ali ibn 'Uthman al-Jullabi al-Hujwiri: *Kashf al-Mahjub.* Translated by R. A. Nicholson (E. J. W. Gibb Memorial, XVII). Leyden, 1911.

Lisan al-Mizan – Shihab al-Din Abu-l-Fadl Ahmad ibn 'Ali ibn Hajar al-'Askalani: *Lisan al-Mizan.* Six volumes. Hyderabad, 1329–31 A. H.

Makrizi – Taki-al-Din Ahmad ibn 'Ali ibn 'Abd al-Kadir ibn Muhammad known as Makrizi: *Kitab al-Khitat.* Two volumes. Bulak, 1270 A. H. – Unless otherwise stated the references are to vol. II.

Makrizi (Fagnan) – E. Fagnan: *Nouveaux textes historiques relatifs a l'Afrique du Nord et a la Sicile.* 1. – La biographie d'Obeyd Allah...... de Makrizi. Published in *Centenario di Michele Amari,* Palermo, 1910, vol. II, 35–86.

Massignon–Louis Massignon: *La Passion d'al-Husain ibn Mansour al-Halladj.* Two volumes. Paris, 1922.

Maturidi – *Kitab Sharh al-Fiqh al-Akbar* .... lil'Imam .... Abi

Mansur Muhammad ibn Muhammad al-Hanafi al-Maturidi al-Samarkandi. Hyderabad, 1321 A. H. Maturidi's authorship of the work has been denied.

Miskawaih – Ahmad ibn Muhammad ibn Miskawaih : *The Eclipse of the 'Abbasid Caliphate.* Edited and Translated by H. F. Amedroz and D. S. Margoliouth. Six volumes and an Index. Oxford, 1920–1.

Mizan – Shams al-Din Abu 'Abdallah Muhammad ibn Ahmad al-Dhahabi : *Mizan al-I'tidal wa-Nakad al-Rijal.* Three volumes. Cairo, 1325.

MS. – Manuscript of Baghdadi's *Al-Fark baina-l-firak.* Ahlwardt's Catalogue of MSS. in Berlin, No. 2800.

Mudawwana – Malik ibn Anas : *Al-Mudawwana al-kubra.* Cairo, 1323.

Muslim – Muslim ibn al-Hajjaj. *Sahih.* With a commentary by Nawawi. Five volumes.

Muh. St. I–II – Ignaz Goldziher : *Muhammedanische Studien.* Two volumes. Halle, 1889–90.

Mukkad, Mukaddasi – Shams-al-Din Abu 'Abdallah Muhammad ibn Ahmad al-Mukaddasi : *Al-Masalik fil-Mamalik.* Edited by M. J. de Goeje (*Bibliotheca Geographorum Arabicorum,* Pars III). Leyden, 1879.

Muruj – Abu-l-Hasan 'Ali ibn al-Husain ibn 'Ali al-Mas'udi : *Kitab Muruj al-Dhahab wa-Ma'adin al-Jawahir.* Edited and Translated by Barbier de Meynard and Pavet de Courteille (Under title *Prairies d'or).* Nine volumes. Paris, 1861–77.

Muwatta – Malik ibn Anas : *Kitab al-Muwatta.* Kazan, 1909.

Naubakhti – Abu-l-Hasan al-Naubakhti : *Firak al-Shi'a.* Edited by Hellmut Ritter. Istanbul, 1933.

Nawawi – Abu Zakariya Yahya Al-Nawawi : *Biographical Dictionary.* Edited by F. Wüstenfeld. Göttingen, 1842–47.

Nujum – Abu-l-Mahasin Taghri Birdi – *Al-Nujum al-Zahira* [Annales]. Edited by Juynboll and Matthes. Two volumes. Leyden, 1855–61.

Nuzhat – Hamdullah al-Mustaufi al-Kazwini : *The Zoological Section of Nuzhatu-l-Qulub.* Edited and Translated by J. Stephenson. London, 1928.

Razi – M. Horten : *Die spekulative und positive Theologie des Islam nach Razi (1209) und ihre Kritik durch Tusi (1273).* Leipzig, 1912.

Sam'ani — 'Abd al-Karim ibn Muhammad al-Sam'ani : *Kitab al-Ansab.* Reproduced in Facsimile by D. S. Margoliouth (E. J. W. Gibb Memorial, XX). Leyden and London, 1912.

Seelye — Kate Chambers Seelye : *Moslem Schisms and Sects* (Part I of the *Kitab al-Fark bain al-Firak* of Baghdadi in Translation). New York, 1919.

Shahr. *or* Shahr. (Haarbrücker) — Abu-l-Fath Muhammad al-Shahrastani : *Kitab al-Milal wal-Nihal,* edited by Cureton. Two volumes, London, 1842—46. — *Religions-Partheien und Philosophen-Schulen.* Theodor Haarbrücker. Two volumes, Halle, 1850—51.

Shiites I, II — Israel Friedlaender : *The Heterodoxies of the Shiites in the Presentation of Ibn Hazm.* Part one : Text and editorial notes. Part two : Commentary. Published in *JAOS,* XXVIII (Jan.—June 1907), 1—80, and XXIX (1908), 1—183, respectively. Also in a separate volume, New Haven, 1909.

Streitschrift — Ignaz Goldziher : *Streitschrift des Gazali gegen die Batiniyya Sekte.* (A detailed presentation of the contents of al-Mustazhiri, with 29 excerpts in Arabic). Leiden, 1916.

Tab. *or* Tabari — Abu Ja'far Muhammad ibn Jarir al-Tabari : *Ta'rikh al-Rusul wal-Muluk* [Annales]. Edited by M. J. de Goeje. Twelve volumes. Leyden, 1879—1901.

Tab. (Zotenberg) — *Chronique de Tabari.* Traduite par Hermann Zotenberg. Four volumes. Paris, 1867—74.

Tanbih — Abu-l-Hasan 'Ali ibn al-Husain ibn 'Ali al-Mas'udi : *Tanbih — Le Livre de l'avertissement et de la revision.* Traduction par Carra de Vaux. Paris, 1896.

Tayalisi — Abu Daud Sulaiman ibn Daud al-Tayalisi : *Musnad.* Hyderabad, 1321 A. H.

Tirmidhi — Abu 'Abdallah Muhammad ibn Isa al-Tirmidhi : *Sahih.* Two volumes.

Umm — Abu 'Abdallah Muhammad ibn Idris al-Shafi'i : *Kitab Al-Umm.* With the *Mukhtasar* of Abu Ibrahim Isma'il ibn Yahya al-Muzani.

Usul — Abu Mansur 'Abd-al-Kahir b. Tahir al-Tamimi al-Baghdadi : *Usul al-Din.* Volume One (Name of Editor not given). Istanbul, 1928.

Utbi — Abu-l-Utbi : *Kitab-i-Yamini.* Translated by James Reynolds. London, 1858.

'Uyun — Ibn Qutaiba : *Uyun al-Akhbar.* Edited by Brockelmann. Berlin, 1900.

Vorlesungen — Ignaz Goldziher : *Vorlesungen ueber dem Islam.* Second edition by Franz Babinger. Heidelberg, 1922.

Wensinck — A. J. Wensinck : *A Handbook of Muhammadan Tradition.* Alphabetically arranged. Leiden, 1927.

Wüstenfeld : *Geschichte d. Fatimidischen Chalifen.* Göttingen, 1880–81.

Ya'kubi — Ahmed ibn Abu Yakub ibn Ja'far ibn Wahb : *Historia.* Edited by M. Th. Houtsma. Two volumes. Leyden, 1883.

Yakut — Abu 'Abdallah Yakut ibn 'Abdallah : *Kitab Mu'jam al-Buldan.* Edited by F. Wuestenfeld. Six volumes. Leipzig, 1866–1870.

Zamakhshari — Abu-l-Kasim Mahmud ibn 'Omar al-Zamakhshari : *Kashshaf 'an Hakaik al-Tanzil.* Edited by W. Nassau Lees. Two volumes. Calcutta, 1856–9.

Zambaur, E..: *Manuel de généalogie et de chronologie.* Hanover, 1972.

Section II

Ahmad ibn Hanbal : *Masnad.* Six volumes. Cairo 1313 A. H.

M. Asin Palacios : *Abenmasarra y su escuela.* Madrid, 1914.

Ibn Hajar al-'Askalani : *A Biographical Dictionary of People Who Knew Mohammad.* Edited by Maulvi Abd-ul-Hai. Four volumes. Calcutta, 1856–1873.

L. Bouvat : *Les Barmecides.* Paris, 1912.

Harold Bowen : *The Life and Times of 'Ali ibn Isa.* Cambridge, 1928.

Browne, E. G. : *A Literary History of Persia.* Volume one. London, 1909.

Idem : A Volume of Oriental Studies, Presented to. Cambridge, 1922.

Rudolph Ernst Brunnow : *Die Charidschiten.* Leiden, 1884.

E. C. Burkitt : *The Religion of the Manichees.* Cambridge, 1925.

Leone Caetani : *Annali dell' Islam. Ten volumes.* Rome, 1905–26.

Arthur Christensen : *Le premier homme et le premier roi.* Stockholm, 1918.

Chwolson, D. : *Die Ssabier und der Ssabismus.* St. Petersburg, 1856.

Henri Galland : *Essai sur les Motazelites.* Paris.

Ignaz Goldziher : *Die Zahiriten.* Leipzig, 1884.

Willi Heffening: *Das islamische Fremdenrecht.* Hanover, 1925.

A. V. W. Jackson: *Zoroaster, The Prophet of Ancient Iran.* New York, 1899.

Ferdinand Justi: *Iranisches Namenbuch.* Marburg, 1895.

H. Lammens: *Le Califat de Yázid Ier.* Beyrouth, 1921.

Louis Massignon: *Essai sur les origines du lexique technique de la mystique musulmane.* Paris, 1922.

Nizam oul-Moulk: *Siasset Nameh.* Transl. by Charles Schefer. Paris, 1893.

William Muir: *The Caliphate. Its Rise, Decline and Fall.* Edited by T. H. Weir. Edinburgh, 1924.

August Mueller: *Der Islam im Morgen- und Abendland.* Two volumes. Berlin, 1885–7.

A. Querry: *Droit Musulman. Recueil de Lois ...... Schiyites.* Two volumes. Paris, 1871–2.

Jalal-al-Din Suyuti: *Al Durar al Hisan fil-Ba'th al Na'im.* Cairo, 1304 A. H.

Jalal-al-Din Suyuti: *History of the Caliphs.* Translated by H. S. Jarret. Calcutta, 1881.

'Ali Tabari: *The Book of Religion and Empire.* Edited and Translated by A. Mingana. Two volumes. Manchester, 1922–3.

A. S. Tritton: *The Caliphs and Their Non-Muslim Subjects.* London, 1930.

J. Wellhausen: *The Arab Kingdom and Its Fall.* Translated by Margaret Graham Weir. Calcutta, 1927.

M. Wolff: *Muhammedanische Eschatalogie.* Arabic Text Edited and Translated. Leipzig, 1872.

Abu Yusuf Yakub: *Kitab al-Kharaj* (Le Livre de l'impôt foncier). Translated by E. Fagnan, Paris, 1921.

Jurji Zaydan: *Umayyads and Abbasids.* Translated by D. S. Margoliouth. (E. J. W. Gibb Memorial). Leyden, 1907.

Part. III

ERE – Encyclopedia of Religion and Ethics.

EI – Encyclopedia of Islam.

Islam – Der Islam.

JA – Journal Asiatique.

JAOS – Journal of the American Oriental Society.

JQR – Jewish Quarterly Review.

REJ – Revue des Etudes Juives.

RMM – Revue du Monde Musulman.

Le Monde Oriental.

ZA – Zeitschrift für Assyriologie.

ZDMG – Zeitschrift der deutschen morgenländischen Gesellschaft.

INDEX

A.

B.

C.

D.

E.

F.

G.

God's greatest Name (al-Ism al-A'tham) 47; 47 n; 50; 50 n; 54.
Goldziher, Ignaz 2 n; 15 n; 20 n; 25 n; 51 n; 57 n; 58 n; 62 n; 71 n; 76 n; 81 n; 92 n; 100 n; 101 n; 104 n; 123 n; 141 n; 160 n; 164 n; 173 n; 175 n.
Graetz, Heinrich 37 n.
Gray, L. H. 87 n.
Greeks 119; 120; 121.
Guyard, S. 71 n; 144 n.

H.

Habir 125,
Hafd al-Fard 16.
Hafiz Ghulam Sarwar 137 n.
Haitiyya 34; 34 n; 40; 90—100; 185.
Hajar 121; 121 n; 123; 161 n.
Hajir 54.
Hajj 119; 176 n.
al-Hajjaj b. Ilat 165 n.
Hakaikiyya 18.
Hakamiyya 32 n.
Hallaj, Abu-l-Mughith al-Husain b. Mansur 73; 80—84; 80; 80 n; 81; 81 n; 82; 82 n; 82; 83 n; 84; 84 n; 86 n.
Hallajiyya 73; 78 n; 80—84; 224.
Hamadan 20 n.
Hamid b. al-Abbas, Abu Muhammad 84; 84 n.
Hamza Ispahani 126 n.
Hanafiyya 4 n.
Hanbalites 20 n.
Hanifa, Banu 38; 142; 225; 228.
Hanifiyya; Hanifites 1 n; 2 n; 4 n; 5 n; 219 n; 222 n.
Harbiyya 40; 56; 59 n.
al-Harith b. Miskin 226.
Harith b. Asad al-Muhasibi, Abu Abdallah 225.
Harith b. Suraij 13 n; 14; 14 n.
Harran 103; 103 n; 123; 124 n; 131; 222 n.
Harun b. Khumarawaih, Abu Musa 124 n.
Harun al-Rashid 5 n; 54 n; 117; 117 n; 118 n.
Harun b. Sa'd al Ijli 71.
Harut 217 n.
Hasan b. Ali 49; 51 n; 60 n; 62; 70; 74; 229.
Hasan al Askari 70 n.
al-Hasan b. al-Hasan 229.
al-Hasan b. Muhammad (*or* al-Fadi) al-Zafarani 11 n.
al-Hasan b. Sanbar 111 n.
Hashim, Banu 61 n.
al-Hawb 215 n.
Heffening 223 n.
Heliogobulus 119 n.
Herat 18 n; 43; 75; 103; 142 n; 161 n.
Hermes 133; 133 n.
al-Hilli 177 n; 191 n.
Himadiyya 40 n; *see* Himariyya.
Himariyya 39; 40; 101—2; 101 n.
Himyarite 152.
Hindoo 16 n; 65 n; 91 n; 209 n.
Hisham (Caliph) 47 n.
Hisham al-Hakam 14 n.
Hisham b. Abd-al-Malik 101 n; 102 n.
Hisham al-Fuwati 188 n.
Hisham ibn al-Hakam al-Rafidi 32; 33 n; 183; 188 n.
Hisham b. Muhammad 211 n.
Hisham ibn Salim al-Jawaliki *or* Juwaliki 33; 33 n; 183.
Hisham b. Ubaidallah al-Razi 226.
Hishamiyya 19 n; 32; 33; 184; 202; 225.

Hit 121; 121 n; 126; 126 n.
Hitti 39 n.
Horten, M. 6 n; 91 n; 93 n.
Houtsma, T. 81 n.
Huart Cl. 110 n.
Hubaira ibn Jubair 43 n.
al-Hudaibiya 167 n; 218; 228.
Hulmaniyya 32; 73; 78–80; 79.
Hulul 73 n.
Huluiiyya 32; 39; 40; 47; 56; 73–86; 74; 78; 79; 80; 81 n; 83; 109; 164; 169; 183 n; 219; 224.
Humaid b. Thaur 155.
Huramiyya 107 n.
Hurkus b. Zahair al-Bajali 212.
Husain b. Abu Mansur 58 n.
Husain (ibn Ali) 45; 45 n; 49; 51 n; 55; 60 n; 62; 62 n; 70; 74; 229.
Husain al-Ahwazi 110 n.
Husain b. Ali b. al-Hasan b. Ali 53 n.
al-Husain b. al-Fadl 201.
Husain b. al-Kasim b. Ubaidallah b. Sulaiman b. Sahb, abu Ali 85; 85 n; 86.
Husain b. Zikrwaih b. Mihrwaih 124; 124 n.
Husainiyya 9 n.

I.

Ibadiyya 27; 103; 103 n; 203 n.
Iblis 3 n; 133; 133 n; 217 n.
Ibn Abu-l-Awja 224.
Ibn Abu Laila, Muhammad b. Abd-al Rahman 160; 160 n.
Ibn al-Arabi 71 n.
Ibn Athir 60 n; 214 n; 219.
Ibn Hajar al-Askalani 165 n.
Ibn Harama 156; 230.
Ibn Haukal 110 n.
Ibn Hazm 4 n; 5 n; 16 n; 20 n; 32 n; 48 n; 51 n; 56 n; 57 n; 62 n; 63 n; 65 n; 67 n; 70 n; 93 n; 95 n; 110 n; 150 n; 173 n; 184 n; 187 n; 188 n; 189 n; 190 n; 191 n; 192 n; 194 n; 202 n; 203 n; 208 n; 210 n; 211 n; 213 n; 214 n; 216 n.
Ibn Jubair 69 n.
Ibn al-Kasim 226.
Ibn Khaldun 211 n; 213 n.
Ibn Kutaiba 60; 61.
Ibn Kutaiba, pseudo — 215 n.
Ibn Labban 65 n.
Ibn Masarra 47 n.
Ibn Muklah 85 n.
Ibn Rawendi 6; 14 n; 188 n.
Ibn Salim al-Basri 189.
Ibn Zikrwaih 110 n.
Ibrahim 76; 144; 145.
Ibrahim b. Abdallah b. al-Hasan b. al-Hasan 53.
Ibrahim b. Ahmad al Marwazy, Abu Ishak 224; 224 n.
Ibrahim b. Muhajir 21; 21 n; 29.
Ibrahim b. Muhammad b. al-Munajjim, Abu Imran 85; 85 n.
Ibrahim b. Muhammad al-Muzakki, Abu Ishak 126; 126 n.
Ibrahim al Nasrabadi, Abu-l-Kasim 82; 82 n.
Ibrahim b. Yahya al-Aslami 34; 34 n.
Ibrahimiyya 34.
Idris 133 n.
Idris b. Abdallah b. al-Hasan 53; 53 n.
al-Iji 138 n; 144 n; 145 n.
Ijl, Banu 58 n; 65 n.
Ikhshidiyya 127.

khwan al-Safa 146 n.
lak, 76 ; 78.
lba *or* Ulba 69 n.
mamiyya *or* Imamite 33 ; 39 ; 41 n ; 44 n ; 49 ; 49 n ; 57 n ; 107 n ; 134 n ; 140 ; 169 ; 213 n ; 225.
ndia 122 ; 122 n ; 130.
rak 46 n ; 47 ; 47 n ; 54 ; 58 ; 58 n ; 109 ; 109 n ; 110 n ; 128 n.
ranian 50 n ; 199 n.
rja 2 ; 2 n.
sa al-Ispahani 37 n.
sa b. Maryam 34 ; 42 ; 45 ; 58 n ; 68 ; 72 ; 83 ; 99 ; 100 ; 136 ; 144 ; 145 ; 185 ; 200.
sa b. Muhammad b. Ali 88 n.
sa b. Musa 52 ; 53.

Jabarites 16 n ; 193 n ; 194 ; 194 n.
Jabarism 34 n.
Jabir b. Abdallah al-Ansari 60 n ; 164 n ; 165 n.
Jabir b. Yezid al Ju'fi 55 ; 55 n ; 60 n.
Jackson, A. V. W. 91 n. ; 92.
Ja'd b. Dirham 101 ; 101 n ; 102 n.
Ja'far b. Abu Talib 59 n.
Ja'far b. Muhammad al-Sadik 49 n ; 62 ; 62 n ; 64 ; 65 ; 65 n ; 71 ; 71 n ; 74 ; 94 ; 108 ; 109 n ; 229.
Jafr (a book) 71.
al-Jahiz 58 n ; 167 n ; 168 ; 177.
Jahm b. Safwan 1 ; 1 n ; 8 n ; 13—15, 13 n ; 14 n ; 187 n ; 190 n ; 209.
Jahmiyya 1 ; 2 n ; 13—15 ; 13 n ; 24 ; 39 ; 159 ; 164 ; 169 ; 170 ; 182 ; 189 ; 194 ; 225 ; 229.
Jaihun 73 ; 73 n ; 75 ; 224.
Jamasp 119 ; 119 n ; 120 ; 123.

Isaac son of Abraham 43 n.
Isawiyya 37 ; 104.
Ishak b. Ibrahim 88 ; 89 n ; 115 ; 115 n.
Ishak Sinjari 113 n.
Ishak b. Suwaid al-Adawi 43 ; 43 n.
Ishak the Turk 75 n.
Ishakiyya 18 ; 75 n ; 89 n.
Ishmael 134 n.
Isma'il b. Abbad al-Sahib 140 ; 140 n.
Isma'il b. Ibrahim b. Ḳabus al-Shirazi al-Daili 14.
Isma'il b. Ja'far al-Sadik 109 ; 110 n.
Isma'iliyya 107 9 ; 109 ; 112 n ; 117 n ; 146 n.
Ispahan 59 n ; 60 ; 61 ; 61 n ; 107 n.
Ithnaashariyya 62 n.
Ivanow V. 116 n.

J.

Jamshid *or* Jimshid 219 ; 219 n.
Janadi 123 n.
al-Jannabi, Abu-l-Kasim Said 111 n.
Janahiyya 39 ; 40 ; 59—61 ; 64 n ; 65 ; 73 ; 74 ; 92 ; 93 ; 169 ; 204 ; 224.
Japhet b. Ali 37 n.
Jarhamiyya 152.
Jarudiyya 169 ; 225.
Jawalikiyya 19 n.
Jawidan b. Sahruk 88.
Jerusalem 18 n.
Jesus 3 n ; 42 n ; 200 n.
Jewish, Jews 5 n ; 19 n ; 38 ; 41 n ; 42 ; 43 ; 44 n ; 45 ; 45 n ; 47 n ; 51 n ; 67 ; 68 ; 92 ; 104 ; 107 ; 134 n ; 136 ; 139 ; 141 n ; 152 ; 172 n ; 182 n ; 184 n ; 185 n ; 200 ; 200 n ; 221 ; 221 n ; 222.
Jibril *or* Jibra'il 46 ; 47 ; 47 n ; 68 ; 75.
Jinn 133 n ; 135.
Joshua *or* Yusha b. Nun 44 n ; 45.

al-Jubba'i 35 ; 93 ; 182 ; 188 ; 191.
al-Junaid 82 ; 82 n.
Jupiter 120 ; 121.
Jurjan 89 ; 107 n ; 112 n ; 115 ; 129 ; 129 n
al-Jurjan, Sawad 90.
Justin Martyr 90 n.

K.

Ka'ba 38 ; 39 ; 117 ; 121 ; 148 ; 200.
al-Ka'bi 37 ; 197 ; 197 n.
Kabus b. Washmkir, Shams al-Ma'ali 129 ; 129 n.
Kadarites 6 n ; 9 ; 10 ; 14 ; 25 ; 27 ; 34 ; 39 ; 43 ; 91 ; 93 ; 93 n ; 94 ; 99 ; 101 ; 105 ; 159 ; 162 ; 164 ; 166 ; 168 ; 169 ; 170 ; 177 ; 182 ; 184 n ; 185 ; 186 ; 187 ; 187 n ; 188 ; 189 ; 190 ; 193 ; 194 ; 195 ; 196 ; 197 ; 198 ; 198 n ; 199 ; 201 ; 203 ; 204 ; 204 n ; 208 ; 209 ; 210 n ; 225 ; 226 ; 229.
al-Kaddah, Abdallah b. Maimun 89 n ; 101 n ; 108 ; 108 n ; 109 ; 109 n ; 111 n ; 121 n.
al-Kaddah, Ahmad b. Abdallah b. Maimun 110 n ; 112 n.
al-Kadir Billahi 85 n ; 122 n.
Kahir al-Falak 127 n.
Kahtaniyya 152.
Kairuan 121 ; 123 ; 127.
Kais, Banu 142 n.
Kaisaniyya 56 n.
al-Kalanisi 217.
Kamiliyya 169 ; 214 n ; 224 ; 228.
Kannawj 122.
Kantarat al-Muhammira 89.
al-Karabisi, al-Husain b. Ali 106 ; 106 n.
Karaites 37 n.
Karbela 45 ; 45 n ; 55.
Karmat, Hamdan 108 n ; 110 ; 110 n ; 111 ; 111 n ; 112 ; 112 n,
Karmatian, Karamita 32 n ; 101 n ; 107 n ; 109 n ; 110 n ; 111 ; 112 ; 114 ; 120 ; 120 n ; 121 n ; 123 n ; 124 n ; 125 ; 125 n ; 126 127 n ; 134 n.
Karramiyya 1 n ; 2 n ; 18 ff ; 18 n ; 19 n 20 n ; 21 ; 22 ; 23 ; 25 ; 26 ; 27 ; 28 ; 29 30 ; 34 ; 35 ; 37 ; 159 n ; 183 ; 184 ; 186 191 ; 193 n ; 201 n ; 203 n ; 216 ; 217.
Kashsh 77 ; 77 n.
al-Kasim b. Isa al-Ijli, Abu Dulaf 88 ; 114.
al-Katif 123 ; 127 n.
Kawakimardan 75 n ; *see* Kaza Kaimun Dat.
Kaza Kaimun Dat 75 ; 75 n.
Kern 2 n.
Kessler 91 n.
Khalefy 107 n.
Khalid b. Abdallah al-Kasri 46 n ; 47 ; 48 n ; 52 ; 58 n ; 101 ; 102 n.
Khalid b. al-Walid 225 ; 225 n.
al-Khalil b. Ahmad 161 ; 161 n.
al-Khalj 76 ; 77.
al-Kharka 166.
al-Khasibi 125 n.
Khattabiyya 32 ; 39 ; 40 ; 62 ; 63 n ; 65 ; 70 ; 73 ; 74 ; 92 ; 93 ; 140 ; 169 ; 201 ; 224 ; 226.
Khawarij, Kharij, Kharijite 1 n ; 5 n ; 15 n ; 27 ; 39 ; 42 ; 42 n ; 43 ; 45 n ; 94 n ; 103 ; 105 ; 105 n ; 152 n ; 159 ; 162 ; 164 ; 168 ; 169 ; 170 ; 174 ; 176 ; 177 ; 205 ; 207 ; 207 n; 209 ; 210 n ; 211 ; 213 n ; 214 n ; 216 ; 224 ; 225 ; 291.
Khawla al-Hanafiyya 225.
Khawwaf 221 n.

L.

M.

N.

O.

P.

R.

Rakashiyya 2 n.
Rakka 124; 124 n; 125 n.
Ramadan, Fast of 39; 90; 204; 205.
al-Ramlah 124; 124 n; 125.
Rawa 221 n.
Rawandiyya 75 n; 92; 93; 94 n; 107 n; 213.
Ra'yaniyya 104.
al-Razi 185 n; 186 n.
Ridda 38 n.
Ritter, H. 46 n.
Romans 119; 120.
Rukn al-Ka'ba 54.
Rusafa 124.
Ruzam b. Sabik. 74 n.
Ruzamiyya *or* Rizamiyya 40; 73; 73 n; 74
75 n; 92 n; 224.

S.

Sa'adya b. Joseph al-Fayyumi 172 n; 182 n; 185 n.
Sabbabiyya 31; 39; 40; 41–45; 55; 73; 74; 93; 140; 169; 201; 223.
Saba'iyya 41 n; (*see* Sabbabiyya)
Sabbath 20 n; 136.
Sabbat al-Madain 42; 44.
Sabians 103; 103 n; 131; 133; 133 n; 200 n; 221; 222; 222 n.
Sab'iyya 107 n; 134 n.
Sachau, Edw. 113 n; 119 n.
Sa'd b. Abu Wakkas 217 n; 218.
Sa'd b. Malik 217 n.
Saggitarius 120.
Sa'id b. Amr al-Harashi 77; 77 n.
Sa'id al-Hasan b. Ahmad b. Abdallah al-Kaddah 111; 111 n.
Sa'id b. Zaid b. Nufail 217 n; 218.
Saidy 107 n.
Sajah b. Harith al-Tamim 201; 201 n; 204.
Salih Kubba 1 n; 6; 8; (*see* al-Salihi).
Salih b. Mudrik 60 n.
al-Salihi 8; 190; 190 n.
Salimiyya 78 n; 81; 81 n.
Salisbury Fragment 116 n.
Salm b. Ahwaz al-Mazini 14; 14 n.
Salm al-Khasir 139 n.
Salm b. Kutaiba 53.
al-Sam'ani 55 n; 62 n; 119 n.
Samanids 29; 129 n; 130.
Samara 3.
Samarra 89 n.
Samaritans 222.
Samarkand 42 n.
San'a 43 n; 123 n.
al-Sanadiki, al-Hasan b. Faraj, Abu-l-Kasim 123; 123 n; 124 n.
Sanbar 126 n.
Sanbar, Banu 111.
Sassanids 120 n.
Sassaniyya 220 n.
Satan 22 n; 26; 54; 55; 68; 75; 100; 102 115; 133; 133 n; 135; 139 n; 148; 183 184; 185; 208; 208 n; 219.
Saturn 120 n; 121; 219 n.
al-Sawad 128.
Sawda' 41 n.
Scandinavian 50 n.
Schacht, J. 172 n.
Schreiner, M. 37 n; 97 n; 98 n.
Seleucids 120 n.
Sem 134 n.
Seth 134 n.
Sha'ban, month of 205.

T.

Ta'limiyya 107 n.
Tamim, Banu 38 ; 46 n ; 201 n.
Tanasukh 46 n ; 60 n ; 64 ; 70 n.
Tanja 53 n.
Tara'ikiyya 18.
Tarsus 161 n.
Tasmiyya 152.
Tatar 122.
Tatius 133 n.
Tawatur 174 ; 175 ; 177.
Tayariyya 59 n.
Teim, Banu 140 ; 140 n ; 141.
Thamud 141.
Thanawiyya 223 ; *see* Dualists ;
Tharwaih 130.
Thauban 1 n ; 5.
Thaubaniyya 1 ; 5.
al-Thauri, Sufyan b. Sa'id b. Masruh 160; 160 n ; 164 n ; 221.
Thumama b. al-Ashras 177 ; 182 ; 195 ; 203 203 n.
Tibet 122.
Tiflis 114 n.
Tigris 84 ; 84 n ; 86 ; 157.
Tirmidh 13 n ; 14.
al-Tirmidhi, Abu 'Isa 165 n.
Transoxania 73 n.
Tughj b. Juff 124 n.
Tulaiha 38 (*see* Talha).
Tuman 4 n.
Tumaniyya 1 ; 4.
Tun 103 ; 103 n.
Turkestan 122 n.
Turkey 121.
Turks 35.
al-Tusi 191 n ; 210 n.
Twelvers *see* Ithna'ashariyya.

U.

Ubai ibn Ka'b 16 ; 16 n.
Ubaid ibn Zurara (b. A'yun ?) 33 n.
Ubaidallah b. Hasan b. Muhammad b. Isma'il 110 n ; 111 ; 112 n ; 123 ; 123 n ; 125 n ; 127 ; 127 n ; 132 ; 135.
Ubaidiyya 2 n.
Uhud, Battle of 168 ; 218 ; 228.
Ukail, Banu 127 n.
Ukkasha b. Mihsan 218 ; 228.
Ulyan b. Dhira' al-Sadusi *or* al-Asadi 69 n.
Ulyaniyya 68 n ; 69 n.
Umar b. Abu Afif al-Azdi 47 n.
Umayya, Banu 140.
Umayyads, Omayyads 2 n ; 14 ; 14 n ; 42 n ; 59 n ; 94 n ; 101 n ; 103 n ; 117 n ; 124 n ; 142 n ; 212 n.
Umm-Walad 166 n.
Umra 176.
Unaisa 201 n.
Ushrusana 42 n.
Uthman 42 n ; 65 ; 70 n ; 140 ; 160 ; 166 ; 169 ; 214 ; 214 n ; 215 ; 215 n.
Uwais al-Karani 228 ; 228 n.

V.

Van Vloten 2 n ; 57 n ; 58 n ; 87 n.
Venus 47.
Veth, P. J. 58 n.
Vishtaspa 119 n.

W.

adi Siba 214.
a'idiyya 2 n.
-Walid 47 n.
alila 53 n; 54 n.
alis 133; 133 n.
Wasil ibn Ata 43 n; 167; 168.
Wasit 85 n; 103.
Wellhausen, J 46 n.
Wensinck 133 n; 175 n.
Wüstenfeld 110 n; 111 n.

Y.

ahya (b. Abdallah) b. al-Hasan 53 n.
ahya b. Aktham 226.
ahya b. al-Mahdi 111 n.
ahya b. Zikrwaih b. Mihrwaih, Abu-l-Kasim 124; 124 n.
aktin 33 n.
-Ya'kubi 225 n.
akut 129 n; 140 n.
azdan 22 n; 117; 117 n; 131; 185.
emen 94 n; 123; 123 n; 124 n; 222 n.
emenite 142 n.
ezid I 45 n.
ezid b. Abu Unaisa 103—4; 103 n; 201; 201 n.
Yezid b. Merwan 103 n.
Yezid b. Omar b. Hubaira 65 n.
Yezidiyya 39; 40; 103—4; 105 n; 224.
Yudasaf 200; 220 n.
Yudghan (al-Ra'i) 104 n.
Yudghaniyya 37 n; 38 n; 104 n.
Yunus b. Abd al-Rahman al-Kummi 33.
Yunus ibn Aun 3; 3 n; 8 n.
Yunus ibn Umar *see* Yunus ibn Aun.
Yunusiyya 1; 1 n; 3; 4; 5; 6 n; 33.
Yusuf b. Diwdad b. Abi Saj, Abu-l-Kasim 125; 125 n.
Yusuf b. Omar al-Thakafi 58.

Z.

abaniyya 217.
a'faraniyya 11; 11 n.
ahirite 20 n; 160; 173.
aidan 108 n; *see* Dhaidhan.
aidiyya 39; 71 n; 140; 160 n; 169; 213 n; 217 n.
akrouya b. Mahrouya Salmani 112 n.
aradusht 119; 120; 122; 132; 200.
arwan 220 n.
arwaniyya 220; 220 n; 221.
emzem Well 121.
Zendik 145; 149; 151; 226.
Ziarids 129 n.
Ziyadiyya 2 n.
Zoroaster 119 n.
Zoroastrianism 220 n.
Zoroastrians 90 n; 118 n.
al-Zubair 15; 15 n; 60; 105; 167; 168; 214; 214 n; 215; 218.
Zurara ibn A'yun al-Rafidi 35; 188.
Zurariyya 35.
Zurkan 7; 7 n.